시원스쿨 토익 실전 1500제

LC LISTENING

시원스쿨 토익
실전 1500제 LC

초판 1쇄 발행 2021년 1월 8일
초판 6쇄 발행 2024년 4월 30일

지은이 정상 시원스쿨어학연구소
펴낸곳 (주)에스제이더블유인터내셔널
펴낸이 양홍걸 이시원

홈페이지 www.siwonschool.com
주소 서울시 영등포구 영신로 166 시원스쿨
교재 구입 문의 02)2014-8151
고객센터 02)6409-0878

ISBN 979-11-6150-437-7 13740
Number 1-110201-02020400-02

시원스쿨 토익

실전 1500제

LC LISTENING

최소의 비용으로 초고속 고득점 달성
시원스쿨 토익 실전 1500제

본 저자는 토익 강의만 10년 이상, 토익 교재를 20권 이상 저술한 사람으로, 이 분야 최고 전문가라는 자부심이 있습니다. 하지만, 완벽한 사람은 없기에 새 교재를 선보일 때마다 두근두근하는 걱정과 기대가 함께 있어왔습니다. 그런데 「시원스쿨 토익 실전 1500제」를 내놓으면서는 오로지 확신만 듭니다. '시원스쿨어학연구소'라는 시험영어 분야 최고 전문가들과 함께 문제를 개발했기 때문입니다.

「시원스쿨 토익 실전 1500제」는 최근 10년간 토익 기출 빅데이터를 완벽하게 분석한 결과를 토대로 최빈출 고난도 문제 유형들을 총 망라하여 900점 이상을 보장하는 실전 모의고사 문제집입니다. 이 교재를 선택한 여러분의 성적 향상은 저와 시원스쿨어학연구소가 책임지겠습니다. 대신, 여러분께서는 다음 세 가지 약속을 반드시 이행해 주셔야 합니다.

첫째, 반드시 TEST 한 회를 실제 시험을 보듯이 집중하고 풀어야 합니다. 중간에 멈추거나 여러 번 나누어 풀면 그 효과가 급격히 떨어진다는 것을 명심하세요.

둘째, 동영상 강의 혹은 교재 해설을 반복해 보면서 가능한 한 완벽하게 이해하려 애써야 합니다. 오답 이유 뿐 아니라 정답 이유까지 말입니다. 맞힌 문제라고 대충 넘겨버리면 결코 원하는 성적을 얻을 수 없습니다. LC도 잘 안 들린 것은 들릴 때까지 반복해서 들어야 합니다.

셋째, 교재 속 어휘/표현은 파트를 막론하고 모두 암기하려 노력합시다. 그 과정에서 어휘 문제 뿐 아니라 독해와 LC 직청직해 능력까지 모두 좋아집니다.

저는 여러분이 시원스쿨랩과 저에게 보여주시는 기대와 사랑을 10배, 100배로 돌려드리겠다는 각오로 게시판의 모든 학습 질문에 명쾌하게 답변드릴 것을 약속 드립니다.

기출 빅데이터를 토대로 한 문제 한 문제 엄선한 「시원스쿨 토익 실전 1500제」는 토익의 빈출 유형들을 총망라하고 있으므로, 15회를 전부 풀고 모든 문제를 철저히 소화한다면, 반드시 900점 이상의 고득점을 달성할 수 있을 것입니다. 「시원스쿨 토익 실전 1500제」를 파트너 삼아 최단 시간 안에 목표 점수를 성취하고, 여러분의 오랜 꿈을 이루시기를 진심으로 바랍니다.

정 상, 시원스쿨어학연구소

목차

왜「시원스쿨 토익 실전 1500제」인가?

01 영어시험 연구 전문 조직이 개발

토익 베스트셀러 집필진, 토익 990점 수십 회 만점자, 토익 콘텐츠 개발 경력 10년의 원어민 연구원, 미국/호주/영국의 명문대학원 석사 출신 영어 테스트 전문가들이 포진한 영어시험 연구 조직인 시원스쿨어학연구소가 직접 개발하였습니다.

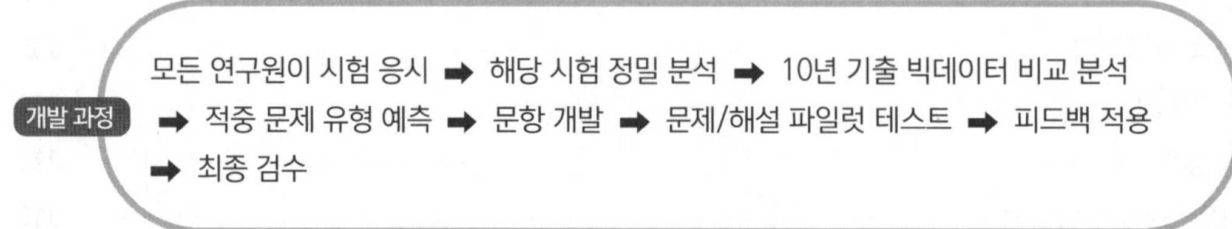

개발 과정
모든 연구원이 시험 응시 ➡ 해당 시험 정밀 분석 ➡ 10년 기출 빅데이터 비교 분석
➡ 적중 문제 유형 예측 ➡ 문항 개발 ➡ 문제/해설 파일럿 테스트 ➡ 피드백 적용
➡ 최종 검수

02 빅데이터 정밀 분석에 기초하여 가장 많이 나오는 것만 수록

지난 10년간의 기출 문제들을 빠짐 없이 분석하여 자주 출제되는 문제 유형과 문장 구조, 어휘와 구문을 모든 문항에 적용하였습니다. 시험에 가장 많이 나오는 것들만 빠르게 공부하여 시간과 에너지 낭비 없이 단기간에 900점 이상을 이룰 수 있습니다.

분석 과정

다음과 같은 심층 분석으로 모든 문항에 토익 출제빈도 및 중요도를 반영

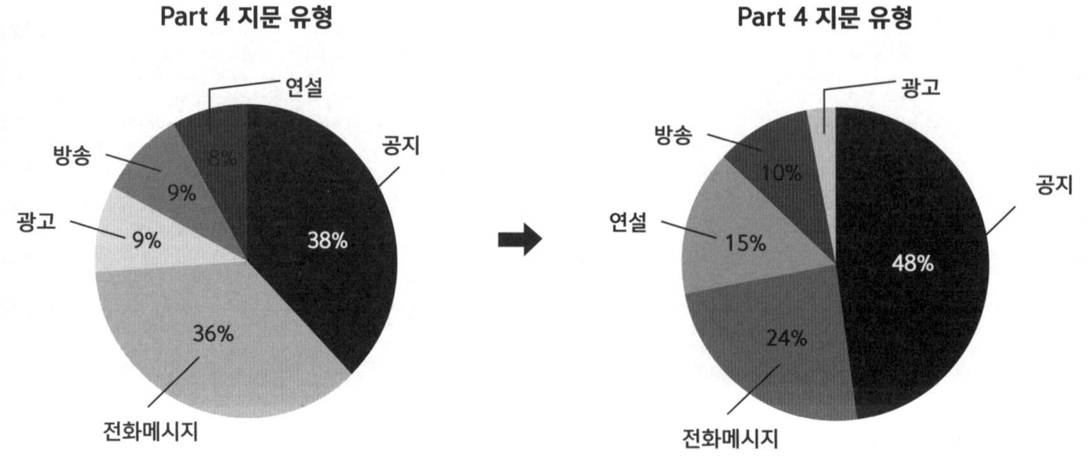

03 토익 실전 모의고사 15회분! 압도적 분량의 최다 실전 문제

토익의 기출 트렌드를 반영한 실전 문제집으로서, 실전 모의고사 총 15회분이라는 압도적으로 많은 양의 실전문제를 실었습니다.

- 기출 트렌드 반영
- 실전 모의고사 15회
  (1회 100문제 X 15회 = 1500문제)

04 900점+ 고득점 직행 보장 문제

지난 10년간의 토익 기출 빅데이터 분석을 통해 고득점을 방해하는 다음과 같은 세 가지 문제 유형을 뽑아 충분히 연습할 수 있게 배치하여 본서를 풀면 고득점으로 직행할 수 있습니다.

- 고수도 틀리는 어려운 문제 유형
- 토익 수험자들이 거의 매번 실수하는 문제 유형
- 기존의 유형과는 달라 당혹스러운 새로운 문제 유형

05 필수 학습 콘텐츠 무료 제공

토익 학습자들의 경제적 부담을 최소화하기 위해 필수 학습 콘텐츠인 **MP3 음원**과 **문제 해설**, **오답노트**, **Answer Sheet**를 무료로 제공합니다. 시원스쿨랩 홈페이지(lab.siwonschool.com)에서 다운로드 할 수 있습니다.

- TEST 15회 MP3 음원 전부 무료 제공
- TEST 15회 해설 전부 무료 제공
- 시원스쿨 토익 오답노트 무료 제공

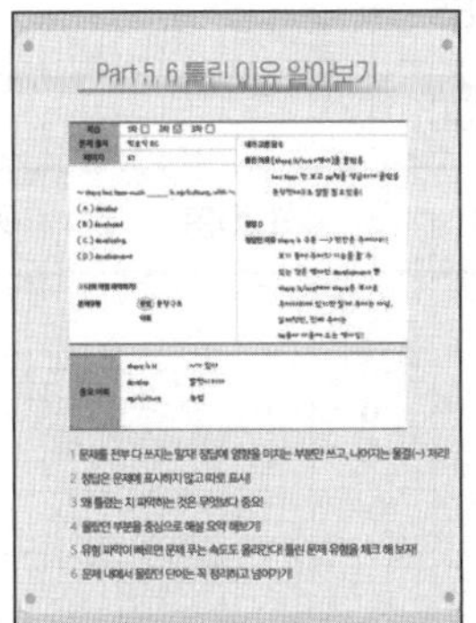

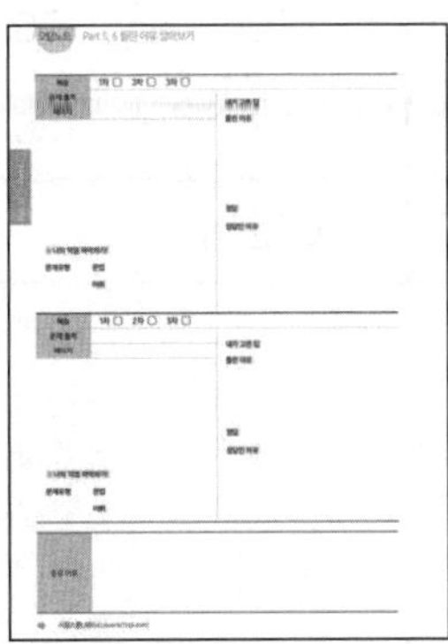

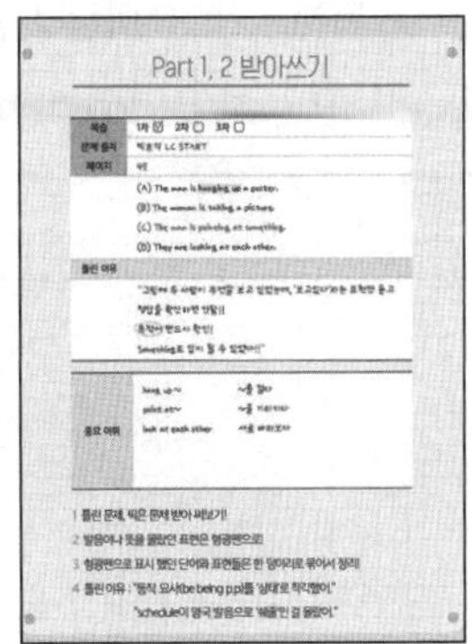

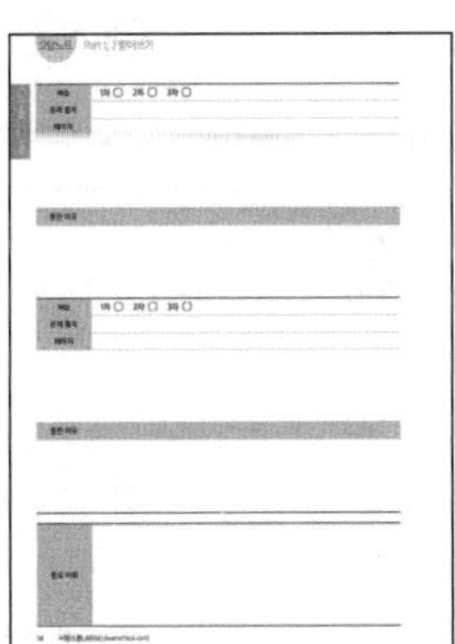

TOEIC이란?

TOEIC은 ETS(Educational Testing Service)가 출제하는 국제 커뮤니케이션 영어 능력 평가 시험(Test Of English for International Communication)입니다. 즉, 토익은 영어로 업무적인 소통을 할 수 있는 능력을 평가하는 시험으로서, 다음과 같은 비즈니스 실무 상황들을 다룹니다.

기업일반	**계약, 협상, 홍보, 영업, 비즈니스 계획, 회의, 행사, 장소 예약**
제조	**공장 관리, 조립라인, 품질관리**
금융과 예산	**은행, 투자, 세금, 회계, 청구**
개발	**연구, 제품개발**
사무실	**회의, 서신 교환(편지, 메모, 전화, 팩스, E-mail 등), 사무용품/가구 주문과 사용**
인사	**입사지원, 채용, 승진, 급여, 퇴직**
부동산	**건축, 설계서, 부동산 매매 및 임대, 전기/가스/수도 설비**
여가	**교통수단, 티켓팅, 여행 일정, 역/공항, 자동차/호텔 예약 및 연기와 취소, 영화, 공연, 전시**

토익 파트별 문항 구성

구성	파트	내용		문항 수 및 문항 번호		시간	배점
Listening Test	Part 1	사진 묘사		6	1-6	45분	495점
	Part 2	질의 응답		25	7-31		
	Part 3	짧은 대화		39 (13지문)	32-70		
	Part 4	짧은 담화		30 (10지문)	71-100		
Reading Test	Part 5	단문 빈칸 채우기 (문법, 어휘)		30	101-130	75분	495점
	Part 6	장문 빈칸 채우기 (문법, 문맥에 맞는 어휘)		16 (4지문)	131-146		
	Part 7	독해	단일 지문	29	147-175		
			이중 지문	10	176-185		
			삼중 지문	15	186-200		
합계				200문제		120분	990 점

접수부터 성적 확인까지

01 접수

- TOEIC 위원회 인터넷 사이트(www.toeic.co.kr)에서 접수 일정을 확인하고 접수합니다.
- 접수 시 최근 6개월 이내 촬영한 jpg 형식의 사진이 필요하므로 미리 준비합니다.
- 토익 응시료는 (2024년 6월 기준) 정기 접수 시 52,500원입니다.
- 시험 30일 전부터는 특별추가접수에 해당하여 추가 비용이 발생하니 잊지 말고 정기 접수 기간에 접수하도록 합니다.

02 시험 당일 할 일

- 아침을 적당히 챙겨 먹습니다. 빈속은 집중력 저하의 주범이고 과식은 졸음을 유발합니다.
- 고사장을 반드시 확인합니다.
- 시험 준비물을 챙깁니다.
  - 신분증 (주민등록증, 운전면허증, 기간 만료 전 여권, 공무원증만 인정. 학생증 안됨. 단, 중고등학생은 국내 학생증 인정)
  - B연필과 깨끗하게 잘 지워지는 지우개 (볼펜이나 사인펜은 안됨. 연필은 뭉툭하게 깎아서 여러 자루 준비)
  - 아날로그 시계 (전자시계는 안됨)
  - 수험표 (필수 준비물은 아님. 수험번호는 시험장에서 감독관이 답안지에 부착해주는 라벨을 보고 적으면 됨)
- 고사장으로 이동하는 동안에는 「시원스쿨 토익 실전 1500제」 LC 음원을 들으며 귀를 예열합니다.
- 최소 30분 전에 입실을 마치고(오전 시험은 오전 9:20까지, 오후 시험은 오후 2:20까지) 지시에 따라 답안지에 기본 정보를 기입한 뒤, 「시원스쿨 토익 실전 1500제」를 풀고나서 정리한 「시원스쿨 토익 오답노트」를 훑어봅니다.
- 안내 방송이 끝나고 시험 시작 전 5분의 휴식시간이 주어지는데, 이때 화장실에 꼭 다녀옵니다.

03 시험 진행

오전 시험	오후 시험	내용
9:30 - 9:45	2:30 - 2:45	답안지 작성 오리엔테이션
9:45 - 9:50	2:45 - 2:50	수험자 휴식시간
9:50 - 10:10	2:50 - 3:10	신분증 확인, 문제지 배부
10:10 - 10:55	3:10 - 3:55	듣기 평가
10:55 - 12:10	3:55 - 5:10	독해 평가

04 성적 확인

- 시험일로부터 9일 후 낮 12시에 한국 TOEIC 위원회 사이트(www.toeic.co.kr)에서 성적이 발표됩니다.

「시원스쿨 토익 실전 1500제」 고득점 보장 학습법

학습 단계	학습 방법	유의 사항
1	시험 문제 풀기	1. 반드시 **실제 시험을 보는 것과 똑같이** 해야 합니다. 2. 휴대폰 전원을 끄고 책상 위에는 연필/지우기/답안지만 놓고, 제한 시간을 지켜 문제를 풉니다. 제한 시간 내에 답안 마킹까지 끝내야 합니다. 3. 100번 문제가 끝날 때까지 중간에 멈추지 않습니다.
2	채점 틀린 문제 다시 풀기	채점 후 바로 틀린 문제의 해설을 보지 말고, 다시 한 번 내 힘으로 풀어봅니다.
3	틀린 문제 완전히 이해하기	1. 틀린 문제는 물론이고, 찍어서 맞은 문제, 맞았지만 헷갈렸던 문제까지 모두 표시해서 **완벽하게 이해**해야 합니다. 2. 해설을 천천히 읽고도 이해가 잘 안된다면 **시원스쿨랩 (lab.siwonschool.com) 홈페이지의 공부 질문하기** 게시판에 질문을 올려주세요. 저자가 직접 답변해 드립니다. 3. 기초가 부족하다고 느끼거나 다양한 실전 전략을 익히고 싶다면 강의 수강을 권장합니다.
4	오답노트 작성하기	1. 시원스쿨랩 홈페이지 교재자료실에서 **시원스쿨 토익 오답노트**를 다운로드 받아 출력해 여러 장 복사해 둡니다. 2. 샘플 예시대로 오답노트를 작성합니다. 3. **[시원스쿨 토익 실전 1500제] 오답노트 전용 파일**에 오답노트지를 보관합니다.
5	추가 복습	1. **오답노트**에 정리한 내용을 확인합니다. 2. 해설지에 정리되어 있는 **어휘/표현**을 외웁니다. 3. 교재 맨 뒤에 나와 있는 **스크립트**를 소리 내어 여러 번 읽습니다. 4. **복습용 음원**을 휴대폰에 넣고 다니며 시간 날 때마다 듣습니다.

「시원스쿨 토익 실전 1500제」 초단기 학습 플랜

실전 문제집은 오랫동안 공부하기 보다는 단기간에 집중적으로 공부하는 것이 효과가 좋습니다. 따라서 15일 동안은 하루에 최소 3시간 이상 할애하여 매일 학습하도록 합니다.

1차 학습_15일 완성

Day 1	Day 2	Day 3	Day 4	Day 5
- TEST 1 풀기 - 채점 및 복습 - 오답노트 정리 - 추가 복습	- TEST 2 풀기 - 채점 및 복습 - 오답노트 정리 - 추가 복습	- TEST 3 풀기 - 채점 및 복습 - 오답노트 정리 - 추가 복습	- TEST 4 풀기 - 채점 및 복습 - 오답노트 정리 - 추가 복습	- TEST 5 풀기 - 채점 및 복습 - 오답노트 정리 - 추가 복습
Day 6	**Day 7**	**Day 8**	**Day 9**	**Day 10**
- TEST 6 풀기 - 채점 및 복습 - 오답노트 정리 - 추가 복습	- TEST 7 풀기 - 채점 및 복습 - 오답노트 정리 - 추가 복습	- TEST 8 풀기 - 채점 및 복습 - 오답노트 정리 - 추가 복습	- TEST 9 풀기 - 채점 및 복습 - 오답노트 정리 - 추가 복습	- TEST 10 풀기 - 채점 및 복습 - 오답노트 정리 - 추가 복습
Day 11	**Day 12**	**Day 13**	**Day 14**	**Day 15**
- TEST 11 풀기 - 채점 및 복습 - 오답노트 정리 - 추가 복습	- TEST 12 풀기 - 채점 및 복습 - 오답노트 정리 - 추가 복습	- TEST 13 풀기 - 채점 및 복습 - 오답노트 정리 - 추가 복습	- TEST 14 풀기 - 채점 및 복습 - 오답노트 정리 - 추가 복습	- TEST 15 풀기 - 채점 및 복습 - 오답노트 정리 - 추가 복습

2차 학습_5일 완성

Day 1	Day 2	Day 3	Day 4	Day 5
- TEST 1~3 다시 풀기 - 채점 및 복습 - 오답노트 정리 - 추가 복습	- TEST 4~6 다시 풀기 - 채점 및 복습 - 오답노트 정리 - 추가 복습	- TEST 7~9 다시 풀기 - 채점 및 복습 - 오답노트 정리 - 추가 복습	- TEST 10~12 다시 풀기 - 채점 및 복습 - 오답노트 정리 - 추가 복습	- TEST 13~15 다시 풀기 - 채점 및 복습 - 오답노트 정리 - 추가 복습

시원스쿨랩이 제안하는 LC 학습법

Part 1_사진 묘사

• Part 1은 이렇다!

* 총 6문항
* 사람 중심의 사진 4~5문항, 사물이나 배경 중심의 사진 1~2문항 출제
* 배경 사진이 가장 고난도
* 6문제를 반드시 모두 맞혀야 함

사람 중심 사진일지라도 주어가 사물로 시작한다면 사물을 유심히 확인해야 하는데, 이때 문형을 통한 오답을 자주 제시한다. 예를 들어, The cars are being parked along the street.(주차되고 있다) The cars have been parked along the street.(주차되어 있다)와 같이 진행 수동형(be being p.p.)과 완료 수동형(have been p.p.)의 시제를 통해서 동작과 상태를 혼동시키는데, 발음이 유사하게 들리기 때문에 실수하기 쉬우므로 주의해야 한다.

• Part 1은 이렇게 대비하자!

1. 빈출 사진 주제에 맞추어 빈출 어휘/표현을 최대한 익혀둔다.
2. 받아쓰기를 통해 어휘와 구를 확실히 듣는 연습을 한다. 받아쓰기를 하면 저절로 반복 듣기와 따라 읽기 연습을 하게 되어 시제 부분이 체득되기 때문에 기본 문형을 확실히 익힐 수 있다.
3. Part 1 은 사람이나 사물의 위치 묘사가 필수이다. above the bed, on each side of the bed, in front of the window 등과 같이 위치를 묘사하는 전치사와 명사를 덩어리로 정리해 둔다.
4. 가장 일반적인 오답 유형인 유사 발음 함정에 빠지지 않기 위해 유사 발음어(walk/work, copy/coffee, lead/read, write/ride, packing/backing, stuck/stacked 등) 를 정리해 둔다.
5. 사물을 포괄적인 단어로 묘사하는 경우가 많다. 예를 들어, 상점에서 파는 cans, juice, paper 등을 item, merchandise, goods 등으로 포괄적으로 표현하는 경우가 많으니 이를 정리해 둔다.

Part 2_질의-응답

• Part 2는 이렇다!

* 총 25문항
* 발음 속도가 빨라지고 예상과 다른 정답이 많이 나오면서 어려워짐
* 문제와 선지 (A)까지가 0.8초로 잠시라도 집중력을 잃으면 정답을 고르기 어렵다.

Where로 물으면 장소, Who가 나오면 사람으로 답하는 직접적인 답변보다 간접적인 응답이나 예상 밖의 응답이 늘고 있다. 단순히 동사, 명사 키워드를 듣고 의미를 아는 것을 묻는 것이 아니라 질문의 의도를 제대로 이해하는지, 질문에서 나올 수 있는 다양한 상황을 생각해 낼 수 있는지를 묻는 것이다. 이러한 능력을 키우기 위해서는 질문의 상황을 우리말로 요약하는 연습이 효과적이다. 그리고 가능한 여러 답변을 생각해 보고 답변을 만들어 보는 방법도 좋다.

• Part 2는 이렇게 대비하자!

질문 학습법

1. 의문문의 문장 구조를 체득하라.

의문문 문장 구조를 파악하기 위한 훈련을 기본적으로 많이 해두어야 한다. 문형을 확실히 이해한 후 받아쓰기 연습을 통해서 완전히 체득한다. 의문문의 기본 문장 구조는 정해져 있기 때문에 그 틀이 체득되면 핵심을 파악하기가 쉬워진다.

2. 질문 내용을 요약하는 연습을 한다.

단어 하나씩 해석하는 것이 아닌 질문 상황 전체를 우리말로 요약하고 이해하는 연습을 한다. 토익에 나오는 상황은 정해져 있기 때문에 빈출 어휘, 문장의 틀 그리고 빈출 상황을 정리해 두면 내용을 이해하기가 쉬워진다.

3. 질문의 소리를 기억하는 연습을 하라.

아무리 연습을 하고 시험장에 들어가도 집중력이 흐려지며 문장의 속도를 따라 잡지 못하는 경우가 발생한다. 이때는 기억나는 키워드로 답을 찾아야 하니 내용어(동사, 명사, 형용사, 부사)를 강하게 읽어가며 문장 속 핵심어를 기억하는 연습을 병행한다.

답변 학습법

1. 다양한 답변을 연습하라.

단순히 질문과 답변을 짝지어 외운다면 예상치 못한 답변이 나올 경우 혼동에 빠질 수 있다. 따라서, 질문과 응답을 단순 암기하는 것이 아닌 상황에 대한 이해와 함께 가능한 답변을 다각도에서 생각하고 만들어 보아야 한다.

2. 오답 유형을 정리하라.

Part 2 문제를 풀 때는 정답을 찾는 느낌보다는 오답을 지우는 방식으로 해야 안전하다. 오답 유형에는 동일 어휘/유사 발음어/파생어를 이용한 소리 함정, 질문에 나온 단어와 연관된 어휘, 주어나 시제 불일치, 다른 의문사 의문문에 대한 답변 등이 있는데 이들을 미리 파악하고 있으면 오답을 쉽게 소거할 수 있어 유리하므로 반드시 정리해 두자.

3. 빈출 정답 유형을 정리하라.

모르겠다(I don't know, I'm not sure), 아직 결정되지 않았다(It hasn't been decided yet.), 게시판을 참고하세요(It should be on the notice board.), 물어볼게요(I'll ask.)와 같이 늘 출제되는 정답 유형들이 있다. 질문을 놓친 경우에 보기에 정답 유형이 있다면 이를 고르면 되므로 이러한 유형들을 암기해 둔다.

Part 3_짧은 대화

• Part 3는 이렇다!

* 대화를 듣고 그 대화에 대한 3개 질문의 답을 찾는 문제
* 총 13개의 대화문에서 39문항 출제
  - 3인 대화문 1~2개 출제
  - 의도파악 문제 2문항 출제
  - 시각자료 문제 3문항 출제

대화가 끝나 문제를 풀려고 하는 순간, 대화 내용이 기억 저편으로 사라져 버리기 일쑤인데, 무엇을 들어야 하는지 모른 채 무작정 들었을 때 이러한 어려움을 겪게 된다. Part 3에서 가장 중요한 능력은 대화를 듣기 전에 문제와 보기의 핵심을 재빨리 파악하는 속독 능력이다. 대화를 100% 들어야 하는 것은 아니다. 문제가 요구하는 부분에 선택 집중 듣기를 하면 정답이 나온다.

• Part 3는 이렇게 대비하자!

질문과 보기 학습

1. 문제 유형은 크게 세 가지로, 전반부 문제(주제, 목적, 대화 장소, 화자의 신분), 중반부의 세부사항 문제(이유, 문제점, 구체적 시간과 장소, 방법) 그리고 후반부의 미래 내용 묻기(특정 시점에서의 행위, 미래 행위, 제안/요청 행위)로 구성된다. 문제 유형을 파악하고 대화문의 어느 부분에 집중해 할지 파악한 후 마음의 준비를 한 후 듣는 연습을 한다.
2. 보기를 읽으며 대화 내용을 예측해 보는 연습을 한다.

대화문 학습

1. 대화문의 첫 문장을 절대 놓치지 않는다.

대화 초반에 등장하는 키워드에서 전체 대화가 그려진다. 세부내용을 묻는 문제 역시 전체 상황을 이해해야 놓치지 않고 잡아 내기 쉽다.

2. 대화문의 전개 패턴을 파악하라. 특히 반전에 주목해라.

대화의 흐름은 대화자 간의 질문과 답변을 통해 앞의 내용과 순조롭게 이어지는 경우와 흐름이 바뀌는 역접으로 나눌 수 있다. 화자가 바뀔 때 다음 사람의 첫 대사를 잘 들어야 흐름을 읽을 수 있음을 반드시 기억하자. 또한 연결어 역시 대화 흐름을 알려준다. 이 두 가지로 흐름을 읽어내자.

3. 말 바꾸어 표현하기를 정리하라.

말 바꾸기는 동사를 유사어로, 명사를 큰 개념 단어로 바꾸는 것이 가장 흔하다. 하지만 문맥 속에서 내용을 요약하는 경우도 있기에 대화의 중요 정보를 보기에서 어떻게 바꾸어 표현하는지를 정리해서 학습해야 한다.

4. 자주 나오는 스토리를 정리하라.

토익에 나오는 스토리는 어느 정도 정해져 있다. 그 안에서 조금 더 구체화 되지만 그래도 큰 줄기를 알면 대화를 이해하고 예측하기가 쉬워진다. 대화문을 학습하며 우리말로 어떤 대화인지 그 이야기를 정리해 두면 좋다.

Part 4_짧은 담화

• Part 4는 이렇다!

* 담화를 듣고 그 담화에 대한3개 질문의 답을 찾는 문제
* 총 10개의 담화문에서 30문항 출제
  - 의도파악 문제 3문항 출제
  - 시각자료 문제 2문항 출제

문제에서 요구하는 특정 정보를 제대로 파악하는 것과 이때 취한 정보가 다른 표현으로 바뀌어 제시된 것을 재빨리 알아 챌 수 있는 기술이 요구되는 점은 Part 3와 같다. 담화 문장의 길이가 길어서 많은 수험생들이 어려워하지만 정해진 유형 중에서 비슷한 내용들이 문제은행 식으로 반복되기 때문에 의외로 쉽게 성적을 올릴 수 있다.

• Part 4는 이렇게 대비하자!

질문과 보기 학습

1. 질문을 꼼꼼히 읽고 답이 나올 부분을 기억해둔다.

질문 유형별로 답이 나올 부분이 지문에 정해져 있다. 주제/목적, 화자/청자와 같은 일반적인 질문은 초반, 세부적인 내용은 중반, 제안/요청/미래 내용은 후반에 등장한다. Part 4의 경우 질문의 순서와 지문에서 언급하는 순서가 거의 일치하므로 미리 문제와 보기를 읽고 키워드에 살짝 표시해둔 후 지문에서 순서대로 나오는 키워드를 잡아내면 쉽다.

2. 보기의 비슷한 내용, 반대 내용을 서로 묶으며 내용을 예측하라.

미리 보기를 보고 서로 비슷한 것과 반대되는 것 등을 정리하면서 담화 내용을 예측해 본다. 보기가 긴 경우 보기의 핵심내용을 요약한다. 반드시 문제를 기억하고 듣되 눈은 보기를 보며 지문 내용을 따라간다.

담화문 학습

1. 담화문의 종류에 따른 전개 방식을 파악하라.

담화의 종류에 따라 구조가 정해져 있고, 그 구조에 따라 논리적으로 내용이 전개되므로, 담화 종류별 전개 방식을 익히고 여기에 맞춰서 답의 단서를 찾는 연습을 하면 된다.

2. 첫 5초, 두 문장에 점수가 달려 있다. 바로 지문의 전개 패턴을 파악하라.

첫 5초 안에 누가, 어디에서, 누구를 대상으로 어떤 이야기를 하고 있는지를 밝히는데, 이를 통해 앞으로 내용이 어떻게 이어질 지 예측할 수 있기 때문에 절대 놓쳐선 안 된다. 대부분의 담화는 주의 환기나 인사말로 시작해 중심 내용을 언급한다. 그 후 세부 사항을 추가 설명하고 마지막으로 요청, 제안 혹은 다음 일정을 설명한다. 중간에 first, lastly, also, moreover, plus, 등의 표현 역시 글의 흐름을 알려주니 이를 잘 이용해 듣도록 하자.

3. 자주 나오는 문제와 정답을 미리 기억하고 예측해 본다.

비슷한 내용들이 문제은행 식으로 반복되므로 시험 전날 그 동안 풀었던 문제집의 문제와 정답 보기만 주욱 보고 가는 것도 도움이 된다. 중간에 내용을 놓쳤다면 내가 정리한 배경 안에서 답을 추려나가 보자. 정답을 맞힐 확률이 높아진다.

4. 시간 관리도 연습해야 한다.

담화문이 나오기 전에 세 문제를 파악하고 들으면서 문제 순서대로 답을 찾고 담화가 끝나면 답 찾기도 끝나야 한다. 문제를 들려주고 푸는 시간을 줄 때는 다음 문제를 준비해야 하며 계속해서 이러한 리듬으로 풀어야 한다. 중간에 놓쳤을 경우는 과감히 찍고 다음 문제로 넘어간다. 한 문제 한 문제가 아니라 전체 30문제를 시원하게 푸는 연습을 여러 번 하고 시험장에 들어가자.

실전모의고사
TEST 1

시작 시간 ________ 시 ________ 분

종료 시간 ________ 시 ________ 분

▸ 중간에 멈추지 말고 처음부터 끝까지 풀어보세요. 문제를 풀 때는 실전처럼 답안지에 마킹하세요.

LISTENING TEST

In the Listening test, you will be asked to demonstrate how well you understand spoken English. The entire Listening test will last approximately 45 minutes. There are four parts, and directions are given for each part. You must mark your answers on the separate answer sheet.

Do not write your answers in your test book.

PART 1

Directions: For each question in this part, you will hear four statements about a picture in your test book. When you hear the statements, you must select the one statement that best describes what you see in the picture. Then find the number of the question on your answer sheet and mark your answer. The statements will not be printed in your test book and will be spoken only one time.

Statement (D), "They are taking photographs," is the best description of the picture, so you should select answer (D) and mark it on your answer sheet.

1.

2.

GO ON TO THE NEXT PAGE

3.

4.

5.

6.

GO ON TO THE NEXT PAGE

PART 2

Directions: You will hear a question or statement and three responses spoken in English. They will not be printed in your test book and will be spoken only one time. Select the best response to the question or statement and mark the letter (A), (B), or (C) on your answer sheet.

7. Mark your answer on your answer sheet.

8. Mark your answer on your answer sheet.

9. Mark your answer on your answer sheet.

10. Mark your answer on your answer sheet.

11. Mark your answer on your answer sheet.

12. Mark your answer on your answer sheet.

13. Mark your answer on your answer sheet.

14. Mark your answer on your answer sheet.

15. Mark your answer on your answer sheet.

16. Mark your answer on your answer sheet.

17. Mark your answer on your answer sheet.

18. Mark your answer on your answer sheet.

19. Mark your answer on your answer sheet.

20. Mark your answer on your answer sheet.

21. Mark your answer on your answer sheet.

22. Mark your answer on your answer sheet.

23. Mark your answer on your answer sheet.

24. Mark your answer on your answer sheet.

25. Mark your answer on your answer sheet.

26. Mark your answer on your answer sheet.

27. Mark your answer on your answer sheet.

28. Mark your answer on your answer sheet.

29. Mark your answer on your answer sheet.

30. Mark your answer on your answer sheet.

31. Mark your answer on your answer sheet.

PART 3

Directions: You will hear some conversations between two or more people. You will be asked to answer three questions about what the speakers say in each conversation. Select the best response to each question and mark the letter (A), (B), (C) or (D) on your answer sheet. The conversations will not be printed in your test book and will be spoken only one time.

32. What kind of business is the man calling?
(A) An amusement park
(B) A concert venue
(C) A restaurant
(D) A movie theater

33. What problem does the man mention?
(A) An employee was disrespectful.
(B) A price is too high.
(C) A scheduling conflict has occurred.
(D) An order quantity is incorrect.

34. What does the woman offer the man as an apology?
(A) A seat upgrade
(B) A free meal
(C) A price reduction
(D) A gift bag

35. What project are the speakers discussing?
(A) Purchasing a building
(B) Hiring new employees
(C) Preparing for an event
(D) Cleaning some rooms

36. What will happen tomorrow?
(A) An inspection will be carried out.
(B) Some equipment will be installed.
(C) A presentation will be given.
(D) Some clients will arrive.

37. What will the woman ask her work crew to do?
(A) Test devices
(B) Attend training
(C) Work overtime
(D) Meet with technicians

38. What problem is the woman having?
(A) She lost her parking permit.
(B) She cannot access a building.
(C) Her ID card has expired.
(D) Her handbag has been stolen.

39. What does the man imply when he says, "I just got here five minutes ago"?
(A) He is sorry for arriving late.
(B) He is unable to answer the question.
(C) He has successfully solved a problem.
(D) He will ask a colleague for assistance.

40. What does the man ask the woman to do?
(A) Return tomorrow morning
(B) Provide a phone number
(C) Submit a report
(D) Contact her supervisor

41. What are the men trying to do?
(A) Decorate a room
(B) Create a meeting agenda
(C) Prepare for interviews
(D) Register for a conference

42. Who is the woman?
(A) An event organizer
(B) An HR manager
(C) A business owner
(D) A job applicant

43. What does the woman ask the men to do?
(A) Go to the cafeteria
(B) Print some documents
(C) Contact a supervisor
(D) Reschedule a lunch meeting

GO ON TO THE NEXT PAGE

44. What is the purpose of the man's call?
(A) To inquire about a product
(B) To find out a doctor's availability
(C) To make a complaint
(D) To schedule a service

45. What does the woman imply when she says, "It won't take more than thirty minutes"?
(A) She will cancel a prior appointment.
(B) The man will get back to work on time.
(C) She will respond to the man later today.
(D) The man should make a booking in advance.

46. What does the man decide to do?
(A) Contact a different company
(B) Reschedule a meeting at work
(C) Visit the business on a different day
(D) Purchase an alternative product

---

47. What does the man like about the apartment building?
(A) The rooftop is available for use.
(B) It was recently built.
(C) His office is located nearby.
(D) It has a large parking area.

48. What does the man say about his brother?
(A) He lives nearby.
(B) He also rents from the realtor.
(C) He works from home.
(D) He recommended the apartment.

49. What does the woman point out about the rental agreement?
(A) It doesn't start until next month.
(B) It requires a safety deposit.
(C) It needs to be revised.
(D) It has a longer duration.

---

50. Where do the speakers most likely work?
(A) At an airport
(B) At a delivery service
(C) At a moving company
(D) At a manufacturing plant

51. What does the woman ask about?
(A) A registration form
(B) A work procedure
(C) An employee benefit
(D) A shift duration

52. According to the man, how can the woman receive additional information?
(A) By visiting a Web site
(B) By calling the head office
(C) By referring to a manual
(D) By consulting a coworker

---

53. Who most likely is the woman?
(A) A lawyer
(B) A financial advisor
(C) A sales representative
(D) A Web designer

54. What does the man want to hire employees to do?
(A) Distribute product catalogs
(B) Install new equipment
(C) Attract new customers
(D) Help with a business relocation

55. Why will the man most likely visit the woman's office?
(A) To take a look at some product samples
(B) To discuss a project in more detail
(C) To interview prospective employees
(D) To make changes to a business contract

---

56. According to the man, what caused some pay slips to be distributed late?
(A) A community event
(B) A computer fault
(C) A schedule conflict
(D) A branch merger

57. What action will be taken to prevent any similar problems?
(A) A payment schedule will be changed.
(B) New equipment will be installed.
(C) A department will be expanded.
(D) Employees will undergo training.

58. What will the man do this afternoon?
(A) Visit the head office
(B) Hold a staff meeting
(C) Submit a payment
(D) Send some receipts

59. What will the visitors see on the tour?
(A) How items are designed
(B) How products are selected
(C) How advertisements are created
(D) How equipment is maintained

60. What are the tour group members permitted to do?
(A) Leave the group
(B) Purchase some items
(C) Handle machinery
(D) Speak to employees

61. What does the tour guide say the company is known for?
(A) Its product packaging
(B) Its large workforce
(C) Its high earnings
(D) Its hiring strategies

Local Restaurants - Private Dining Rooms

Restaurant	Seating Capacity
Four Kings	15
Antonidas	25
Willow	40
Garibaldi's	55

62. What information about the meal did the woman receive yesterday?
(A) The event budget
(B) The guest list
(C) The menu options
(D) The reservation time

63. Look at the graphic. Which restaurant do the speakers choose?
(A) Four Kings
(B) Antonidas
(C) Willow
(D) Garibaldi's

64. What does the man say he will take care of?
(A) Organizing transportation
(B) Preparing a speech
(C) Making a payment
(D) Notifying employees

GO ON TO THE NEXT PAGE

Club President (Anita Laing)	
Club Vice President (James Sorrell)	
Club Treasurer (Matthew Anderson)	Club Secretary (Penelope Grossman)

65. What type of club do the speakers most likely belong to?
(A) A tennis club
(B) A bowling club
(C) A badminton club
(D) A rock climbing club

66. Look at the graphic. Which position is being discussed?
(A) Club President
(B) Club Vice President
(C) Club Treasurer
(D) Club Secretary

67. What will the man do next?
(A) Change a schedule
(B) Make an announcement
(C) Visit headquarters
(D) Create a poster

TriCore Fitness Center
Additional Services

Service	Price
Fitness assessment	$5
Yoga class	$8
Meal planning	$15
Private trainer	$25

68. Look at the graphic. How much will the woman pay for a service?
(A) $5
(B) $8
(C) $15
(D) $25

69. What does the man say about the evening?
(A) The facility is usually crowded.
(B) The parking area is poorly lit.
(C) There are more lockers available.
(D) Complimentary drink is provided.

70. What does the man say the woman will need to show?
(A) A certificate
(B) A form of identification
(C) A medical report
(D) A receipt

PART 4

Directions: You will hear some talks given by a single speaker. You will be asked to answer three questions about what the speaker says in each talk. Select the best response to each question and mark the letter (A), (B), (C), or (D) on your answer sheet. The talks will not be printed in your test book and will be spoken only one time.

71. What product is the speaker selling?
(A) A computer database
(B) A product scanner
(C) An online chat program
(D) A household appliance

72. What does the speaker say the product will help avoid?
(A) Shipping errors
(B) Slow service
(C) High costs
(D) Staff complaints

73. What will the speaker do next?
(A) Give a demonstration
(B) Introduce a colleague
(C) Discuss a payment plan
(D) Distribute pamphlets

---

74. Who is Pricilla Nichols?
(A) A food critic
(B) A chef
(C) A business owner
(D) A property developer

75. What project is Pricilla Nichols currently involved in?
(A) Raising money for charity
(B) Opening a cooking institute
(C) Introducing a new magazine
(D) Expanding a business overseas

76. What does the speaker say Pricilla Nichols plans to do?
(A) Publish an article
(B) Recruit new employees
(C) Give out a scholarship
(D) Renovate a building

---

77. What has caused a delay?
(A) An overbooking error
(B) A security concern
(C) Misplaced luggage
(D) Inclement weather

78. Why does the speaker say, "Gate 12 has several amenities"?
(A) To promote some new airport features
(B) To encourage listeners to stay close
(C) To describe some special offers
(D) To recommend a restaurant

79. According to the speaker, how can the listeners receive more information?
(A) By speaking to an airline employee
(B) By visiting the information desk
(C) By waiting for further announcements
(D) By checking a notice board

---

80. What happened yesterday?
(A) A recruitment event ended.
(B) A building underwent renovations.
(C) A community fair took place.
(D) An environmental project began.

81. Why does the speaker say Assange Corporation was selected?
(A) It has an excellent reputation.
(B) It offered to work for free.
(C) It is based locally.
(D) It has the largest workforce.

82. What is the city council hoping to do?
(A) Boost tourism
(B) Create new jobs
(C) Construct property
(D) Attract foreign investment

GO ON TO THE NEXT PAGE →

83. What does the speaker mention about herself?

(A) She lives in a nearby town.
(B) She works for the local government.
(C) She is in charge of a committee.
(D) She does research in the area.

84. According to the speaker, why will the group make frequent stops?

(A) To use the facilities
(B) To listen to lectures
(C) To enjoy the scenery
(D) To eat snacks

85. According to the speaker, what can the listeners do on a Web site?

(A) View a map
(B) Write a comment
(C) Place an order
(D) Read an article

---

86. What is the speaker calling about?

(A) A lost shipment
(B) A job opening
(C) A missing document
(D) An available apartment

87. What does the speaker say has changed?

(A) A departure time
(B) A bank account
(C) A business location
(D) A utility expense

88. Why does the speaker say, "my parents are moving next week"?

(A) She wants to reserve a moving truck.
(B) She needs the listener to hurry.
(C) She has to make travel arrangements.
(D) She must cancel an appointment.

---

89. What is the speaker mainly discussing?

(A) A hiring strategy
(B) A company policy
(C) A customer complaint
(D) A business deal

90. What are the listeners asked to do?

(A) Attract new customers
(B) Participate in group activities
(C) Tidy their workspaces
(D) Lead training sessions

91. What does the speaker say he will do after the meeting?

(A) Hold interviews
(B) Prepare for a trip
(C) Visit a department store
(D) Post a document

---

92. What is the message mainly about?

(A) Organizing a welcome party
(B) Planning a product launch
(C) Designing new merchandise
(D) Reserving accommodations

93. What does the speaker imply when he says, "Don't forget what happened in March"?

(A) He wants the listener to send him some information.
(B) He is apologizing for a delay to a project.
(C) He does not want to encounter similar problems.
(D) He suggests that the listener reschedule an event.

94. What is the speaker going to do this afternoon?

(A) Survey some customers
(B) Review some advertisements
(C) Compare potential venues
(D) Visit the head office

Thursday	Friday	Saturday	Sunday
Rainy	Rainy	Cloudy	Partly cloudy

95. What event is being described?

(A) A store opening
(B) A park dedication
(C) A community sale
(D) A local festival

96. According to the speaker, what can the listeners find on a Web site?

(A) An event map
(B) A registration sheet
(C) A list of rules
(D) An introductory video

97. Look at the graphic. Which day is the event being held?

(A) Thursday
(B) Friday
(C) Saturday
(D) Sunday

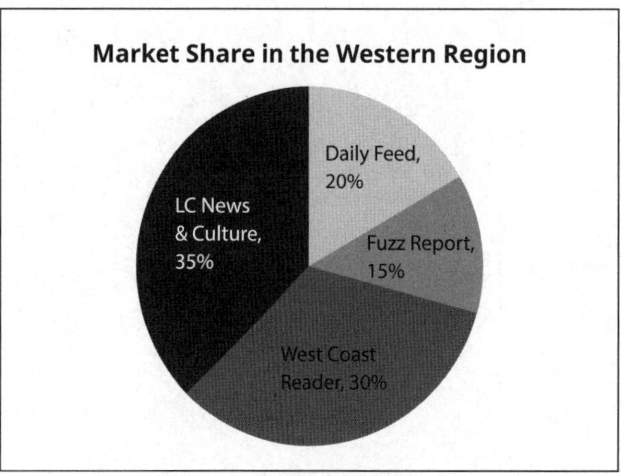

98. According to the speaker, what was mentioned in the company newsletter?

(A) An office will be ready ahead of schedule.
(B) The company has been nominated for an award.
(C) A product release date has been delayed.
(D) The company has come under new ownership.

99. What problem does the speaker mention?

(A) Shipments are delayed.
(B) Positions are vacant.
(C) Content quality has dropped.
(D) Costs have increased.

100. Look at the graphic. Which company may be acquired?

(A) LC News & Culture
(B) Daily Feed
(C) Fuzz Report
(D) West Coast Reader

This is the end of the Listening Test. Turn to Part 5 in your test book.

정답 및 스크립트 p.228 / 점수 환산표 p.363

실전모의고사
TEST 2

시작 시간 ________시 ________분

종료 시간 ________시 ________분

▸ 중간에 멈추지 말고 처음부터 끝까지 풀어보세요. 문제를 풀 때는 실전처럼 답안지에 마킹하세요.

LISTENING TEST

In the Listening test, you will be asked to demonstrate how well you understand spoken English. The entire Listening test will last approximately 45 minutes. There are four parts, and directions are given for each part. You must mark your answers on the separate answer sheet.

Do not write your answers in your test book.

PART 1

Directions: For each question in this part, you will hear four statements about a picture in your test book. When you hear the statements, you must select the one statement that best describes what you see in the picture. Then find the number of the question on your answer sheet and mark your answer. The statements will not be printed in your test book and will be spoken only one time.

Statement (D), "They are taking photographs," is the best description of the picture, so you should select answer (D) and mark it on your answer sheet.

1.

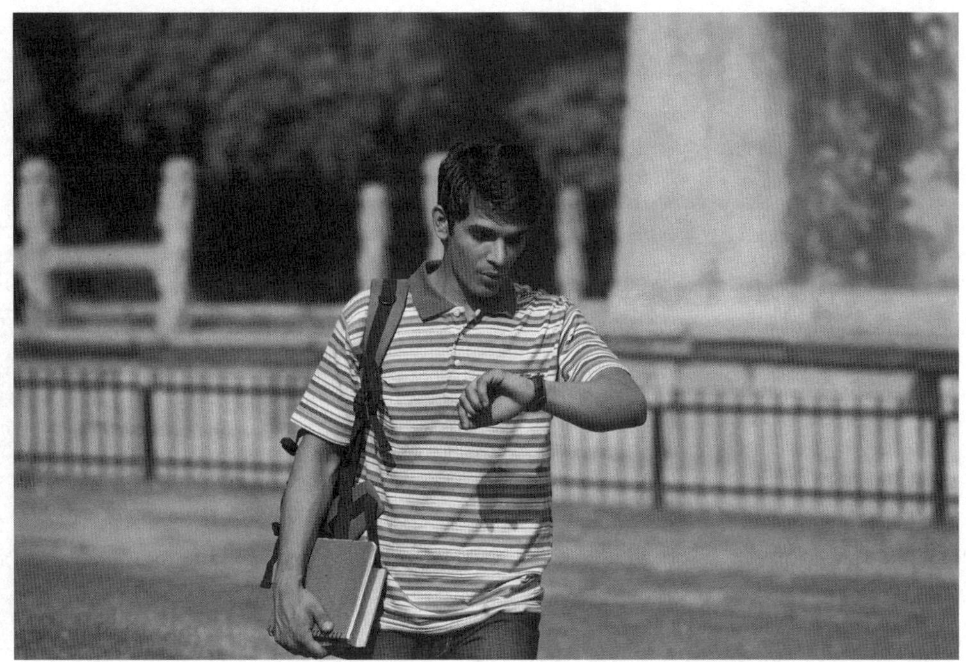

2.

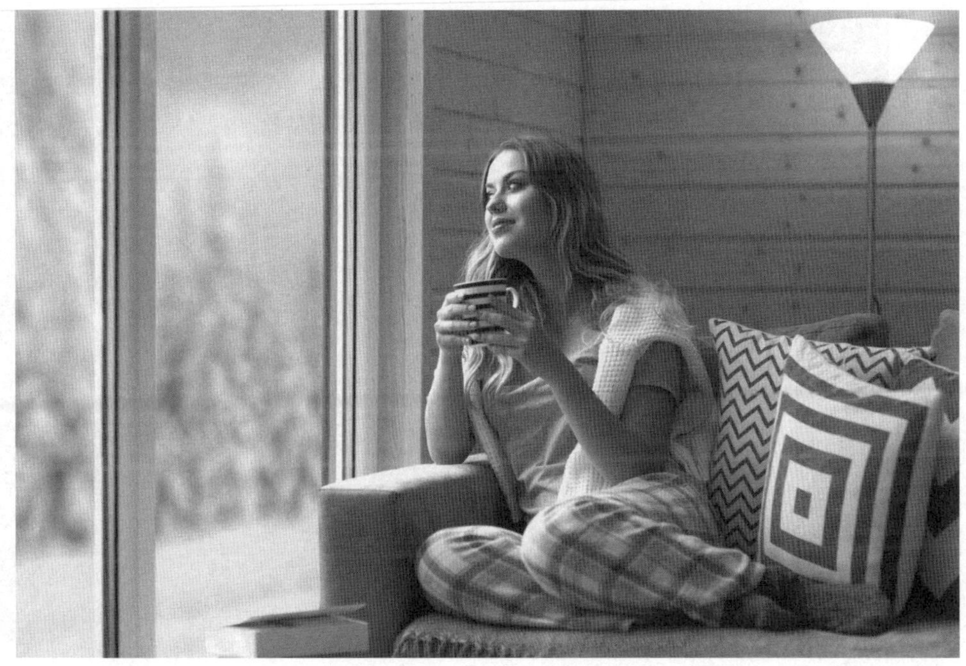

GO ON TO THE NEXT PAGE

3.

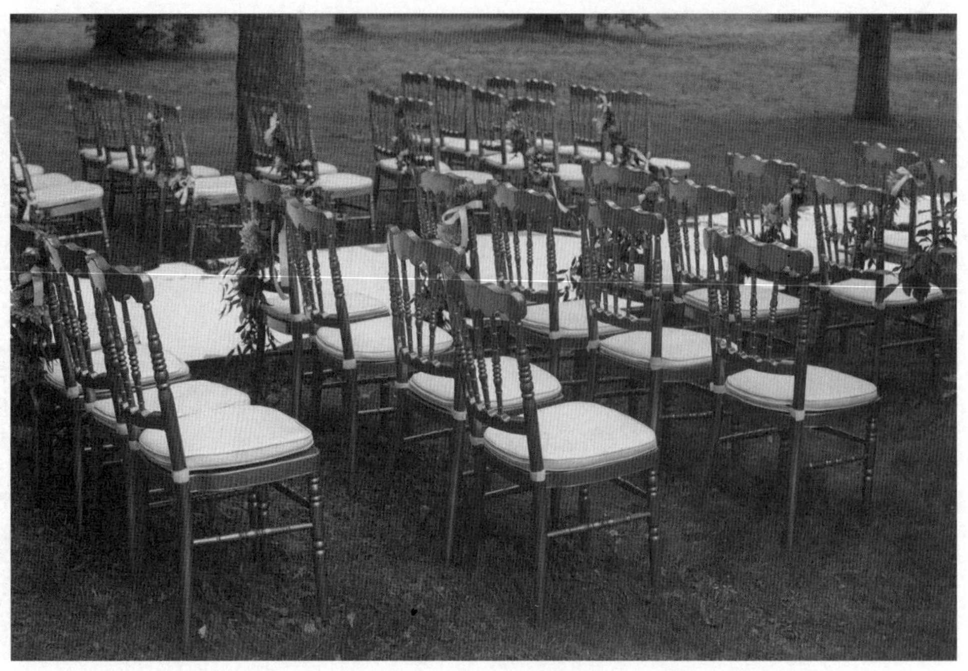

4.

5.

6.

GO ON TO THE NEXT PAGE

PART 2

Directions: You will hear a question or statement and three responses spoken in English. They will not be printed in your test book and will be spoken only one time. Select the best response to the question or statement and mark the letter (A), (B), or (C) on your answer sheet.

7. Mark your answer on your answer sheet.

8. Mark your answer on your answer sheet.

9. Mark your answer on your answer sheet.

10. Mark your answer on your answer sheet.

11. Mark your answer on your answer sheet.

12. Mark your answer on your answer sheet.

13. Mark your answer on your answer sheet.

14. Mark your answer on your answer sheet.

15. Mark your answer on your answer sheet.

16. Mark your answer on your answer sheet.

17. Mark your answer on your answer sheet.

18. Mark your answer on your answer sheet.

19. Mark your answer on your answer sheet.

20. Mark your answer on your answer sheet.

21. Mark your answer on your answer sheet.

22. Mark your answer on your answer sheet.

23. Mark your answer on your answer sheet.

24. Mark your answer on your answer sheet.

25. Mark your answer on your answer sheet.

26. Mark your answer on your answer sheet.

27. Mark your answer on your answer sheet.

28. Mark your answer on your answer sheet.

29. Mark your answer on your answer sheet.

30. Mark your answer on your answer sheet.

31. Mark your answer on your answer sheet.

PART 3

Directions: You will hear some conversations between two or more people. You will be asked to answer three questions about what the speakers say in each conversation. Select the best response to each question and mark the letter (A), (B), (C) or (D) on your answer sheet. The conversations will not be printed in your test book and will be spoken only one time.

32. Where does the woman most likely work?
(A) At a hair salon
(B) At a pharmacy
(C) At a health clinic
(D) At a restaurant

33. Why does the woman apologize?
(A) A product is sold out.
(B) An employee made a mistake.
(C) A sale has ended.
(D) An order is not ready.

34. What does the woman remind the man to pick up?
(A) Coupons
(B) Snacks
(C) A catalogue
(D) A membership card

35. What are the speakers mainly discussing?
(A) A promotion
(B) A repair
(C) A product
(D) A schedule

36. What does the man explain to the woman?
(A) He is not accepting more applications.
(B) He is working on another task.
(C) He will prepare an orientation.
(D) He will leave early today.

37. Why does the woman want to use the room today?
(A) To conduct interviews
(B) To meet with some guests
(C) To perform employee evaluations
(D) To participate in a teleconference

38. Where do the men most likely work?
(A) A film studio
(B) A department store
(C) A television network
(D) A construction agency

39. What does the woman say she is surprised about?
(A) A price decrease
(B) A management change
(C) A refund policy
(D) A late delivery

40. What information will the woman be asked to provide?
(A) A business address
(B) A bank account number
(C) A reservation time
(D) A policy revision

41. What type of business is the woman visiting?
(A) A movie theater
(B) A bookstore
(C) An office supply store
(D) A mobile phone vendor

42. What does the woman imply when she says, "I'm leaving for a vacation tonight"?
(A) She will visit another store location.
(B) She has already made a reservation.
(C) She is looking forward to relaxing.
(D) She needs to make a purchase today.

43. What does the woman ask the man to do?
(A) Contact a distributor
(B) Rearrange a display
(C) Check an online store
(D) Provide a discount

GO ON TO THE NEXT PAGE

44. What happened in March?

(A) An employee was hired.
(B) A store was relocated.
(C) A vacation was scheduled.
(D) An online store was launched.

45. According to the woman, what do customers like about the business?

(A) The friendly staff
(B) The store location
(C) The return policy
(D) The variety of goods

46. What does the woman offer to do?

(A) Contact a colleague
(B) Visit the post office
(C) Submit new designs
(D) Create a survey

---

47. What are the speakers mainly discussing?

(A) A retirement dinner
(B) A gym membership
(C) A club activity
(D) A vacation plan

48. Who is Thelma Pierce?

(A) A department manager
(B) A former coworker
(C) A product designer
(D) A professional athlete

49. What will the speakers most likely do at 6:30?

(A) Hold a meeting
(B) Depart for a trip
(C) Repair some equipment
(D) Attend a party

---

50. What service does Fetzer Solutions provide?

(A) Office renovations
(B) Payroll accounting
(C) Market analysis
(D) Performance reviews

51. What did the man's company do three months ago?

(A) It relocated its office.
(B) It received special recognition.
(C) It hired additional staff.
(D) It released a new product.

52. What does Isabelle offer to do?

(A) Provide a discount
(B) Alter a schedule
(C) Estimate an expense
(D) Ship a package

---

53. Why is the man calling?

(A) To express an opinion
(B) To check on an application
(C) To correct an error
(D) To inquire about a subscription

54. What does the woman imply when she says, "most of our employees started out at smaller companies"?

(A) The company has grown quickly.
(B) There are several job openings.
(C) The employees have been recently hired.
(D) The man lacks experience.

55. What will the man do next?

(A) Cancel a request
(B) Schedule a meeting
(C) E-mail a document
(D) Contact a supervisor

---

56. What does the woman say she has done?
(A) Arranged travel plans
(B) Scheduled an interview
(C) Read an article
(D) Filed a report

57. What type of product is being discussed?
(A) An exercise machine
(B) A massage chair
(C) A television
(D) A mattress

58. What will take place tomorrow?
(A) A product test
(B) A training session
(C) A company trip
(D) An investor visit

59. Where is the woman planning to go this morning?
(A) To an airport
(B) To a university
(C) To a hotel
(D) To a restaurant

60. What is the woman surprised about?
(A) A transportation fee
(B) A building location
(C) A travel schedule
(D) An event cancelation

61. What does the man give the woman?
(A) A map
(B) A receipt
(C) A ticket
(D) A timetable

Stacy's Used Phone Shop Fun-in-the-Sun Weekend Sale!		
15% off Thursday only	20% off Friday only	25% off Saturday only

62. What do the speakers mention about a mobile phone?
(A) It is waterproof.
(B) It has good battery life.
(C) It has a new screen.
(D) It has a lot of storage space.

63. Look at the graphic. On which day is the man making a purchase?
(A) Thursday
(B) Friday
(C) Saturday
(D) Sunday

64. What additional service does the man ask about?
(A) Data plans
(B) Product exchanges
(C) In-store repairs
(D) Free accessories

GO ON TO THE NEXT PAGE

Welcome to Version 2.1!

Sample install ○
Quick install ○
Full install ○
Pro install ○

[Cancel] [OK]

65. What does the man say he is trying to do?
(A) Save a document
(B) View a video
(C) Delete a program
(D) Modify an image

66. Look at the graphic. Which option does the woman suggest selecting?
(A) Sample install
(B) Quick install
(C) Full install
(D) Pro install

67. Where will the speakers most likely go next?
(A) To a cafeteria
(B) To a budget review
(C) To a sales meeting
(D) To a product demonstration

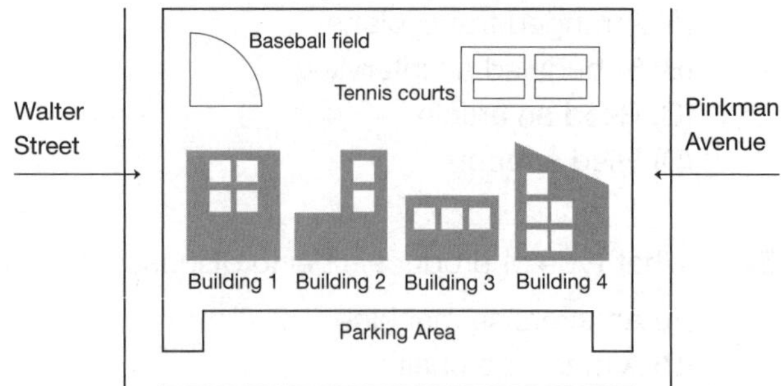

68. What are the speakers mainly discussing?
(A) A business presentation
(B) A radio interview
(C) A sports match
(D) A musical performance

69. Look at the graphic. Which building is Badger Studios located in?
(A) Building 1
(B) Building 2
(C) Building 3
(D) Building 4

70. What does the woman tell the man to do in the lobby?
(A) Wait for a short time
(B) Take the elevator
(C) Pick up a parking pass
(D) Register at the desk

PART 4

Directions: You will hear some talks given by a single speaker. You will be asked to answer three questions about what the speaker says in each talk. Select the best response to each question and mark the letter (A), (B), (C), or (D) on your answer sheet. The talks will not be printed in your test book and will be spoken only one time.

71. What products does the company sell?
(A) Laundry detergents
(B) Pool supplies
(C) Home appliances
(D) Gardening tools

72. What does the speaker emphasize about the products?
(A) They are long lasting.
(B) They are locally made.
(C) They are inexpensive.
(D) They are difficult to find.

73. What is being offered for free this month?
(A) Consultation
(B) Delivery
(C) Repairs
(D) Training classes

---

74. Why is the speaker calling?
(A) To check the status of an order
(B) To schedule equipment repairs
(C) To discuss a project schedule
(D) To respond to a request

75. What does the speaker mean when he says, "It's not up to me"?
(A) He is unable to change a deadline.
(B) He needs assistance with some work.
(C) He cannot authorize a purchase.
(D) He has no experience in finance.

76. What does the speaker suggest the listener do?
(A) Create a report
(B) Submit a receipt
(C) Compare prices
(D) Delay a project

---

77. What kind of business does the speaker work for?
(A) A travel agency
(B) A clothing manufacturer
(C) A publishing company
(D) An accounting firm

78. What is the purpose of the meeting?
(A) To recruit some new talent
(B) To demonstrate a technique
(C) To announce a new business plan
(D) To explain a vacation policy

79. What will the next speaker talk about?
(A) A project schedule
(B) A promotion opportunity
(C) A marketing plan
(D) A budget increase

---

80. Where does the speaker most likely work?
(A) A concert hall
(B) A hotel
(C) A movie theater
(D) An amusement park

81. What does the speaker mean when she says, "we always value our customers"?
(A) She is advertising a limited time offer.
(B) She would like feedback about a program.
(C) She has recommended a premium service.
(D) She wants to make up for a mistake.

82. What does the caller ask the listener to do?
(A) Send a message
(B) Change a payment method
(C) Visit a Web page
(D) Arrive early

GO ON TO THE NEXT PAGE

83. What is the purpose of the speech?

(A) To announce a company merger
(B) To introduce an award recipient
(C) To select a new CEO
(D) To promote a new product

84. What industry does Topher De La Rosa work in?

(A) Web development
(B) Architecture
(C) Graphic design
(D) Fashion

85. According to the speaker, what does Topher De La Rosa plan to do?

(A) Reveal a product
(B) Make a donation to charity
(C) Open locations overseas
(D) Relocate offices

---

86. What product does the speaker's company make?

(A) Plastic utensils
(B) Chocolates
(C) Household cleaners
(D) Baked goods

87. What is the speaker calling about?

(A) A change to an order
(B) A suggestion for a new design
(C) A location for a meeting
(D) A problem with some packaging

88. What does the speaker request?

(A) Product samples
(B) A partial refund
(C) Expedited shipping
(D) A second order

---

89. Where do the listeners most likely work?

(A) At a construction company
(B) At a manufacturing plant
(C) At an architecture firm
(D) At a publishing agency

90. What does the speaker recommend the listeners do?

(A) Provide work-related incentives
(B) Increase staff vacation use
(C) Reduce employee tardiness
(D) Spend time with new employees

91. What will the speaker most likely do next?

(A) Demonstrate a technique
(B) Arrange a dinner
(C) Introduce a book
(D) Schedule a trip

---

92. What will the convention focus on?

(A) Films
(B) Comic books
(C) Model building
(D) Sports cars

93. What does the speaker imply when he says, "But, have you checked them recently"?

(A) Some data hasn't been updated.
(B) Attendance has dropped.
(C) A sales strategy is effective.
(D) Some employees have been absent.

94. What advice does the speaker ask for?

(A) Where to find sponsors
(B) When to send invitations
(C) Who to nominate for an award
(D) How to organize the floor space

"August Nights"		
- Table of Contents -		
Introduction	...	2
Act 1	...	10
Act 2	...	21
Act 3	...	39

95. What does the speaker thank the listeners for?

(A) Wearing costumes
(B) Sharing ideas
(C) Arriving early
(D) Bringing refreshments

96. Look at the graphic. Which section will the listeners cover today?

(A) Introduction
(B) Act 1
(C) Act 2
(D) Act 3

97. What does the speaker say about the afternoon session?

(A) It will be rescheduled.
(B) A special guest will attend.
(C) Some equipment will not be available.
(D) The listeners must make a payment.

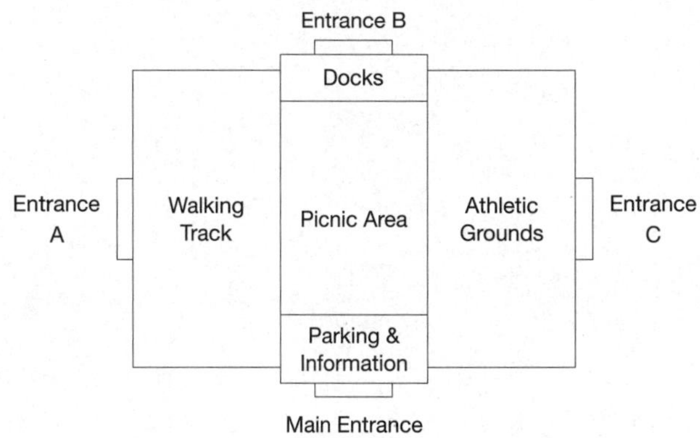

98. What is the purpose of the meeting?

(A) To prepare for an event
(B) To create a park map
(C) To train new employees
(D) To make a reservation

99. Look at the graphic. Which entrance will guests use on Saturday?

(A) Main Entrance
(B) Entrance A
(C) Entrance B
(D) Entrance C

100. What does the speaker say will happen in the picnic area?

(A) A speech will be given.
(B) A DJ will perform.
(C) A contest will be held.
(D) A meal will be served.

This is the end of the Listening Test. Turn to Part 5 in your test book.

정답 및 스크립트 p.237 / 점수 환산표 p.363

GO ON TO THE NEXT PAGE

실전모의고사
TEST 3

TEST 3 MP3

TEST 3 해설

시작 시간 ________시 ________분

종료 시간 ________시 ________분

▸중간에 멈추지 말고 처음부터 끝까지 풀어보세요. 문제를 풀 때는 실전처럼 답안지에 마킹하세요.

LISTENING TEST

In the Listening test, you will be asked to demonstrate how well you understand spoken English. The entire Listening test will last approximately 45 minutes. There are four parts, and directions are given for each part. You must mark your answers on the separate answer sheet.

Do not write your answers in your test book.

PART 1

Directions: For each question in this part, you will hear four statements about a picture in your test book. When you hear the statements, you must select the one statement that best describes what you see in the picture. Then find the number of the question on your answer sheet and mark your answer. The statements will not be printed in your test book and will be spoken only one time.

Statement (D), "They are taking photographs," is the best description of the picture, so you should select answer (D) and mark it on your answer sheet.

1.

2.

GO ON TO THE NEXT PAGE

3.

4.

5.

6.

TEST 3

GO ON TO THE NEXT PAGE

PART 2

Directions: You will hear a question or statement and three responses spoken in English. They will not be printed in your test book and will be spoken only one time. Select the best response to the question or statement and mark the letter (A), (B), or (C) on your answer sheet.

7. Mark your answer on your answer sheet.
8. Mark your answer on your answer sheet.
9. Mark your answer on your answer sheet.
10. Mark your answer on your answer sheet.
11. Mark your answer on your answer sheet.
12. Mark your answer on your answer sheet.
13. Mark your answer on your answer sheet.
14. Mark your answer on your answer sheet.
15. Mark your answer on your answer sheet.
16. Mark your answer on your answer sheet.
17. Mark your answer on your answer sheet.
18. Mark your answer on your answer sheet.
19. Mark your answer on your answer sheet.
20. Mark your answer on your answer sheet.
21. Mark your answer on your answer sheet.
22. Mark your answer on your answer sheet.
23. Mark your answer on your answer sheet.
24. Mark your answer on your answer sheet.
25. Mark your answer on your answer sheet.
26. Mark your answer on your answer sheet.
27. Mark your answer on your answer sheet.
28. Mark your answer on your answer sheet.
29. Mark your answer on your answer sheet.
30. Mark your answer on your answer sheet.
31. Mark your answer on your answer sheet.

PART 3

Directions: You will hear some conversations between two or more people. You will be asked to answer three questions about what the speakers say in each conversation. Select the best response to each question and mark the letter (A), (B), (C) or (D) on your answer sheet. The conversations will not be printed in your test book and will be spoken only one time.

32. Why is the man speaking to the woman?
(A) To invite her to an event
(B) To offer assistance
(C) To inquire about tickets
(D) To ask for directions

33. What event is the man planning to attend?
(A) A musical performance
(B) A sporting event
(C) A professional seminar
(D) A job interview

34. What does the woman advise the man to do?
(A) Take a different subway line
(B) Wait for a shuttle bus
(C) Go to a destination on foot
(D) Use a specific parking facility

---

35. Where is the conversation most likely taking place?
(A) A bakery
(B) A restaurant
(C) A company event
(D) A pharmacy

36. According to the woman, what has caused a problem?
(A) Some equipment is malfunctioning.
(B) She ran out of ingredients.
(C) A payment was not sent.
(D) An employee is absent.

37. What does the woman offer to do?
(A) Provide an alternative
(B) Expedite a service
(C) Recommend another business
(D) Deliver a product

---

38. Where does the conversation probably take place?
(A) A taxi stop
(B) An airport
(C) A bus station
(D) A city center

39. What are the women concerned about?
(A) Checking their luggage
(B) Finding a hotel
(C) Missing a reservation
(D) Saving some money

40. What does the man suggest the women do?
(A) Download an app
(B) Order a drink
(C) Call a cab
(D) Use a travel card

---

41. Who most likely are the speakers?
(A) Computer technicians
(B) Real estate agents
(C) Web developers
(D) Bank clerks

42. What are the speakers mainly discussing?
(A) A system error
(B) A new employee
(C) A pay request
(D) A work schedule

43. What does the man suggest the woman do?
(A) Call a specialist
(B) Provide a refund
(C) Offer a discount
(D) Cancel a service

GO ON TO THE NEXT PAGE

44. Why does the woman ask for a recommendation?
(A) She is entertaining clients.
(B) She is new to the city.
(C) She is in charge of a company outing.
(D) She is organizing a party.

45. What does the man say about the tickets?
(A) Some are more expensive.
(B) They currently cost less.
(C) They are likely sold out.
(D) VIP sections are available.

46. What does the woman say she will do right away?
(A) Order tickets
(B) Send a message
(C) Cancel a reservation
(D) Finish a project

---

47. What does the man say he needs?
(A) A signed document
(B) A bank account number
(C) A business address
(D) A client's phone number

48. What does the woman imply when she says, "Oh, I just got on the subway"?
(A) She is reassuring the man.
(B) She is happy to be leaving work.
(C) She cannot assist the man.
(D) She should have taken a taxi.

49. What does the man decide to do?
(A) Check a Web site
(B) Return to the office
(C) Send an e-mail
(D) Reschedule a meeting

---

50. Where do the speakers most likely work?
(A) A furniture store
(B) A hardware store
(C) A moving company
(D) A clothing shop

51. What has caused a problem?
(A) Some products are not available.
(B) A delivery has not arrived.
(C) A special event is canceled.
(D) The prices are too high.

52. What do the speakers decide to do?
(A) Extend store hours
(B) Offer a refund
(C) Accept monthly payments
(D) Provide additional benefits

---

53. What are the speakers discussing?
(A) Applying for a job opening
(B) Participating in an exhibition
(C) Attending a lecture series
(D) Arranging a business trip

54. What problem does the man mention?
(A) He is still in an employment contract.
(B) He will be attending another event.
(C) He does not have enough experience.
(D) He cannot take any time off to travel.

55. What does the woman say to reassure the man?
(A) The interview can be done online.
(B) The event will be in another city.
(C) Several openings are still available.
(D) The deadline has been changed.

---

56. Who most likely are the speakers?

(A) Landscapers
(B) Lawyers
(C) Athletes
(D) Graphic designers

57. Why does the man say, "They've hired us before, right"?

(A) To criticize a coworker
(B) To assign a task
(C) To ask about a client
(D) To cancel an agreement

58. How does the man want to change the contract?

(A) By adding overtime pay
(B) By including more workers
(C) By removing a refund policy
(D) By permitting deadline extensions

---

59. What type of business does the man work for?

(A) An office supplies store
(B) A publishing company
(C) An advertising agency
(D) A library

60. What does the man say the business is known for?

(A) Its customer service
(B) Its low prices
(C) Its convenient location
(D) Its high quality products

61. What is the problem with the delivery?

(A) An address is incorrect.
(B) A shipping fee is too expensive.
(C) The delivery arrived late.
(D) The order is incomplete.

Destination	Departure
New York City	2:20
Pittsburgh	Sold out
Baltimore	3:30
New York City	Canceled
Pittsburgh	4:40
Baltimore	6:00

62. Look at the graphic. What is the departure time of the flight that the man will take?

(A) 2:20
(B) 3:30
(C) 4:40
(D) 6:00

63. What does the woman ask the man about?

(A) The limits on a budget
(B) His progress on a report
(C) Some revisions to a speech
(D) His attendance at a dinner

64. What does the woman volunteer to do?

(A) Record an event
(B) Reschedule some plans
(C) Send an address
(D) Book a hotel room

GO ON TO THE NEXT PAGE

Monthly Rates per Package		
Individual	U.S. only	$5.00
Family	U.S. only	$9.00
Family Deluxe	North America	$12.00
Family Global	North America, Europe, Asia	$15.00

65. Who most likely is the woman?
(A) A customer service representative
(B) A travel agent
(C) A store attendant
(D) An international courier

66. Look at the graphic. Which monthly rate will the man pay?
(A) $5.00
(B) $9.00
(C) $12.00
(D) $15.00

67. What will the man most likely do next?
(A) Upgrade a service
(B) Choose a delivery option
(C) Provide payment information
(D) Notify a colleague

MyWeather-Nashville, TN
Extended Forecast

Monday	26°	Thunderstorms
Tuesday	25°	Sunny
Wednesday	24°	Rainy
Thursday	28°	Sunny

68. What activity are the speakers mainly discussing?
(A) A park opening
(B) A statue unveiling
(C) A holiday celebration
(D) A community fair

69. Look at the graphic. Which day do the speakers choose?
(A) Monday
(B) Tuesday
(C) Wednesday
(D) Thursday

70. What does the woman say she will do?
(A) Contact a news agency
(B) Prepare a speech
(C) Provide refreshments
(D) Hire a photographer

PART 4

Directions: You will hear some talks given by a single speaker. You will be asked to answer three questions about what the speaker says in each talk. Select the best response to each question and mark the letter (A), (B), (C), or (D) on your answer sheet. The talks will not be printed in your test book and will be spoken only one time.

71. What does the store most likely sell?

(A) Home furnishings
(B) Electronic goods
(C) Camping gear
(D) Art supplies

72. What does the speaker say has been extended?

(A) An application period
(B) A seasonal sale
(C) A renovation deadline
(D) A grand opening event

73. Why does the speaker apologize?

(A) Business hours have changed.
(B) A parking area is closed.
(C) Vouchers are no longer accepted.
(D) A branch will be relocated.

---

74. What is being advertised?

(A) A travel consulting service
(B) An accounting program
(C) A data storage service
(D) A home security device

75. What has the business received an award for?

(A) Its customer service
(B) Its innovative designs
(C) Its hiring policies
(D) Its low prices

76. What offer does the speaker mention?

(A) Free installation
(B) A discounted price
(C) A premium membership
(D) A product demonstration

---

77. Who is the speaker?

(A) An event organizer
(B) A musician
(C) A TV host
(D) A museum curator

78. According to the speaker, what is Gatlinburg most known for?

(A) Its hotels
(B) Its writers
(C) Its musicians
(D) Its shopping centers

79. Why does the speaker say, "Yes, that Enrique Marquez"?

(A) To correct the pronunciation of a name
(B) To highlight the popularity of a celebrity
(C) To make an addition to an itinerary
(D) To blame someone for an error

---

80. What is the main topic of the broadcast?

(A) An education project
(B) A local festival
(C) A public library
(D) A recycling service

81. What will the listeners now be able to do?

(A) Reserve a facility
(B) Extend a membership
(C) Participate in a contest
(D) Receive text alerts

82. Why does the speaker say, "I'll give it a try, too"?

(A) To criticize a strategy
(B) To support a service
(C) To assist with an effort
(D) To offer instructions

GO ON TO THE NEXT PAGE

83. What is the speaker mainly talking about?
(A) Participating in a special event
(B) Applying for a gym membership
(C) Attending a company dinner
(D) Planning a vacation schedule

84. Who is Miranda Tucker?
(A) A lawyer
(B) A fitness instructor
(C) A chef
(D) A public official

85. What will the speaker do next?
(A) Hand out a registration sheet
(B) Prepare some snacks
(C) Revise a document
(D) Share a Web address

---

86. What is the topic of today's program?
(A) Lowering shipping costs
(B) Investing in diverse markets
(C) Increasing online sales
(D) Expanding a business overseas

87. According to the speaker, what did Ashley Reynolds recently do?
(A) Teach a class
(B) Speak at an event
(C) Launch a Web site
(D) Break a record

88. What are the listeners encouraged to do?
(A) Post comments online
(B) Listen to the next episode
(C) Attend a lecture
(D) Support a sponsor

---

89. Who most likely is the speaker?
(A) A landscaper
(B) A construction manager
(C) An interior designer
(D) A furniture store owner

90. What does the speaker mean when she says, "we can't stretch that far"?
(A) A project is delayed.
(B) A schedule is too busy.
(C) An item is sold out.
(D) A budget is limited.

91. What has the speaker sent to the listener?
(A) Business documents
(B) Product samples
(C) Building blueprints
(D) Store receipts

---

92. What type of business does the speaker work for?
(A) A fitness center
(B) A pharmaceutical company
(C) A medical clinic
(D) A financial firm

93. What will happen on Thursday?
(A) Some officials will hold an inspection.
(B) A journalist will conduct some interviews.
(C) Some shareholders will visit a facility.
(D) A CEO will announce a new product.

94. What are the listeners asked to do?
(A) Attend a presentation
(B) Prepare some data
(C) Rearrange an office
(D) Delay some work

Counter 1 Sausages	Counter 2 Steaks	Counter 3 Chicken	Counter 4 Fish

95. What is the store celebrating?
(A) A business anniversary
(B) A national holiday
(C) A new location
(D) A store renovation

96. When will the event end?
(A) In an hour
(B) This evening
(C) Tomorrow
(D) Next week

97. Look at the graphic. Which deli counter contains items with an additional discount?
(A) Counter 1
(B) Counter 2
(C) Counter 3
(D) Counter 4

Business:
The Redwood

Health Checklist:
✓ Food storage
✓ Prep area
✓ Employee hygiene
✓ Dining area

Comments:
Inspection failed - Refrigeration

Agent:
Jenn Hines

98. Where does the speaker work?
(A) At a pharmacy
(B) At a farm
(C) At a restaurant
(D) At a grocery store

99. Look at the graphic. Which section of the report does the speaker ask about?
(A) Business
(B) Health Check-list
(C) Comments
(D) Agent

100. What does the speaker say he is concerned about?
(A) Paying staff members on time
(B) Keeping up with a competitor
(C) Leaving for a vacation
(D) Participating in a local event

This is the end of the Listening Test. Turn to Part 5 in your test book.

정답 및 스크립트 p.246 / 점수 환산표 p.363

GO ON TO THE NEXT PAGE

실전모의고사

TEST 4

TEST 4 MP3

TEST 4 해설

시작 시간 ________시 ________분

종료 시간 ________시 ________분

▸ 중간에 멈추지 말고 처음부터 끝까지 풀어보세요. 문제를 풀 때는 실전처럼 답안지에 마킹하세요.

LISTENING TEST

In the Listening test, you will be asked to demonstrate how well you understand spoken English. The entire Listening test will last approximately 45 minutes. There are four parts, and directions are given for each part. You must mark your answers on the separate answer sheet.

Do not write your answers in your test book.

PART 1

Directions: For each question in this part, you will hear four statements about a picture in your test book. When you hear the statements, you must select the one statement that best describes what you see in the picture. Then find the number of the question on your answer sheet and mark your answer. The statements will not be printed in your test book and will be spoken only one time.

Statement (D), "They are taking photographs," is the best description of the picture, so you should select answer (D) and mark it on your answer sheet.

1.

TEST 4

2.

GO ON TO THE NEXT PAGE

3.

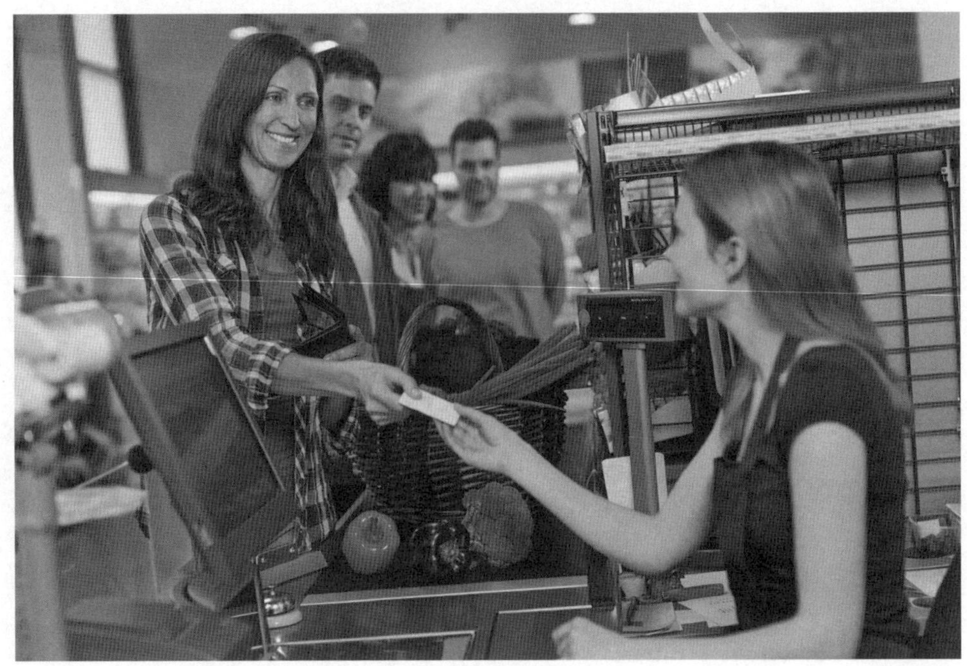

4.

5.

6.

GO ON TO THE NEXT PAGE

PART 2

Directions: You will hear a question or statement and three responses spoken in English. They will not be printed in your test book and will be spoken only one time. Select the best response to the question or statement and mark the letter (A), (B), or (C) on your answer sheet.

7. Mark your answer on your answer sheet.

8. Mark your answer on your answer sheet.

9. Mark your answer on your answer sheet.

10. Mark your answer on your answer sheet.

11. Mark your answer on your answer sheet.

12. Mark your answer on your answer sheet.

13. Mark your answer on your answer sheet.

14. Mark your answer on your answer sheet.

15. Mark your answer on your answer sheet.

16. Mark your answer on your answer sheet.

17. Mark your answer on your answer sheet.

18. Mark your answer on your answer sheet.

19. Mark your answer on your answer sheet.

20. Mark your answer on your answer sheet.

21. Mark your answer on your answer sheet.

22. Mark your answer on your answer sheet.

23. Mark your answer on your answer sheet.

24. Mark your answer on your answer sheet.

25. Mark your answer on your answer sheet.

26. Mark your answer on your answer sheet.

27. Mark your answer on your answer sheet.

28. Mark your answer on your answer sheet.

29. Mark your answer on your answer sheet.

30. Mark your answer on your answer sheet.

31. Mark your answer on your answer sheet.

PART 3

Directions: You will hear some conversations between two or more people. You will be asked to answer three questions about what the speakers say in each conversation. Select the best response to each question and mark the letter (A), (B), (C) or (D) on your answer sheet. The conversations will not be printed in your test book and will be spoken only one time.

32. What are the speakers mainly discussing?
(A) Correcting a mistake
(B) Releasing a product
(C) Attending an event
(D) Placing an order

33. According to the woman, how should the man submit information?
(A) By using a Web site
(B) By calling a number
(C) By visiting a store
(D) By completing a form

34. What does the man say will happen next month?
(A) A business will close.
(B) A competition will be held.
(C) A membership will start.
(D) An award will be given.

35. What product is being discussed?
(A) A cleaning solution
(B) An electronic device
(C) A piece of furniture
(D) A vehicle

36. What does the woman like about the product?
(A) It has a variety of models.
(B) It is inexpensive.
(C) It is guaranteed to last for a long time.
(D) It is made with a special material.

37. What does Nathan agree to do?
(A) Lend an item
(B) Call a store
(C) Share a coupon
(D) Place an order

38. What is the woman calling about?
(A) A product exchange
(B) A special offer
(C) A payment error
(D) A store location

39. What does the woman say she is worried about?
(A) The store hours
(B) A late delivery
(C) The additional costs
(D) A purchase date

40. What does the man remind the woman to bring?
(A) An identification card
(B) A receipt
(C) A sales catalogue
(D) A piece of equipment

41. Why does the man congratulate the woman?
(A) She completed a training course.
(B) She published an article.
(C) She negotiated a deal.
(D) She won an award.

42. Where do the speakers most likely work?
(A) At a news agency
(B) At a museum
(C) At an advertising firm
(D) At a vehicle manufacturer

43. What will take place on Friday?
(A) A dinner
(B) A presentation
(C) A grand opening
(D) An interview

TEST 4

GO ON TO THE NEXT PAGE

44. What does the woman need help doing?
(A) Collecting tickets
(B) Arranging a schedule
(C) Cleaning an area
(D) Fixing some equipment

45. Why does Mitch say, "A film in Theater A just finished"?
(A) To assign a task
(B) To recommend a change
(C) To explain a delay
(D) To correct an error

46. What will the woman most likely do next?
(A) Purchase an item
(B) Update an itinerary
(C) Introduce a film
(D) Speak with a supervisor

---

47. Where does the man work?
(A) A utility company
(B) A landscaping agency
(C) A construction firm
(D) A hardware shop

48. What does the man want to do?
(A) Renew a contract
(B) Rent some equipment
(C) Hire temporary help
(D) Request a repair

49. What does the woman ask the man to do?
(A) Pay a deposit fee
(B) Provide some personal information
(C) Attend a training session
(D) Arrive early for a service

---

50. What problem does the woman mention?
(A) A TV will not turn on.
(B) A key does not work.
(C) A bathroom needs to be restocked.
(D) A device will not open.

51. What will the man ask Philip to do?
(A) Prepare a meal
(B) Replace some equipment
(C) Clean a room
(D) Provide transportation

52. What does the man suggest the woman do?
(A) Take some photographs
(B) Store some items
(C) Book a tour
(D) Make a payment

---

53. What question does the woman have about a promotional campaign?
(A) Why it uses different posters
(B) Why it focuses on women
(C) Why it is not nationwide
(D) Why it has a short duration

54. Which department does the man most likely work in?
(A) Research and Development
(B) Accounting
(C) Graphic Design
(D) Human Resources

55. What does the woman ask to see?
(A) A magazine article
(B) A product design
(C) A television interview
(D) A marketing plan

---

56. What does the man say is a problem?
(A) A shipment has not gone out.
(B) Employees are causing technical issues.
(C) An employee orientation is insufficient.
(D) A deadline is too soon.

57. How does the woman propose solving the problem?
(A) By hiring a consultant
(B) By transferring some employees
(C) By changing a policy
(D) By giving a presentation

58. What does the woman ask the man to do?
(A) Complete some training
(B) Cancel a meeting
(C) Install some software
(D) Compile a list

---

59. What are the speakers mainly discussing?
(A) A software development
(B) A sales report
(C) A travel itinerary
(D) A business opening

60. What does the woman imply when she says, "Wow! That wasn't what I was expecting"?
(A) She isn't ready for a presentation.
(B) She disagrees with a plan.
(C) She wasn't involved in a project.
(D) She is happy about some news.

61. What will the woman receive soon?
(A) A project timeline
(B) A return ticket
(C) An updated device
(D) A survey result

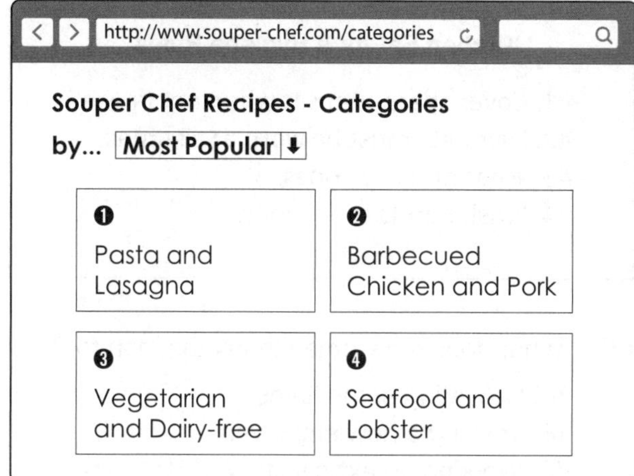

62. What project is the man working on?
(A) Hosting a retirement party
(B) Planning a wedding
(C) Catering an event
(D) Opening a restaurant

63. Look at the graphic. Which category will the woman most likely search?
(A) Category 1
(B) Category 2
(C) Category 3
(D) Category 4

64. Why does the man recommend using recipes from souper-chef.com?
(A) The recipes are simple to make.
(B) The company employs several famous chefs.
(C) The recipes use diverse ingredients.
(D) The company updates the site frequently.

TEST 4

GO ON TO THE NEXT PAGE

Kitchen Safety & Hygiene Rules

#1. Cover sharp utensils when not in use.
#2. Hair nets must be worn at all times.
#3. Wear non-slip shoes.
#4. Wash hands every hour.

65. What does the woman thank the man for?

(A) Delivering some items
(B) Training a new employee
(C) Working an extra shift
(D) Providing a ride to work

66. What happened to the man this afternoon?

(A) He slept through an alarm.
(B) He made a purchase.
(C) He felt sick.
(D) He got caught in bad weather.

67. Look at the graphic. Which safety & hygiene rule are the speakers discussing?

(A) #1
(B) #2
(C) #3
(D) #4

Brand:	Rupture Farms
Item:	Sal's Frozen Burrito
Flavor:	Spicy Chicken
Heating instructions:	Microwave - 3 minutes
Serving size:	1

68. What does the woman say they will need to do?

(A) Change an ingredient
(B) Increase advertising
(C) Hire more employees
(D) Visit a location

69. What does the man suggest?

(A) Holding a demonstration
(B) Attending an event
(C) Launching a Web site
(D) Changing some deadlines

70. Look at the graphic. Which section of the label will the man need to revise?

(A) Item
(B) Flavor
(C) Heating instructions
(D) Serving size

PART 4

Directions: You will hear some talks given by a single speaker. You will be asked to answer three questions about what the speaker says in each talk. Select the best response to each question and mark the letter (A), (B), (C), or (D) on your answer sheet. The talks will not be printed in your test book and will be spoken only one time.

71. What is the speaker calling about?
(A) A computer repair
(B) A missing shipment
(C) A printing order
(D) A store location

72. According to the speaker, what will take place on March 3?
(A) A new store will open.
(B) A magazine will be released.
(C) A special offer will end.
(D) A lease will begin.

73. What does the speaker say is available on a Web site?
(A) A product listing
(B) A price calculator
(C) A delivery tracker
(D) An event calendar

---

74. What kind of company does the speaker work for?
(A) Publishing
(B) Software development
(C) Online advertising
(D) Web design

75. What are the listeners asked to do first?
(A) Register on a Web site
(B) Choose a desk
(C) Make a name tag
(D) Select a meal

76. What does the speaker say is available in the back of the room?
(A) Refreshments
(B) Maps
(C) T-shirts
(D) Office supplies

---

77. Who is the speaker most likely talking to?
(A) New employees
(B) Potential investors
(C) Local business owners
(D) Tour group members

78. What does the speaker mean when he says, "Ms. Dawson will discuss the town's history this afternoon"?
(A) The listeners should try to be on time.
(B) He apologizes for a change in schedule.
(C) He advises the listeners to register for an event.
(D) The listeners' questions will be answered.

79. What will the listeners most likely do next?
(A) Tour a market
(B) Watch a presentation
(C) Enjoy a meal
(D) Read some information

---

80. What does the speaker apologize for?
(A) Missing a social event
(B) Changing a deadline
(C) Turning in a late assignment
(D) Forgetting to send an e-mail

81. According to the survey, what are customers dissatisfied with?
(A) The writing quality
(B) The subscription costs
(C) The online content
(D) The delivery schedule

82. What will happen on Tuesday?
(A) A job opening will be posted.
(B) A Web site will be updated.
(C) A book will be published.
(D) An investor will visit a department.

GO ON TO THE NEXT PAGE →

83. What is the news report mainly about?
(A) A new law
(B) A community center
(C) A health program
(D) A sports league

84. According to the speaker, what will Heads Up Development do?
(A) Conduct a survey
(B) Hire instructors
(C) Open a local branch
(D) Organize a conference

85. What are the listeners invited to do?
(A) Review a proposal
(B) Volunteer for a program
(C) Donate some supplies
(D) Contact an official

---

86. What type of industry does the speaker work in?
(A) Training
(B) Manufacturing
(C) Recruitment
(D) Sales

87. Why does the speaker say, "they're enjoying their highest employee retention rate ever"?
(A) To explain a process
(B) To offer a job
(C) To describe a work environment
(D) To give an example

88. What does the speaker say he will do next week?
(A) Go on a leave
(B) Place an ad
(C) Publish some research
(D) Arrange a meeting

---

89. What is the purpose of the talk?
(A) To announce a store sale
(B) To promote a new product
(C) To provide details about an event
(D) To describe the rules of a contest

90. What feature of the sneakers does the speaker mention?
(A) Improved grip
(B) Automatic lacing
(C) Additional cushioning
(D) Color changing

91. What will the speaker most likely do next?
(A) Distribute samples
(B) Introduce a colleague
(C) Give a demonstration
(D) Answer questions

---

92. Why is the speaker canceling today's meeting?
(A) A personal matter came up.
(B) Some clients have arrived early.
(C) A meeting room is unavailable.
(D) There was a scheduling error.

93. According to the speaker, what was the listener's proposal about?
(A) Ways to improve customer service
(B) Recommendations for a promotion
(C) Reasons for opening a new office
(D) Requests for vacation leave

94. What does the speaker imply when she says, "We'll discuss it more later"?
(A) She will call back soon.
(B) She wants to read other reports.
(C) She is surprised by a rental fee.
(D) She thinks a change is not helpful.

Parking Directory

Entrances A - C ----- Red Lot
Entrances D - F ----- Orange Lot
Entrances G - I ----- Yellow Lot
Entrances J - L ----- Green Lot

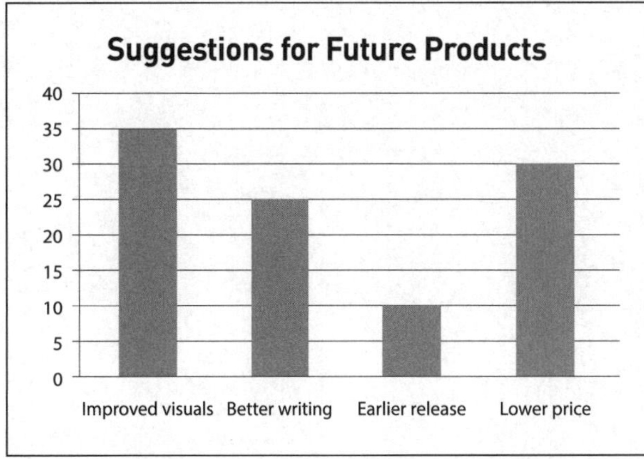

95. What will most likely be discussed at the meeting?
(A) A business merger
(B) A leasing agreement
(C) An event schedule
(D) An advertising deal

96. What should the listener do at the ticket booth?
(A) Contact the speaker
(B) Check a map
(C) Join a tour
(D) Pick up a guest pass

97. Look at the graphic. Which entrance is the speaker's office located at?
(A) Entrance A
(B) Entrance D
(C) Entrance G
(D) Entrance J

98. Who most likely are the listeners?
(A) Game developers
(B) TV producers
(C) Film directors
(D) Book publishers

99. Look at the graphic. Which category is the speaker concerned about?
(A) Improved visuals
(B) Better writing
(C) Earlier release
(D) Lower price

100. What has the company decided to do?
(A) Work with another company
(B) Hire additional employees
(C) Delay an announcement
(D) Open a new office

This is the end of the Listening Test. Turn to Part 5 in your test book.

정답 및 스크립트 p.255 / 점수 환산표 p.363

GO ON TO THE NEXT PAGE

실전모의고사
TEST 5

시작 시간 ________시 ________분

종료 시간 ________시 ________분

▸ 중간에 멈추지 말고 처음부터 끝까지 풀어보세요. 문제를 풀 때는 실전처럼 답안지에 마킹하세요.

LISTENING TEST

In the Listening test, you will be asked to demonstrate how well you understand spoken English. The entire Listening test will last approximately 45 minutes. There are four parts, and directions are given for each part. You must mark your answers on the separate answer sheet.

Do not write your answers in your test book.

PART 1

Directions: For each question in this part, you will hear four statements about a picture in your test book. When you hear the statements, you must select the one statement that best describes what you see in the picture. Then find the number of the question on your answer sheet and mark your answer. The statements will not be printed in your test book and will be spoken only one time.

Statement (D), "They are taking photographs," is the best description of the picture, so you should select answer (D) and mark it on your answer sheet.

1.

TEST 5

2.

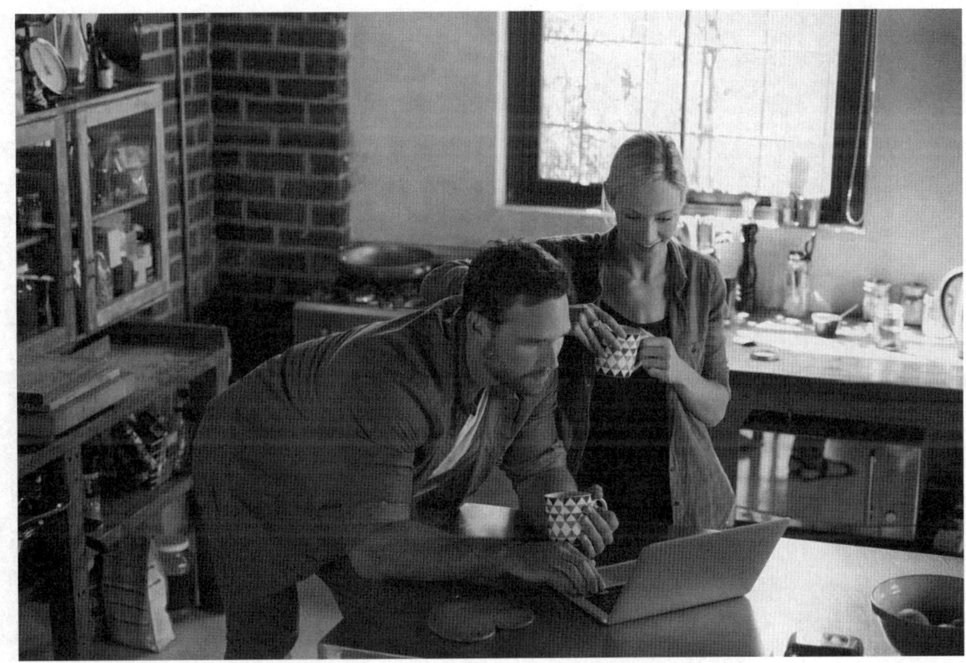

GO ON TO THE NEXT PAGE →

3.

4.

5.

6.

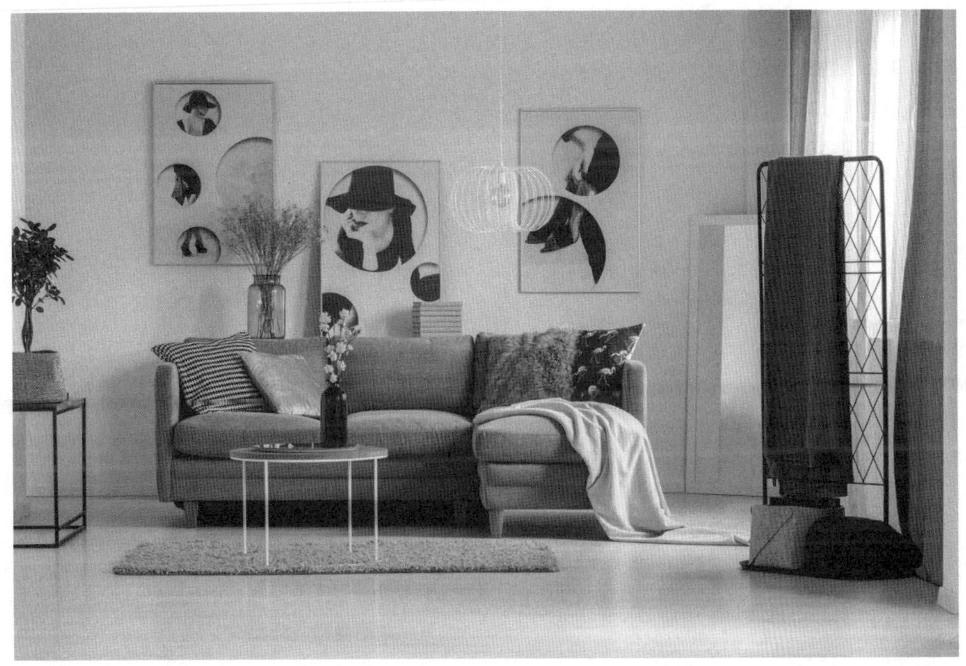

TEST 5

GO ON TO THE NEXT PAGE

PART 2

Directions: You will hear a question or statement and three responses spoken in English. They will not be printed in your test book and will be spoken only one time. Select the best response to the question or statement and mark the letter (A), (B), or (C) on your answer sheet.

7. Mark your answer on your answer sheet.
8. Mark your answer on your answer sheet.
9. Mark your answer on your answer sheet.
10. Mark your answer on your answer sheet.
11. Mark your answer on your answer sheet.
12. Mark your answer on your answer sheet.
13. Mark your answer on your answer sheet.
14. Mark your answer on your answer sheet.
15. Mark your answer on your answer sheet.
16. Mark your answer on your answer sheet.
17. Mark your answer on your answer sheet.
18. Mark your answer on your answer sheet.
19. Mark your answer on your answer sheet.
20. Mark your answer on your answer sheet.
21. Mark your answer on your answer sheet.
22. Mark your answer on your answer sheet.
23. Mark your answer on your answer sheet.
24. Mark your answer on your answer sheet.
25. Mark your answer on your answer sheet.
26. Mark your answer on your answer sheet.
27. Mark your answer on your answer sheet.
28. Mark your answer on your answer sheet.
29. Mark your answer on your answer sheet.
30. Mark your answer on your answer sheet.
31. Mark your answer on your answer sheet.

PART 3

Directions: You will hear some conversations between two or more people. You will be asked to answer three questions about what the speakers say in each conversation. Select the best response to each question and mark the letter (A), (B), (C) or (D) on your answer sheet. The conversations will not be printed in your test book and will be spoken only one time.

32. Where does the woman work?
(A) At a utility provider
(B) At a waste management facility
(C) At a catering company
(D) At a storage rental agency

33. Why is the man calling?
(A) To promote a new business
(B) To schedule a meeting
(C) To explain a late payment
(D) To ask about a service

34. What will the man most likely do next?
(A) Sign a contract
(B) Provide a document
(C) Check an amount
(D) Order some supplies

---

35. What is the topic of the conversation?
(A) Film
(B) Television
(C) Theater
(D) Technology

36. What caused a problem?
(A) Faulty equipment
(B) Scheduling errors
(C) Missed deadlines
(D) Low sales

37. What will the listeners hear next?
(A) A song
(B) An advertisement
(C) A weather forecast
(D) A speech

---

38. What does the man want to do?
(A) File a complaint
(B) Arrange a tour
(C) Reserve a room
(D) Purchase some tickets

39. What is the man asked to choose?
(A) A departure time
(B) A beverage option
(C) A donation amount
(D) A shirt design

40. What does the woman suggest doing?
(A) Eating at a restaurant
(B) Arriving early
(C) Returning an item
(D) Joining a membership program

---

41. Where do the speakers most likely work?
(A) At a concert venue
(B) At a radio station
(C) At a music store
(D) At a printing shop

42. What does the woman say she dislikes doing?
(A) Making advertisements
(B) Selling merchandise
(C) Moving some equipment
(D) Updating a Web site

43. What does the man say he will bring to work tomorrow?
(A) An art sample
(B) A magazine article
(C) A microphone
(D) A festival flyer

GO ON TO THE NEXT PAGE

44. What does the man offer to do?

(A) Place an order
(B) Make a reservation
(C) Give a ride
(D) Share an umbrella

45. According to the man, what happened last week?

(A) A shipment was lost.
(B) A client visited.
(C) A car broke down.
(D) A lease began.

46. Why does the woman say, "a special part had to be shipped from overseas"?

(A) To recommend a service
(B) To explain a delay
(C) To highlight a product's value
(D) To express excitement over a purchase

---

47. Where do the speakers work?

(A) At a TV station
(B) At a publishing agency
(C) At an accounting firm
(D) At a newspaper company

48. What were the speakers surprised by?

(A) The job requirements
(B) The difficulty of questions
(C) The quality of the applicants
(D) The starting pay

49. What has Josh been asked to do next?

(A) Prepare a workspace
(B) Begin some paperwork
(C) Introduce a new employee
(D) Make some phone calls

---

50. Who most likely is the man?

(A) A client
(B) A consultant
(C) An investor
(D) An executive

51. What does the woman ask for?

(A) An identification number
(B) An address
(C) An assessment
(D) A reference

52. What does the man receive?

(A) A job offer
(B) A salary bonus
(C) A letter of recommendation
(D) A gift

---

53. Who is the man?

(A) A travel agent
(B) A landscaper
(C) A groundskeeper
(D) A guest

54. What problem does the woman mention?

(A) Some equipment needs to be replaced.
(B) An area is inaccessible.
(C) Proper maintenance is difficult.
(D) Customer complaints have increased.

55. What does the man say he will complete in two weeks?

(A) A product model
(B) A work contract
(C) A business review
(D) A repayment plan

---

56. What are the speakers mainly discussing?
(A) A product catalog
(B) A company logo
(C) An advertising campaign
(D) An employee handbook

57. What problem does the woman mention?
(A) Some fonts are difficult to read.
(B) Some materials are too expensive.
(C) Some documents are missing.
(D) Some colors are unappealing.

58. What do the men agree to do?
(A) Give a presentation
(B) Make some revisions
(C) Order some supplies
(D) Conduct market research

---

59. What type of product is being discussed?
(A) A computer program
(B) A kitchen appliance
(C) A musical instrument
(D) A personal vehicle

60. Which product feature is the man most proud of?
(A) The compact size
(B) The ease of use
(C) The energy efficiency
(D) The low cost

61. Why does the man say, "my favorite soccer team is playing that night"?
(A) To share an interest
(B) To regret a missed opportunity
(C) To request a favor
(D) To turn down an invitation

Destination	Cost
Southside	$8
River Bend	$12
Uncanny Valley	$14
Polaris	$16

62. Look at the graphic. Where is the woman going?
(A) Southside
(B) River Bend
(C) Uncanny Valley
(D) Polaris

63. Why does the man say the trip will cost extra?
(A) Fuel prices are currently high.
(B) It is late at night.
(C) There will be multiple stops.
(D) There is a lot of traffic.

64. What does the man remind the woman to do?
(A) Take her belongings
(B) Leave a review
(C) Make a payment
(D) Use a map

GO ON TO THE NEXT PAGE

Tour	Available Tickets
9:00 A.M.	Sold out
10:00 A.M.	4
11:00 A.M.	1
2:00 P.M.	5

65. What do the speakers plan to tour?

(A) A train station
(B) A government building
(C) A state park
(D) A car factory

66. What does the woman remind the man about?

(A) Changing a travel itinerary
(B) Submitting a report
(C) Checking out of a hotel
(D) Bringing a passport

67. Look at the graphic. Which tour will the speakers buy tickets for?

(A) 9:00 A.M.
(B) 10:00 A.M.
(C) 11:00 A.M.
(D) 2:00 P.M.

Moss's Café
Sandwich Menu

#1. Ham & Mustard
#2. Ham & Cheese
#3. Turkey & Bacon
#4. Turkey & Ham

68. Why is the woman surprised?

(A) A sandwich is selling well.
(B) A special offer has ended.
(C) A conference was cancelled.
(D) A business is busy.

69. Look at the graphic. Which item will be removed from the menu?

(A) #1
(B) #2
(C) #3
(D) #4

70. What will the man probably do next?

(A) Prepare an ingredient
(B) Make a delivery
(C) Order supplies
(D) Help a customer

PART 4

Directions: You will hear some talks given by a single speaker. You will be asked to answer three questions about what the speaker says in each talk. Select the best response to each question and mark the letter (A), (B), (C), or (D) on your answer sheet. The talks will not be printed in your test book and will be spoken only one time.

71. What kind of a business does the speaker manage?
(A) A restaurant
(B) A sports store
(C) A grocery store
(D) A movie theater

72. Why should the listener come to work early tomorrow?
(A) To set up a display
(B) To clean a workspace
(C) To train employees
(D) To deal with a customer

73. What does the speaker offer the listener?
(A) An extra vacation day
(B) A complimentary meal
(C) A bonus payment
(D) An event ticket

---

74. What is being advertised?
(A) An electronic device
(B) A restaurant
(C) A fitness class
(D) A health food

75. What does the speaker mean when she says, "Stop what you are doing"?
(A) She thinks the listeners should take regular breaks.
(B) She recommends buying a different item.
(C) She wants the listeners to pay attention.
(D) She is advising the listeners to avoid certain foods.

76. According to the speaker, what can listeners do on a Web site?
(A) Enter a contest
(B) Join a mailing list
(C) Find business locations
(D) Place an order

---

77. Who most likely are the listeners?
(A) Video game developers
(B) Electrical engineers
(C) Audio technicians
(D) Technology journalists

78. According to the speaker, what aspect of the new software is particularly interesting?
(A) Compatibility with new technology
(B) Extended storage space
(C) Faster processing speeds
(D) Enhanced messaging features

79. What does the speaker say will happen on Friday?
(A) An update will be released.
(B) Some product tests will occur.
(C) A package will arrive.
(D) A demonstration will take place.

---

80. What does the speaker ask the listeners to do?
(A) Work extra hours
(B) Keep track of some inventory
(C) Help with the cleaning
(D) Wear a new uniform

81. What does the speaker imply when she says, "This isn't your first night"?
(A) The listeners don't need some information.
(B) Customers have been pleased with the service.
(C) The listeners have made several mistakes.
(D) A training session was cancelled.

82. What does the speaker say about the employee meals?
(A) They can only be ordered after a shift.
(B) They cannot be a dinner special.
(C) They must be eaten in the kitchen.
(D) They no longer require payment.

GO ON TO THE NEXT PAGE

83. Why is a new program being started?

(A) To raise money
(B) To attract more visitors
(C) To provide education
(D) To promote an exhibition

84. What are the listeners invited to do?

(A) Donate money to the museum
(B) Enroll children in classes
(C) Sign up for a membership
(D) Join a local history tour

85. Who is Olivia Treadwell?

(A) A curator
(B) An exhibitor
(C) A historian
(D) A professor

---

86. What is the talk mainly about?

(A) An orientation session
(B) A policy update
(C) A vacation itinerary
(D) A company trip

87. According to the speaker, what will change soon?

(A) A department name
(B) The weather
(C) A floor layout
(D) Working hours

88. What does the speaker want the listeners to do next?

(A) Send a memo
(B) Make a reservation
(C) Review a schedule
(D) Visit a location

---

89. Who most likely is the speaker?

(A) A land developer
(B) A professor
(C) A photographer
(D) A park guide

90. Why does the speaker say, "I always enjoy visiting Sumac Falls"?

(A) To disagree with a decision
(B) To offer a suggestion
(C) To compare different activities
(D) To share some plans

91. What is planned for 6 o'clock?

(A) A rehearsal
(B) A dinner
(C) A lecture
(D) A game

---

92. What does the speaker say has recently been announced?

(A) A venue change
(B) Ticket prices
(C) Contest winners
(D) Additional performers

93. According to the speaker, what makes some people dislike the festival?

(A) The food
(B) The costs
(C) The crowds
(D) The site

94. What will the speaker do next?

(A) Attend a concert
(B) Introduce a special guest
(C) Purchase a ticket
(D) Interview some people

Claire's Thursday Schedule	
1:00	Fitness class
2:00	Video review
3:00	Phone interview
4:00	Sectional practice
5:00	Solo rehearsal

95. What does the speaker want to discuss with the listener?

(A) Adding another performance
(B) Reviewing some applications
(C) Changing a venue location
(D) Planning an award ceremony

96. What does the speaker say she will lead tomorrow morning?

(A) A fundraising event
(B) A press interview
(C) A group practice
(D) A recording session

97. Look at the graphic. When will the speaker and the listener most likely meet?

(A) 2:00
(B) 3:00
(C) 4:00
(D) 5:00

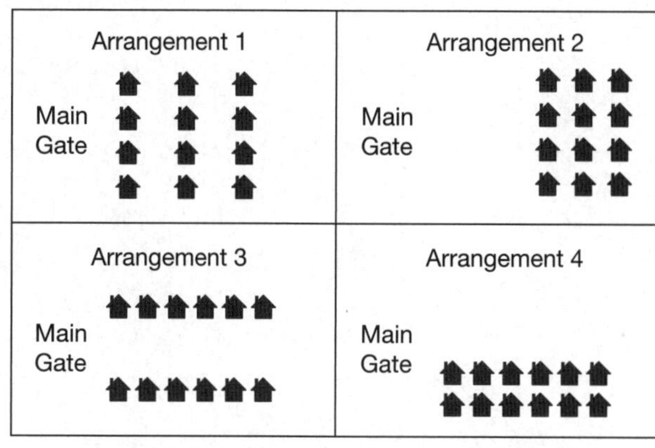

98. What kind of event is being organized?

(A) A career day
(B) A craft fair
(C) A sporting event
(D) A food festival

99. Why is the speaker expecting attendance to be high?

(A) The event has been advertised online.
(B) The event is free to attend.
(C) The venue is conveniently located.
(D) The event was promoted by a celebrity.

100. Look at the graphic. Which arrangement will be used in Leland Park?

(A) Arrangement 1
(B) Arrangement 2
(C) Arrangement 3
(D) Arrangement 4

TEST 5

This is the end of the Listening Test. Turn to Part 5 in your test book.

정답 및 스크립트 p.264 / 점수 환산표 p.363

GO ON TO THE NEXT PAGE

실전모의고사
TEST 6

TEST 6 MP3

TEST 6 해설

시작 시간 ________ 시 ________ 분

종료 시간 ________ 시 ________ 분

▸ 중간에 멈추지 말고 처음부터 끝까지 풀어보세요. 문제를 풀 때는 실전처럼 답안지에 마킹하세요.

LISTENING TEST

In the Listening test, you will be asked to demonstrate how well you understand spoken English. The entire Listening test will last approximately 45 minutes. There are four parts, and directions are given for each part. You must mark your answers on the separate answer sheet.

Do not write your answers in your test book.

PART 1

Directions: For each question in this part, you will hear four statements about a picture in your test book. When you hear the statements, you must select the one statement that best describes what you see in the picture. Then find the number of the question on your answer sheet and mark your answer. The statements will not be printed in your test book and will be spoken only one time.

Statement (D), "They are taking photographs," is the best description of the picture, so you should select answer (D) and mark it on your answer sheet.

1.

2.

GO ON TO THE NEXT PAGE

3.

4.

5.

6.

GO ON TO THE NEXT PAGE

PART 2

Directions: You will hear a question or statement and three responses spoken in English. They will not be printed in your test book and will be spoken only one time. Select the best response to the question or statement and mark the letter (A), (B), or (C) on your answer sheet.

7. Mark your answer on your answer sheet.
8. Mark your answer on your answer sheet.
9. Mark your answer on your answer sheet.
10. Mark your answer on your answer sheet.
11. Mark your answer on your answer sheet.
12. Mark your answer on your answer sheet.
13. Mark your answer on your answer sheet.
14. Mark your answer on your answer sheet.
15. Mark your answer on your answer sheet.
16. Mark your answer on your answer sheet.
17. Mark your answer on your answer sheet.
18. Mark your answer on your answer sheet.
19. Mark your answer on your answer sheet.
20. Mark your answer on your answer sheet.
21. Mark your answer on your answer sheet.
22. Mark your answer on your answer sheet.
23. Mark your answer on your answer sheet.
24. Mark your answer on your answer sheet.
25. Mark your answer on your answer sheet.
26. Mark your answer on your answer sheet.
27. Mark your answer on your answer sheet.
28. Mark your answer on your answer sheet.
29. Mark your answer on your answer sheet.
30. Mark your answer on your answer sheet.
31. Mark your answer on your answer sheet.

PART 3

Directions: You will hear some conversations between two or more people. You will be asked to answer three questions about what the speakers say in each conversation. Select the best response to each question and mark the letter (A), (B), (C) or (D) on your answer sheet. The conversations will not be printed in your test book and will be spoken only one time.

32. What is the purpose of the conversation?
(A) To resolve some complaints
(B) To compare cable services
(C) To evaluate a product
(D) To install some equipment

33. What department does the man work in?
(A) Accounting
(B) Customer Service
(C) Information Technology
(D) Marketing

34. What does the man suggest?
(A) Updating a Web site
(B) Recording a message
(C) Sending a pamphlet
(D) Hiring more staff

35. What complaint does the man have about the breakfast service?
(A) The operating hours are too short.
(B) The food is not good.
(C) The dining area is crowded.
(D) The price is too high.

36. What does the woman suggest the man do?
(A) Come to the breakfast earlier
(B) Eat at a different location
(C) Order a meal from room service
(D) Wait until lunchtime to eat

37. Why does the man reject the woman's suggestion?
(A) He does not want to spend extra money.
(B) He does not want to wake up earlier.
(C) He does not want to eat alone.
(D) He does not want to leave the hotel.

38. What type of event is being discussed?
(A) A theatrical play
(B) A sports game
(C) A music festival
(D) A movie premiere

39. What do the men decide to do?
(A) Check a schedule
(B) Leave the office early
(C) Use public transportation
(D) Upgrade some tickets

40. What will the woman most likely do next?
(A) Make a phone call
(B) Send an e-mail
(C) Print some documents
(D) Make a reservation

41. What are the speakers discussing?
(A) A news article
(B) A vacation plan
(C) An upcoming performance
(D) A new product

42. What does the man say he will do this afternoon?
(A) Finish an assignment
(B) Visit a location
(C) Contact a client
(D) Watch a video

43. What does the woman suggest?
(A) Attracting more investors
(B) Confirming a reservation
(C) Decreasing a price
(D) Adding to a schedule

GO ON TO THE NEXT PAGE

44. What feature does the woman mention about the Point Hotel?

(A) The low price
(B) The well-reviewed restaurants
(C) The beautiful scenery
(D) The friendly customer service

45. What does the man say he has done?

(A) He made a special request.
(B) He arranged a pick-up service.
(C) He booked a flight.
(D) He spoke with some colleagues.

46. What does the woman invite the man to do?

(A) Attend a sporting event
(B) Go sightseeing
(C) Share a cab
(D) Swim in the ocean

---

47. What type of business do the speakers work for?

(A) A marketing firm
(B) A construction company
(C) A real estate agency
(D) A publishing company

48. What did Natalie Romanov suggest?

(A) Joining a class
(B) Signing up for another seminar
(C) Holding a training session
(D) Reading a book

49. What does the woman say she will do?

(A) Reschedule an appointment
(B) Make a purchase
(C) Contact a colleague
(D) Copy a document

---

50. What does the woman ask the man to do?

(A) Set up some equipment
(B) Review some data
(C) Contact the clients
(D) Reserve a meeting space

51. What does the woman plan to do today?

(A) Visit the head office
(B) Prepare a room
(C) Conduct interviews
(D) Lead a training class

52. Why does the woman say, "I just joined the firm"?

(A) To show concern about too much responsibility
(B) To express gratitude for a career opportunity
(C) To ask the man for his advice on a decision
(D) To explain why she is unable to assist the man

---

53. Why did the men travel to Miami?

(A) To open a new store
(B) To inspect a factory
(C) To attend a conference
(D) To acquire new business

54. What problem does Thomas say he had?

(A) He was late to a meeting.
(B) He forgot some information.
(C) He lost an important document.
(D) He didn't keep any receipts.

55. According to the woman, what will be included in a handbook?

(A) Product listings
(B) Survey data
(C) Employee information
(D) Store locations

---

56. What are the speakers planning to do in November?

(A) Play a concert
(B) Record an album
(C) Begin a lease
(D) Purchase some instruments

57. What does the man mean when he says, "I think there are some apartments next door"?

(A) A room will be noisy.
(B) He wants to rent a room.
(C) Another location is preferable.
(D) Several stores are nearby.

58. What does the woman say she will do?

(A) Move some equipment
(B) Hire a professional
(C) Sign a document
(D) Speak with a contractor

---

59. Where does the conversation most likely take place?

(A) At an interview
(B) At a university
(C) At a trade exhibition
(D) At a factory

60. What does the woman's company sell?

(A) Navigation equipment
(B) Home appliances
(C) Heavy machinery
(D) Engine parts

61. How does the woman prefer to be contacted?

(A) By social media
(B) By fax
(C) By e-mail
(D) By telephone

Don't miss the event of the year!
Saturday, July 18, 6:00 P.M.

RSVP to Kayla Briggs: 555-0987

Menu Choices

1 - Shrimp alfredo pasta
2 - Grilled fish and vegetables
3 - Lemon roasted chicken
4 - Three bean casserole

62. What kind of event is being held?

(A) An awards ceremony
(B) A charity dinner
(C) A grand opening
(D) A sales promotion

63. Look at the graphic. Which meal will the man have?

(A) Choice 1
(B) Choice 2
(C) Choice 3
(D) Choice 4

64. What does the woman encourage the man to do?

(A) Drive to the event
(B) Invite a friend
(C) Make a donation
(D) Sign a guest list

TEST 6

GO ON TO THE NEXT PAGE

Altoona Fitness Center	
Towel rental (per item)	$1.50
Membership card replacement	$5.00
Equipment deposit (per day)	$10.00
Class registration (per week)	$25.00

65. What does the woman say will happen soon?
(A) A facility will close.
(B) Some equipment will be repaired.
(C) A class will start.
(D) A special offer will end.

66. Look at the graphic. How much will the man have to pay?
(A) $1.50
(B) $5.00
(C) $10.00
(D) $25.00

67. What will the man most likely do next?
(A) Complete a document
(B) Make a reservation
(C) Purchase an item
(D) Leave a card

 **Pay utilities at second floor accounting office**	❷ **All guests must sign in at the first floor lobby**
❸ **Parks Departments closed on Mondays**	❹ **Police department located next door**

68. Look at the graphic. Which sign did the man refer to?
(A) Sign 1
(B) Sign 2
(C) Sign 3
(D) Sign 4

69. Why is the man at the city hall?
(A) To pay a fine
(B) To meet an official
(C) To tour a building
(D) To apply for a permit

70. What does the woman give to the man?
(A) A pamphlet
(B) A ticket
(C) A city map
(D) A schedule

PART 4

Directions: You will hear some talks given by a single speaker. You will be asked to answer three questions about what the speaker says in each talk. Select the best response to each question and mark the letter (A), (B), (C), or (D) on your answer sheet. The talks will not be printed in your test book and will be spoken only one time.

71. According to the speaker, what is being delayed?
(A) A grand opening
(B) A move-in date
(C) A delivery time
(D) A job contract

72. Why does the speaker apologize?
(A) Some repairs were not done.
(B) An employee missed a meeting.
(C) A payment is higher than expected.
(D) Some information was incorrect.

73. What does the speaker ask the listener to do?
(A) Sign a form
(B) Open an account
(C) Purchase some furniture
(D) Recruit some helpers

74. What is the speaker helping to organize?
(A) A fundraiser
(B) A company trip
(C) A merger
(D) A retirement dinner

75. What does the speaker say she will do later today?
(A) Make a reservation
(B) Submit a report
(C) Prepare a presentation
(D) Promote an employee

76. What does the speaker ask the listeners to do?
(A) Forward an e-mail
(B) Visit a Web site
(C) Attend a workshop
(D) Gather some information

77. Who is visiting the agency this weekend?
(A) An executive
(B) A celebrity
(C) A designer
(D) A writer

78. What did the speaker send to the listener?
(A) The address of a café
(B) A flight itinerary
(C) Tickets to an event
(D) Promotional items

79. Why does the speaker say, "you have my cell phone number"?
(A) To request frequent updates
(B) To confirm contact information
(C) To change a meeting time
(D) To offer additional help

80. Where is the announcement being made?
(A) In a TV studio
(B) In a movie theater
(C) In a sports stadium
(D) In a department store

81. What problem does the speaker mention?
(A) A product is sold out.
(B) An event has been delayed.
(C) A price will increase.
(D) The weather will be bad.

82. According to the speaker, why should the listeners talk with a staff member?
(A) To request a refund
(B) To report a missing item
(C) To sign up for a membership
(D) To purchase a ticket

GO ON TO THE NEXT PAGE

83. Who is the speaker talking to?
(A) Construction workers
(B) New tenants
(C) Security guards
(D) Prospective clients

84. What does the speaker imply when she says, "The elevators are equipped with scanners"?
(A) Listeners can only use the stairs.
(B) Listeners will need to use their cards.
(C) Some renovations are finished.
(D) The elevator has the newest technology.

85. What does the speaker say has recently changed?
(A) A transportation route
(B) A floor layout
(C) A store location
(D) An employee handbook

---

86. Where does the speaker most likely work?
(A) At a department store
(B) At a factory
(C) At a library
(D) At a post office

87. What problem does the speaker report?
(A) A large order is due.
(B) A manager is absent.
(C) A delivery is missing.
(D) Some equipment has malfunctioned.

88. What will the speaker allow the listener to do?
(A) Receive a promotion
(B) Take a longer break
(C) Claim overtime pay
(D) Change a schedule

---

89. What does the speaker remind the listeners to do by Wednesday?
(A) Attend a training class
(B) Sign up for a trip
(C) Submit measurements
(D) Purchase equipment

90. What good news does the speaker mention?
(A) The restaurant received a positive review.
(B) A menu has been modified.
(C) New employees have been recruited.
(D) Many reservations have been made.

91. Why does the speaker say, "our system is currently being updated"?
(A) To request assistance
(B) To explain a delay
(C) To praise a colleague's work
(D) To suggest some improvements

---

92. What does the speaker thank the listeners for?
(A) Working overtime
(B) Postponing a vacation
(C) Participating in a survey
(D) Attending a seminar

93. In which division do the listeners most likely work?
(A) Marketing
(B) Accounting
(C) Sales
(D) Development

94. What does the speaker say she will provide?
(A) Bonus pay
(B) Holiday time
(C) Dinner
(D) Accommodations

Delaney Country Club

· Name: David Wells
· ID Number: 11278
· Valid From: 01/26
· Valid Untill: 07/25
· Parking Space: 89

95. Which department is the speaker calling?
(A) Marketing
(B) Administration
(C) Human Resources
(D) Public Relations

96. Look at the graphic. What information does the speaker say is incorrect?
(A) 11278
(B) 01/26
(C) 07/25
(D) 89

97. What does the speaker ask the listener to do?
(A) Issue a new card
(B) Return a call
(C) Arrange a meeting
(D) Provide instructions

Wire World Floor Directory
Fourth Floor: Cameras
Third Floor: Computers
Second Floor: Televisions & Monitors
First Floor: Game Consoles & Mobile Phones

98. Why is the sale being held?
(A) To celebrate a holiday
(B) To prepare for a store closing
(C) To promote a new product
(D) To thank long-term employees

99. Look at the graphic. Which floor is the sale on?
(A) The first floor
(B) The second floor
(C) The third floor
(D) The fourth floor

100. According to the speaker, what is available on a Web site?
(A) An additional sale
(B) A product review
(C) A promotional video
(D) A membership application

This is the end of the Listening Test. Turn to Part 5 in your test book.

정답 및 스크립트 p.273 / 점수 환산표 p.363

실전모의고사
TEST 7

TEST 7 MP3

TEST 7 해설

시작 시간 ________시 ________분

종료 시간 ________시 ________분

▸중간에 멈추지 말고 처음부터 끝까지 풀어보세요. 문제를 풀 때는 실전처럼 답안지에 마킹하세요.

LISTENING TEST

In the Listening test, you will be asked to demonstrate how well you understand spoken English. The entire Listening test will last approximately 45 minutes. There are four parts, and directions are given for each part. You must mark your answers on the separate answer sheet.

Do not write your answers in your test book.

PART 1

Directions: For each question in this part, you will hear four statements about a picture in your test book. When you hear the statements, you must select the one statement that best describes what you see in the picture. Then find the number of the question on your answer sheet and mark your answer. The statements will not be printed in your test book and will be spoken only one time.

Statement (D), "They are taking photographs," is the best description of the picture, so you should select answer (D) and mark it on your answer sheet.

1.

2.

TEST 7

GO ON TO THE NEXT PAGE

3.

4.

5.

6.

TEST 7

GO ON TO THE NEXT PAGE

PART 2

Directions: You will hear a question or statement and three responses spoken in English. They will not be printed in your test book and will be spoken only one time. Select the best response to the question or statement and mark the letter (A), (B), or (C) on your answer sheet.

7. Mark your answer on your answer sheet.
8. Mark your answer on your answer sheet.
9. Mark your answer on your answer sheet.
10. Mark your answer on your answer sheet.
11. Mark your answer on your answer sheet.
12. Mark your answer on your answer sheet.
13. Mark your answer on your answer sheet.
14. Mark your answer on your answer sheet.
15. Mark your answer on your answer sheet.
16. Mark your answer on your answer sheet.
17. Mark your answer on your answer sheet.
18. Mark your answer on your answer sheet.
19. Mark your answer on your answer sheet.
20. Mark your answer on your answer sheet.
21. Mark your answer on your answer sheet.
22. Mark your answer on your answer sheet.
23. Mark your answer on your answer sheet.
24. Mark your answer on your answer sheet.
25. Mark your answer on your answer sheet.
26. Mark your answer on your answer sheet.
27. Mark your answer on your answer sheet.
28. Mark your answer on your answer sheet.
29. Mark your answer on your answer sheet.
30. Mark your answer on your answer sheet.
31. Mark your answer on your answer sheet.

PART 3

Directions: You will hear some conversations between two or more people. You will be asked to answer three questions about what the speakers say in each conversation. Select the best response to each question and mark the letter (A), (B), (C) or (D) on your answer sheet. The conversations will not be printed in your test book and will be spoken only one time.

32. Why is the woman calling?
(A) To inquire about a service
(B) To cancel a subscription
(C) To participate in a survey
(D) To order a product

33. According to the man, what has recently changed?
(A) A contract length
(B) A delivery fee
(C) A business location
(D) A package deal

34. What does the man offer to do?
(A) Refund a payment
(B) Provide a free trial
(C) Speak to a supervisor
(D) Install some equipment

---

35. Where are the speakers?
(A) At a restaurant
(B) At a festival
(C) At a grocery store
(D) At a farm

36. Why is the man expecting more customers than usual?
(A) An advertisement was successful.
(B) An apartment complex opened.
(C) A competitor went out of business.
(D) A new product became popular.

37. What does the man say he did?
(A) He posted a job opening.
(B) He met with a contractor.
(C) He ordered more inventory.
(D) He reorganized a workspace.

---

38. What product are the speakers discussing?
(A) Fabrics
(B) Vehicle parts
(C) Furniture
(D) Electronic equipment

39. What does Elizabeth suggest?
(A) Launching a new product
(B) Opening another office
(C) Increasing a budget
(D) Improving a Web site

40. What does the man propose?
(A) Closing a factory
(B) Reorganizing a department
(C) Purchasing a business
(D) Delaying a project

---

41. What are the speakers working on?
(A) A musical performance
(B) A theater production
(C) An art exhibition
(D) A short film

42. Why does the man say, "the opening night is still this Friday"?
(A) Many people are interested in coming.
(B) A brochure has incorrect information.
(C) He needs to hire additional staff.
(D) He is surprised by a change.

43. What does the woman say she will do next?
(A) Contact a colleague
(B) Finish a project
(C) Change a location
(D) Cancel an event

GO ON TO THE NEXT PAGE

44. What does the woman notify the man about?
(A) A job opening
(B) A research finding
(C) An extended deadline
(D) A meeting agenda

45. According to the woman, what recently happened in her department?
(A) Some equipment was upgraded.
(B) Employees were transferred.
(C) A supervisor retired.
(D) Some funding was decreased.

46. What does the man say he will do next?
(A) Submit a report
(B) Contact some coworkers
(C) Revise a document
(D) Plan a vacation

---

47. What does the woman ask the man to create?
(A) A product review
(B) A customer survey
(C) A test model
(D) An expense report

48. According to the woman, why was the man selected for the project?
(A) He is receiving a promotion.
(B) He is the only employee available.
(C) He has asked for extra work.
(D) He has relevant work experience.

49. What does the woman suggest the man do?
(A) Visit a worksite
(B) Refer to a Web site
(C) Work on the weekend
(D) Attend a demonstration

---

50. What industry do the speakers work in?
(A) Travel
(B) Food
(C) Manufacturing
(D) Finance

51. What is the woman concerned about?
(A) Purchasing new equipment
(B) Hiring additional employees
(C) Moving to another location
(D) Accepting a contract

52. Why will the speakers go to Albany?
(A) A conference is being held.
(B) A client is visiting.
(C) A business is closing.
(D) A commercial is being filmed.

---

53. Where are the speakers?
(A) A luxury hotel
(B) A national monument
(C) A commercial complex
(D) A private estate

54. Why does the woman say, "The client wants the conference hall's carpet shampooed"?
(A) To complain about a fee
(B) To ask for help
(C) To alter a plan
(D) To win a contract

55. What do the speakers agree to do at 4 o'clock?
(A) Change shifts
(B) Store some equipment
(C) Meet with a customer
(D) Drink some coffee

---

56. Where does the man most likely work?
(A) An art gallery
(B) A library
(C) An office supply store
(D) An accounting office

57. What problem does the woman mention about a printer?
(A) It will not print in color.
(B) It jams frequently.
(C) It runs out of ink quickly.
(D) It is too large.

58. What does the man tell the woman to do?
(A) Restart a computer
(B) Visit a Web site
(C) Purchase a warranty
(D) Request a refund

59. According to the man, what did some people complain about?
(A) Food quality
(B) Faulty equipment
(C) Showing times
(D) Limited parking

60. Why does the woman say she is not concerned?
(A) Reviews were positive.
(B) Sales were increased.
(C) Clients were pleased.
(D) Attendance was high.

61. What does the man suggest?
(A) Reducing participation
(B) Extending a schedule
(C) Raising ticket prices
(D) Holding a contest

Area Zip Codes	
Townsville	50010
Grand Rapids	50011
Silver Pines	50012
Hamilton	50013

62. What is the man having trouble with?
(A) Purchasing a ticket
(B) Sending a package
(C) Selling some real estate
(D) Making a payment

63. Look at the graphic. Which code should the man use?
(A) 50010
(B) 50011
(C) 50012
(D) 50013

64. What does the woman say will happen soon?
(A) A delivery will arrive.
(B) A map will be drawn.
(C) A Web site will be updated.
(D) A driver will be hired.

TEST 7

GO ON TO THE NEXT PAGE

Howdy Hardware Store
"Always the right fool for the job!"

Flash Sale!
June 6 - June 8

· Buy one hammer, Get 100 pack of nails
· Buy one wrench set, Get 25 12mm nuts
· Buy one screwdriver set, Get 50 2 inch screws
· Buy one saw, Get 1 saw guide

65. What does the woman say she will send by e-mail?
(A) Some measurements
(B) A photograph
(C) A color sample
(D) Some contract information

66. Look at the graphic. Which items will the woman receive for free?
(A) Nails
(B) Screws
(C) Nuts
(D) Saw guide

67. What does the man say he will do this afternoon?
(A) Contact a distributor
(B) Extend a sale
(C) Prepare an order
(D) Close early

Train Number	Departure	Arrival
3098	7:10 A.M.	11:50 A.M.
2076	7:45 A.M.	12:30 P.M.
2045	8:10 A.M.	12:50 P.M.
1097	8:35 A.M.	1:05 P.M.

68. Why does the man apologize?
(A) A store is no longer open.
(B) A phone number was changed.
(C) A Web site is down for maintenance.
(D) A train service has been delayed.

69. Look at the graphic. What train will the woman most likely take?
(A) 3098
(B) 2076
(C) 2045
(D) 1097

70. What does the woman say she will do in London?
(A) Participate in a tour
(B) Attend an interview
(C) View some exhibits
(D) Purchase some items

PART 4

Directions: You will hear some talks given by a single speaker. You will be asked to answer three questions about what the speaker says in each talk. Select the best response to each question and mark the letter (A), (B), (C), or (D) on your answer sheet. The talks will not be printed in your test book and will be spoken only one time.

71. What type of business is being advertised?
(A) A restaurant
(B) A hotel
(C) A convenience store
(D) A bank

72. What will the listeners be able to do starting in April?
(A) Join a rewards program
(B) Enter a contest
(C) Purchase new products
(D) Apply for a job

73. Why does the speaker invite the listeners to visit a Web site?
(A) To download an application
(B) To print a coupon
(C) To check store hours
(D) To place an order

---

74. What is the purpose of the session?
(A) To offer instruction
(B) To reveal a product
(C) To present an award
(D) To announce a merger

75. Who is Mr. Wentz?
(A) A graphic artist
(B) An entrepreneur
(C) A software developer
(D) A technology journalist

76. What will take place after Mr. Wentz's talk?
(A) A dinner buffet
(B) An award ceremony
(C) An after party
(D) A video presentation

---

77. According to the speaker, what is special about the hotel?
(A) It was built long ago.
(B) It has a theater.
(C) Celebrities often stay there.
(D) It is near a landmark.

78. Who is Lucas?
(A) A government official
(B) A chef
(C) A business owner
(D) A designer

79. Why does the speaker say, "I've seen it several times"?
(A) He wants to change his plans.
(B) He is suggesting an activity.
(C) He can perform a task by himself.
(D) He knows where to find a lost item.

---

80. What is the main purpose of the talk?
(A) To coordinate a project
(B) To introduce a new member
(C) To decide on a budget
(D) To elect an officer

81. What does the speaker say Tony Chappitz recently did?
(A) He ran for political office.
(B) He moved to the area.
(C) He opened a new business.
(D) He retired from his job.

82. What will the speaker do later today?
(A) Order some food
(B) Submit a request
(C) Sign a contract
(D) Lead a tour

TEST 7

GO ON TO THE NEXT PAGE

83. Who is the speaker?

(A) A store owner
(B) A salesperson
(C) A delivery driver
(D) A chef

84. What does the company sell?

(A) Electronics
(B) Furniture
(C) Office equipment
(D) Cooking utensils

85. What does the speaker imply when she says, "nobody has come"?

(A) She realized a product is unpopular.
(B) She thinks a schedule was wrong.
(C) Some colleagues are running late.
(D) The directions were incorrect.

---

86. What kind of business does Ms. Park manage?

(A) A bank
(B) A department store
(C) An architecture agency
(D) A legal firm

87. What kind of software will Ms. Park discuss?

(A) Video editing
(B) Scheduling
(C) Designing
(D) Accounting

88. What are the listeners encouraged to do?

(A) Purchase a product
(B) Call in with questions
(C) Download a sample
(D) Visit a Web site

---

89. What does the speaker mean when she says, "We've all read the reviews"?

(A) The reviews should not have been available.
(B) New reviews are coming out soon.
(C) The listeners know a product has been poorly received.
(D) The listeners are excited to try an item.

90. What does Paige's report indicate?

(A) Online media sources are becoming more successful.
(B) The company should advertise to different customers.
(C) A market has become very competitive.
(D) A product is in demand overseas.

91. What does the speaker ask the listeners to do?

(A) Share some ideas
(B) Visit a store
(C) Proofread a draft
(D) Update a Web site

---

92. What is the talk mainly about?

(A) Updated computer programs
(B) New office equipment
(C) A seminar itinerary
(D) Company policies

93. Why did the company choose the product?

(A) It was part of a package deal.
(B) It is easy to fix.
(C) It has several new features.
(D) It is lightweight.

94. What does the speaker say is offered with the product?

(A) A store coupon
(B) A free month of service
(C) An extra cable
(D) An extended warranty

Adelphia Music Hall

Thunderclap's Super Concert

Opening Act: The Loose Cuffs
Start Time: 8:00 P.M.
Section: G
Cost: $45

95. According to the speaker, what has caused a problem?

(A) Faulty equipment
(B) An injury
(C) Bad traffic
(D) A miscommunication

96. Look at the graphic. According to the speaker, what piece of information on the ticket will change?

(A) Opening Act
(B) Start Time
(C) Section
(D) Cost

97. What does the speaker say the listeners can receive?

(A) A free snack
(B) A full refund
(C) A band t-shirt
(D) A store coupon

Advertising Today Conference February 15	
8:00	Marketing to the Youth, Peggy Olstein
9:00	Advertising Ethics, Lane Pryce
10:00	Power of Branding, Yujin Kang
11:00	Online Advertising - Issues and Challenges, Sally Draper
12:00	Lunch

98. What is the purpose of the call?

(A) To request a payment
(B) To offer an apology
(C) To cancel an event
(D) To ask for feedback

99. Look at the graphic. Who is the speaker calling?

(A) Peggy Olstein
(B) Lane Pryce
(C) Yujin Kang
(D) Sally Draper

100. What does the speaker ask the listener to do?

(A) Review some notes
(B) Watch a video
(C) Attend a meeting
(D) Send an e-mail

This is the end of the Listening Test. Turn to Part 5 in your test book.

정답 및 스크립트 p.282 / 점수 환산표 p.363

GO ON TO THE NEXT PAGE →

실전모의고사
TEST 8

TEST 8 MP3

TEST 8 해설

시작 시간 ________시 ________분

종료 시간 ________시 ________분

▸중간에 멈추지 말고 처음부터 끝까지 풀어보세요. 문제를 풀 때는 실전처럼 답안지에 마킹하세요.

LISTENING TEST

In the Listening test, you will be asked to demonstrate how well you understand spoken English. The entire Listening test will last approximately 45 minutes. There are four parts, and directions are given for each part. You must mark your answers on the separate answer sheet.

Do not write your answers in your test book.

PART 1

Directions: For each question in this part, you will hear four statements about a picture in your test book. When you hear the statements, you must select the one statement that best describes what you see in the picture. Then find the number of the question on your answer sheet and mark your answer. The statements will not be printed in your test book and will be spoken only one time.

Statement (D), "They are taking photographs," is the best description of the picture, so you should select answer (D) and mark it on your answer sheet.

1.

2.

GO ON TO THE NEXT PAGE

3.

4.

5.

6.

TEST 8

GO ON TO THE NEXT PAGE

PART 2

Directions: You will hear a question or statement and three responses spoken in English. They will not be printed in your test book and will be spoken only one time. Select the best response to the question or statement and mark the letter (A), (B), or (C) on your answer sheet.

7. Mark your answer on your answer sheet.

8. Mark your answer on your answer sheet.

9. Mark your answer on your answer sheet.

10. Mark your answer on your answer sheet.

11. Mark your answer on your answer sheet.

12. Mark your answer on your answer sheet.

13. Mark your answer on your answer sheet.

14. Mark your answer on your answer sheet.

15. Mark your answer on your answer sheet.

16. Mark your answer on your answer sheet.

17. Mark your answer on your answer sheet.

18. Mark your answer on your answer sheet.

19. Mark your answer on your answer sheet.

20. Mark your answer on your answer sheet.

21. Mark your answer on your answer sheet.

22. Mark your answer on your answer sheet.

23. Mark your answer on your answer sheet.

24. Mark your answer on your answer sheet.

25. Mark your answer on your answer sheet.

26. Mark your answer on your answer sheet.

27. Mark your answer on your answer sheet.

28. Mark your answer on your answer sheet.

29. Mark your answer on your answer sheet.

30. Mark your answer on your answer sheet.

31. Mark your answer on your answer sheet.

PART 3

Directions: You will hear some conversations between two or more people. You will be asked to answer three questions about what the speakers say in each conversation. Select the best response to each question and mark the letter (A), (B), (C) or (D) on your answer sheet. The conversations will not be printed in your test book and will be spoken only one time.

32. What is the woman trying to do?
(A) Install equipment
(B) File some documents
(C) Access a room
(D) Locate a store

33. What does the man tell the woman to do?
(A) Post a notice
(B) Change a schedule
(C) Move her workstation
(D) Request a repair

34. What does the man say about Marriott Supplies?
(A) It is having a sale.
(B) It is located nearby.
(C) It opens early.
(D) It sent a shipment.

35. How did the man hear about Raffles Restaurant?
(A) From a colleague
(B) From a newspaper ad
(C) From a Web site
(D) From a radio commercial

36. According to the woman, what makes Raffles Restaurant different from its competitors?
(A) It has lower prices.
(B) It has a larger dining area.
(C) It has longer business hours.
(D) It has more locations.

37. What will the man do in October?
(A) Entertain some clients
(B) Leave his job
(C) Celebrate his birthday
(D) Hire new staff

38. According to the woman, why is the restaurant moving to a new location?
(A) The utilities are cheaper.
(B) The kitchen is larger.
(C) The rent is lower.
(D) The area is better.

39. What addition has the woman requested?
(A) A walk-in refrigerator
(B) A mini café
(C) An outside eating area
(D) An employee parking lot

40. According to the woman, why must the work be completed in August?
(A) A leasing contract will end.
(B) A competitor will be opening.
(C) A local event is taking place.
(D) Employees need to be trained.

41. What goal does the man have?
(A) To appear on a TV program
(B) To invent a device
(C) To develop software
(D) To found a business

42. What does the woman offer to do for the man?
(A) Lend him some books
(B) Contact a friend
(C) Arrange an interview
(D) Get tickets for an event

43. What information does the man ask for?
(A) An event date
(B) A telephone number
(C) A business location
(D) An e-mail address

GO ON TO THE NEXT PAGE

44. What are the speakers discussing?
(A) A training session
(B) An upcoming trip
(C) A site inspection
(D) A community fair

45. What would the woman like to do?
(A) Arrange accommodation
(B) Lead an activity
(C) Change a venue
(D) Give a speech

46. What does the man say he will do?
(A) Contact a hotel
(B) Hold a staff meeting
(C) Update a schedule
(D) Post a notice

---

47. What type of product are the speakers discussing?
(A) Computer keyboards
(B) Office chairs
(C) Home appliances
(D) Safety equipment

48. According to the woman, what information was disappointing?
(A) Market research feedback
(B) Monthly sales figures
(C) Product design costs
(D) Advertising expenses

49. What does the woman suggest doing?
(A) Extending a deadline
(B) Revising a design
(C) Placing an advertisement
(D) Meeting with a supervisor

---

50. Why is the woman surprised?
(A) A client cancelled a meeting.
(B) A city area has been renovated.
(C) A shop is well designed.
(D) A price is lower than expected.

51. Why does the woman meet with the man?
(A) She would like to open a store.
(B) She is conducting an interview.
(C) She is looking for a distributor.
(D) She plans to launch a Web site.

52. What does the man say about his clients?
(A) Many of them sell their products internationally.
(B) They produce a low volume of goods.
(C) They mainly market to young adults.
(D) Some of them have expanded their businesses.

---

53. What does the man imply when he says, "It's already past 5:30"?
(A) He thinks a deadline is unrealistic.
(B) He wants to leave the office soon.
(C) He is running late for a meeting.
(D) He will check on a late delivery.

54. What is the woman concerned about?
(A) The date of a meeting
(B) The changes to a design
(C) The effect of a policy
(D) The cost of a project

55. Why does the woman apologize?
(A) She forgot to inform a client.
(B) She cannot attend an event.
(C) She did not respond to a message.
(D) She was absent for a meeting.

---

56. Where are the speakers?

(A) At a product launch
(B) At an annual banquet
(C) At a training event
(D) On a staff vacation

57. What project are the men working on?

(A) Attracting new suppliers
(B) Creating an ad campaign
(C) Opening a retail location
(D) Redesigning a Web site

58. What does the woman say she was in charge of?

(A) Designing a range of cosmetics
(B) Organizing a company event
(C) Recruiting sales representatives
(D) Conducting market research

59. What did Mr. Molson dislike about a bicycle frame?

(A) The color
(B) The shape
(C) The weight
(D) The logo

60. Why does the man say, "The project schedule says we should be completely finished by this Friday"?

(A) He will be available to assist the woman next week.
(B) He is relieved that a project is almost done.
(C) He thinks a schedule is wrong.
(D) He is concerned about a deadline.

61. What does the woman say she will do?

(A) Postpone an event
(B) Contact the CEO
(C) Test a product
(D) Call a staff meeting

Conference Talks	
9:00 A.M.	Peter Maynard
9:45 A.M.	
10:30 A.M.	Karen Singh
11:15 A.M.	
1:30 P.M.	
2:15 P.M.	Oliver Kantor
3:00 P.M.	

62. Why is the man waiting to finish a seminar schedule?

(A) Some speakers have not responded.
(B) A venue might be changed.
(C) He is working on another task.
(D) The event has been postponed.

63. Look at the graphic. When will Paul Butler give a talk?

(A) At 9:45 A.M.
(B) At 11:15 A.M.
(C) At 1:30 P.M.
(D) At 3:00 P.M.

64. Why is the woman going to an event space?

(A) To meet with speakers
(B) To put up decorations
(C) To check equipment
(D) To distribute flyers

TEST 8

GO ON TO THE NEXT PAGE →

Invoice - Catalog Printing	
Up to 5 pages	$5 per catalog
6 to 10 pages	$15 per catalog
11 to 15 pages	$25 per catalog
16 to 20 pages	$30 per catalog

65. What does the woman say she will do with the printed catalogs?

(A) Distribute them in a store
(B) Take them to a convention
(C) Mail them to customers
(D) Place them in a store room

66. Look at the graphic. Which amount will be refunded to the woman?

(A) $5
(B) $15
(C) $25
(D) $30

67. What does the man say his colleague will do?

(A) Provide directions to a business
(B) Print an additional catalog
(C) Check credit card information
(D) Transfer items to a vehicle

Building Entrance

Reserved CFO	Available Space 1	Reserved President		Reserved CEO	Available Space 2	Reserved Sales Director
Client Parking	Client Parking	Available Space 3		Available Space 4	Client Parking	Client Parking

68. What department does the woman work in?

(A) Sales
(B) Human Resources
(C) Administration
(D) Marketing

69. What information does the woman ask for?

(A) An employee ID number
(B) A license plate number
(C) A telephone number
(D) A credit card number

70. Look at the graphic. Which space has been assigned to the man?

(A) Space 1
(B) Space 2
(C) Space 3
(D) Space 4

PART 4

Directions: You will hear some talks given by a single speaker. You will be asked to answer three questions about what the speaker says in each talk. Select the best response to each question and mark the letter (A), (B), (C), or (D) on your answer sheet. The talks will not be printed in your test book and will be spoken only one time.

71. Where does the listener work?
(A) A farm
(B) A factory
(C) A government agency
(D) A transportation company

72. What is the speaker mainly discussing?
(A) Signing a contract
(B) Hiring new staff
(C) Scheduling deliveries
(D) Obtaining a certificate

73. What does the speaker ask the listener to submit?
(A) A billing address
(B) An order size
(C) A payment method
(D) A store location

74. Where most likely does the speaker work?
(A) At a coffee shop
(B) At a historical landmark
(C) At a community center
(D) At a museum

75. Why does the speaker say, "The weather should be clear all morning"?
(A) To suggest rescheduling an activity
(B) To recommend going outside
(C) To confirm that an event will take place
(D) To advise the listeners to return tomorrow

76. What does the speaker say is happening this week?
(A) A live performance
(B) A special contest
(C) A renovation project
(D) A recruitment fair

77. What is the advertisement mainly about?
(A) A job vacancy
(B) A store sale
(C) A branch closure
(D) A business relocation

78. What type of business is being advertised?
(A) A furniture store
(B) An interior design firm
(C) A hardware shop
(D) A tool rental agency

79. According to the speaker, what can the listeners do on a Web site?
(A) Fill out a form
(B) Find business locations
(C) Contact customer services
(D) View an inventory

80. What is Alberto Lorentz planning to do?
(A) Receive a promotion
(B) Lead a hiring committee
(C) Launch a company Web site
(D) Open a new department

81. What company policy does the speaker mention?
(A) Sending staff to work abroad
(B) Conducting frequent media interviews
(C) Training employees in multiple fields
(D) Utilizing new technology in the office

82. According to the speaker, why should the listeners talk to a manager?
(A) To attend a presentation
(B) To join an office club
(C) To volunteer for an assignment
(D) To conduct a performance review

GO ON TO THE NEXT PAGE

83. What is the purpose of the talk?
(A) To give instructions to workers
(B) To welcome potential investors
(C) To describe an upcoming event
(D) To talk about a company's success

84. What does the woman recommend the listeners do?
(A) Speak with employees
(B) Attend a seminar
(C) View a product range
(D) Ask questions

85. What will the listeners do next?
(A) Read promotional materials
(B) Form into groups
(C) Meet a business owner
(D) Take a break for lunch

---

86. What department does the speaker work in?
(A) Information Technology
(B) Maintenance
(C) Customer Relations
(D) Marketing

87. What is the topic of the workshop?
(A) Updating computer software
(B) Improving work efficiency
(C) Communicating with other offices
(D) Using a security system

88. What will the listeners do next?
(A) Take a tour
(B) Receive a card
(C) Review some data
(D) Create a password

---

89. What is the speaker calling about?
(A) Coffee mugs
(B) T-shirts
(C) Baseball caps
(D) Flyers

90. What does the speaker offer the listener?
(A) Complimentary items
(B) A product discount
(C) Free shipping
(D) A membership

91. What does the speaker imply when he says, "We don't have many orders to fill this week"?
(A) He is disappointed about a decline in business.
(B) He recommends that the listener postpone an order.
(C) He can get started on the listener's order right away.
(D) He will be available to attend a special event.

---

92. Why is the speaker qualified to host the show?
(A) She has an academic qualification.
(B) She has won several awards.
(C) She is experienced in her field.
(D) She has published a book.

93. Why does the speaker say, "hosting a dinner party can be rather expensive"?
(A) To recommend eating out
(B) To acknowledge a common opinion
(C) To remind listeners to book in advance
(D) To disagree with a critic's opinion

94. What will the speaker most likely do next?
(A) Provide some advice
(B) Prepare a meal
(C) Compare some restaurants
(D) Review equipment

Landmark 1

Landmark 2

Landmark 3

Landmark 4

95. What does the speaker say that passengers are now permitted to do?

(A) Exit the vehicle
(B) Turn on a screen
(C) Use a bathroom
(D) Eat snacks

96. Look at the graphic. Where most likely is the bus now?

(A) Near Landmark 1
(B) Near Landmark 2
(C) Near Landmark 3
(D) Near Landmark 4

97. According to the speaker, how can the listeners get more information?

(A) By listening for updates
(B) By reading a guidebook
(C) By visiting a Web site
(D) By checking a map

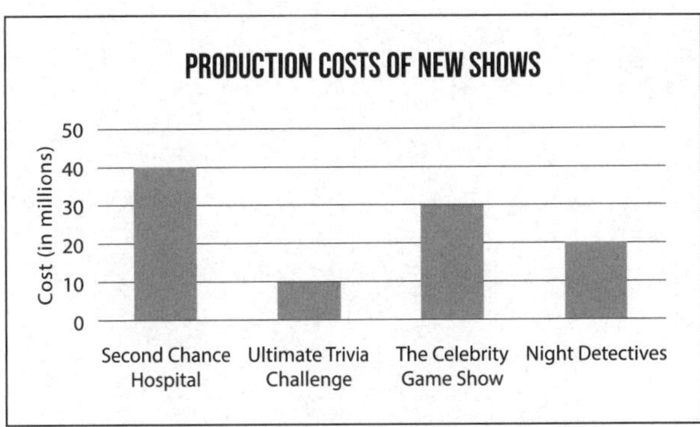

98. Who most likely are the listeners?

(A) Possible investors
(B) Movie audience
(C) Company executives
(D) Television critics

99. Look at the graphic. Which show will most likely be acquired?

(A) Second Chance Hospital
(B) Ultimate Trivia Challenge
(C) The Celebrity Game Show
(D) Night Detectives

100. What will Robert Oras talk about next?

(A) Some survey results
(B) A recent promotion
(C) A business expense
(D) A project schedule

TEST 8

This is the end of the Listening Test. Turn to Part 5 in your test book.

정답 및 스크립트 p.291 / 점수 환산표 p.363

GO ON TO THE NEXT PAGE

실전모의고사
TEST 9

TEST 9 MP3

TEST 9 해설

시작 시간 ________시 ________분

종료 시간 ________시 ________분

▸중간에 멈추지 말고 처음부터 끝까지 풀어보세요. 문제를 풀 때는 실전처럼 답안지에 마킹하세요.

LISTENING TEST

In the Listening test, you will be asked to demonstrate how well you understand spoken English. The entire Listening test will last approximately 45 minutes. There are four parts, and directions are given for each part. You must mark your answers on the separate answer sheet.

Do not write your answers in your test book.

PART 1

Directions: For each question in this part, you will hear four statements about a picture in your test book. When you hear the statements, you must select the one statement that best describes what you see in the picture. Then find the number of the question on your answer sheet and mark your answer. The statements will not be printed in your test book and will be spoken only one time.

Statement (D), "They are taking photographs," is the best description of the picture, so you should select answer (D) and mark it on your answer sheet.

1.

2.

GO ON TO THE NEXT PAGE

3.

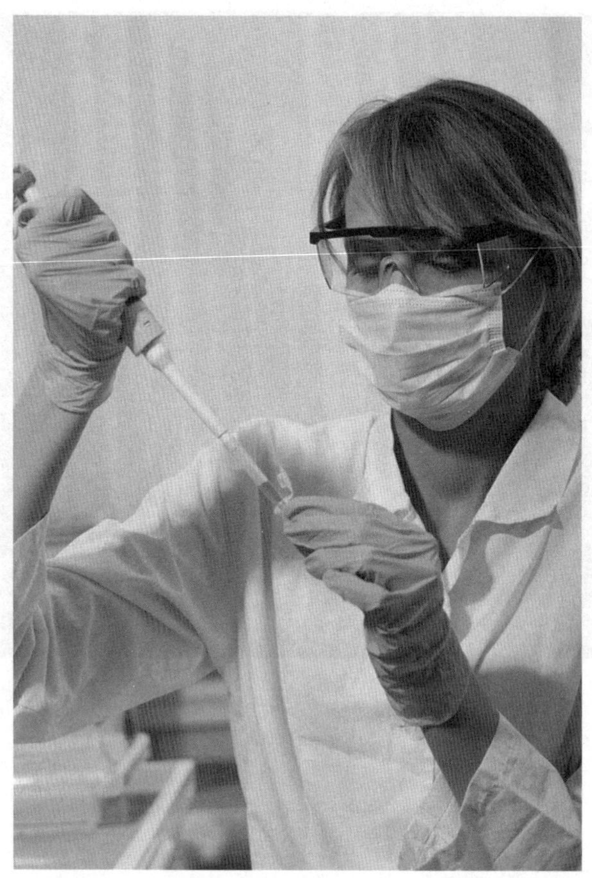

4.

5.

6.

GO ON TO THE NEXT PAGE

PART 2

Directions: You will hear a question or statement and three responses spoken in English. They will not be printed in your test book and will be spoken only one time. Select the best response to the question or statement and mark the letter (A), (B), or (C) on your answer sheet.

7. Mark your answer on your answer sheet.

8. Mark your answer on your answer sheet.

9. Mark your answer on your answer sheet.

10. Mark your answer on your answer sheet.

11. Mark your answer on your answer sheet.

12. Mark your answer on your answer sheet.

13. Mark your answer on your answer sheet.

14. Mark your answer on your answer sheet.

15. Mark your answer on your answer sheet.

16. Mark your answer on your answer sheet.

17. Mark your answer on your answer sheet.

18. Mark your answer on your answer sheet.

19. Mark your answer on your answer sheet.

20. Mark your answer on your answer sheet.

21. Mark your answer on your answer sheet.

22. Mark your answer on your answer sheet.

23. Mark your answer on your answer sheet.

24. Mark your answer on your answer sheet.

25. Mark your answer on your answer sheet.

26. Mark your answer on your answer sheet.

27. Mark your answer on your answer sheet.

28. Mark your answer on your answer sheet.

29. Mark your answer on your answer sheet.

30. Mark your answer on your answer sheet.

31. Mark your answer on your answer sheet.

PART 3

Directions: You will hear some conversations between two or more people. You will be asked to answer three questions about what the speakers say in each conversation. Select the best response to each question and mark the letter (A), (B), (C) or (D) on your answer sheet. The conversations will not be printed in your test book and will be spoken only one time.

32. What are the speakers mainly discussing?
(A) A training schedule
(B) A catering menu
(C) A billing fee
(D) A reservation

33. What does the woman warn the man about?
(A) A weather forecast
(B) A staff shortage
(C) Some ongoing renovations
(D) A price increase

34. According to the woman, what is scheduled for Saturday afternoon?
(A) A theater performance
(B) A community event
(C) A product demonstration
(D) A free meal

---

35. What are the speakers mainly discussing?
(A) A branch opening
(B) A work assignment
(C) A company policy
(D) A job promotion

36. What is Alison concerned about?
(A) The cost of tickets
(B) The size of a workload
(C) The schedule for a workshop
(D) The distance to a location

37. What will the company provide to the women?
(A) A rental vehicle
(B) Free accommodation
(C) Travel reimbursement
(D) A monthly bonus

---

38. What type of product is being discussed?
(A) Cell phone
(B) Laptop
(C) Photocopier
(D) Camera

39. What did the market research group like about the product?
(A) Its weight
(B) Its appearance
(C) Its price
(D) Its battery life

40. What will the speakers most likely do this afternoon?
(A) Compile survey results
(B) Meet with some colleagues
(C) Change a product design
(D) Review some advertisements

---

41. What is the man selling?
(A) A kitchen appliance
(B) A used vehicle
(C) A fitness machine
(D) A piece of furniture

42. What will the man do this weekend?
(A) Start a new job
(B) Leave for a vacation
(C) Hold a garage sale
(D) Move to a new home

43. What does the man imply when he says, "I've had calls all morning"?
(A) He is apologizing to the woman for being busy.
(B) He was unable to perform a task on time.
(C) He would prefer to meet the woman tomorrow.
(D) He wants the woman to make a decision quickly.

GO ON TO THE NEXT PAGE

44. What are the speakers mainly discussing?
(A) A company Web site
(B) A local business
(C) A recent promotion
(D) A work policy

45. What does the woman say she enjoys doing?
(A) Contacting potential customers
(B) Creating staff surveys
(C) Collaborating with other departments
(D) Planning company events

46. What does the man say about Mr. Price?
(A) He was recently hired.
(B) He works at different locations.
(C) He is currently on vacation.
(D) He has won several awards.

---

47. What is the purpose of the woman's visit?
(A) To purchase electronic equipment
(B) To hire an advertising agency
(C) To reserve a hotel room
(D) To rent out a recording studio

48. Why is the woman unable to work with Mr. Crank?
(A) He has been relocated to another branch.
(B) His services are too expensive.
(C) He has started a new company.
(D) He has changed professions.

49. What does the man suggest the woman do?
(A) Review the company guidelines
(B) Listen to some music
(C) Leave her contact information
(D) Borrow some video cassettes

---

50. What are the speakers mainly discussing?
(A) A business proposal
(B) A sales report
(C) A building blueprint
(D) A company merger

51. What does the woman imply when she says, "Kevin worked at Holden Construction"?
(A) She thinks Kevin's opinion might be valuable.
(B) She believes that Kevin deserves a promotion.
(C) She wants Kevin to lead an upcoming project.
(D) She will ask Kevin to accompany her on a trip.

52. What does the man suggest?
(A) Postponing a presentation
(B) Visiting a client's workplace
(C) Having a lunch meeting
(D) Changing an advertising plan

---

53. What are the speakers talking about?
(A) Films
(B) Televisions
(C) Mobile phones
(D) Video games

54. What problem does the man mention?
(A) Some software is malfunctioning.
(B) Staff members are behind schedule.
(C) A supervisor is displeased.
(D) A project has become expensive.

55. What is the man asked to do?
(A) Prepare a demonstration
(B) Change a deadline
(C) Hire additional help
(D) Contact a superior

---

56. Where do the speakers most likely work?
(A) At a transportation service
(B) At a restaurant
(C) At an office supply store
(D) At a bank

57. What does the man ask about?
(A) The speed of a service
(B) The duration of a contract
(C) The cost of a product
(D) The location of a shipment

58. What does the man tell the woman to do?
(A) Read some reviews
(B) Download an application
(C) Update a Web site
(D) Contact some coworkers

---

59. What problem does the man mention?
(A) He forgot to send an e-mail.
(B) He needs directions to a meeting.
(C) He left his wallet at home.
(D) He has to make a phone call.

60. Where are the speakers?
(A) A library
(B) A grocery store
(C) A fitness center
(D) A print shop

61. What does the woman suggest the man do?
(A) Speak with a manager
(B) Use a coupon
(C) Visit another location
(D) Eat in the cafeteria

Welford Building - Tenant List	
Floor	Tenant
2 - 3	Triton Software
4 - 6	Kobold Engineering
7 - 8	Bourne IT Solutions
9 - 12	Quest Electronics

62. Look at the graphic. Which company does Mr. Mulder most likely work for?
(A) Triton Software
(B) Kobold Engineering
(C) Bourne IT Solutions
(D) Quest Electronics

63. Why is the man running late?
(A) He had a business meeting.
(B) He got stuck in traffic.
(C) He went to the wrong location.
(D) His vehicle broke down.

64. What does the woman give to the man?
(A) A map
(B) A questionnaire
(C) An ID card
(D) An application form

GO ON TO THE NEXT PAGE →

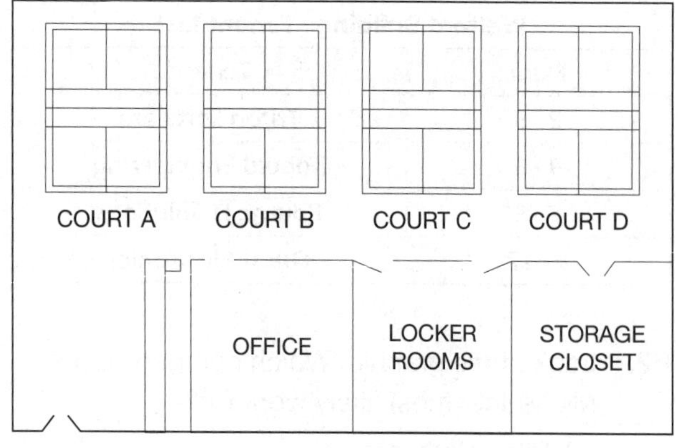

Guardian Supplies

Black Pen	x 10	......	$15
Brown Envelopes	X 20	......	$5
Ink Toner	x 2	......	$30
Printer Paper (1 pack)		......	$10
	Total	......	$60

Thank you for shopping at Guardian Supplies!

65. Why is the woman calling?
(A) To inquire about a booking fee
(B) To ask about equipment rental
(C) To request directions to a sports center
(D) To change a reservation time

66. Look at the graphic. Which badminton court has the woman reserved?
(A) Court A
(B) Court B
(C) Court C
(D) Court D

67. What does the man suggest?
(A) Arriving earlier
(B) Checking a schedule
(C) Using a locker
(D) Taking a class

68. Where does the man work?
(A) At a bank
(B) At a post office
(C) At an office supply store
(D) At a legal firm

69. What problem does the woman mention?
(A) Some equipment has broken down.
(B) A special offer has ended.
(C) Some products are unavailable.
(D) An employee made an error.

70. Look at the graphic. What amount will be refunded to the man?
(A) $5
(B) $10
(C) $15
(D) $30

PART 4

Directions: You will hear some talks given by a single speaker. You will be asked to answer three questions about what the speaker says in each talk. Select the best response to each question and mark the letter (A), (B), (C), or (D) on your answer sheet. The talks will not be printed in your test book and will be spoken only one time.

71. Why does the speaker call the listener?
(A) To explain an additional fee
(B) To encourage participation in a survey
(C) To notify her of a mistake
(D) To inform her that a product is available

72. What can the listener request?
(A) A free sample
(B) Delivery service
(C) Store membership
(D) A full refund

73. What does the speaker remind the listener about?
(A) A closing time
(B) A leftover cost
(C) A store location
(D) An online offer

---

74. What department does the speaker work in?
(A) Human Resources
(B) Quality Assurance
(C) Maintenance
(D) Customer Service

75. What does the speaker need help with?
(A) Gaining entry to the factory
(B) Operating a vehicle
(C) Selecting office supplies
(D) Locating a missing item

76. Why does the problem have to be solved soon?
(A) The deadline for a project is approaching.
(B) Some equipment is being replaced.
(C) A shipment must be sent out on time.
(D) A client meeting is scheduled to be held.

---

77. According to the speaker, what is scheduled to happen next month?
(A) A service will be expanded.
(B) Student interns will be hired.
(C) Customer surveys will be distributed.
(D) The price for investment tips will be lowered.

78. What are employees asked to verify?
(A) That customers have a minimum amount of money.
(B) That a child's parent has an account with them.
(C) That account applicants are currently employed.
(D) That a potential customer lives in the city.

79. Why have some customers praised the bank recently?
(A) Customer requests are processed very quickly.
(B) Its rates are lower than its competitors.
(C) Its Web site is simple to use.
(D) Its employees have given good financial advice.

---

80. Where is the announcement being made?
(A) In a financial institution
(B) In a shopping mall
(C) In a coffee shop
(D) In a fitness center

81. What does the speaker imply when she says, "That's all it takes"?
(A) A business prefers a specific payment method.
(B) An event will be finished early.
(C) A procedure is simple to complete.
(D) A location is easy to find.

82. Why are listeners encouraged to visit a Web site?
(A) To view a schedule
(B) To complete a form
(C) To print coupons
(D) To read about new services

GO ON TO THE NEXT PAGE →

83. What kind of business do the listeners most likely work for?
(A) A bank
(B) A finance company
(C) A law firm
(D) An architecture agency

84. What news does the speaker share with the listeners?
(A) A renovation project will be started.
(B) A promotion will be given.
(C) Performance reviews will be held.
(D) An awards ceremony is being planned.

85. What does the speaker ask the listeners to submit by the end of the week?
(A) Tax information
(B) Office relocation requests
(C) Expense reports
(D) Work schedules

---

86. What is being discussed?
(A) A recent review
(B) A company vehicle
(C) A change in management
(D) A parking service

87. What is Gaston Grill and Bistro hoping to do?
(A) Reduce complaints
(B) Recruit more employees
(C) Promote a product
(D) Improve a rating

88. What are the listeners asked to review?
(A) A contract
(B) A map
(C) An application
(D) An article

---

89. What is the broadcast mainly about?
(A) Local events
(B) Sports results
(C) Business updates
(D) Gardening tips

90. What are the listeners reminded to do by Wednesday afternoon?
(A) Make a payment
(B) Cancel a membership
(C) Place an order
(D) Attend a fair

91. What does the speaker imply when he says, "frequent showers are expected"?
(A) Listeners should purchase an umbrella.
(B) A schedule depends on the weather.
(C) An earlier report included incorrect information.
(D) Listeners should conserve water.

---

92. What is being advertised?
(A) A fitness device
(B) A skin lotion
(C) A health food
(D) A recipe book

93. What does the speaker say is special about the product?
(A) It is only sold online.
(B) It is imported from abroad.
(C) Its price has been reduced.
(D) It is manufactured locally.

94. What does the speaker imply when she says, "Millions can't be wrong"?
(A) A bulk order is preferred.
(B) A product is already popular.
(C) A company is becoming profitable.
(D) A business has multiple branches.

Watersports Rowing Expo	
Youth	500 meters
Beginner	1 kilometer
Amateur	2 kilometer
Professional	5 kilometer

95. What is Reynold's Boating and Tours providing?
(A) Transportation
(B) Safety gear
(C) Prizes
(D) Accommodations

96. Look at the graphic. Which race is canceled?
(A) Youth
(B) Beginner
(C) Amateur
(D) Professional

97. What are the participants reminded to do?
(A) Participate in a survey
(B) Support a sponsor
(C) Purchase a ticket
(D) Upload some pictures

DEPARTMENT	TYPICAL PAPER USES	MONTHLY PAPER USAGE LIMITS
Accounting	Pay slips, financial reports	1,800 sheets
Marketing	Flyers, posters, pamphlets	2,400 sheets
Sales	Sales reports, sales contracts	3,000 sheets
Personnel	Employment contracts, memos	3,500 sheets

98. What is the speaker mainly discussing?
(A) Reducing waste
(B) Saving energy
(C) Boosting profits
(D) Increasing work speed

99. What does the speaker say happened last week?
(A) Employees were hired.
(B) Departments were merged.
(C) New products were launched.
(D) Equipment was replaced.

100. Look at the graphic. In which department does the speaker work?
(A) Accounting
(B) Marketing
(C) Sales
(D) Personnel

This is the end of the Listening Test. Turn to Part 5 in your test book.

정답 및 스크립트 p.300 / 점수 환산표 p.363

GO ON TO THE NEXT PAGE

실전모의고사

TEST 10

시작 시간 ________시 ________분

종료 시간 ________시 ________분

▸중간에 멈추지 말고 처음부터 끝까지 풀어보세요. 문제를 풀 때는 실전처럼 답안지에 마킹하세요.

LISTENING TEST

In the Listening test, you will be asked to demonstrate how well you understand spoken English. The entire Listening test will last approximately 45 minutes. There are four parts, and directions are given for each part. You must mark your answers on the separate answer sheet.

Do not write your answers in your test book.

PART 1

Directions: For each question in this part, you will hear four statements about a picture in your test book. When you hear the statements, you must select the one statement that best describes what you see in the picture. Then find the number of the question on your answer sheet and mark your answer. The statements will not be printed in your test book and will be spoken only one time.

Statement (D), "They are taking photographs," is the best description of the picture, so you should select answer (D) and mark it on your answer sheet.

1.

2.

GO ON TO THE NEXT PAGE

3.

4.

5.

6.

GO ON TO THE NEXT PAGE

PART 2

Directions: You will hear a question or statement and three responses spoken in English. They will not be printed in your test book and will be spoken only one time. Select the best response to the question or statement and mark the letter (A), (B), or (C) on your answer sheet.

7. Mark your answer on your answer sheet.

8. Mark your answer on your answer sheet.

9. Mark your answer on your answer sheet.

10. Mark your answer on your answer sheet.

11. Mark your answer on your answer sheet.

12. Mark your answer on your answer sheet.

13. Mark your answer on your answer sheet.

14. Mark your answer on your answer sheet.

15. Mark your answer on your answer sheet.

16. Mark your answer on your answer sheet.

17. Mark your answer on your answer sheet.

18. Mark your answer on your answer sheet.

19. Mark your answer on your answer sheet.

20. Mark your answer on your answer sheet.

21. Mark your answer on your answer sheet.

22. Mark your answer on your answer sheet.

23. Mark your answer on your answer sheet.

24. Mark your answer on your answer sheet.

25. Mark your answer on your answer sheet.

26. Mark your answer on your answer sheet.

27. Mark your answer on your answer sheet.

28. Mark your answer on your answer sheet.

29. Mark your answer on your answer sheet.

30. Mark your answer on your answer sheet.

31. Mark your answer on your answer sheet.

PART 3

Directions: You will hear some conversations between two or more people. You will be asked to answer three questions about what the speakers say in each conversation. Select the best response to each question and mark the letter (A), (B), (C) or (D) on your answer sheet. The conversations will not be printed in your test book and will be spoken only one time.

32. What does the man want to do?
(A) Purchase a new television
(B) Get his TV reception repaired
(C) Cancel an unnecessary service
(D) Enter a competition

33. What will happen this evening?
(A) The man will go to a fitness center.
(B) A sales promotion will end.
(C) The man will watch a sporting event.
(D) A product will be delivered.

34. According to the woman, what will the man be charged for?
(A) A late payment
(B) A service upgrade
(C) Tickets for a soccer game
(D) A contract cancellation

35. What are the speakers mainly discussing?
(A) A sporting event
(B) A seminar about poverty
(C) A film release
(D) A political gathering

36. What is the man's problem?
(A) Tickets are no longer available.
(B) He has to work on Saturday.
(C) Prices for an event are too expensive.
(D) He will be out of town this weekend.

37. What does the woman offer to do?
(A) Send the man's résumé to her boss
(B) Let the man use her ticket
(C) Give the man a ride
(D) Speak with a business owner

38. What does the man say will happen on Friday?
(A) A Web site will launch.
(B) A renovation project will begin.
(C) A competition will be held.
(D) A business will open.

39. What did the women do this morning?
(A) Set up displays
(B) Cleaned a workspace
(C) Distributed flyers
(D) Purchased supplies

40. What does the man ask Bella to do?
(A) Conduct job interviews
(B) Lead a training session
(C) Place advertisements
(D) Contact staff members

41. Who most likely are the speakers?
(A) Janitors
(B) Plumbers
(C) Architects
(D) Painters

42. Why is the man unable to help the woman?
(A) He is leaving to go on vacation.
(B) He must train a new employee.
(C) He cannot find transportation.
(D) He is not qualified.

43. What does the man suggest the woman do?
(A) Request a new assignment
(B) Hire a part-time worker
(C) Ask a coworker for help
(D) Take a training course

GO ON TO THE NEXT PAGE →

44. What is the woman concerned about?
(A) Choosing a venue for an event
(B) Hiring a chef for a restaurant
(C) Finding a coffee supplier
(D) Selecting a name for her business

45. What does the man say he will do?
(A) Visit a potential restaurant site
(B) Report the results of a study
(C) Contact the woman in the afternoon
(D) Review some résumés

46. What is scheduled to happen in March?
(A) A company executive will retire.
(B) A business will relocate.
(C) The results of an inspection will be announced.
(D) A restaurant will start a new service.

---

47. Where is the conversation taking place?
(A) In a restaurant
(B) In a bus terminal
(C) In an airport
(D) In a hotel

48. What problem does the woman mention?
(A) She has misplaced an item.
(B) She is running late for a meeting.
(C) She cannot access a room.
(D) She has arrived at the wrong location.

49. What do the men agree to do?
(A) Speak with coworkers
(B) Provide a refund
(C) Upgrade a service
(D) Reschedule an event

---

50. What is the man interested in doing?
(A) Signing an apartment lease
(B) Postponing a celebration
(C) Booking a space for an event
(D) Renovating an office

51. What did the woman want to get?
(A) An updated inventory
(B) A list of clients
(C) A price estimate
(D) Information about a room

52. What does the man suggest the woman do?
(A) Check out a Web site
(B) E-mail a document
(C) Visit a building
(D) Fill out an application

---

53. What does the woman imply when she says, "Finally"?
(A) She thinks a project took too long to complete.
(B) She has an important topic to discuss.
(C) She is pleased that a decision has been made.
(D) She wants the man to complete a task.

54. What does the man say about Mr. Cowell?
(A) He is planning to leave the company.
(B) He has helped increase the company's profits.
(C) He will interview potential job candidates.
(D) He will take on a new role next month.

55. What will the speakers do next?
(A) Make some coffee
(B) Attend a meeting
(C) Purchase a gift
(D) Arrange a celebration

---

56. Why is the company making changes to workers' salaries?
(A) A recent business deal was less successful than expected.
(B) The company's profits have increased drastically.
(C) A law was passed by the government.
(D) The company has not hired enough workers.

57. What is an additional result of the pay change?
(A) Employees will work longer hours.
(B) The company can retain its workers.
(C) Foreign investors can be attracted.
(D) The company will receive an award.

58. What will happen soon?
(A) More workers will join the company.
(B) A new company policy will be announced.
(C) The company will open up a new branch.
(D) Employees will negotiate new contracts.

---

59. Where do the speakers work?
(A) At a bank
(B) At a restaurant
(C) At a post office
(D) At a hospital

60. Why has the woman been asked to visit headquarters?
(A) To submit a report
(B) To oversee training
(C) To attend a board meeting
(D) To join a business luncheon

61. What does the man mean when he says, "Leave it to me"?
(A) He would like a copy of an interview schedule.
(B) He suggests that the woman cancel a trip.
(C) He will contact some job candidates.
(D) He plans to depart at the same time as the woman.

Post Office Branch	Supervisor
Glendale Street	Ms. Prescott
Foreman Road	Mr. Gupta
Rowan Avenue	Ms. Anders
Yale Boulevard	Mr. Lubick

62. What is the man trying to do?
(A) Buy some stamps
(B) Send some packages
(C) Pick up a delivery
(D) Obtain a refund

63. What does the woman ask for?
(A) An invoice number
(B) A delivery address
(C) A piece of ID
(D) An estimated weight

64. Look at the graphic. What branch does the woman work at?
(A) Glendale Street
(B) Foreman Road
(C) Rowan Avenue
(D) Yale Boulevard

GO ON TO THE NEXT PAGE

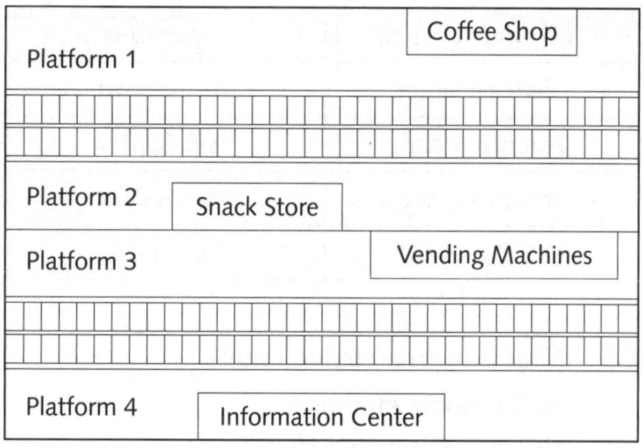

Platform 1
Coffee Shop

Platform 2
Snack Store

Platform 3
Vending Machines

Platform 4
Information Center

65. Who most likely is the man?
(A) A train driver
(B) A maintenance worker
(C) A passenger
(D) A ticket agent

66. What does the woman ask about?
(A) Train delays
(B) Special discounts
(C) Food availability
(D) Seat upgrades

67. Look at the graphic. Which platform will the woman go to next?
(A) Platform 1
(B) Platform 2
(C) Platform 3
(D) Platform 4

Burnaby Jazz Festival Afternoon Schedule	
1:45 P.M. – 2:15 P.M.	Jerome Lewis
2:30 P.M. – 3:15 P.M.	Otto Manfred
3:30 P.M. – 4:15 P.M.	Catriona Salford
4:30 P.M. – 5:30 P.M.	Lou Garland

68. Who most likely are the speakers?
(A) Event organizers
(B) Concert performers
(C) Music critics
(D) Magazine editors

69. What does the man mention about the jazz festival?
(A) It will be broadcast online.
(B) It has sold out of tickets.
(C) It is being held in several venues.
(D) It will be covered in a magazine.

70. Look at the graphic. When will the speakers probably meet?
(A) At 2:15 P.M.
(B) At 3:15 P.M.
(C) At 4:15 P.M.
(D) At 5:30 P.M.

PART 4

Directions: You will hear some talks given by a single speaker. You will be asked to answer three questions about what the speaker says in each talk. Select the best response to each question and mark the letter (A), (B), (C), or (D) on your answer sheet. The talks will not be printed in your test book and will be spoken only one time.

71. Where does the speaker most likely work?
(A) At a real estate office
(B) At a magazine company
(C) At an architectural firm
(D) At a bank

72. What problem is reported?
(A) A deadline has passed.
(B) A bill was not paid in full.
(C) A building violated a safety rule.
(D) A meeting must be cancelled.

73. What does the speaker say he might do tomorrow?
(A) Refund an item
(B) Put a service on hold
(C) Turn in a report
(D) Send out some merchandise

---

74. What is the purpose of the contest?
(A) To decide on a location for a trip
(B) To create a company logo
(C) To rename the company
(D) To select the best employee

75. According to the speaker, why should workers go to the Human Resources Department?
(A) To apply for a job opening
(B) To get an application form
(C) To hand in a design
(D) To vote on a contest winner

76. What will take place on September 20?
(A) A merger deal will be signed.
(B) Additional staff will be hired.
(C) Ms. Perkins will be promoted.
(D) A new design will be revealed.

---

77. What kind of business is being advertised?
(A) A grocery store
(B) A fitness center
(C) A sporting goods store
(D) A hardware store

78. When is the store's grand opening?
(A) On Sunday
(B) On Monday
(C) On Wednesday
(D) On Friday

79. How can customers become a member?
(A) By turning in a form
(B) By visiting a Web site
(C) By contacting the manager
(D) By attending the grand opening

---

80. What information should the listeners look for on a Web site?
(A) An event map
(B) Directions
(C) A price list
(D) Available parking

81. Why is the event at the Boston Club expected to be popular?
(A) Admission is free.
(B) A famous band will play.
(C) There are many food specials.
(D) The location is convenient.

82. Why does the speaker say, "the Boston Club has limited capacity"?
(A) To criticize a decision
(B) To explain a price
(C) To warn about safety conditions
(D) To stress a suggestion

GO ON TO THE NEXT PAGE →

83. What problem has the caller discovered?
(A) He submitted the wrong poster design.
(B) He provided the wrong delivery address.
(C) He forgot to order some materials.
(D) He misplaced a Web site address.

84. What event is scheduled for next weekend?
(A) A career fair
(B) A drama production
(C) A musical performance
(D) A graphic design convention

85. What does the caller offer to do?
(A) Pay a fee in advance
(B) Cancel a previous order
(C) Reschedule an event
(D) Visit a business location

---

86. Who most likely are the listeners?
(A) Sales representatives
(B) Financial advisors
(C) Potential customers
(D) Department managers

87. What does the speaker mean when she says, "We wish we could offer more"?
(A) She wants to provide new benefits to customers.
(B) She acknowledges that the listeners are disappointed.
(C) She hopes to expand a product range in the future.
(D) She wants the listeners to offer their suggestions.

88. What will the listeners probably do next?
(A) Watch a video clip
(B) Test new products
(C) Begin a tour
(D) Review a budget

---

89. Where most likely are the listeners?
(A) At a leadership workshop
(B) At an awards show
(C) At a store opening
(D) At an anniversary celebration

90. According to the speaker, what has been the most important aspect of his work?
(A) Giving large amounts of money
(B) Influencing governmental policy
(C) Assisting others in person
(D) Organizing charity events

91. What will the speaker probably talk about next?
(A) The importance of student volunteering
(B) The social effects of some natural disasters
(C) Methods of conserving water
(D) Tactics for soliciting donations

---

92. What is the speaker mainly discussing?
(A) A sports competition
(B) A grand opening event
(C) A community art fair
(D) A musical performance

93. What did the city council do last month?
(A) It resurfaced a road.
(B) It modified a park.
(C) It renovated a building.
(D) It donated funds to charity.

94. What does the speaker mean when she says, "that has yet to be confirmed"?
(A) Ticket prices might increase.
(B) A schedule might change.
(C) A planning permit has not been granted.
(D) Local celebrities are likely to participate.

Box Office Earnings – July	
1. Dreams of Flight	$115 million
2. The Lost Talisman	$105 million
3. Star Voyager	$72 million
4. Summer Sonnet	$35 million
5. Eastern Winds	$24 million

95. Who most likely is the speaker?

(A) A theater owner
(B) A magazine writer
(C) A radio show host
(D) A movie critic

96. Look at the graphic. How much money did Brad Ford's new movie make in July?

(A) $115 million
(B) $105 million
(C) $72 million
(D) $35 million

97. What does the speaker say about Eastern Winds?

(A) It has been poorly received.
(B) It was released one week ago.
(C) It features an award-winning actor.
(D) It was expensive to produce.

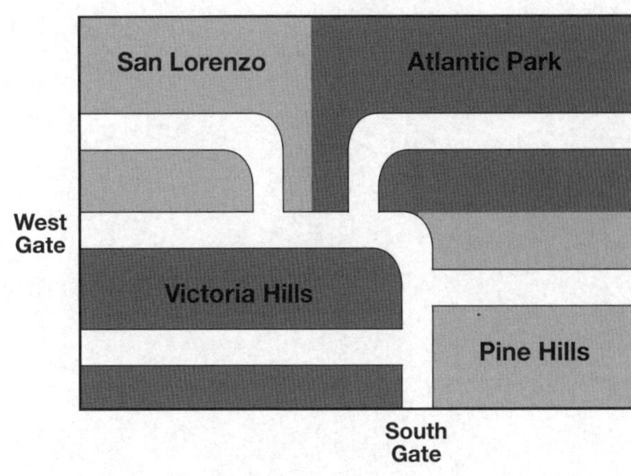

98. Why is the speaker calling?

(A) To describe a company's services
(B) To request a deadline extension
(C) To point out an error with some work
(D) To confirm the details of a project

99. What does the speaker say he will do on Saturday?

(A) Leave an entrance unlocked
(B) Submit a payment to a business
(C) Rent some extra equipment
(D) Provide additional instructions

100. Look at the graphic. Which neighborhood is the speaker's house located in?

(A) San Lorenzo
(B) Atlantic Park
(C) Victoria Hills
(D) Pine Hills

This is the end of the Listening Test. Turn to Part 5 in your test book.

정답 및 스크립트 p.309 / 점수 환산표 p.363

GO ON TO THE NEXT PAGE

실전모의고사
TEST 11

시작 시간 ________시 ________분

종료 시간 ________시 ________분

▸ 중간에 멈추지 말고 처음부터 끝까지 풀어보세요. 문제를 풀 때는 실전처럼 답안지에 마킹하세요.

LISTENING TEST

In the Listening test, you will be asked to demonstrate how well you understand spoken English. The entire Listening test will last approximately 45 minutes. There are four parts, and directions are given for each part. You must mark your answers on the separate answer sheet.

Do not write your answers in your test book.

PART 1

Directions: For each question in this part, you will hear four statements about a picture in your test book. When you hear the statements, you must select the one statement that best describes what you see in the picture. Then find the number of the question on your answer sheet and mark your answer. The statements will not be printed in your test book and will be spoken only one time.

Statement (D), "They are taking photographs," is the best description of the picture, so you should select answer (D) and mark it on your answer sheet.

1.

2.

GO ON TO THE NEXT PAGE

3.

4.

5.

6.

TEST 11

GO ON TO THE NEXT PAGE

PART 2

Directions: You will hear a question or statement and three responses spoken in English. They will not be printed in your test book and will be spoken only one time. Select the best response to the question or statement and mark the letter (A), (B), or (C) on your answer sheet.

7. Mark your answer on your answer sheet.

8. Mark your answer on your answer sheet.

9. Mark your answer on your answer sheet.

10. Mark your answer on your answer sheet.

11. Mark your answer on your answer sheet.

12. Mark your answer on your answer sheet.

13. Mark your answer on your answer sheet.

14. Mark your answer on your answer sheet.

15. Mark your answer on your answer sheet.

16. Mark your answer on your answer sheet.

17. Mark your answer on your answer sheet.

18. Mark your answer on your answer sheet.

19. Mark your answer on your answer sheet.

20. Mark your answer on your answer sheet.

21. Mark your answer on your answer sheet.

22. Mark your answer on your answer sheet.

23. Mark your answer on your answer sheet.

24. Mark your answer on your answer sheet.

25. Mark your answer on your answer sheet.

26. Mark your answer on your answer sheet.

27. Mark your answer on your answer sheet.

28. Mark your answer on your answer sheet.

29. Mark your answer on your answer sheet.

30. Mark your answer on your answer sheet.

31. Mark your answer on your answer sheet.

PART 3

Directions: You will hear some conversations between two or more people. You will be asked to answer three questions about what the speakers say in each conversation. Select the best response to each question and mark the letter (A), (B), (C) or (D) on your answer sheet. The conversations will not be printed in your test book and will be spoken only one time.

32. What event did the woman miss?
(A) A theatrical performance
(B) A press conference
(C) A book tour reading
(D) A product demonstration

33. Why did the woman miss the event?
(A) The roads were too congested.
(B) She was returning from vacation.
(C) The schedule was recently changed.
(D) She was in a car accident.

34. What does the man suggest the woman do?
(A) Invest in his company
(B) Subscribe to a media publication
(C) Write a report about a recent meeting
(D) Retrieve a newspaper from his office

35. What is the man having problems with?
(A) Confirming a delivery
(B) Installing an appliance
(C) Developing software
(D) Ordering a device

36. What happened while the man was on his lunch break?
(A) An item was delivered.
(B) The woman printed a document.
(C) A department held a meeting.
(D) An electrical device broke.

37. What does the woman tell the man to do?
(A) Look for a manual
(B) Take a class
(C) Make an appointment
(D) E-mail a technician

38. What are the speakers mainly discussing?
(A) A company excursion
(B) A restaurant's grand opening
(C) A coworker's birthday
(D) A department merger

39. What problem does the man mention?
(A) A business has closed.
(B) A colleague is off work.
(C) A special offer has ended.
(D) An event has been postponed.

40. What do the women intend to do?
(A) Revise a menu
(B) Compare prices
(C) Prepare some food
(D) Post a notice

41. Where do the speakers most likely work?
(A) At a restaurant
(B) At an electronics store
(C) At a catering company
(D) At a newspaper

42. What are the speakers discussing?
(A) Ordering a meal
(B) Improving worker benefits
(C) Increasing a product's price
(D) Expanding a menu

43. What does the man suggest doing?
(A) Enlarging a work space
(B) Changing business hours
(C) Buying extra equipment
(D) Spending more on advertising

GO ON TO THE NEXT PAGE →

44. Where is the conversation taking place?
(A) In an office
(B) In a restaurant
(C) In a car
(D) In a park

45. What will the woman do this morning?
(A) Meet with a client
(B) Inspect a construction site
(C) Interview for a job
(D) Lead an orientation

46. What does the woman imply when she says, "It should be empty right now"?
(A) She thinks a business is closing early.
(B) She is certain that the food is sold out.
(C) She can get to an appointment on time.
(D) She recommends visiting a different store.

---

47. What is the conversation mainly about?
(A) Building a production facility
(B) Investing in the woman's company
(C) Decreasing a department's staff
(D) Purchasing another business

48. What are the speakers worried about?
(A) The efficiency of factories
(B) An impending deadline
(C) Quarterly sales figures
(D) The rising price of resources

49. What does the woman say she will do next week?
(A) Negotiate a price
(B) Delay an appointment
(C) Give a presentation
(D) Tour a factory

---

50. Where do the speakers most likely work?
(A) At a music store
(B) At a movie theater
(C) At a conference hall
(D) At a sports stadium

51. Why do the men want to leave work early?
(A) They are concerned about traffic.
(B) They want to avoid road maintenance.
(C) They are going out for a meal.
(D) They are attending an event.

52. What does the woman ask Philip to do?
(A) Clean an office
(B) Set up some equipment
(C) Put up some posters
(D) File some documents

---

53. What does the man mean when he says, "We'd better watch our levels"?
(A) Some noise is too loud.
(B) Some stock is running low.
(C) Profits are lower than expected.
(D) The business should save energy.

54. What has caused a problem?
(A) A shortage of staff
(B) A change to a schedule
(C) A computer malfunction
(D) A lack of communication

55. What will the man probably do next?
(A) Hold an employee meeting
(B) Repair a piece of equipment
(C) Visit a different business
(D) Speak with some customers

---

56. What are the speakers discussing?
(A) A talk by the head of a firm
(B) The retirement of a CEO
(C) An upcoming career fair
(D) The success of a new product

57. What has Mr. Cobb done for the field of electronics?
(A) He has pioneered new technologies.
(B) He has invested in young companies.
(C) He has trained promising engineers.
(D) He has broadened the consumer base.

58. What does the man ask the woman to do?
(A) Purchase tickets for employees
(B) Speak with a member of Mr. Cobb's staff
(C) Conduct an interview with Mr. Cobb
(D) Contact a department of the university

---

59. What are the speakers mainly discussing?
(A) Buying a new monitor
(B) Going to see a movie
(C) Installing new software
(D) Replacing a faulty part

60. What does the man offer to do?
(A) Loan the woman a computer
(B) Teach the woman to use a program
(C) Give the woman a coupon
(D) Repair a device for the woman

61. What is the woman's problem?
(A) Her computer is out-of-date.
(B) Her coupon has expired.
(C) She doesn't have a store membership.
(D) She could not afford a new product.

Willard County Airshow

Date/Time:
April 26th, 10 a.m. - 6 p.m.

Location:
Willard Fairgrounds

Admission Fee:
Adults: $8 / Children: $4

Parking Fee: $2 per vehicle

62. Who most likely is the man?
(A) A ticket seller
(B) An event organizer
(C) A fairgrounds employee
(D) A print shop worker

63. Look at the graphic. What information on the poster should be changed?
(A) Date/Time
(B) Location
(C) Admission Fee
(D) Parking Fee

64. What will the woman probably do next?
(A) Make a payment
(B) Purchase some items
(C) Review a document
(D) Contact a supervisor

GO ON TO THE NEXT PAGE

Psion Full HD TVs	Screen Size
K5100	40 inch
K5300	43 inch
K6300	49 inch
K6500	55 inch

65. What are the speakers preparing for?
(A) A product launch
(B) A staff orientation
(C) A client meeting
(D) An interview session

66. What is the woman concerned about?
(A) The size of a room
(B) The price of a device
(C) The quality of a screen
(D) The length of a warranty

67. Look at the graphic. Which television will the man most likely buy?
(A) K5100
(B) K5300
(C) K6300
(D) K6500

Inbox		
Name	**Subject**	**Time**
Dan Continenza	Meeting minutes	8:37 A.M.
Martin Trese	Training guide revisions	9:14 A.M.
Ryan Nutter	FileSafe (Download Link)	9:45 A.M.
John Montgomery	Market research report	10:07 A.M.

68. Look at the graphic. What is the name of the man speaking?
(A) Dan Continenza
(B) Martin Trese
(C) Ryan Nutter
(D) John Montgomery

69. How will the woman help the man?
(A) By responding to an e-mail
(B) By signing for a package
(C) By proofreading a document
(D) By testing a program

70. Why will the woman be absent from a meeting?
(A) She has to meet with a client.
(B) She will travel to another country.
(C) She is not involved in the project.
(D) She is leading a training session.

PART 4

Directions: You will hear some talks given by a single speaker. You will be asked to answer three questions about what the speaker says in each talk. Select the best response to each question and mark the letter (A), (B), (C), or (D) on your answer sheet. The talks will not be printed in your test book and will be spoken only one time.

71. What is the speaker calling about?
(A) An apartment lease renewal
(B) An incomplete service
(C) A broken kitchen appliance
(D) An unpaid bill

72. What does the speaker say she will do tomorrow?
(A) Order a replacement part
(B) Go on vacation
(C) Move to a new home
(D) Contact a repair man

73. What is the listener asked to do?
(A) Send a monthly check
(B) Visit the speaker's office
(C) Read a contract
(D) Provide product information

---

74. What will be made in the new facility?
(A) Video cameras
(B) Television commercials
(C) News broadcasts
(D) A monthly publication

75. According to the speaker, where will the new facility be?
(A) In the company's headquarters
(B) In a shopping center
(C) In a government building
(D) In an overseas branch

76. According to the speaker, what is an advantage of the new facility?
(A) The company's workforce can be expanded.
(B) Press events can be held there.
(C) Product development speed will increase.
(D) Advertising campaigns can be launched promptly.

---

77. Where most likely are the listeners?
(A) At a restaurant
(B) At an airport
(C) At a department store
(D) At a hotel

78. What are the speaker's instructions mainly about?
(A) Some special equipment
(B) A company Web site
(C) An office expansion
(D) A budget restriction

79. What does the speaker imply when she says, "Sean will be in later"?
(A) Sean is in charge of customer service.
(B) Sean is knowledgeable about an issue.
(C) Too many employees are working.
(D) Staff will be observed by a superior.

---

80. Who most likely are the listeners?
(A) Gym members
(B) Factory workers
(C) Fitness instructors
(D) Safety officers

81. How are the new machines better than the previous ones?
(A) They are more powerful.
(B) They take up less space.
(C) They have more features.
(D) They are easier to assemble.

82. What will Mr. Kang do?
(A) Set up some new equipment
(B) Describe available fitness classes
(C) Install some new exercise programs
(D) Explain the operation of a machine

GO ON TO THE NEXT PAGE →

83. Where does the speaker most likely work?
(A) At a manufacturing company
(B) At an interior design firm
(C) At a real estate agency
(D) At a hardware store

84. Why does the speaker say, "We're finally ready to go"?
(A) She plans to attend an upcoming event.
(B) She wants the listener to accompany her.
(C) She is happy to relocate her business.
(D) She is excited to begin some work.

85. What is the listener reminded to do?
(A) Make a payment
(B) Complete a form
(C) Approve a work schedule
(D) Check some samples

---

86. What is the purpose of the message?
(A) To inquire about a charge
(B) To complain about a faulty product
(C) To schedule a delivery
(D) To discuss a missing item

87. What does the speaker say about the Web site?
(A) It contains helpful videos.
(B) It lacks some information.
(C) It has too many advertisements.
(D) It requires a membership.

88. What does the speaker request?
(A) A printed copy
(B) A replacement part
(C) An e-mail attachment
(D) A product demonstration

---

89. What is the speaker mainly discussing?
(A) New employees
(B) Marketing strategies
(C) Sales figures
(D) Customer complaints

90. What does the speaker mean when she says, "This just won't do"?
(A) New equipment is insufficient.
(B) Staff performance must improve.
(C) A company event will be canceled.
(D) A dining area will be rearranged.

91. What will the listeners do next?
(A) Attend a training session
(B) Clean a workplace
(C) Order new supplies
(D) Collect customer feedback

---

92. What department does the speaker work in?
(A) Sales
(B) Customer service
(C) Marketing
(D) Purchasing

93. What is scheduled to happen in April?
(A) A new branch of a restaurant will open.
(B) A food item's ingredients will change.
(C) An advertising campaign will begin.
(D) An employee's contract will expire.

94. What does the speaker ask the listener to do?
(A) Send a cost estimate
(B) Reduce the price of a menu item
(C) Provide a business address
(D) Expedite a delivery

Package	Price Per Month
Standard	$19.99
Premium	$24.99
Unlimited	$29.99
Platinum	$34.99

95. What is the main purpose of the message?
(A) To extend a contract
(B) To inquire about a bill
(C) To schedule repairs
(D) To request an upgrade

96. What is the speaker most pleased with?
(A) The connection speed
(B) The customer service
(C) The movie selection
(D) The monthly data allowance

97. Look at the graphic. Which package does the speaker currently have?
(A) Standard
(B) Premium
(C) Unlimited
(D) Platinum

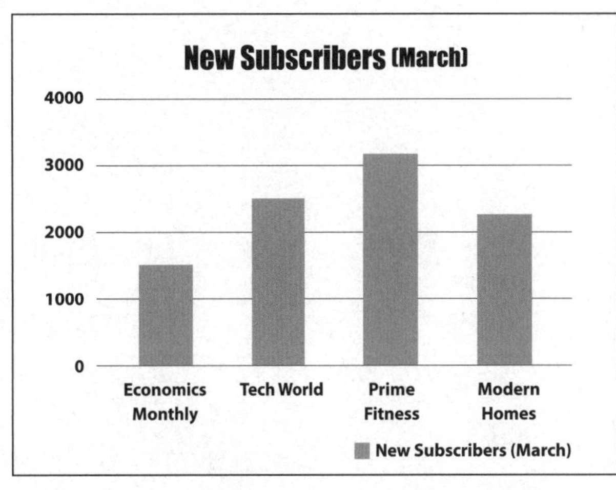

98. Who most likely is the speaker?
(A) An HR manager
(B) A company owner
(C) A customer service adviser
(D) A magazine writer

99. According to the speaker, what happened in March?
(A) A new magazine was launched.
(B) Free gifts were offered.
(C) A subscription fee was reduced.
(D) Articles were published online.

100. Look at the graphic. Which magazine will the speaker discuss next?
(A) Economics Monthly
(B) Tech World
(C) Prime Fitness
(D) Modern Homes

This is the end of the Listening Test. Turn to Part 5 in your test book.

정답 및 스크립트 p.318 / 점수 환산표 p.363

GO ON TO THE NEXT PAGE

실전모의고사
TEST 12

TEST 12 MP3

TEST 12 해설

시작 시간 ________시 ________분

종료 시간 ________시 ________분

▸중간에 멈추지 말고 처음부터 끝까지 풀어보세요. 문제를 풀 때는 실전처럼 답안지에 마킹하세요.

LISTENING TEST

In the Listening test, you will be asked to demonstrate how well you understand spoken English. The entire Listening test will last approximately 45 minutes. There are four parts, and directions are given for each part. You must mark your answers on the separate answer sheet.

Do not write your answers in your test book.

PART 1

Directions: For each question in this part, you will hear four statements about a picture in your test book. When you hear the statements, you must select the one statement that best describes what you see in the picture. Then find the number of the question on your answer sheet and mark your answer. The statements will not be printed in your test book and will be spoken only one time.

Statement (D), "They are taking photographs," is the best description of the picture, so you should select answer (D) and mark it on your answer sheet.

1.

2.

TEST 12

GO ON TO THE NEXT PAGE

3.

4.

5.

TEST 12

6.

GO ON TO THE NEXT PAGE

PART 2

Directions: You will hear a question or statement and three responses spoken in English. They will not be printed in your test book and will be spoken only one time. Select the best response to the question or statement and mark the letter (A), (B), or (C) on your answer sheet.

7. Mark your answer on your answer sheet.

8. Mark your answer on your answer sheet.

9. Mark your answer on your answer sheet.

10. Mark your answer on your answer sheet.

11. Mark your answer on your answer sheet.

12. Mark your answer on your answer sheet.

13. Mark your answer on your answer sheet.

14. Mark your answer on your answer sheet.

15. Mark your answer on your answer sheet.

16. Mark your answer on your answer sheet.

17. Mark your answer on your answer sheet.

18. Mark your answer on your answer sheet.

19. Mark your answer on your answer sheet.

20. Mark your answer on your answer sheet.

21. Mark your answer on your answer sheet.

22. Mark your answer on your answer sheet.

23. Mark your answer on your answer sheet.

24. Mark your answer on your answer sheet.

25. Mark your answer on your answer sheet.

26. Mark your answer on your answer sheet.

27. Mark your answer on your answer sheet.

28. Mark your answer on your answer sheet.

29. Mark your answer on your answer sheet.

30. Mark your answer on your answer sheet.

31. Mark your answer on your answer sheet.

PART 3

Directions: You will hear some conversations between two or more people. You will be asked to answer three questions about what the speakers say in each conversation. Select the best response to each question and mark the letter (A), (B), (C) or (D) on your answer sheet. The conversations will not be printed in your test book and will be spoken only one time.

32. Where does the conversation most likely take place?
(A) In a flower shop
(B) In a factory
(C) In a car rental agency
(D) In an auto shop

33. What is the problem?
(A) The woman ran out of fuel.
(B) The woman crashed her car.
(C) A vehicle won't start.
(D) A car has a flat tire.

34. What does the man say he will do next?
(A) Retrieve some tools
(B) Give the woman a ride
(C) Check the wire connections
(D) Deliver some merchandise

35. In which department do the speakers work?
(A) Advertising
(B) Sales
(C) Accounting
(D) Human Resources

36. What does the man suggest that the women do?
(A) Arrange a workspace
(B) Print a document
(C) Make a reservation
(D) Begin some training

37. What does Priyanka Kapoor ask for?
(A) Some work samples
(B) A menu
(C) An e-mail address
(D) Some office supplies

38. Why was the restaurant recommended to the man?
(A) It is running a special promotion.
(B) It has good vegetarian options.
(C) It has hired a new head chef.
(D) It has a wide range of desserts.

39. What does the woman say is happening next month?
(A) The restaurant is adding a new pasta dish.
(B) Entrée prices will go up.
(C) A home delivery service will begin.
(D) A food supplier is changing.

40. What will the woman most likely do next?
(A) Check an item's ingredients
(B) Bring out a food sample
(C) Print out a receipt
(D) Give the man some change

41. Why is the man calling the woman?
(A) To book a taxi
(B) To request a refund
(C) To confirm an order
(D) To complain about a service

42. What does the woman suggest?
(A) Paying online
(B) Applying for an account
(C) Making a donation
(D) Subscribing to a magazine

43. What does the woman offer to do?
(A) Send the man a free gift
(B) Deliver an item in person
(C) Reduce the price of some merchandise
(D) Ask her boss to call the man

GO ON TO THE NEXT PAGE

44. What is the main topic of the conversation?
(A) A skills workshop
(B) A fundraising event
(C) A recruitment fair
(D) A seasonal sale

45. What does Desmond mention about Rickard Avenue?
(A) It is known for heavy traffic.
(B) It is currently inaccessible.
(C) It is located far away from a venue.
(D) It has many parking spaces.

46. What does the woman suggest?
(A) Having a meal together
(B) Using public transportation
(C) Following alternate directions
(D) Renting some equipment

---

47. According to the man, what was the company unable to do?
(A) Provide a refund
(B) Upload a document
(C) Process a payment
(D) Host a conference

48. What does the man offer to do for the woman?
(A) Arrange transportation
(B) Make a reservation
(C) Carry some luggage
(D) Clean a room

49. Why does the woman need to leave soon?
(A) Traffic will be bad.
(B) A store is closing.
(C) A meeting will start.
(D) Some visitors have arrived.

---

50. What is the woman doing on Wednesday?
(A) Starting a new job
(B) Hosting a fundraiser
(C) Attending a conference
(D) Appearing on a news show

51. Why does the woman say, "You are the event organizer, after all"?
(A) To explain a promotion
(B) To criticize an error
(C) To assign a responsibility
(D) To justify a request

52. What does the man need to do on Wednesday?
(A) Visit some contributors
(B) Pick up an order
(C) Make a bank deposit
(D) Finish a design

---

53. What does the woman mention about the posters?
(A) They will be displayed the following week.
(B) They will be sent to international offices.
(C) They will be printed solely in black and white.
(D) They will be distributed to clients.

54. What problem does the man report?
(A) There is incorrect information on the poster.
(B) He has to leave the office early.
(C) Delivery prices have risen recently.
(D) Some ink will take too long to dry.

55. What does the woman recommend doing?
(A) E-mailing a document to each branch
(B) Posting information on a message board
(C) Using a professional service
(D) Purchasing a new office appliance

---

56. Where most likely are the speakers?
(A) At a clinic
(B) At a sporting event
(C) At a pharmacy
(D) At a spa

57. What does the man mean when he says, "I've never used it before"?
(A) He is surprised by some results.
(B) He is upset about making a mistake.
(C) He would prefer to try a different product.
(D) He is hoping to receive some information.

58. Where will the speakers most likely go next?
(A) To a drive-thru service
(B) To a nearby park
(C) To a photo printer
(D) To a phone store

59. What about the woman impressed the man?
(A) Her writing style
(B) Her interview performance
(C) Her letters of reference
(D) Her educational experience

60. Why does the woman say she is interested in the job?
(A) She would like to have more flexible hours.
(B) She wants to cover more serious topics.
(C) Her current employer is going out of business.
(D) She wants a much higher pay rate.

61. According to the man, what does the job require?
(A) A deep knowledge about fashion
(B) Familiarity with international cuisine
(C) A willingness to travel abroad
(D) Experience in managing others

Zane's Office Supplies

Monthly
Membership Coupon

Spend $25 → 5% off
Spend $50 → 10% off
Spend $75 → 15% off
Spend $100 → 20% off

Enter discount code AQ4233
at checkout

62. What is the woman trying to buy?
(A) Keyboards
(B) Ink
(C) Staples
(D) Paper

63. Look at the graphic. Which discount should the woman receive?
(A) 5% off
(B) 10% off
(C) 15% off
(D) 20% off

64. What does the man offer to do?
(A) Update a catalogue
(B) Arrange a delivery
(C) Provide additional savings
(D) Check with a coworker

GO ON TO THE NEXT PAGE

Otterbein University
Annual Literature Festival
April 17 – April 20

Hanby Hall, 7 P.M.
Free admission

65. What project will the speakers be working on?
(A) Creating some advertisements
(B) Relocating an office
(C) Planning a business trip
(D) Opening a restaurant

66. Look at the graphic. Which date will the woman attend the festival?
(A) April 17
(B) April 18
(C) April 19
(D) April 20

67. Who is Charles Kinney?
(A) A designer
(B) A professor
(C) A writer
(D) A business owner

Corsair Airways Flight CA 56, July 25 Toronto to London, One-way Ticket	
Standard Economy	$1,500
Premium Economy	$2,100
Business Traveler	$4,500
Business Plus	$5,200

68. Where is the conversation most likely taking place?
(A) At an airport
(B) In a hotel
(C) In a travel agency
(D) On an airplane

69. Look at the graphic. What type of ticket does the woman purchase?
(A) Standard Economy
(B) Premium Economy
(C) Business Traveler
(D) Business Plus

70. What special request does the woman make?
(A) She would prefer to take a later flight.
(B) She would like a specific meal.
(C) She requires transportation to a hotel.
(D) She wants a room with a nice view.

PART 4

Directions: You will hear some talks given by a single speaker. You will be asked to answer three questions about what the speaker says in each talk. Select the best response to each question and mark the letter (A), (B), (C), or (D) on your answer sheet. The talks will not be printed in your test book and will be spoken only one time.

71. What will listeners most likely do when they finish writing?
(A) Gather together for a meal
(B) Present their papers to the class
(C) Listen to a speech
(D) Watch a short film

72. What does the speaker remind listeners about?
(A) The deadline for a payment
(B) A common negotiating error
(C) An upcoming assignment
(D) The cancellation of a class

73. What does the speaker say can be found on a Web site?
(A) Next month's schedule
(B) A speaker's profile
(C) A list of workshop fees
(D) Potential topic ideas

74. What kind of event is being discussed?
(A) A staff training workshop
(B) A recruitment fair
(C) A product launch
(D) An annual office party

75. According to the speaker, what can listeners do by e-mail?
(A) Request an information package
(B) Reserve a ticket for the event
(C) Sign up to be a volunteer
(D) Inquire about job opportunities

76. Why should listeners arrive early on Monday?
(A) To register for a company event
(B) To attend a product demonstration
(C) To meet with the personnel manager
(D) To help clean up the offices

77. What is the speaker mainly discussing?
(A) A food fair
(B) A catering company
(C) A grand opening
(D) A recipe book

78. What does the speaker mean when she says, "I've had better"?
(A) She was disappointed with a meal.
(B) She thinks a price was too high.
(C) She is pleased about some improvements.
(D) She plans to return to a business.

79. What will the speaker talk about next?
(A) Business locations
(B) Upcoming events
(C) Menu options
(D) Cooking tips

80. Who most likely is the message for?
(A) A government official
(B) A marketing executive
(C) A corporate accountant
(D) A potential client

81. Why is the speaker calling?
(A) To delay a scheduled delivery
(B) To update his contact information
(C) To alter an agreement
(D) To request a refund

82. What does the speaker say he will do tomorrow?
(A) Specify a deadline
(B) Submit his resignation
(C) Process an order
(D) Sign a contract

GO ON TO THE NEXT PAGE

83. Where is the talk taking place?
(A) In a factory
(B) In a restaurant
(C) In a supermarket
(D) In a hospital

84. Why does the speaker say, "It's his first day"?
(A) To suggest holding a celebration
(B) To excuse a coworker's mistake
(C) To ask the listeners for some feedback
(D) To remind the listeners to be helpful

85. According to the speaker, what will happen on Tuesday?
(A) Additional workers will be hired.
(B) A training workshop will be held.
(C) Performance reviews will be carried out.
(D) Employees will gather for a meal.

---

86. Who most likely is the speaker?
(A) A head chef
(B) A supermarket manager
(C) A farmer
(D) A food critic

87. What problem does the speaker mention?
(A) A shipment of supplies has arrived late.
(B) Customers are not getting their orders quickly.
(C) Operating hours have to be decreased.
(D) Public Health Standards have not been met.

88. What are the station leaders expected to do?
(A) Work an extra hour each evening
(B) Talk about a pay cut with the employer
(C) Teach workers a new safety procedure
(D) Notify workers of their new schedule

---

89. What has the speaker recently done?
(A) Remodeled a house
(B) Published a book
(C) Attended a concert
(D) Moved to a new city

90. What does the speaker want to discuss?
(A) Researching local building regulations
(B) Negotiating a lower price for real estate
(C) Applying for construction permits
(D) Improving the appearance of properties

91. What does the speaker encourage listeners to do?
(A) Join a mailing list
(B) Tour a facility
(C) Order a novel
(D) Visit a Web site

---

92. Why is the speaker calling?
(A) To recommend some tourist destinations
(B) To extend an invitation to an event
(C) To confirm arrangements for a trip
(D) To discuss accommodation options

93. What will the speaker do on Friday?
(A) Demonstrate a product
(B) Speak at a conference
(C) Join a city tour
(D) Travel to the airport

94. What does the speaker mean when she says, "our flight is at 12"?
(A) An itinerary has been changed.
(B) The listener's preferred flight was unavailable.
(C) There will be no time for sightseeing.
(D) A meeting might need to be canceled.

Cabin Name	Details
Maple Cabin	3 bedrooms/2 bathrooms
Sunrise Cabin	4 bedrooms/2 bathrooms
Creek Cabin	5 bedrooms/3 bathrooms
Rocky Cabin	6 bedrooms/3 bathrooms

95. Who most likely is the speaker?

(A) A tour guide
(B) A travel agent
(C) A park employee
(D) A climbing instructor

96. Look at the graphic. Which cabin has been reserved for the listener?

(A) Maple Cabin
(B) Sunrise Cabin
(C) Creek Cabin
(D) Rocky Cabin

97. What should the listener do on Saturday?

(A) Fill out a form
(B) Make a payment
(C) Rent equipment
(D) Present a form of ID

Grill Cleaning Process

Step 1	Remove food scraps from grill using scraper
Step 2	Turn off grill and allow to cool for at least 5 minutes
Step 3	Apply anti-grease solution and scrub grill surface
Step 4	Clean grill surface using cloths and soapy water

98. What is the purpose of the talk?

(A) To introduce new kitchen equipment
(B) To discuss customer complaints
(C) To welcome new employees
(D) To review safety guidelines

99. Look at the graphic. Which step does the speaker want to change?

(A) Step 1
(B) Step 2
(C) Step 3
(D) Step 4

100. What will probably happen next?

(A) Some equipment will be repaired.
(B) A restaurant will open for business.
(C) A demonstration will be given.
(D) Some floors will be mopped.

This is the end of the Listening Test. Turn to Part 5 in your test book.

정답 및 스크립트 p.327 / 점수 환산표 p.363

GO ON TO THE NEXT PAGE

실전모의고사

TEST 13

TEST 13 MP3

TEST 13 해설

시작 시간 ________시 ________분

종료 시간 ________시 ________분

▸ 중간에 멈추지 말고 처음부터 끝까지 풀어보세요. 문제를 풀 때는 실전처럼 답안지에 마킹하세요.

LISTENING TEST

In the Listening test, you will be asked to demonstrate how well you understand spoken English. The entire Listening test will last approximately 45 minutes. There are four parts, and directions are given for each part. You must mark your answers on the separate answer sheet.

Do not write your answers in your test book.

PART 1

Directions: For each question in this part, you will hear four statements about a picture in your test book. When you hear the statements, you must select the one statement that best describes what you see in the picture. Then find the number of the question on your answer sheet and mark your answer. The statements will not be printed in your test book and will be spoken only one time.

Statement (D), "They are taking photographs," is the best description of the picture, so you should select answer (D) and mark it on your answer sheet.

1.

2.

GO ON TO THE NEXT PAGE

3.

4.

5.

6.

GO ON TO THE NEXT PAGE

PART 2

Directions: You will hear a question or statement and three responses spoken in English. They will not be printed in your test book and will be spoken only one time. Select the best response to the question or statement and mark the letter (A), (B), or (C) on your answer sheet.

7. Mark your answer on your answer sheet.
8. Mark your answer on your answer sheet.
9. Mark your answer on your answer sheet.
10. Mark your answer on your answer sheet.
11. Mark your answer on your answer sheet.
12. Mark your answer on your answer sheet.
13. Mark your answer on your answer sheet.
14. Mark your answer on your answer sheet.
15. Mark your answer on your answer sheet.
16. Mark your answer on your answer sheet.
17. Mark your answer on your answer sheet.
18. Mark your answer on your answer sheet.
19. Mark your answer on your answer sheet.
20. Mark your answer on your answer sheet.
21. Mark your answer on your answer sheet.
22. Mark your answer on your answer sheet.
23. Mark your answer on your answer sheet.
24. Mark your answer on your answer sheet.
25. Mark your answer on your answer sheet.
26. Mark your answer on your answer sheet.
27. Mark your answer on your answer sheet.
28. Mark your answer on your answer sheet.
29. Mark your answer on your answer sheet.
30. Mark your answer on your answer sheet.
31. Mark your answer on your answer sheet.

PART 3

Directions: You will hear some conversations between two or more people. You will be asked to answer three questions about what the speakers say in each conversation. Select the best response to each question and mark the letter (A), (B), (C) or (D) on your answer sheet. The conversations will not be printed in your test book and will be spoken only one time.

32. Where are the speakers?
(A) In a flower shop
(B) At a restaurant
(C) At a factory
(D) At a travel agency

33. What will the man do now?
(A) Have lunch with the woman
(B) Return to his workplace
(C) Order some equipment
(D) Make a phone call

34. What will happen next month?
(A) A business will relocate.
(B) A training course will begin.
(C) A plant will start operating.
(D) An inspection will be carried out.

---

35. What is wrong with the woman's computer?
(A) A program was not properly installed.
(B) The monitor is cracked.
(C) The keyboard isn't functioning.
(D) A virus has deleted her work files.

36. What does the man suggest the woman do?
(A) Have her computer checked
(B) Call a service center
(C) Have a look at a user manual
(D) Order some extra parts

37. What does the woman want to know?
(A) How to update some software
(B) How to get to a service center
(C) How much some repairs will cost
(D) How to travel to Clarksdale

---

38. What have the speakers been doing?
(A) Placing advertisements
(B) Ordering party supplies
(C) Decorating a workplace
(D) Distributing invitations

39. What is the man surprised about?
(A) The attendance at an event
(B) The cost of some equipment
(C) The size of an event budget
(D) The selected date of an event

40. What has Isabel been asked to do next?
(A) Send a notification to staff
(B) Conduct an interview
(C) Book accommodations
(D) Arrange live entertainment

---

41. What is the woman concerned about?
(A) Her cell phone is faulty.
(B) Her monthly payment is late.
(C) Her phone bills are too high.
(D) Her phone contract was canceled.

42. What does the man suggest the woman do?
(A) Use fewer minutes each month
(B) Contact a customer representative
(C) Change mobile phone services
(D) Get a telephone membership card

43. What will the woman probably do next?
(A) Visit a phone shop
(B) Buy a new cell phone
(C) Go to the man's office
(D) Call a phone company

GO ON TO THE NEXT PAGE

44. Why is the woman going to Toronto next week?
(A) To visit her colleagues
(B) To go sightseeing
(C) To exhibit some work
(D) To meet the man

45. What did the man intend to do?
(A) Show the woman around town
(B) Pick the woman up from the airport
(C) Visit the woman's office in Chicago
(D) Recommend a hotel to the woman

46. What does the woman suggest to the man?
(A) Attending an exhibition together
(B) Collaborating on a project
(C) Meeting at a later date
(D) Extending the length of a trip

---

47. What are the speakers discussing?
(A) A store membership plan
(B) The opening of a new store
(C) The start day of a sale
(D) A new range of products

48. What does the woman say will happen on April 2?
(A) A store will close for a national holiday.
(B) New employees will begin work.
(C) An advertising campaign will start.
(D) Promotional flyers will be mailed out.

49. What will the speakers probably do next?
(A) Revise a newspaper ad
(B) Make a TV commercial
(C) Contact a customer
(D) Speak to a colleague

---

50. Where is this conversation most likely taking place?
(A) At a bookstore
(B) At a newsstand
(C) At a library
(D) At a grocery store

51. What does the woman want to do?
(A) Sign up for a membership
(B) Order an item
(C) Borrow a book
(D) Change her shipping address

52. What does the man suggest that the woman do?
(A) Pay some outstanding charges
(B) Try another store location
(C) Write down her date of birth
(D) Leave a partial payment

---

53. What have the speakers been working on?
(A) Building blueprints
(B) Web site designs
(C) Online advertisements
(D) Product packaging

54. What does the man mean when he says, "What's wrong with today"?
(A) He is disappointed with the woman's work.
(B) He wants to begin a task immediately.
(C) He is too busy to offer assistance today.
(D) He wants to know the reason for an error.

55. What will the woman probably do next?
(A) Contact a supervisor
(B) Make a phone call
(C) Print some documents
(D) E-mail some designs

---

56. Why does the woman want to go to the personnel office?

(A) To pick up a uniform
(B) To submit some documents
(C) To report a missing item
(D) To interview for a job

57. What does the man say about the employee handbook?

(A) He thinks it needs a floor plan.
(B) He distributed copies of it at a meeting.
(C) He has recently revised it.
(D) He has placed it on the third floor.

58. What will the man get for the woman?

(A) A parking permit
(B) A work schedule
(C) An access card
(D) An application form

---

59. What type of event does the man want to attend?

(A) A music concert
(B) A theatrical play
(C) A sports competition
(D) A comedy show

60. Why does the woman apologize?

(A) A device is not working.
(B) A box office is already closed.
(C) An event has been rescheduled.
(D) A ticket price has increased.

61. What does the woman imply when she says, "There's no need to rush"?

(A) A business is staying open late.
(B) The venue is not far away.
(C) There are plenty of tickets available.
(D) The man should consider a different event.

Customer's Name	Complaint
Gary Noonan	Service was too slow
Anjit Singh	Employee was rude
Jacob Lillard	Hours not as advertised
Michelle Bertolli	Products not available

62. Where do the speakers work?

(A) At a restaurant
(B) At a grocery store
(C) At a bank
(D) At a hotel

63. Look at the graphic. Which customer is being discussed?

(A) Gary Noonan
(B) Anjit Singh
(C) Jacob Lillard
(D) Michelle Bertolli

64. What does the man ask the woman to do?

(A) Train some employees
(B) Contact a customer
(C) Update a Web site
(D) Put up some signs

GO ON TO THE NEXT PAGE

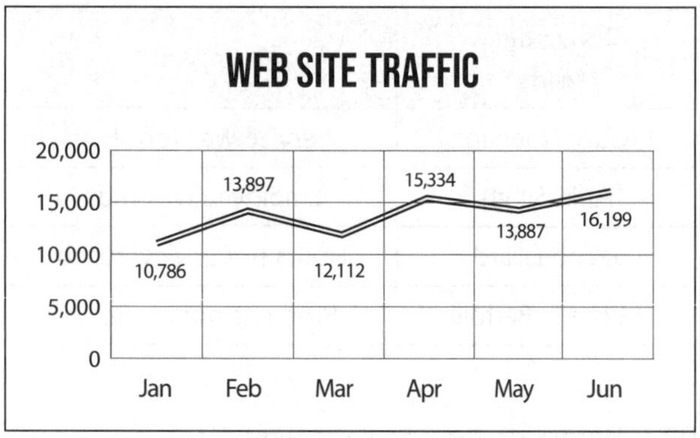

WEB SITE TRAFFIC

	Jan	Feb	Mar	Apr	May	Jun
Web site traffic	10,786	13,897	12,112	15,334	13,887	16,199

(Y-axis: 0, 5,000, 10,000, 15,000, 20,000)

65. Who most likely is the man?

(A) A Web designer
(B) A market researcher
(C) An HR manager
(D) A business owner

66. Look at the graphic. When did the company redesign its Web site?

(A) In March
(B) In April
(C) In May
(D) In June

67. According to the man, what does the company intend to do?

(A) Recruit skilled computer programmers
(B) Improve its consumer satisfaction rating
(C) Place advertisements online
(D) Launch a new range of merchandise

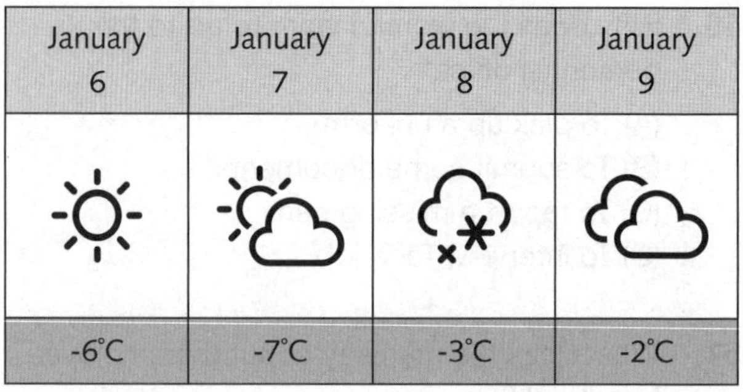

January 6	January 7	January 8	January 9
-6°C	-7°C	-3°C	-2°C

68. What type of event are the speakers preparing for?

(A) A sports competition
(B) A musical performance
(C) A street parade
(D) A fireworks display

69. Look at the graphic. On what date is the event scheduled to take place?

(A) January 6
(B) January 7
(C) January 8
(D) January 9

70. What does the woman suggest?

(A) Changing the event date
(B) Inviting a public official
(C) Recruiting some volunteers
(D) Arranging an alternative venue

PART 4

Directions: You will hear some talks given by a single speaker. You will be asked to answer three questions about what the speaker says in each talk. Select the best response to each question and mark the letter (A), (B), (C), or (D) on your answer sheet. The talks will not be printed in your test book and will be spoken only one time.

71. What is the problem with the customer's sweater?
(A) It is the wrong size.
(B) It is the wrong color.
(C) It is no longer on sale.
(D) It is no longer being manufactured.

72. Why are the boots arriving later than expected?
(A) They were sent to the wrong store.
(B) The company has a shortage of the item.
(C) They are being sent from a different location.
(D) They were ordered later than the other items.

73. What does the speaker request that the listener do?
(A) Place another order
(B) Send a payment
(C) Return an item
(D) Make a decision

74. What is the purpose of the talk?
(A) To announce a policy change
(B) To inform staff about sales figures
(C) To request financial contributions
(D) To introduce an award winner

75. What was mentioned about the overseas sales division?
(A) It was opened in March.
(B) It recently completed a project.
(C) It has struggled to make a profit.
(D) It includes the firm's top salespeople.

76. What contribution has Christine Espinoza made to the company?
(A) She trained new staff in several branches.
(B) She helped boost the company's earnings.
(C) She developed a successful marketing strategy.
(D) She launched a new product.

77. Where is the announcement being made?
(A) At a music festival
(B) In a community center
(C) At a sports stadium
(D) In a shopping mall

78. What problem does the speaker mention?
(A) A vehicle has been damaged.
(B) A parking lot is full.
(C) An entrance has been blocked.
(D) A worker has been injured.

79. Why does the speaker say, "there's no penalty"?
(A) To advise the listeners to make a purchase
(B) To encourage a listener to come forward
(C) To apologize for a delay to an event
(D) To promote a limited-time offer

80. What does the speaker mention about Smooth Java?
(A) It provides a quiet atmosphere.
(B) It offers live musical performances.
(C) It features an outdoor seating area.
(D) It is the largest coffee shop in Seattle.

81. According to the speaker, what food can customers order at Smooth Java?
(A) Chocolate
(B) Baked goods
(C) Ice cream
(D) Candy

82. What will Smooth Java do from next month?
(A) Begin offering discounts
(B) Introduce a new service
(C) Hire more workers
(D) Extend its beverage line

GO ON TO THE NEXT PAGE →

83. What is the purpose of the talk?
(A) To present some findings
(B) To train staff members
(C) To discuss the aims of a project
(D) To announce a new schedule

84. According to the speaker, what needs to be improved?
(A) Office communication
(B) Work environment
(C) Customer service
(D) Online advertising

85. What does the speaker suggest?
(A) Installing a new computer system
(B) Hiring additional employees
(C) Holding meetings more often
(D) Implementing some office rules

---

86. According to the speaker, why is now a good time to purchase a home?
(A) New construction is taking place everywhere.
(B) Interest rates are higher than ever before.
(C) Banks are offering larger loans.
(D) More people are selling their houses.

87. What are listeners recommended to do?
(A) Call to schedule a financial consultation
(B) Subscribe online for a publication
(C) Sell their house as soon as possible
(D) Look through a company's catalog

88. What can listeners do on Mountain Realty's Web site?
(A) Download an application form
(B) View properties for sale
(C) Chat with an estate agent
(D) Apply for a loan

---

89. Why does the speaker thank the listeners?
(A) They conducted several interviews.
(B) They attended a training session.
(C) They shared ideas about a product.
(D) They broke a sales record.

90. According to the speaker, what is scheduled for next week?
(A) A job fair
(B) An awards dinner
(C) A product launch
(D) An office relocation

91. What does the speaker imply when she says, "there's a lot of room"?
(A) The employees will be comfortable.
(B) New equipment will be installed.
(C) The company is overspending.
(D) A living space can be shared.

---

92. What is the talk mainly about?
(A) A construction project
(B) A restaurant opening
(C) A company merger
(D) A change in management

93. What does the speaker mention about Burt Avenue?
(A) There will be heavy traffic.
(B) It was featured in an internet video.
(C) It is closed for maintenance.
(D) Several new clothing stores are opening there.

94. What does the speaker imply when he says, "there are only three locations in the Midwest"?
(A) A franchise should open more branches.
(B) A company is still small.
(C) More employees need to be trained.
(D) A business will attract many customers.

Like: 91%
Dislike: 9%

Like: 95%
Dislike: 5%

Like: 89%
Dislike: 11%

Like: 98%
Dislike: 2%

95. Who are the listeners?

(A) New employees
(B) Potential investors
(C) Regular customers
(D) Focus group members

96. According to the speaker, what does the company intend to do next year?

(A) Launch new merchandise
(B) Restructure management
(C) Alter product packaging
(D) Open several stores

97. Look at the graphic. What type of ice cream does the speaker give to the listeners?

(A) Papaya
(B) Guava
(C) Lychee
(D) Mango

The Carlton Hotel

Special rates available from December 1 to December 31!

Stay for 2 nights ---
--- pay for only 1!

Stay for 5 nights ---
--- pay for only 3!

Stay for 7 nights ---
--- pay for only 4!

Stay for 10 nights ---
--- pay for only 6!

98. Why is the speaker calling?

(A) To inquire about a lost item
(B) To complain about a staff member
(C) To make another reservation
(D) To point out a billing error

99. Look at the graphic. For how many days did the speaker probably stay at the hotel?

(A) Two
(B) Five
(C) Seven
(D) Ten

100. What is the listener asked to do?

(A) Send a payment
(B) Return the call
(C) Change a check-in date
(D) Check a room

This is the end of the Listening Test. Turn to Part 5 in your test book.

정답 및 스크립트 p.336 / 점수 환산표 p.363

실전모의고사
TEST 14

시작 시간 ________ 시 ________ 분

종료 시간 ________ 시 ________ 분

▸ 중간에 멈추지 말고 처음부터 끝까지 풀어보세요. 문제를 풀 때는 실전처럼 답안지에 마킹하세요.

LISTENING TEST

In the Listening test, you will be asked to demonstrate how well you understand spoken English. The entire Listening test will last approximately 45 minutes. There are four parts, and directions are given for each part. You must mark your answers on the separate answer sheet.

Do not write your answers in your test book.

PART 1

Directions: For each question in this part, you will hear four statements about a picture in your test book. When you hear the statements, you must select the one statement that best describes what you see in the picture. Then find the number of the question on your answer sheet and mark your answer. The statements will not be printed in your test book and will be spoken only one time.

Statement (D), "They are taking photographs," is the best description of the picture, so you should select answer (D) and mark it on your answer sheet.

1.

2.

GO ON TO THE NEXT PAGE

3.

4.

5.

6.

TEST 14

GO ON TO THE NEXT PAGE

PART 2

Directions: You will hear a question or statement and three responses spoken in English. They will not be printed in your test book and will be spoken only one time. Select the best response to the question or statement and mark the letter (A), (B), or (C) on your answer sheet.

7. Mark your answer on your answer sheet.
8. Mark your answer on your answer sheet.
9. Mark your answer on your answer sheet.
10. Mark your answer on your answer sheet.
11. Mark your answer on your answer sheet.
12. Mark your answer on your answer sheet.
13. Mark your answer on your answer sheet.
14. Mark your answer on your answer sheet.
15. Mark your answer on your answer sheet.
16. Mark your answer on your answer sheet.
17. Mark your answer on your answer sheet.
18. Mark your answer on your answer sheet.
19. Mark your answer on your answer sheet.
20. Mark your answer on your answer sheet.
21. Mark your answer on your answer sheet.
22. Mark your answer on your answer sheet.
23. Mark your answer on your answer sheet.
24. Mark your answer on your answer sheet.
25. Mark your answer on your answer sheet.
26. Mark your answer on your answer sheet.
27. Mark your answer on your answer sheet.
28. Mark your answer on your answer sheet.
29. Mark your answer on your answer sheet.
30. Mark your answer on your answer sheet.
31. Mark your answer on your answer sheet.

PART 3

Directions: You will hear some conversations between two or more people. You will be asked to answer three questions about what the speakers say in each conversation. Select the best response to each question and mark the letter (A), (B), (C) or (D) on your answer sheet. The conversations will not be printed in your test book and will be spoken only one time.

32. Why is the man calling?
(A) To inquire about making a delivery
(B) To request dry cleaning
(C) To report a problem with a room
(D) To order room service

33. What does the woman say about the express service?
(A) It is only available after 12 P.M.
(B) It is more expensive.
(C) It is not being offered today.
(D) It takes up to 48 hours.

34. What does the woman offer to do?
(A) Send over a technician
(B) Transfer the man's call
(C) Give the man a room upgrade
(D) Have an item picked up

---

35. What type of business do the speakers most likely work for?
(A) An interior design firm
(B) A courier service
(C) A catering company
(D) A vacation resort

36. What does Emma say she will do?
(A) Send an invoice
(B) Prepare an event space
(C) Deliver some items
(D) Pick up a client

37. What does the man recommend?
(A) Visiting a different business
(B) Taking an alternative route
(C) Using public transportation
(D) Rescheduling an appointment

---

38. What are the speakers discussing?
(A) Proposed topics for a conference
(B) The launch of a publication
(C) The difficulty of speaking in public
(D) Attendance figures from a recent event

39. Who most likely is David Reese?
(A) A conference attendee
(B) An author
(C) The woman's colleague
(D) A film maker

40. What will the man do tomorrow?
(A) Visit a factory
(B) Give a speech
(C) Read a book
(D) Work in his office

---

41. What problem is mentioned?
(A) A product is sold out.
(B) A delivery has been delayed.
(C) Sales have decreased.
(D) Some merchandise is overpriced.

42. What does the woman recommend?
(A) Ordering a different brand
(B) Placing a larger order
(C) Offering a discount
(D) Rearranging the display

43. What is the man's concern?
(A) He received complaints from customers.
(B) Customers might go to competing stores.
(C) The purchasing manager is absent.
(D) Betafix is no longer being produced.

TEST 14

GO ON TO THE NEXT PAGE →

44. Where most likely do the speakers work?
(A) In a factory
(B) In an electronics store
(C) In a clothing shop
(D) In a supermarket

45. What does the woman ask Harry to do?
(A) Set up a sign
(B) Clean a room
(C) Speak to a customer
(D) Fill out a report

46. What reminder does the woman give to the men?
(A) That a delivery will arrive soon
(B) That a training session has been postponed
(C) That a business is closing early
(D) That she needs them to work this weekend

---

47. What is the woman worried about?
(A) Scheduling a department meeting
(B) Negotiating contract details
(C) Approving a schedule change
(D) Meeting a project deadline

48. What has the woman's department done recently?
(A) Hired more accountants
(B) Completed a joint project
(C) Secured several new contracts
(D) Relocated to a new office

49. What does the man offer to do?
(A) Train some newly hired employees
(B) Send the woman an expense report
(C) Assign employees to the woman's department
(D) Organize a special event

---

50. Who most likely are the speakers?
(A) Financial advisors
(B) Construction workers
(C) Real estate agents
(D) Cinema employees

51. What does the man mean when he says, "that's only the beginning"?
(A) An initial payment is required.
(B) Construction is behind schedule.
(C) Additional projects are planned.
(D) Several houses are up for sale.

52. What will the man probably do next?
(A) Update a Web site
(B) Tour a building
(C) Review some documents
(D) Contact a landlord

---

53. Who most likely are the speakers?
(A) Restaurant servers
(B) Store clerks
(C) Hotel receptionists
(D) Event coordinators

54. What problem is mentioned by the speakers?
(A) There are not enough flowers.
(B) An order was not placed in time.
(C) The room is not large enough.
(D) Attendance is higher than expected.

55. What is Bob currently doing?
(A) Purchasing flowers
(B) Picking up some plates
(C) Borrowing a few chairs
(D) Collecting some food

---

56. What kind of company do the speakers work for?

(A) An accounting firm
(B) A computer manufacturer
(C) An electronics store
(D) A software developer

57. What is mentioned about the EZBooks software?

(A) It is more advanced than AccountTec.
(B) Its price has recently been reduced.
(C) It is the best-selling product of its kind.
(D) It can be used in combination with AccountTec.

58. What will the woman most likely do next?

(A) Start work on a new product
(B) Go over some figures
(C) Contact her friend
(D) Obtain customer feedback

---

59. What do the speakers want to do?

(A) See a live performance
(B) Enter a contest
(C) Attend a conference
(D) Watch a movie

60. What does the woman mean when she says, "Go right ahead"?

(A) The man should keep walking straight.
(B) The man is welcome to pay.
(C) The man may borrow her phone.
(D) The man has taken a wrong turn.

61. What problem does the man mention?

(A) A business is closed.
(B) A Web site is offline.
(C) Some tickets are unavailable.
(D) Credit cards are not accepted.

Biotechnology	Laboratory 1A
Plant Biology	Laboratory 1B
Microbiology	Laboratory 2A
Biochemistry	Laboratory 2B

62. What does the woman ask for help with?

(A) Using a door entry system
(B) Accessing her e-mail account
(C) Changing a company database
(D) Obtaining a parking permit

63. Why does the man suggest the woman visit his department?

(A) To have her fingerprint scanned
(B) To enter her details into a system
(C) To have her keycard replaced
(D) To create a new computer account

64. Look at the graphic. Which laboratory does the woman work in?

(A) Laboratory 1A
(B) Laboratory 1B
(C) Laboratory 2A
(D) Laboratory 2B

GO ON TO THE NEXT PAGE

SATURDAY	SUNDAY	MONDAY	TUESDAY
Stormy	Partly Cloudy	Sunny	Light Rain

65. Look at the graphic. When will the man arrive on Nessus Island?

(A) On Saturday
(B) On Sunday
(C) On Monday
(D) On Tuesday

66. What activity is the man looking forward to?

(A) Scuba diving
(B) Swimming
(C) Fishing
(D) Sunbathing

67. How long will the man be on vacation?

(A) Three days
(B) One week
(C) Two weeks
(D) Three weeks

	Morning	Afternoon	Evening
Tour A	Sloane Castle	Pickton Market	Waterfront Walk
Tour B	Waterfront Walk	Sloane Castle	Pickton Market
Tour C	Sloane Castle	Waterfront Walk	Pickton Market
Tour D	Pickton Market	Sloane Castle	Waterfront Walk

68. Why is the man calling?

(A) To get details about a tour
(B) To extend an invitation
(C) To make a payment
(D) To cancel a booking

69. Look at the graphic. Which tour did the man sign up for?

(A) Tour A
(B) Tour B
(C) Tour C
(D) Tour D

70. What information does the woman ask for?

(A) A booking reference
(B) A telephone number
(C) A credit card number
(D) A street address

PART 4

Directions: You will hear some talks given by a single speaker. You will be asked to answer three questions about what the speaker says in each talk. Select the best response to each question and mark the letter (A), (B), (C), or (D) on your answer sheet. The talks will not be printed in your test book and will be spoken only one time.

71. What item's listing has an incorrect photograph?

(A) The printer
(B) The portable heater
(C) The ceiling fan
(D) The air conditioner

72. What does the speaker say about the A-70 model?

(A) It was launched a year ago.
(B) It has been discounted.
(C) It appears on a Web site.
(D) It is no longer being sold.

73. According to the message, what is the speaker going to do now?

(A) Send out some brochures
(B) Contact a printing company
(C) Wait for Josh to return a call
(D) Update the company's Web site

---

74. Where is the talk taking place?

(A) At a staff orientation
(B) At a recruitment fair
(C) At an awards banquet
(D) At a product launch

75. What does the speaker mean when she says, "You won't believe it"?

(A) She believes the listeners will doubt some data.
(B) She thinks the listeners will be impressed.
(C) She would prefer to revise some details.
(D) She is proud of the company's revenue.

76. What will the listeners receive?

(A) Complimentary gifts
(B) Product catalogs
(C) Discount vouchers
(D) Event invitations

---

77. Where is the talk taking place?

(A) In a supermarket
(B) In a production plant
(C) At a farmer's market
(D) At a trade show

78. What will take place next?

(A) A talk about cheese
(B) A cooking class
(C) A sampling session
(D) A tour of a facility

79. What are listeners encouraged to do before they leave?

(A) Feed some animals
(B) Visit a gift shop
(C) Sign up for a newsletter
(D) Speak to some employees

---

80. What will the company give the listeners?

(A) A flexible work schedule
(B) A personal office
(C) Free consultations
(D) Business cards

81. Who most likely are the listeners?

(A) A market survey group
(B) Customer service representatives
(C) Members of the Advertising Department
(D) Management trainees

82. According to the speaker, why should listeners go to Ms. Bucher's office?

(A) To receive professional advice
(B) To pick up a request form
(C) To deal with complaints
(D) To view a commercial

GO ON TO THE NEXT PAGE →

TEST 14

83. Who most likely is Batima Attam?
(A) A singer
(B) A concert promoter
(C) A dancer
(D) A guitar player

84. What does the speaker say about the brothers?
(A) They played their first concert last year.
(B) They will not appear at this year's concert.
(C) They will perform live on the radio show.
(D) They released an album last month.

85. What will listeners most likely hear next?
(A) An advertisement for an event
(B) A song from a new album
(C) An interview with a director
(D) A review of a new television show

---

86. Who most likely are the listeners?
(A) Hotel guests
(B) Tour guides
(C) Maintenance workers
(D) News anchors

87. What is the purpose of the talk?
(A) To announce an expansion
(B) To demonstrate a new product
(C) To organize a floor plan
(D) To outline a workshop itinerary

88. What does the speaker imply when he says, "there are snacks available in the lobby"?
(A) The listeners should get food from the lobby.
(B) The listeners are mistaken about a location.
(C) The listeners will meet in the lobby.
(D) The listeners should use their coupons.

---

89. Who most likely is the speaker?
(A) A corporate recruiter
(B) A customer service manager
(C) A workshop instructor
(D) A software developer

90. What are the listeners asked to do?
(A) Provide some feedback
(B) Take a performance-based test
(C) Participate in a discussion
(D) Test some new products

91. What will the speaker most likely do next?
(A) Attend a training seminar
(B) Discuss business strategies
(C) Take questions from listeners
(D) Distribute some information

---

92. Who are the listeners?
(A) Safety inspectors
(B) Potential investors
(C) New recruits
(D) Repair technicians

93. What does the speaker mean when he says, "You have several options"?
(A) The listeners can participate in various activities.
(B) The listeners may choose where to eat.
(C) The listeners can take public transportation.
(D) The listeners may use any payment method.

94. What will the listeners do this afternoon?
(A) Meet department supervisors
(B) Watch a procedure demonstration
(C) Learn how to use equipment
(D) Attend a training seminar

Deer Horn National Park Trails	Length (Kilometers)	Difficulty (1=Easy, 5=Hard)
Swallow Tail Ridge	3.5	3
Green Moss Valley	4.2	2
Lonely Spire Peak	10.5	5
Old Merchant Trail	8.1	4

95. What is the main purpose of the talk?
(A) To describe new amenities
(B) To recommend a trail
(C) To outline park rules
(D) To welcome new staff

96. What does the woman warn the listeners about?
(A) Wild animals
(B) Poor weather
(C) Steep cliffs
(D) Slippery surfaces

97. Look at the graphic. Which trail will the listeners see today?
(A) Swallow Tail Ridge
(B) Green Moss Valley
(C) Lonely Spire Peak
(D) Old Merchant Trail

98. What is the speaker mainly discussing?
(A) A fundraising project
(B) A health and safety inspection
(C) A company relocation
(D) An employee complaint

99. Look at the graphic. Which bin did the speaker empty earlier?
(A) Food
(B) Paper
(C) Metal
(D) Plastic

100. What will the speaker do next?
(A) Give a demonstration
(B) Post a schedule
(C) Schedule appointments
(D) Check some equipment

This is the end of the Listening Test. Turn to Part 5 in your test book.

정답 및 스크립트 p.345 / 점수 환산표 p.363

GO ON TO THE NEXT PAGE

실전모의고사

TEST 15

시작 시간 ________시 ________분

종료 시간 ________시 ________분

▸ 중간에 멈추지 말고 처음부터 끝까지 풀어보세요. 문제를 풀 때는 실전처럼 답안지에 마킹하세요.

LISTENING TEST

In the Listening test, you will be asked to demonstrate how well you understand spoken English. The entire Listening test will last approximately 45 minutes. There are four parts, and directions are given for each part. You must mark your answers on the separate answer sheet.

Do not write your answers in your test book.

PART 1

Directions: For each question in this part, you will hear four statements about a picture in your test book. When you hear the statements, you must select the one statement that best describes what you see in the picture. Then find the number of the question on your answer sheet and mark your answer. The statements will not be printed in your test book and will be spoken only one time.

Statement (D), "They are taking photographs," is the best description of the picture, so you should select answer (D) and mark it on your answer sheet.

1.

2.

TEST 15

GO ON TO THE NEXT PAGE

3.

4.

5.

6.

TEST 15

GO ON TO THE NEXT PAGE

PART 2

Directions: You will hear a question or statement and three responses spoken in English. They will not be printed in your test book and will be spoken only one time. Select the best response to the question or statement and mark the letter (A), (B), or (C) on your answer sheet.

7. Mark your answer on your answer sheet.
8. Mark your answer on your answer sheet.
9. Mark your answer on your answer sheet.
10. Mark your answer on your answer sheet.
11. Mark your answer on your answer sheet.
12. Mark your answer on your answer sheet.
13. Mark your answer on your answer sheet.
14. Mark your answer on your answer sheet.
15. Mark your answer on your answer sheet.
16. Mark your answer on your answer sheet.
17. Mark your answer on your answer sheet.
18. Mark your answer on your answer sheet.
19. Mark your answer on your answer sheet.
20. Mark your answer on your answer sheet.
21. Mark your answer on your answer sheet.
22. Mark your answer on your answer sheet.
23. Mark your answer on your answer sheet.
24. Mark your answer on your answer sheet.
25. Mark your answer on your answer sheet.
26. Mark your answer on your answer sheet.
27. Mark your answer on your answer sheet.
28. Mark your answer on your answer sheet.
29. Mark your answer on your answer sheet.
30. Mark your answer on your answer sheet.
31. Mark your answer on your answer sheet.

PART 3

Directions: You will hear some conversations between two or more people. You will be asked to answer three questions about what the speakers say in each conversation. Select the best response to each question and mark the letter (A), (B), (C) or (D) on your answer sheet. The conversations will not be printed in your test book and will be spoken only one time.

32. Where does the man work?
(A) At a university
(B) At a travel agency
(C) At a local newspaper company
(D) At a publishing company

33. What does the man say about his current position?
(A) The commute is long.
(B) He is happy with his work.
(C) There is a lot of vacation time.
(D) His coworkers are friendly.

34. What does the man offer to do for the woman?
(A) Give her a discount
(B) Recommend some books
(C) Contact his employer
(D) Buy her a best seller

35. What is the main topic of the conversation?
(A) A store sale
(B) A product demonstration
(C) A live performance
(D) A book signing

36. What problem does the man mention?
(A) There are limited tickets available.
(B) A business is located far away.
(C) A work schedule is not ready.
(D) An order did not arrive on time.

37. What will the women probably do next?
(A) Check an inventory
(B) Speak to a supervisor
(C) Visit a different business
(D) Revise a document

38. What are the speakers planning to talk about tomorrow?
(A) Museum exhibits
(B) A job opening
(C) Travel plans
(D) Menu options

39. Why did the woman contact the restaurant?
(A) To have food delivered
(B) To ask about the hours of operation
(C) To request a specialty dish
(D) To book a table for lunch

40. What does the man suggest?
(A) Changing an appointment time
(B) Inviting someone else to a meeting
(C) Closing a business early for the day
(D) Raising the price of a product

41. What type of event is being planned?
(A) A sports contest
(B) An awards ceremony
(C) A company retreat
(D) An orientation session

42. What does the man ask about?
(A) Accommodations
(B) Transportation
(C) Activities
(D) Costs

43. What does the venue offer for free?
(A) Parking
(B) Meals
(C) Electronic equipment
(D) Internet service

GO ON TO THE NEXT PAGE

44. Why is the man at the shop?
(A) To write an art review
(B) To return a purchase
(C) To interview for a position
(D) To see some items in person

45. What does the woman's shop sell?
(A) Paintings
(B) Films
(C) Furniture
(D) Books

46. Why does the woman mention the recycled materials?
(A) To suggest a place to reuse a product
(B) To provide information about her artistic training
(C) To recommend a special community project
(D) To explain why her products are well reviewed

---

47. What is the woman planning to purchase?
(A) An artwork
(B) An electronic appliance
(C) A new apartment
(D) A piece of furniture

48. What does the man imply when he says, "You'll be lucky"?
(A) He agrees with the woman's choice.
(B) He thinks a product is sold out.
(C) He expects a price to be higher.
(D) He can help the woman with a purchase.

49. What does the man recommend the woman do?
(A) Check an online store
(B) Use a discount coupon
(C) Purchase a product warranty
(D) Consider a different brand

---

50. What is the problem?
(A) A food delivery has not arrived yet.
(B) A credit card is no longer valid.
(C) A menu item is not available.
(D) A loan application was denied.

51. Why is the man concerned?
(A) He needs to place a large order.
(B) A recipe's ingredient is out of stock.
(C) An event venue is already booked.
(D) He sent a payment late.

52. What does the man say he will do?
(A) Request emergency funds
(B) Use a coupon
(C) Postpone a staff party
(D) Contact a restaurant manager

---

53. Why is the woman calling?
(A) To issue a complaint
(B) To apply for a job
(C) To schedule a training session
(D) To give an annual survey

54. What is the man's problem?
(A) One of his departments is understaffed.
(B) Some of his employees are not qualified.
(C) He failed an important examination.
(D) He has recently lost his job.

55. What does the woman say she did?
(A) Submitted some documents
(B) Requested a job promotion
(C) Tested some applicants
(D) Updated an online database

---

56. Where do the speakers work?
(A) At a department store
(B) In a manufacturing plant
(C) At a restaurant
(D) In a sports center

57. What does the man imply when he says, "Pedro has been here since 6 A.M."?
(A) Pedro may be able to answer a question.
(B) Pedro has made a mistake.
(C) Pedro should be allowed to leave.
(D) Pedro substituted for a coworker.

58. What does the woman ask the man to do?
(A) Lock a door
(B) Clean a workstation
(C) Make a delivery
(D) Speak to clientele

---

59. Where most likely does the woman work?
(A) At a department store
(B) At a grocery store
(C) At a catering service
(D) At an amusement park

60. What will happen at 7 o'clock on August 12?
(A) Wine will stop being served at a party.
(B) A live musical performance will begin.
(C) The man will give a public speech.
(D) Family members will join a corporate party.

61. According to the woman, what are the wristbands for?
(A) To gain entry into a company function
(B) To verify that someone can drink wine
(C) To indicate who is a client of the company
(D) To signify that someone wants a vegetarian meal

Meeting Room	
Time	**Reserved By**
9:00 A.M. – 10:30 A.M.	Jeremy Douglas
10:40 A.M. – 12:15 P.M.	Maria Lundgren
1:45 P.M. – 3:00 P.M.	Allan Ripley
3:10 P.M. – 4:30 P.M.	Dawn Olsen

62. Look at the graphic. When does the woman want to use the meeting room?
(A) At 9:00 A.M.
(B) At 10:40 A.M.
(C) At 1:45 P.M.
(D) At 3:10 P.M.

63. What does the man suggest?
(A) Rescheduling a meeting
(B) Practicing a presentation
(C) Contacting some clients
(D) Using a different room

64. What will the woman probably do next?
(A) Set up some equipment
(B) Make a phone call
(C) Enter a door code
(D) Review some paperwork

GO ON TO THE NEXT PAGE

Mr. Kenneth Hunter – While You Were Out...	
Greta Wickens	Would like you to send a receipt
Pauline Smith	Would like you to arrange a meeting
Fiona Stewart	Would like you to lead a training workshop
Wendy Cosgrove	Would like you to contact a client

65. Look at the graphic. What is the name of the woman the man is calling?
(A) Greta Wickens
(B) Pauline Smith
(C) Fiona Stewart
(D) Wendy Cosgrove

66. What is the woman currently working on?
(A) A recruitment plan
(B) An advertising campaign
(C) A work shift schedule
(D) A building design

67. What does the man suggest the woman do?
(A) Send an e-mail
(B) Visit his office
(C) Contact another colleague
(D) Attend a presentation

Boarding Group	Rows
A	43-49
B	36-42
C	30-35
D	20-29

68. What are the speakers mainly discussing?
(A) Upgrading tickets
(B) Meeting colleagues
(C) Purchasing gifts
(D) Having some food

69. Why is the man concerned?
(A) A price is too high.
(B) A ticket has incorrect information.
(C) A store is closing.
(D) A flight is departing soon.

70. Look at the graphic. What boarding group do the speakers belong to?
(A) Group A
(B) Group B
(C) Group C
(D) Group D

PART 4

Directions: You will hear some talks given by a single speaker. You will be asked to answer three questions about what the speaker says in each talk. Select the best response to each question and mark the letter (A), (B), (C), or (D) on your answer sheet. The talks will not be printed in your test book and will be spoken only one time.

71. Who is Molly Singer?
(A) An architect
(B) A magazine editor
(C) A real estate agent
(D) An interior designer

72. What does the speaker say about the television show, House Guru?
(A) It focuses on improving homes.
(B) It offers advice on buying property.
(C) It will begin airing next month.
(D) It has declined in popularity.

73. What will Molly Singer discuss today?
(A) Recycling household items
(B) Saving energy in the home
(C) Tips for making one's home secure
(D) Creative ways to decorate rooms

---

74. What problem does the speaker mention?
(A) His company has sold out of an item.
(B) The air conditioner in his office has broken.
(C) Delivery service is not currently available.
(D) He is going on vacation next week.

75. According to the speaker, what will happen on Monday?
(A) Free delivery service will become unavailable.
(B) A new employee will begin working.
(C) His company will unveil a new product.
(D) Repairs to a vehicle will be finished.

76. What does the speaker say he will do today?
(A) Transfer money to the listener
(B) Give a message to his sales staff
(C) Order a machine part
(D) Drive to the listener's home

---

77. What is the speaker mainly discussing?
(A) A busy work period
(B) A change to a policy
(C) A hiring strategy
(D) An error in a report

78. What does the speaker mention about the company?
(A) Its profits have been declining.
(B) It is opening a second location.
(C) It has reduced an advertising budget.
(D) It has remodeled its headquarters.

79. What does the speaker mean when he says, "it's too late"?
(A) A store will be closing soon.
(B) A colleague has left for the day.
(C) A decision cannot be reversed.
(D) A meeting must be rescheduled.

---

80. Who most likely are the listeners?
(A) Technical support advisors
(B) Online marketing experts
(C) Computer store owners
(D) Self-employed programmers

81. According to the speaker, what are many people doing?
(A) Launching new Web sites
(B) Creating their own software applications
(C) Using computers inefficiently
(D) Applying for technology-related jobs

82. What does the speaker say is available at a reasonable price?
(A) Memory upgrades
(B) Regular maintenance work
(C) New office software
(D) Computer skills workshops

GO ON TO THE NEXT PAGE

83. Why does the speaker say, "Three weeks is a long time to wait for an appointment"?
(A) To file a complaint
(B) To blame some employees
(C) To express understanding
(D) To arrange an itinerary

84. What does the speaker say will happen next month?
(A) A product will be available.
(B) An advertisement will appear.
(C) A meal will be provided.
(D) A lease will begin.

85. What does the speaker ask for help with?
(A) Evaluating job candidates
(B) Rearranging a workspace
(C) Contacting a client
(D) Installing new equipment

---

86. Where does the speaker most likely work?
(A) A furniture store
(B) A textile factory
(C) An office supply retailer
(D) A carpet outlet

87. What problem does the speaker report?
(A) A supplier has gone out of business.
(B) A deadline cannot be met.
(C) A product has been recalled.
(D) A delivery has been delayed.

88. What does the speaker offer to do?
(A) Visit the listener
(B) Sign a contract
(C) Provide a refund
(D) Pay a fee

---

89. What is the main purpose of the talk?
(A) To announce conference topics
(B) To explain a security procedure
(C) To introduce a contest winner
(D) To summarize a tour agenda

90. Where does the speaker work?
(A) At a science museum
(B) At a restaurant
(C) At a food factory
(D) At a farmer's market

91. What does the speaker say the spokesperson will do?
(A) Demonstrate a product
(B) Discuss a video
(C) Hand out souvenirs
(D) Prepare a meal

---

92. What type of product is the speaker promoting?
(A) A cell phone
(B) An exercise machine
(C) A kitchen appliance
(D) A vacuum cleaner

93. What does the speaker mean when she says, "you'll barely know it's there"?
(A) The product is a convenient size.
(B) The product has a plain appearance.
(C) The product is easy to carry around.
(D) The product makes little noise.

94. What will the speaker do next?
(A) Give a demonstration
(B) Distribute samples
(C) Answer questions
(D) Introduce another product

< Alton Community Center – Swimming Pool >

Lane 1	Beginners
Lane 2	Intermediate
Lane 3	Advanced
Lane 4	Water Aerobics

95. What is the main purpose of the talk?
(A) To describe some activities
(B) To announce a schedule change
(C) To introduce an instructor
(D) To attract new class members

96. Look at the graphic. Which lane will the listeners use?
(A) Lane 1
(B) Lane 2
(C) Lane 3
(D) Lane 4

97. What will the speaker do next month?
(A) Replace some equipment
(B) Launch a new class
(C) Move overseas
(D) Open a business

Hanley's Department Store

4F	Electronics
3F	Furniture
2F	Fashion
1F	Cosmetics

98. What is being announced?
(A) A seasonal sale
(B) A promotion opportunity
(C) A grand opening event
(D) An incentive program

99. Look at the graphic. Where most likely do the listeners work?
(A) On the 1st floor
(B) On the 2nd floor
(C) On the 3rd floor
(D) On the 4th floor

100. What are the listeners required to do at the end of each work shift?
(A) Tidy a work area
(B) Attend a meeting
(C) Submit data
(D) Log out of a system

This is the end of the Listening Test. Turn to Part 5 in your test book.

정답 및 스크립트 p.354 / 점수 환산표 p.363

GO ON TO THE NEXT PAGE

정답

스크립트

TEST 1

정답

PART 1

1. (D) **2**. (A) **3**. (A) **4**. (B) **5**. (D) **6**. (C)

PART 2

7. (B) **8**. (A) **9**. (C) **10**. (A) **11**. (C) **12**. (C) **13**. (A) **14**. (C) **15**. (A) **16**. (A) **17**. (B) **18**. (A) **19**. (A)
20. (C) **21**. (C) **22**. (A) **23**. (C) **24**. (B) **25**. (A) **26**. (A) **27**. (C) **28**. (A) **29**. (B) **30**. (A) **31**. (B)

PART 3

32. (B) **33**. (D) **34**. (C) **35**. (D) **36**. (B) **37**. (C) **38**. (A) **39**. (B) **40**. (B) **41**. (C) **42**. (B) **43**. (A) **44**. (D)
45. (B) **46**. (C) **47**. (A) **48**. (A) **49**. (D) **50**. (B) **51**. (B) **52**. (D) **53**. (D) **54**. (C) **55**. (B) **56**. (B) **57**. (B)
58. (D) **59**. (B) **60**. (B) **61**. (B) **62**. (B) **63**. (D) **64**. (D) **65**. (A) **66**. (C) **67**. (D) **68**. (B) **69**. (D) **70**. (B)

PART 4

71. (B) **72**. (B) **73**. (D) **74**. (C) **75**. (B) **76**. (C) **77**. (D) **78**. (B) **79**. (C) **80**. (D) **81**. (B) **82**. (C) **83**. (D)
84. (C) **85**. (B) **86**. (D) **87**. (B) **88**. (B) **89**. (B) **90**. (B) **91**. (D) **92**. (B) **93**. (C) **94**. (D) **95**. (C) **96**. (A)
97. (C) **98**. (A) **99**. (B) **100**. (C)

PART 1

1. (A) He's leaving the office.
(B) He's rearranging the table.
(C) He's facing a window.
(D) He's writing some notes.

2. (A) The woman is trying on shoes.
(B) The woman is putting items on a shelf.
(C) The woman is hanging clothes on racks.
(D) The woman is paying for her purchase.

3. (A) A streetlamp is being repaired.
(B) A ladder is lying on the ground.
(C) Some trees are being trimmed.
(D) Some scaffolding has been erected against a building.

4. (A) The women are entering a park.
(B) One of the women is posing for a photograph.
(C) One of the women is posting a sign.
(D) The women are standing next to a fence.

5. (A) An instructor is writing on a whiteboard.
(B) Some desks are being arranged in a classroom.
(C) Some people are sitting on the floor.
(D) An audience is listening to a lecturer.

6. (A) A briefcase has been left on a chair.
(B) Some papers are scattered on the ground.
(C) A laptop computer is on a table.
(D) A lamp is being turned on.

PART 2

7. When did you last go to yoga class?
(A) The other gym.
(B) Earlier this month.
(C) No, she was first.

8. Where will your soccer team be playing?
(A) At the sports field on Miller Road.
(B) A new player from London.
(C) Every Saturday afternoon.

9. How long will the meeting be?
(A) To discuss the budget.
(B) Tuesday, at 9.
(C) Just half an hour.

10. Would you like to go to the coffee shop with me?
(A) Yes, I could do with a break.
(B) Coffee with sugar, please.
(C) They have the biggest menu.

11. Why did you order the desks from another store?
(A) On Friday morning.
(B) Off of their Web site.
(C) The selection was better.

12. Who's the workshop instructor for the morning session?
(A) In the conference room on the third floor.
(B) It's mandatory for all staff.
(C) It's Mr. Horton from Marketing.

13. How do I get to the nearest post office?
(A) There are branch listings online.
(B) Just to buy some stamps.
(C) No, it didn't take long.

14. The light in the store room isn't very bright.
(A) It's a nice day to walk outside.
(B) No, they're stored in a different room.
(C) Yes, it's hard to see.

15. Do you want to travel together to the convention?
(A) I'm not sure I'm able to attend.
(B) It was a good decision to take a train.
(C) I'd be happy to lend a hand.

16. Isn't it supposed to snow tomorrow?
(A) Yes, I believe so.
(B) We'll know by next week.
(C) In the weather forecast.

17. Why was I charged an additional fee for the laptop repair?
(A) I'm planning to get it fixed tomorrow.
(B) Let me check with the technician.
(C) Thanks, I appreciate it.

18. Didn't Rebecca attend night classes at Trent University?
(A) Yes, I think she did.
(B) A degree in graphic design.
(C) I prefer to work in the evenings.

19. Where will the tennis open be held next year?
(A) It's in Boston again.
(B) She won last time.
(C) Toward the end of spring.

20. Could you give me some advice on my speech?
(A) His talk was very well received.
(B) I'm afraid we've already run out.
(C) Sure, but can you wait until 4?

21. Your food order will be ready for pickup at 7 P.M.
(A) Just pick anything for me.
(B) There aren't any tables available.
(C) Thanks, I'll return then.

22. Do we have any more brown envelopes?
(A) They're usually at the reception desk.
(B) You can leave them in my office.
(C) Just some promotional leaflets.

23. Did you check the presentation slides?
(A) It'll be presented after the meeting.
(B) They don't accept checks.
(C) Yes, they're all ready.

24. Wasn't it Barry's turn to clean the staff break room?
(A) That's a great idea.
(B) He swapped with Peter.
(C) I'll turn it off for you.

25. Where's the best place to get Chinese food?
(A) Mr. Lee just went out for some last night.
(B) You should book a table in advance.
(C) I wasn't impressed with their menu.

26. Would you prefer a seat near the screen or one further back?
(A) I'd rather not be too close.
(B) Sure, I'm looking forward to the movie.
(C) The films are screened twice a day.

27. Our car rental period can be extended, right?
(A) There are several near the airport.
(B) These vehicles are second-hand.
(C) Did you check the agreement?

28. What did you think of the celebration on Saturday?
(A) The fireworks were spectacular.
(B) Yes, but I'll arrive a little late.
(C) For the town's 250th birthday.

29. When will the software be installed?
(A) No, I haven't used it yet.
(B) The IT technician just arrived.
(C) It deletes all harmful files.

30. Could you look at this complaint from one of our customers?
(A) Oh, I've had a few similar ones.
(B) It's been a highly positive response.
(C) Usually about our delivery times.

31. The delivery's scheduled for Monday, right?
(A) I have some free time today.
(B) You'd better check with Jim.
(C) At the warehouse entrance.

PART 3

Questions 32-34 refer to the following conversation.

M: Hi, this is Peter Evans. This morning, I used your Web site to book tickets for a show at your concert hall in October.
W: Just a moment... Yes, I have your reservation. Is there anything else you need?
M: Well, I just read the confirmation that came in my e-mail, and the number of tickets was incorrect. I purchased three tickets, but the confirmation is only for two.
W: Oh, that's odd. Well, I can fix that for you right away. And since it must have been a problem with our site, I'll give you a 10% discount on your third ticket.

32. What kind of business is the man calling?
33. What problem does the man mention?
34. What does the woman offer the man as an apology?

Questions 35-37 refer to the following conversation.

M: Hi, Bella. I heard that you and your work crew have been busy cleaning all the empty offices on the fifth floor. Is it going well?
W: Definitely. In fact, I'd say we're ahead of schedule.
M: That's great! The reason I asked is that our CEO just told me that the air conditioning units and telephones are going to be installed tomorrow. Is there any chance you'll be done before then?
W: Oh, then that just gives us one day to finish. I guess I can ask my work crew to stay late this evening to wrap everything up. Then the offices will be ready for the technicians arriving tomorrow.
M: I'd really appreciate that. Thanks.

35. What project are the speakers discussing?
36. What will happen tomorrow?
37. What will the woman ask her work crew to do?

Questions 38-40 refer to the following conversation.

W: Excuse me. I think my company parking permit must have fallen out of my handbag at some point. Did anyone hand one in here at the security desk?

M: Oh... I just got here five minutes ago. Where do you think it might've fallen out of your bag?

W: Well, I used it when I arrived for work at 8:30 this morning, and then I thought I put it in my bag. It could be anywhere really.

M: I think the best thing to do is to give me your name and number. Then I can give you a call if it turns up anywhere.

38. What problem is the woman having?
39. What does the man imply when he says, "I just got here five minutes ago"?
40. What does the man ask the woman to do?

Questions 41-43 refer to the following conversation with three speakers.

M1: Hi, Arnold. Here is the list of job candidates coming in for interviews this afternoon. Is the conference room ready for us to use?

M2: Yes, I just need to get hold of all the candidates' résumés and application forms. I think the human resources manager still has them.

M1: Right. I'm calling her now. Elizabeth, I'm in the conference room with Arnold. We still need to get the forms for the candidates before they arrive.

W: Oh, of course! But, I was just about to take a break for lunch.

M1: We'd be happy to join you for lunch somewhere, and then we can get the documents from you.

W: Great. I was just planning to head to the cafeteria. Can you meet me there? I'll make sure I bring everything you need.

41. What are the men trying to do?
42. Who is the woman?
43. What does the woman ask the men to do?

Questions 44-46 refer to the following conversation.

M: Good morning. I'd like to make an appointment to have some viruses removed from my laptop. Can I bring it in sometime today?

W: I'm afraid our technicians have no time available today, and we're closed on Sundays. We could fit you in on Monday at around noon.

M: Hmm... That's during my lunch break, but I need to be back at my office by 1 P.M. at the latest.

W: It won't take more than thirty minutes.

M: Well, I don't want to risk being late, as I have an important meeting that day. I'd better just wait until next weekend.

W: That will work, too. How about 10 A.M. on Saturday?

M: That will be perfect, thanks. See you then.

44. What is the purpose of the man's call?
45. What does the woman imply when she says, "It won't take more than thirty minutes"?
46. What does the man decide to do?

Questions 47-49 refer to the following conversation.

W: It's great that you finally have the chance to see the apartment for yourself. The pictures online don't really do it justice.

M: I think I'll love it. I'm especially excited about the open space on the rooftop. I've always wanted to keep a garden, and it should be a good spot for one.

W: I think that's a wonderful idea. Now, I know this residential area is a bit far from downtown, but that means it's quieter, too.

M: Oh, I don't mind. My brother actually lives around here, so I can see him more often.

W: Fantastic! And one last thing: these leases are actually for 24-months, which is longer than a typical agreement.

47. What does the man like about the apartment building?
48. What does the man say about his brother?
49. What does the woman point out about the rental agreement?

Questions 50-52 refer to the following conversation.

M: Hello, KyungMi. Today will be your first day on your own in FleetFox Couriers Eastern Distribution Center. Do you have any questions before you start?
W: The past week of training covered a lot, but I'm still unsure of how to sort international deliveries. How do I do it again?
M: Oh, it really isn't any different from domestic deliveries. Scan them as you normally would, but just be sure to place them on Conveyor Belt C.
W: That's easy enough. I'm all set, then.
M: You'll do fine. And if you need to know anything else, just ask Daniel in the next station. He's worked here for a while.

50. Where do the speakers most likely work?
51. What does the woman ask about?
52. According to the man, how can the woman receive additional information?

Questions 53-55 refer to the following conversation.

W: Good morning. Thanks for calling Sirius Digital Solutions. How can I help?
M: Hi, my name is Benjamin Stark. I need someone to create a new Web site for my business and I heard your firm can produce great results.
W: I certainly aim to please my clients. What type of site are you hoping for?
M: Well, I'm hiring several new salespeople to draw more customers to my business. But in order to meet the increased demand, I'll need to create a fully functional online store, instead of just distributing traditional catalogs. Do you think you could handle that?
W: No problem. But, online stores can be fairly complicated projects. Let's meet at my office so that we can talk about all the details in person. Would 4 P.M. this Thursday suit you?

53. Who most likely is the woman?
54. What does the man want to hire employees to do?
55. Why will the man most likely visit the woman's office?

Questions 56-58 refer to the following conversation.

W: Jeremy, what's going on with the payroll system at your branch? I heard that the monthly pay slips for around 50 of your employees were handed out two days late.
M: The problem is with our staff database. The current system uses outdated computers, so there are often errors when calculating employee work hours. I had to manually calculate work hours for those employees because the system crashed again.
W: Oh... Well, has anything been done to avoid a similar situation in the future?
M: Yes, we're finally getting new computers installed this week. I just purchased them this morning.
W: I'm glad to hear that. And I'd appreciate it if you could e-mail the receipts for those to head office this afternoon.
M: No problem. I'll get them to you by 4 P.M.

56. According to the man, what caused some pay slips to be distributed late?
57. What action will be taken to prevent any similar problems?
58. What will the man do this afternoon?

Questions 59-61 refer to the following conversation with three speakers.

M1: Welcome to this tour of Everglade Fruit Orchard. I'll be showing you how we choose the very best fruits and discard those that aren't quite good enough. Now, before we begin, does anyone have any questions?
W: Yes, I was wondering if we can purchase some fruit at the end of the tour.
M1: Some of our fruits are only for distribution to retailers, but we will allow you to buy some of our apples.
W: Apples? That's what I was hoping to hear. Thanks!
M1: Are there any more questions before we set off?
M2: I heard this orchard employs over one hundred people. What do they all do here?
M1: Actually, we have more employees than any other orchard in the country. Most of them are involved with picking and packaging our fruit.

59. What will the visitors see on the tour?
60. What are the tour group members permitted to do?

61. What does the tour guide say the company is known for?

Questions 62-64 refer to the following conversation and table.

W: I think we should move a little faster with our planning of the company's year-end banquet, Miguel. I received the full list of attendees from the head of personnel last evening, so we can go ahead and make a reservation somewhere.
M: Sounds great. So, obviously we need to find a nice place that has a private dining room we can use for our event. I've narrowed it down to this list of four options.
W: Well, I've eaten at Willow before, and the food was excellent. But there will be more than 40 employees attending the banquet. We'll need a private dining room that can accommodate everyone, so let's reserve the biggest one.
M: You're right. I'll let you figure out the best date for the meal. Then I'll send a memo to our staff and let them know the plan.

62. What information about the meal did the woman receive yesterday?
63. Look at the graphic. Which restaurant do the speakers choose?
64. What does the man say he will take care of?

Questions 65-67 refer to the following conversation and diagram.

W: Hi, James. I think you and I and the other committee members at our tennis club need to have a meeting. We need to discuss potential replacements for Matthew Anderson, since he's moving overseas next month.
M: Good idea, but it's going to be hard to replace him. Matthew's been with us for a long time. We'll need someone who really understands all the finances involved with running our tennis club.
W: Yes, but I think we have some suitable individuals among our current members. Can you advertise the position to everyone?
M: Sure. I'll start by designing a poster that we can put up in club headquarters.

65. What type of club do the speakers most likely belong to?
66. Look at the graphic. Which position is being discussed?
67. What will the man do next?

Questions 68-70 refer to the following conversation and price list.

M: Welcome back to the TriCore Fitness Center.
W: Thanks. Here's my membership ID.
M: I noticed you haven't signed up for any of our additional services yet. Our new meal planning program has become very popular.
W: Actually, I want to join the yoga class.
M: Oh, fantastic. It starts at 6 o'clock and ends at 7. The instructor always makes healthy juice for everyone in the evening after class, so plan to stick around a bit longer. Maybe until around 7:15.
W: That sounds fine. Will my name be on a list or something?
M: That's right. Just show the instructor any piece of ID with your name on it.

68. Look at the graphic. How much will the woman pay for a service?
69. What does the man say about the evening?
70. What does the man say the woman will need to show?

PART 4

Questions 71-73 refer to the following talk.

Thanks for visiting our exhibit here at the technology convention. We're here to show you an effective way to allow your customers to scan their own products and pay for their purchases. Please take a look at our new line of barcode scanners. I bet you've experienced long lines of customers and slow service on busy days in your store. Well, our new devices can solve that! Customers can scan and pay for goods themselves, more quickly and easily. Now, I'd like to give each of you a pamphlet that describes our new products in more detail.

71. What product is the speaker selling?
72. What does the speaker say the product will help avoid?
73. What will the speaker do next?

Questions 74-76 refer to the following broadcast.

This is Alexander Knight on WPRK Talk Radio, and you're listening to 'What's On the Menu?', the bi-weekly program about local food and eating out. Our special guest tonight is Pricilla Nichols, the owner of the popular Italian restaurant on Twelfth Avenue, Primo Pasta. Pricilla is here to explain more about a special project she's involved in. She's one of several local entrepreneurs funding a new culinary school that is scheduled to open in Los Angeles later this year. And she'll be offering scholarships to several promising young chefs in our area. It's a pleasure to have you on the show, Pricilla.

74. Who is Pricilla Nichols?
75. What project is Pricilla Nichols currently involved in?
76. What does the speaker say Pricilla Nichols plans to do?

Questions 77-79 refer to the following announcement.

Attention, all passengers waiting to board Flight 035 to Toronto. Due to strong winds and heavy snow, your flight will be delayed for a minimum of one hour. Your luggage has already been loaded onto the plane, and we will be ready to go as soon as the snowstorm stops. Don't go too far. Gate 12 has several amenities. If we're lucky, you may be able to board the plane sooner than expected. I'll keep you informed about any changes to the situation, so keep listening. We appreciate your understanding.

77. What has caused a delay?
78. Why does the speaker say, "Gate 12 has several amenities"?
79. According to the speaker, how can the listeners receive more information?

Questions 80-82 refer to the following broadcast.

You're listening to Radio Rochdale, and now it's time for your local news. Yesterday, a project to clean up Thorpe River started. The river has grown polluted over the past few years, and the city council has finally decided to address the problem. The waste management firm, Assange Corporation, was selected to lead the clean-up efforts. Several firms bid to do the work, but the contract was offered to Assange Corporation after it promised to complete the task without taking any payment for the work. The city council is hoping to build new homes on the banks of the river once the clean-up is complete.

80. What happened yesterday?
81. Why does the speaker say Assange Corporation was selected?
82. What is the city council hoping to do?

Questions 83-85 refer to the following tour information.

Good morning, everyone. It looks like we'll have beautiful weather for today's hike through Thurston Forest. My name is Sonya, and I've been studying the plants and wildlife in the area for 15 years, so if you have any questions, just ask! We'll start off at a fairly quick pace, but once we get further into the forest, we'll stop frequently to admire several gorgeous waterfalls and some truly stunning views. The trail ends near the small town of Beverly, so we'll have lunch there. And if you enjoy today's hike, please leave a comment for us on our Web site!

83. What does the speaker mention about herself?
84. According to the speaker, why will the group make frequent stops?
85. According to the speaker, what can the listeners do on a Web site?

Questions 86-88 refer to the following telephone message.

Hello, Mr. Killian. This is Jessica Lowe. We met last week about the apartment on Market Street. I'm calling because I haven't heard back from you about receiving my deposit for the lease. I recently started using a new bank account, so I'm wondering if that might have caused a problem with my transfer. Anyway, I would really appreciate an update. I'm living back at home right now, and umm... my parents are moving next week. Just call me back at 555-3210. Thanks.

86. What is the speaker calling about?
87. What does the speaker say has changed?
88. Why does the speaker say, "my parents are moving next week"?

Questions 89-91 refer to the following excerpt from a meeting.

The final thing to discuss at this staff meeting is our team bonding policy. The concept behind this new program is to encourage all of you, our employees, to build better relationships and improve communication with one another. We feel that the best way to do that is for staff to join company-led clubs. Therefore, we have organized clubs for bowling, badminton, and hiking. If you sign up to join any of these, you'll receive a gift certificate for Darcy's Department Store. To sign up for a club, you'll need to add your name to the sign-up sheet. I'll post that on the notice board right after this meeting.

89. What is the speaker mainly discussing?
90. What are the listeners asked to do?
91. What does the speaker say he will do after the meeting?

Questions 92-94 refer to the following telephone message.

Hey Mustafa, it's Donald. I'm calling you to discuss the event to celebrate the launch of our new range of washing machines. We need to make sure that everything is organized so that it's a success. For example, the product displays, the live music, and most importantly – thinking back to the disappointing launch earlier this year for our new microwave line – how we're going to attract enough consumers to our store for the event. Don't forget what happened in March. Anyway, I'm planning to visit our headquarters this afternoon to speak with you and the other marketing managers in person. Let me know what time you'll be free for a chat.

92. What is the message mainly about?
93. What does the speaker imply when he says, "Don't forget what happened in March"?
94. What is the speaker going to do this afternoon?

Questions 95-97 refer to the following news report and weather forecast.

Locals are excited for the upcoming Pottsville Community Yard Sale, which is returning for its third year. Held outside at Lakeview Park, the event gives everyone the chance to sell secondhand clothes, old tools and equipment, or even handmade crafts. And for shoppers, it's a great way to meet others and buy some truly unique items. If you're interested in attending, you can visit the city Web site to see a map of the vendor layout, which is updated daily as new participants join. As for the weather, our streak of rainy days will be over by then, but there still won't be any sun all day, so be sure to dress warmly.

95. What event is being described?
96. According to the speaker, what can the listeners find on a Web site?
97. Look at the graphic. Which day is the event being held?

Questions 98-100 refer to the following excerpt from a meeting and pie chart.

Hello, and thanks for coming to this meeting. As you read in this morning's newsletter, preparations for our new West Coast office have progressed faster than we anticipated. We'll actually be able to open it soon; however, we still need to hire a lot of staff to fill all the positions. To solve this problem, the board of directors has decided to buy out an independent Web publisher in the area to absorb its work force. The small Web site we've chosen currently holds 15% of the Western region's market share. This is the perfect size for our goals.

98. According to the speaker, what was mentioned in the company newsletter?
99. What problem does the speaker mention?
100. Look at the graphic. Which company may be acquired?

TEST 2

정답

PART 1

1. (A) **2**. (C) **3**. (A) **4**. (C) **5**. (A) **6**. (D)

PART 2

7. (B) **8**. (A) **9**. (C) **10**. (A) **11**. (B) **12**. (B) **13**. (C) **14**. (B) **15**. (C) **16**. (C) **17**. (B) **18**. (A) **19**. (A)
20. (C) **21**. (A) **22**. (A) **23**. (B) **24**. (B) **25**. (C) **26**. (A) **27**. (C) **28**. (A) **29**. (C) **30**. (A) **31**. (A)

PART 3

32. (A) **33**. (B) **34**. (A) **35**. (B) **36**. (B) **37**. (B) **38**. (C) **39**. (C) **40**. (C) **41**. (B) **42**. (D) **43**. (C) **44**. (D)
45. (D) **46**. (A) **47**. (C) **48**. (B) **49**. (D) **50**. (D) **51**. (C) **52**. (C) **53**. (B) **54**. (D) **55**. (C) **56**. (C) **57**. (B)
58. (A) **59**. (C) **60**. (B) **61**. (B) **62**. (B) **63**. (A) **64**. (D) **65**. (B) **66**. (C) **67**. (D) **68**. (B) **69**. (A) **70**. (D)

PART 4

71. (B) **72**. (C) **73**. (B) **74**. (D) **75**. (C) **76**. (A) **77**. (C) **78**. (C) **79**. (A) **80**. (C) **81**. (D) **82**. (A) **83**. (B)
84. (D) **85**. (C) **86**. (B) **87**. (D) **88**. (A) **89**. (C) **90**. (B) **91**. (C) **92**. (B) **93**. (C) **94**. (D) **95**. (C) **96**. (C)
97. (B) **98**. (A) **99**. (C) **100**. (B)

PART 1

1. (A) He's checking his watch.
(B) He's removing his jacket.
(C) He's carrying a laptop computer.
(D) He's looking in his backpack.

2. (A) The woman is switching off a lamp.
(B) The woman is opening some curtains.
(C) The woman is seated by a window.
(D) The woman is pouring coffee into a mug.

3. (A) Chairs are arranged in rows.
(B) Some trees are being trimmed.
(C) Grass is being mowed.
(D) Flowers have been put in a vase.

4. (A) The men are talking to each other.
(B) One of the men is serving food on a plate.
(C) One of the women is wearing a hat.
(D) A menu is being examined.

5. (A) Some people are walking toward an archway.
(B) A notice is being hung on a post.
(C) A roof is being repaired.
(D) Some shoppers are trying on hats.

6. (A) Some people are watching a video.
(B) Some people are setting up a meeting room.
(C) Some people are writing on a notepad.
(D) Some people are listening to a presentation.

PART 2

7. Where can I store these leftover decorations?
(A) No, it won't work.
(B) Somewhere in the basement.
(C) They're in aisle 9.

8. Can you please check my engine?
(A) Just a minute.
(B) I don't know his name.
(C) It was a while ago.

9. How do I get to the outlet mall from here?
(A) It's a popular brand.
(B) A new television.
(C) Just keep going straight.

10. Do you know where Eric is?
(A) Check the cafeteria.
(B) I already learned how to do it.
(C) Wasn't it at 9 o'clock?

11. You checked all the applications, right?
(A) A few references.
(B) I did this morning.
(C) A high starting salary.

12. How many tour members have signed up this week?
(A) I already saw the sign.
(B) At least 100, I think.
(C) Probably around five hours.

13. Would you like to send this by boat or by plane?
(A) They can carry it further.
(B) Two tickets, please.
(C) What's the difference?

14. How much is a full engine service?
(A) We provide express service.
(B) There's a special offer right now.
(C) Four engineers.

15. Why is the community center closed this week?
(A) No, I didn't hear anything.
(B) Several local residents were there.
(C) Because it's being renovated.

16. We should make the schedule for the training session.
(A) Around fifteen people.
(B) Overtime and personal leave.
(C) I have time this morning.

17. When can I pick up the cake?
(A) Just pick your favorite.
(B) Any time before the party.
(C) At the grocery store.

18. I don't know how to use the new fax machine.
(A) I haven't tried it yet.
(B) OK. I look forward to it.
(C) Sending signed documents.

19. Who put together the slideshow for the year-end dinner?
(A) Shelley from Human Resources.
(B) I don't know how to.
(C) Oh, a couple weeks ago.

20. Why did Mr. and Mrs. Smith cancel their session?
(A) No, it's OK.
(B) Around 9 o'clock last night.
(C) They had to go out of town.

21. I need feedback on our product's performance.
(A) The data isn't ready yet.
(B) The project looks promising.
(C) Put it back after you're done.

22. Would you like the beef or the pork?
(A) Is the pork salty?
(B) I'll take it.
(C) I just brought it out.

23. Wasn't the sales meeting pushed back to next week?
(A) They've been low lately.
(B) Right, to Monday afternoon.
(C) Some staff didn't attend.

24. You transferred from the Hong Kong office, didn't you?
(A) I referred to the instructions.
(B) No, that was Brandon.
(C) A permanent work visa.

25. Won't you be closed during the summer?
(A) It's not far by taxi.
(B) Don't open another box yet.
(C) No, but the menu will be limited.

26. I'd like to schedule a checkup with Dr. Bolero.
(A) He's at the Marietta branch now.
(B) No, 1 o'clock doesn't work for us.
(C) We accept credit cards, too.

27. Why haven't you printed the invitations yet?
(A) For the anniversary dinner.
(B) Five copies, please.
(C) We're out of paper.

28. Who can I contact about donating some artwork to the museum?
(A) Read these guidelines first.
(B) Yes, by the end of the month.
(C) Mostly landscapes and portraits.

29. Didn't he win an award for that article?
(A) A new publisher.
(B) The display case is full.
(C) That was his colleague.

30. Do you think our restaurant should find a new vendor for our ingredients?
(A) The current prices are reasonable.
(B) Three boxes of tomatoes.
(C) An increased delivery fee.

31. Is the traffic on the highway always like this?
(A) Only when there's road work.
(B) That's fine. We can take my car.
(C) Get off at Maple Street.

PART 3

Questions 32-34 refer to the following conversation.

W: Hello, welcome to TrueYoo Beauty Salon. What can I do for you?
M: Good afternoon. I have an appointment with Tricia at 2 o'clock. I'm Glenn Park.
W: Oh… I can't find your name here.
M: Well, I called yesterday in the evening and made the appointment.
W: I see. We had a new employee who was training last night. She must have taken your call and forgotten to write down the details. I'm sorry. We're not busy, if you could just wait 10 minutes.
M: That's fine. I don't mind.
W: Thanks for understanding. Oh, and after you pay, be sure to pick up some vouchers for some great hair care products from the front desk.

32. Where does the woman most likely work?
33. Why does the woman apologize?
34. What does the woman remind the man to pick up?

Questions 35-37 refer to the following conversation.

W: Oh, Jeremy, there you are. Have you had a chance to check out the problem I mentioned yesterday? I think there's an issue with the heater in Conference Room B.
M: Ah.. not yet. I've been setting up the new workspaces for the part-time workers we recently hired. I'll get to it as soon as I finish.
W: Great. And let me know if it can't be fixed right away. I'm planning to host our visiting clients in that room later this afternoon, so I'll change the location if it's still too chilly in there.

35. What are the speakers mainly discussing?
36. What does the man explain to the woman?
37. Why does the woman want to use the room today?

Questions 38-40 refer to the following conversation with three speakers.

W: Hi, I'm calling from Hanover Hardware. We've had some problems with the studio producing our commercial, so we need to change the dates of the airtime we purchased.

M1: Okay. You won't get a refund for the unused time, though.
W: Really? I'm surprised we'd still have to pay.
M1: Let me check with my manager. Mr. Fleming, someone from Hanover Hardware wants to change the dates for their commercial time. Will they get a refund?
M2: Well, the network has a policy that allows for one schedule change if it's a daytime slot. Did they reserve a time in the afternoon or in the evening?
M1: I don't know. I'll ask her right now.

38. Where do the men most likely work?
39. What does the woman say she is surprised about?
40. What information will the woman be asked to provide?

Questions 41-43 refer to the following conversation.

W: Hello. I've started reading the *Midnight Eye* series, but it looks like you only have the first book on your shelves. Do you have the sequel in the back by any chance?
M: Ah... that title sold out very quickly. However, our weekly delivery from our distributor comes in tomorrow. Then we will have plenty of copies.
W: I'm leaving for a vacation tonight...
M: I see. Well, I could suggest several similar detective novels you could try.
W: Oh, I really want to find out what happens next. Would you see if you have an e-reader version available on your online store? Then I could just read it on my phone application.

41. What type of business is the woman visiting?
42. What does the woman imply when she says, "I'm leaving for a vacation tonight"?
43. What does the woman ask the man to do?

Questions 44-46 refer to the following conversation.

M: Good morning, Salma. I was looking at the figures, and our sales have increased a lot since we opened our online store back in March.
W: I know. Our customers like the collection of different styles we offer online. There are even more choices than what we sell in the store.
M: Exactly. But, how do you think we could make it even better?
W: I'm not sure. Do you have any ideas?
M: Well, I was thinking about offering a premium service. Perhaps it could have exclusive offers and expedited shipping.
W: Yeah, that would be good. I'll call the warehouse manager and see what kind of shipping options we could arrange.

44. What happened in March?
45. According to the woman, what do customers like about the business?
46. What does the woman offer to do?

Questions 47-49 refer to the following conversation.

W1: Good afternoon, Tina. I saw your post about starting a biking club here in the company. I was wondering, could people who don't work here join too?
W2: I suppose so. Anyone would be welcome to join our biking trips.
W1: Well, I don't even have a bike, but do you remember Thelma Pierce? She used to work with me in sales. Anyways, she's a real biking enthusiast. She even cycled across Europe.
W2: Wow, that's impressive. She should definitely join us then. We have our company's end-of-quarter party tonight at 6:30, but I can give her a call afterward. Then I'll let her know more about the club.

47. What are the speakers mainly discussing?
48. Who is Thelma Pierce?
49. What will the speakers most likely do at 6:30?

Questions 50-52 refer to the following conversation with three speakers.

W1: Welcome, and thanks for choosing Fetzer Solutions. My name is Susan, and this is Isabelle. Our company can help analyze your employees' performances and attitudes about their work environment.
M: Thanks. It will be helpful to have the reviews done by an outside company. The employees will be more honest.
W2: I'm wondering... why are you interested in our services at the moment?
M: Well, Isabelle, we just doubled our staff three months ago in anticipation of market growth, and I want to make sure everyone is comfortable in their new positions.

W2: Great. There are several service packages that should suit your needs then. And with some basic information, I can give you an idea of the cost.

50. What service does Fetzer Solutions provide?
51. What did the man's company do three months ago?
52. What does Isabelle offer to do?

Questions 53-55 refer to the following conversation.

M: Hi, my name is Wes Taylor. I turned in an application for the copy editor position at your publishing house earlier this week. I wanted to call and follow up on it.
W: Hello, Mr. Taylor. I haven't seen it yet, but since you're on the line, tell me about yourself.
M: Oh, let's see. I studied journalism at university, and I just graduated in the spring.
W: Good for you. However, most of our employees started out at smaller companies.
M: That's what I figured. If it helps, though, I was the head editor of my university newspaper.
W: Interesting. Would I be able to see an issue you worked on?
M: Sure, I can e-mail you a digital copy now.

53. Why is the man calling?
54. What does the woman imply when she says, "most of our employees started out at smaller companies"?
55. What will the man do next?

Questions 56-58 refer to the following conversation.

M: Hello, Rosita. Have you had the chance to read the article I sent you about new trends in the hotel industry?
W: Yes, and I believe it gives us a good idea about how to market our newest line of massage chairs.
M: Indeed. Apparently, hotels around the country are creating relaxing lounge areas for guests. We should focus on the largest franchises.
W: Well, we'll have a product trial session tomorrow. We can ask the participants how they would feel about using one in a hotel.

56. What does the woman say she has done?
57. What type of product is being discussed?
58. What will take place tomorrow?

Questions 59-61 refer to the following conversation.

W: Excuse me. I just landed and I'd like to arrange a taxi to take me to the Sandford Hotel in the business district. And I need to get there quickly, as I'm giving a lecture there at 10 A.M.
M: Certainly, but that hotel is in the theater district, not the business district.
W: Oh, really? I'm sure I read online that it's located there.
M: You're probably confusing it with the Sandringham Hotel on Markley Avenue.
W: Hmm... you might be right! Anyway, I'd like to get going as soon as possible.
M: No problem. It's a flat fee of $18 from here to your destination. We accept cash or credit card.
W: I think I have cash. Here you are.
M: Thank you. Now, just take this receipt and present it to the next taxi driver in line outside this airport terminal.

59. Where is the woman planning to go this morning?
60. What is the woman surprised about?
61. What does the man give the woman?

Questions 62-64 refer to the following conversation and coupon.

W: Hello, sir. Is there anything I can help you with today?
M: Yes, I'm interested in purchasing this phone. It has a long-lasting battery, right?
W: That's correct. That model supposedly has the best battery life on the market.
M: Oh, I almost forgot about this coupon, too.
W: Well, if you can wait to buy it on Saturday, you could get 25 percent off.
M: Ah, I see that. My mobile phone just broke and I need one for work. I'll just have to take the 15 percent discount. Does it still come with a free case and headphones, though?
W: It does, but we're currently sold out of cases that fit that model.

62. What do the speakers mention about a mobile phone?
63. Look at the graphic. On which day is the man making a purchase?
64. What additional service does the man ask about?

Questions 65-67 refer to the following conversation and computer window.

W: Hello, Connor. When are you leaving for the product demonstration in the Research Department?
M: Oh, I'm just about to go. But, perhaps you'll know. I'm trying to watch a video I downloaded, but when I try to open it, this window pops up.
W: That's because of the latest system update. You'll have to re-install the media player, and it gives you a few options for how to do it.
M: Well, which is best?
W: Don't choose the fourth; it's too complicated. A few other people in the Sales Department used the third option, and I didn't hear any complaints.
M: Ok, I'll try that too, and then I'll head to the demonstration.

65. What does the man say he is trying to do?
66. Look at the graphic. Which option does the woman suggest selecting?
67. Where will the speakers most likely go next?

Questions 68-70 refer to the following conversation and office park map.

W: Hello, Mr. Goodman. It's Skyler, the producer from the ABQ Radio Show. I went over our schedule, and we would love you to come in and do an on-air interview. How does Thursday at 10 A.M. work for you?
M: Oh, fantastic. Let me check my planner... Yes, I'm free at that time.
W: Good to hear. Badger Studios, where we record, is part of a business complex. Our building is on Walter Street, right in front of the baseball field.
M: OK, I'll be able to find it. Which floor are you on?
W: The ninth floor, but while you're in the lobby, you'll need to sign in at the security desk.

68. What are the speakers mainly discussing?
69. Look at the graphic. Which building is Badger Studios located in?
70. What does the woman tell the man to do in the lobby?

PART 4

Questions 71-73 refer to the following advertisement.

Do you own a small to mid-sized pool? Then you're all too familiar with how difficult it is to keep it clean and well-maintained. That's why Rafferty's Pool Surplus is here to help. We have everything you need to keep your pool water crystal clear in any season. We have top-of-the-line equipment, from aquatic vacuums to durable covers, and strong yet safe chemical cleaners. And we have all of this for the lowest prices you can find, guaranteed! Check out our online store to see just how low the prices are. And for this month only, we're offering free delivery for any online purchase!

71. What products does the company sell?
72. What does the speaker emphasize about the products?
73. What is being offered for free this month?

Questions 74-76 refer to the following telephone message.

Hi, Rachel. This is Frank Johnson in Accounting returning your call. You mentioned that you would like to buy ten new laptops for your department on the fourth floor. I understand that your current equipment is out of date, and you have several important projects coming up, and I would love to approve your request. Unfortunately, however, it's not up to me. When it comes to such large purchases, you need to speak directly with the chief financial officer. It's also a good idea to prepare a report for him, detailing why you feel this is a good use of the company's funds. If you have any questions about that, please get in touch.

74. Why is the speaker calling?
75. What does the speaker mean when he says, "it's not up to me"?
76. What does the speaker suggest the listener do?

Questions 77-79 refer to the following excerpt from a meeting.

As you're all aware, most people know our company for publishing entertaining and informative travel guides. However, I've asked you all here to announce that we are going to start releasing fictional novels set in exotic locations. If it goes well, we'll consider expanding into nonfiction stories, too. We've already begun talking to several talented writers, but this new direction will require quite a few other changes to our usual procedures. It will also require a lot of planning, so Meriam, the head editor, will talk to us now about the project timeline we expect to follow.

77. What kind of business does the speaker work for?
78. What is the purpose of the meeting?
79. What will the next speaker talk about?

Questions 80-82 refer to the following telephone message.

Good afternoon. My name is Sophia, and I work at the Athena Grand Cinema. Around 11 o'clock this morning, you purchased four movie tickets for a showing at 8:15 this evening via our mobile app. There was an error with the system, though, and that showing was actually already sold out. I'm sorry to say that your current tickets are invalid. However, we still have seats available for that same movie at 6:45, 7:50, and 9:20 tonight. Of course, I can't make a change until I can confirm your preference. And since we always value our customers, I'm applying a 20% discount to your purchase. Just text me at 555-0845 with your preferred movie time, and I'll take care of the rest.

80. Where does the speaker most likely work?
81. What does the speaker mean when she says, "we always value our customers"?
82. What does the caller ask the listener to do?

Questions 83-85 refer to the following speech.

Good evening, everyone, and thanks for coming out to tonight's Designer of the Year awards ceremony. This year's winner was a clear choice – Topher De La Rosa, owner and head designer of Rosen Fashionwear. Topher started working by himself out of his studio apartment just four years ago, but he worked hard, entering jackets, dresses, and footwear in fashion shows across the country. He has now transformed his small label into an internationally recognized brand, designing not only clothing but furniture and handbags as well. His stores are found all over the country, and he has plans to open several branches in Europe and Asia later this year. Everyone, please give a round of applause for Topher De La Rosa!

83. What is the purpose of the speech?
84. What industry does Topher De La Rosa work in?
85. According to the speaker, what does Topher De La Rosa plan to do?

Questions 86-88 refer to the following telephone message.

Good afternoon. This is James calling from Tudor Chocolates. The plastic packaging you made for our holiday set just arrived. Unfortunately, I noticed a mistake with it. Some of the dimensions are incorrect, so the chocolate pieces don't fit securely. They might come loose before the customer even opens the box. We don't have time to redo the order, so we'll just have to make it work somehow. Next time, though, I'd appreciate it if you sent some samples of your goods for us to check. Doing so will help us avoid any future confusion.

86. What product does the speaker's company make?
87. What is the speaker calling about?
88. What does the speaker request?

Questions 89-91 refer to the following excerpt from a meeting.

Thanks for taking the time to come in. I wanted to talk to you because you all lead a different department here at New Branch Architecture. While your teams' goals are different, some managing skills are important in any field. For instance, to be productive, you probably think that your staff shouldn't take much time off. However, you should encourage your employees to use their vacation time. It helps reduce stress and promote creativity, especially when working on building designs. I've read about the benefits thoroughly in this book by a famous British architect, and I'd like you all to take a look.

89. Where do the listeners most likely work?
90. What does the speaker recommend the listeners do?
91. What will the speaker most likely do next?

Questions 92-94 refer to the following excerpt from a meeting.

All right, everyone, our big Midtown Comic Book Convention is only a month away, so we have a lot to cover today. Our biggest concern is increasing ticket sales, which we've struggled with in the past. We're trying to sell e-tickets this year so people around the world can access the convention and participate in its events over the Internet. I was skeptical that this would help our sales. But, have you checked them recently? If this keeps up, we'll definitely use this strategy next year, too. Also, we need to finalize our floor plan. Do you have any suggestions for where we should place the comic book vendors? They were too far from the entrance last year.

92. What will the convention focus on?
93. What does the speaker imply when he says, "But, have you checked them recently"?
94. What advice does the speaker ask for?

Questions 95-97 refer to the following announcement and table of contents.

Good morning, cast, and welcome to the third day of our table reading for our next play, "August Nights". First of all, thank you all for coming in an hour earlier than we planned. We have a lot to cover today, and this shows just how dedicated you all are to our production. Now, go ahead and open your scripts to page 21, and we'll pick up from where we ended yesterday. Oh, keep in mind that this afternoon's session will be quite important. Eugene Williams, the author of the play, will be here, and you'll want to make a good impression.

95. What does the speaker thank the listeners for?
96. Look at the graphic. Which section will the listeners cover today?
97. What does the speaker say about the afternoon session?

Questions 98-100 refer to the following excerpt from a meeting and floor plan.

Good morning, everyone. As you know, the Wilmore Society has reserved Namsae Park on Saturday night for their annual fundraising gala. Their members will do the decorations, but we'll still take care of the park security. One thing to keep in mind is that the guests will not be using the main park entrance. They'll have dinner beforehand on a river boat, so all attendees will enter through the opposite end at the docks. And since a DJ will be playing in the picnic area, we'll need to store some of the tables in order to make room for a dance floor.

98. What is the purpose of the meeting?
99. Look at the graphic. Which entrance will guests use on Saturday?
100. What does the speaker say will happen in the picnic area?

TEST 3

정답

PART 1

1. (D) **2**. (C) **3**. (D) **4**. (D) **5**. (D) **6**. (B)

PART 2

7. (C) **8**. (B) **9**. (B) **10**. (A) **11**. (A) **12**. (C) **13**. (C) **14**. (A) **15**. (C) **16**. (C) **17**. (B) **18**. (A) **19**. (A)
20. (A) **21**. (C) **22**. (C) **23**. (A) **24**. (B) **25**. (B) **26**. (B) **27**. (B) **28**. (A) **29**. (C) **30**. (A) **31**. (C)

PART 3

32. (D) **33**. (B) **34**. (C) **35**. (A) **36**. (D) **37**. (A) **38**. (C) **39**. (C) **40**. (D) **41**. (D) **42**. (A) **43**. (B) **44**. (D)
45. (B) **46**. (B) **47**. (D) **48**. (C) **49**. (A) **50**. (A) **51**. (D) **52**. (D) **53**. (B) **54**. (D) **55**. (A) **56**. (A) **57**. (C)
58. (D) **59**. (B) **60**. (B) **61**. (D) **62**. (C) **63**. (D) **64**. (C) **65**. (A) **66**. (D) **67**. (C) **68**. (B) **69**. (B) **70**. (A)

PART 4

71. (C) **72**. (B) **73**. (B) **74**. (C) **75**. (A) **76**. (B) **77**. (A) **78**. (C) **79**. (B) **80**. (C) **81**. (D) **82**. (B) **83**. (A)
84. (C) **85**. (A) **86**. (C) **87**. (B) **88**. (B) **89**. (C) **90**. (D) **91**. (B) **92**. (B) **93**. (C) **94**. (D) **95**. (B) **96**. (B)
97. (A) **98**. (C) **99**. (C) **100**. (B)

PART 1

1. (A) She's serving food on a plate.
(B) She's wiping a counter.
(C) She's mixing food in a bowl.
(D) She's holding a container.

2. (A) A woman is moving some furniture.
(B) A woman is opening a window.
(C) A woman is looking in a drawer.
(D) A woman is wiping a desk.

3. (A) Some bushes are being trimmed.
(B) There are lampposts along the walkway.
(C) A driver is getting out of a vehicle.
(D) Some bicycles have been parked outdoors.

4. (A) One of the men is putting on boots.
(B) The woman is sitting in a waiting area.
(C) One of the men is reaching for a tree.
(D) Two people are holding a bag open.

5. (A) Some people are waiting in line at an entrance.
(B) Customers are being served at a food counter.
(C) Some people are waiting to be seated.
(D) A buffet table has been prepared for a meal.

6. (A) A bridge is being constructed.
(B) Trees are growing along a river.
(C) People are getting into a boat.
(D) Some boats are tied to a pier.

PART 2

7. When did Mr. Davis start working here?
(A) In Marketing.
(B) He carpools with the others.
(C) Not too long ago.

8. Where's the office library?
(A) From 9 A.M. to 5 P.M.
(B) On the third floor.
(C) A book on management.

9. How often do you travel to Europe?
(A) It's about 800 dollars.
(B) Every summer.
(C) I moved there in March.

10. May I thank a few people before the start of the show?
(A) Go ahead, but be quick.
(B) He'll show you after we're done.
(C) The ending really surprised me.

11. Have the new editions arrived yet?
(A) Maybe tomorrow.
(B) Did he catch the bus?
(C) $10 each.

12. Will you notify our suppliers about the new policy?
(A) There are more in storage.
(B) We supply fresh ingredients.
(C) I just sent an e-mail.

13. When will their next album be released?
(A) Several new songs.
(B) The lease is about to end.
(C) Sometime next year.

14. Why is Ruthie not here today?
(A) Maybe she's at the corporate office.
(B) Every Saturday.
(C) No, it's not.

15. Which service should we use to ship these products?
(A) Less than a week.
(B) You could give it a try.
(C) The cheapest one.

16. How much does a monthly subscription cost?
(A) You can register on our Web site.
(B) Yes, I read every issue.
(C) Well, you have a few options.

17. Isn't the dinner with the Arts Committee tonight?
(A) A table for eight, please.
(B) I completely forgot.
(C) Yes, we had a great time.

18. Have you learned how to request vacation time?
(A) Yes, Emily showed me this morning.
(B) Visiting my family.
(C) Sometime near the end of the month.

19. We need three copies of the contract.
(A) Kate already has one.
(B) The second floor printer.
(C) I don't need any more coffee.

20. Should we have the lunch meeting at the restaurant on Clement Street?
(A) We can't get a reservation now.
(B) To discuss a design.
(C) I'll have the soup and salad.

21. Where are the IT request forms?
(A) Yes, a new keyboard.
(B) Later this afternoon.
(C) Kyle can take care of it.

22. Didn't you say you'd like to buy a vacuum cleaner?
(A) No, from an online store.
(B) By the washing machine.
(C) Yes, my old one broke.

23. Whose turn is it to take the minutes?
(A) I'll do it again.
(B) Turn right after the light.
(C) Just take a picture.

24. Hi, I'm here for my appointment with Dr. Durat.
(A) Well, that is a good point.
(B) Fill out this form first, please.
(C) Drop it off at the pharmacy.

25. You signed up for the advanced accounting class, right?
(A) Some bills were overdue.
(B) No, there weren't any more spots.
(C) She holds a degree in economics.

26. Do you think we should trim the tree again, or just remove it?
(A) Thanks, it looks great.
(B) It provides a lot of shade.
(C) At the gardening store.

27. Where can I get my security pass?
(A) First thing in the morning.
(B) Check with your supervisor.
(C) Between 8 and 10.

28. Why don't I update the employee titles in the database?
(A) You could do that?
(B) There's another case here.
(C) It was delivered this morning.

29. Have you heard what people are saying about that show?
(A) She missed the meeting.
(B) I thought your painting was beautiful.
(C) All right, let's watch something else.

30. Are you going to tell Dan about the new deadline, or should I?
(A) It was your decision.
(B) No, they haven't heard yet.
(C) Wednesday at noon.

31. The bus to the airport is almost here.
(A) I booked the rental car.
(B) London, for a week.
(C) Tell Martin to hurry.

PART 3

Questions 32-34 refer to the following conversation.

M: Excuse me, could you tell me where the nearest subway station is?
W: Of course. Umm... You just need to continue walking down this street for two blocks, and then turn left at the bank. Then walk for one block, and take another left. You'll see the Hyland Street subway station right in front of you. It's on Line 2.
M: Does that subway line go to the riverfront area? I have tickets for a soccer game that starts in 20 minutes at Winkleman Stadium.
W: Yes, but to be honest, the stadium isn't that far from here. I'm sure you could walk there in about twenty minutes. It might be quicker than waiting on a subway.

32. Why is the man speaking to the woman?
33. What event is the man planning to attend?
34. What does the woman advise the man to do?

Questions 35-37 refer to the following conversation.

M: Good afternoon. I called in a cake order earlier this morning, and it was supposed to be ready by now. Here's the pickup number.
W: Oh, right. I have your order details right here. However, one of the bakers became ill and couldn't come in today. Now I'm way behind schedule. Do you mind waiting another hour?
M: Well, I actually need the cake for a retirement party tonight, and I'm leaving for it soon.
W: I see. Well, if it's okay with you, I have another cake that's already made, and the customer cancelled his order. I believe it's similar to what you wanted.

35. Where is the conversation most likely taking place?
36. According to the woman, what has caused a problem?
37. What does the woman offer to do?

Questions 38-40 refer to the following conversation with three speakers.

W1: Oh, no! The schedule just changed again, Imogene. Now it says the next bus to Arlington won't be here for another 30 minutes.

TEST 3

W2: We can't wait that long. We still have to get downtown from the station, so we'd definitely miss our dinner reservation. It will be cancelled after 6:30.
W1: Let's see if we can ask for some help... Excuse me, if we can't wait for the bus to Arlington, is there another way to get there? We need to be downtown as soon as possible.
M: Well, there's a subway station a couple blocks away. It runs frequently. You'll have to transfer once, but it won't cost any extra if you use your metro card.

38. Where does the conversation probably take place?
39. What are the women concerned about?
40. What does the man suggest the women do?

Questions 41-43 refer to the following conversation.

W: Jonas, a bank customer is here about a late fee on her loan repayment. It's usually automatically deducted from her checking account, but the transfer didn't go through yesterday.
M: Well, yesterday was a holiday.
W: Right, so there shouldn't be a late fee. I don't know how to fix it, though. The late fee was already charged first thing this morning.
M: Hmm.. I'm not sure. For now... Why don't you go ahead and transfer a refund for the fee into her checking account? I'll fix the record on her credit report later.

41. Who most likely are the speakers?
42. What are the speakers mainly discussing?
43. What does the man suggest the woman do?

Questions 44-46 refer to the following conversation.

W: Elliot, you go to baseball games fairly often, right?
M: Yeah, at least once a month.
W: I'm planning my friend's birthday party for next Saturday, and I thought it might be fun to go to a game. Are there any good ones that day?
M: Well, two strong teams will face each other at Three River Stadium. And you're in luck. There's a big discount on the tickets right now to draw more fans to the games.
W: Oh, perfect! Do you know of any places we could eat around there, too?
M: Honestly, just buy food at the ball park. The chili dogs are fantastic.
W: Ok. I'll message my friends right now and see if they're interested. Thanks!

44. Why does the woman ask for a recommendation?
45. What does the man say about the tickets?
46. What does the woman say she will do right away?

Questions 47-49 refer to the following conversation.

W: Bryan?
M: Hi, Melissa. I'm sorry to call after hours, but I know you usually work late at the office. Could you find the home number for our new client, Mr. Mason? I don't have it.
W: Oh, I just got on the subway. I left earlier than usual for an appointment. Is it urgent?
M: Well, there was a big development in his case, but I can't get through to his cell phone.
W: Hmm...that's odd. I'd go back and find it, but I'm already running late. Perhaps there's another number listed on his company's Web site.
M: I'll have to try that. Have a nice evening, Melissa.

47. What does the man say he needs?
48. What does the woman imply when she says, "Oh, I just got on the subway"?
49. What does the man decide to do?

Questions 50-52 refer to the following conversation.

M: I think I know why our mattress sales are down. I've visited some of our competitors' stores, and our prices are always higher than theirs.
W: I agree. A lot of customers come into our store to test how the mattresses feel, but then they leave and buy one somewhere else.
M: That's a real problem. Any ideas on how we can fix this?
W: Well, there isn't much we can do about the prices, but we can include other benefits with a sale. Possibly offering free delivery, or throwing in a two-year warranty at no extra cost.
M: Actually, that's a good plan. Then customers would be more likely to buy from our store.

50. Where do the speakers most likely work?

51. What has caused a problem?
52. What do the speakers decide to do?

Questions 53-55 refer to the following conversation.

W: Hello, Mr. Nielson. This is Penelope calling from the Metro Art Gallery. You left a message saying you're interested in taking part in our upcoming Young Artists Exhibition.
M: I did. I think it would be a good opportunity for me to get some more exposure.
W: I agree. Before we can extend an invitation, though, you need to do an interview with the gallery directors.
M: Oh... that will be difficult. I don't have any vacation time right now that I could use to travel to Chicago.
W: Oh, don't worry about that. The interview can be done over the Internet via webcam. We just need to arrange a time that's suitable for everyone.

53. What are the speakers discussing?
54. What problem does the man mention?
55. What does the woman say to reassure the man?

Questions 56-58 refer to the following conversation.

W: Hiro, I looked over the landscape design you're making for the new football stadium. I'm really impressed!
M: I like it, too. But the clients have a new request for the plans every day, so I don't know what they really want. They've hired us before, right?
W: Yes, to work on some other properties. You can see the old work in the archives. It might help.
M: Hmm... I'll do that. All these changes are making the deadline very tight, though. It's definitely time to change how we make our contracts.
W: How so?
M: We should simply be able to extend the deadline if there are additional requests.

56. Who most likely are the speakers?
57. Why does the man say, "They've hired us before, right"?
58. How does the man want to change the contract?

Questions 59-61 refer to the following conversation.

W: Hello, I'm from Milton Publishing. I have your order of textbooks here for delivery.
W: Wonderful! I'm surprised it arrived so quickly. Fast delivery and fantastic prices: I'm glad we ordered from Milton!
M: You know, we are recognized for having the best prices in educational materials among our competitors. I'll go ahead and unload your order after you sign this receipt.
W: Okay. But... It says there are only 25 books here. That's only half of what I ordered. There must be a mistake.
M: Oh, really? I'm so sorry. Let me call my manager. I'll get this taken care of as fast as possible.

59. What type of business does the man work for?
60. What does the man say the business is known for?
61. What is the problem with the delivery?

Questions 62-64 refer to the following conversation and sign.

M: Roxanne, it's Jaeden. I'm sorry, but I waited too long to buy a last-minute ticket, and now the flight has completely sold out. I'll have to catch the next flight to Pittsburgh.
W: Ah, I warned you! Do you think you'll make it in time for the client dinner, or should I cancel it?
M: I can if I take a taxi straight from the airport, but I definitely won't arrive until after 6 o'clock.
W: Well, I'll message you the restaurant address so you'll know where to go.
M: Thanks. You're the best!

62. Look at the graphic. What is the departure time of the flight that the man will take?
63. What does the woman ask the man about?
64. What does the woman volunteer to do?

TEST 3

Questions 65-67 refer to the following conversation and chart.

W:	New-View Video, how can I help you today?
M:	Hello. I'd like to sign up for your Internet video streaming service for my family. However, my son is currently living in Europe. Can he use it there?
W:	Sure, as long as you sign up for the Family Global package.
M:	Good to hear. Oh, and the first month is a free trial, right?
W:	That's correct. You won't be charged for the global service until next month, but we still need payment details when you register.
M:	All right. Let me give you my credit card information. Just a second.

65. Who most likely is the woman?
66. Look at the graphic. Which monthly rate will the man pay?
67. What will the man most likely do next?

Questions 68-70 refer to the following conversation and phone app.

M:	The weather is going to be terrible this weekend. We have to choose another date for the memorial statue unveiling at Gramercy Park.
W:	Check out the forecast on my weather app. You know, we could have it on a weekday.
M:	True. And look here. Sunny and 25° C would be perfect. Let's do it then.
W:	I'll call WTAP News to let the reporters know when to come.
M:	Ah, I'm glad you remembered. I hope there aren't any other big news stories planned for that day.

68. What activity are the speakers mainly discussing?
69. Look at the graphic. Which day do the speakers choose?
70. What does the woman say she will do?

PART 4

Questions 71-73 refer to the following recorded message.

Thank you for calling Rocky Mountain Goods, the best place in town for all your camping equipment and outdoor clothing. Unfortunately, the store is closed right now. Our normal business hours are 9 A.M. to 6 P.M., Monday through Saturday. Our customers will be pleased to know that due to surplus stock of tents and sleeping bags, our summer sale has been extended by an additional two weeks. If you plan to visit our store, however, please note that our parking lot is closed for resurfacing, so you will need to park elsewhere. We apologize for the inconvenience.

71. What does the store most likely sell?
72. What does the speaker say has been extended?
73. Why does the speaker apologize?

Questions 74-76 refer to the following advertisement.

If you've ever lost an important electronic file, then you want to make sure it never happens again. Byte Bank by InnoTech Industries can help guarantee that your data stays safe and accessible whether you're at the office, at home, or even on vacation. With Byte Bank, you can simply upload any file to our online storage cloud and then view it from any device with an Internet connection. And if you ever have any issues, you can contact our 24/7 customer service team, which recently won the National Better Service Award. Would you like to give Byte Bank a try before paying full price? For a limited time, you can receive half-off your first three months of service.

74. What is being advertised?
75. What has the business received an award for?
76. What offer does the speaker mention?

Questions 77-79 refer to the following announcement.

I'd like to thank you all for coming out to the final night of the Gatlinburg Music Festival. I really enjoyed planning it again this year. Now, as you're all aware, this town has always been famous for being the home of some of the best country and folk guitarists and singers. But this fall, we'll experience something new and exciting, as well as a little different. I've just finished making arrangements with electronic musician and DJ Enrique Marquez, who's agreed to perform at our very own Mulch Theater on April 4. Yes, that Enrique Marquez. It's guaranteed to be a great time and a memorable evening, so make sure you reserve your tickets early.

77. Who is the speaker?
78. According to the speaker, what is Gatlinburg most known for?
79. Why does the speaker say, "Yes, that Enrique Marquez"?

Questions 80-82 refer to the following broadcast.

Good evening, I'm Randal Richards, and tonight's main story is about a new service provided by the city library that should help local residents. Community readers always worry about forgetting the due dates of their books and videos. Well now, a new service has been introduced by the library that will send an automated text message to users to remind them of an approaching return date. The message will tell you the materials you need to return and by when. No more returning your books, hoping they aren't already late. I'll give it a try, too.

80. What is the main topic of the broadcast?
81. What will the listeners now be able to do?
82. Why does the speaker say, "I'll give it a try, too"?

Questions 83-85 refer to the following excerpt from a meeting.

There's one last thing. Please remember that March will be our company's fitness month. I know we've been busy lately, but the company wants everyone to make their health a priority. That's why we'll be dedicating four hours a week of office time to healthy activities. Since eating right is also an important part of fitness, local chef Miranda Tucker will be giving weekly cooking demonstrations that will teach us how to prepare simple, nutritious, and delicious meals. So if any of you would like to attend her classes, or any of our other planned activities, sign up on this sheet that I'll pass around.

83. What is the speaker mainly talking about?
84. Who is Miranda Tucker?
85. What will the speaker do next?

Questions 86-88 refer to the following broadcast.

Welcome back to this episode of Business Insider. Today, we'll be discussing how small businesses can expand their online presence and boost Web site sales. A successful small business can't just be a local corner shop nowadays, so it's crucial to learn how to use the Internet to reach as many customers as possible. Joining us later will be Ashley Reynolds, an expert in business Web design and the keynote speaker at this year's BizTech Conference. She'll talk about how your business can utilize effective search algorithms to really stand out online. And if you like what you learn today, be sure to tune in again tomorrow as we continue discussing another aspect of modern business: social media advertising.

86. What is the topic of today's program?
87. According to the speaker, what did Ashley Reynolds recently do?
88. What are the listeners encouraged to do?

Questions 89-91 refer to the following telephone message.

Hello, this is Evelyn calling from Anfield Home Designs. I received your message regarding the changes you want to make to the bedroom and living room designs I sent to you. It should be possible to change the dining table to the solid oak one you selected, but it's just a little higher in price. You also mentioned that you wanted to swap the sofa and chair set for the more expensive leather ones, but... we can't stretch that far. Finally, regarding the carpet that you want to change, please take a look at the samples that I have sent to you by courier. I'm sure you'll find a color you like.

89. Who most likely is the speaker?
90. What does the speaker mean when she says, "we can't stretch that far"?
91. What has the speaker sent to the listener?

Questions 92-94 refer to the following excerpt from a meeting.

Sorry to call this quick meeting, but I just found out that our major shareholders will be visiting the lab this Thursday for a tour. They're very interested in how we make our new fast-acting headache medicine since they expect it will make the company a lot of money. When they arrive on Thursday, I will guide them through our facility. I know you're all busy, but on that day, please postpone your other projects and make sure you're working on this specific medicine when we stop by your section. After they see how it's made, you can resume your other tasks.

92. What type of business does the speaker work for?
93. What will happen on Thursday?
94. What are the listeners asked to do?

Questions 95-97 refer to the following announcement and deli counter.

Good afternoon, Rex-Mart shoppers! In honor of the national holiday, we're offering huge sales on a variety of summer goods today. Most deals can be found in our flyer, but we're also announcing new savings every hour until 7 P.M., when we'll close early for the holiday. For instance, just now, we've started a special deal at our deli for 10 percent off on all meats. The counters are fully stocked with everything you might need for a nice barbecue – sausages, steaks, chicken, and even fresh fish. And until the end of the hour, the sausages will be an additional 15 percent off. You really don't want to miss a sale like this!

95. What is the store celebrating?
96. When will the event end?
97. Look at the graphic. Which deli counter contains items with an additional discount?

Questions 98-100 refer to the following telephone message and inspection report.

Hello, this is Ron Pert from The Redwood, the small diner on Terrace Avenue. You stopped by yesterday to do a routine health inspection of our restaurant. Umm.. I'm leaving this message because I'm scanning over the ticket, and it seems incomplete. It looks to me that we passed everything on the top half of the sheet. But toward the bottom, there's nothing that indicates why we failed the inspection. What exactly is wrong with our refrigeration? I'd really like to know as quickly as possible so I can fix it. I'm concerned because a new burger franchise opened in town, and we'll lose a lot of business to it if we don't open again soon.

98. Where does the speaker work?
99. Look at the graphic. Which section of the report does the speaker ask about?
100. What does the speaker say he is concerned about?

TEST 4

정답

PART 1

1. (C) **2**. (C) **3**. (D) **4**. (A) **5**. (D) **6**. (B)

PART 2

7. (A) **8**. (B) **9**. (A) **10**. (A) **11**. (A) **12**. (A) **13**. (A) **14**. (B) **15**. (B) **16**. (A) **17**. (C) **18**. (B) **19**. (B)
20. (C) **21**. (B) **22**. (C) **23**. (C) **24**. (A) **25**. (C) **26**. (C) **27**. (C) **28**. (B) **29**. (C) **30**. (A) **31**. (B)

PART 3

32. (D) **33**. (A) **34**. (B) **35**. (C) **36**. (D) **37**. (A) **38**. (A) **39**. (D) **40**. (B) **41**. (A) **42**. (C) **43**. (B) **44**. (D)
45. (B) **46**. (D) **47**. (A) **48**. (B) **49**. (B) **50**. (D) **51**. (B) **52**. (A) **53**. (A) **54**. (C) **55**. (A) **56**. (B) **57**. (D)
58. (D) **59**. (A) **60**. (D) **61**. (A) **62**. (C) **63**. (C) **64**. (C) **65**. (C) **66**. (D) **67**. (C) **68**. (B) **69**. (D) **70**. (C)

PART 4

71. (C) **72**. (A) **73**. (B) **74**. (B) **75**. (C) **76**. (B) **77**. (D) **78**. (D) **79**. (C) **80**. (B) **81**. (C) **82**. (A) **83**. (B)
84. (B) **85**. (D) **86**. (C) **87**. (D) **88**. (A) **89**. (B) **90**. (B) **91**. (C) **92**. (B) **93**. (C) **94**. (D) **95**. (D) **96**. (D)
97. (C) **98**. (A) **99**. (B) **100**. (B)

PART 1

1. (A) She's turning on a copy machine.
(B) She's typing on a keyboard.
(C) She's putting a document on a copier.
(D) She's writing a list on a notepad.

2. (A) He's entering a building.
(B) He's resting against a lamppost.
(C) He's cycling in a city.
(D) He's parking a vehicle on a street.

3. (A) A shop assistant is giving a woman a bag.
(B) Some people are entering a supermarket.
(C) A cashier is putting merchandise into a basket.
(D) Some customers are waiting in line.

4. (A) There are lampposts along the walkway.
(B) Some people are running in a race.
(C) A man is sweeping sand off a path.
(D) Some pedestrians are crossing the street.

5. (A) The man is placing documents on a table.
(B) The woman is handing a menu to a customer.
(C) The man is organizing his workplace.
(D) They're standing behind a counter.

6. (A) Pillows are being arranged on a sofa.
(B) Some reading material is on the floor.
(C) A cabinet drawer has been left open.
(D) A window is facing a street.

PART 2

7. Where do you usually buy your vegetables?
(A) At a stall in the market.
(B) Sure, I'll go with you.
(C) The tomatoes are delicious.

8. What kinds of products does your business manufacture?
(A) That's our best-selling model.
(B) Kitchen appliances.
(C) At various retail stores.

9. Do you know how to use the new self-service checkouts?
(A) Yes, I can help you.
(B) They're next to aisle 20.
(C) We check out at 10 A.M.

10. Pardon me. Is this your ID card?
(A) Oh, I was looking for that.
(B) I'll have it this afternoon.
(C) No, my car is out front.

11. When's the movie theater offering the special deal?
(A) All this month.
(B) A well-known director.
(C) Buy one, get one free.

12. Should I stack the boxes in the warehouse?
(A) Please, if you would.
(B) I opened it already.
(C) Another large order.

13. Could you please take these reports to the conference room?
(A) Sure. Which one are you using?
(B) At the end of the hall.
(C) A large projector screen.

14. Who's the new store supervisor?
(A) She'll do well.
(B) George decided to stay, actually.
(C) It's at the end of Maple Street.

15. This briefcase is on sale, right?
(A) Here's the latest document.
(B) I'm sorry, but it isn't.
(C) In case you want another.

16. When does the train leave?
(A) Check the tickets.
(B) From Platform 10.
(C) It's much faster than by bus.

17. Do you have time to talk about the new designs over dinner?
(A) They're posted online.
(B) The soup was delicious.
(C) I'm completely booked.

18. Should we drive or take a bus to the stadium?
(A) I'd be happy to.
(B) The subway would be best.
(C) A baseball game.

19. Are you signed up for the safety training?
(A) 9 to 12 tomorrow.
(B) I did it last week.
(C) On the factory floor.

20. Hasn't the annual budget been approved yet?
(A) That's good to know.
(B) A yearly spending increase.
(C) The CEO is reviewing it.

21. I'm traveling to Barcelona for my summer vacation.
(A) It's two stops away.
(B) Which airline will you use?
(C) Where was your hotel?

22. Where should we hang the banner?
(A) From the print shop.
(B) Some tape will work.
(C) It's too windy out here.

23. Attendance at your book club increased, right?
(A) Check the library.
(B) A novel by Anne Smith.
(C) Yes, a lot of students joined.

24. Make sure you put on safety goggles whenever you use this machine.
(A) Sure, I'll keep that in mind.
(B) It will be installed tomorrow.
(C) No, I haven't heard anything.

25. How was the parade yesterday?
(A) That sounds fun.
(B) From 10 to 12.
(C) It wasn't what I expected.

26. What is this suit made of?
(A) Made in Italy.
(B) Let's get your measurements.
(C) It's a wool and linen blend.

27. We can start the slideshow after the speech if you'd like.
(A) Let's meet inside.
(B) Only ten minutes long.
(C) Yes, that will work.

28. Who's picking up the investors from the train station?
(A) The 5:38 train.
(B) It should be in the e-mail.
(C) Coming from Birmingham.

29. How did the client like the artwork?
(A) Maybe another day.
(B) A family portrait.
(C) You don't want to know.

30. Which of the sandwich options is the least popular in the café?
(A) We just collected the surveys this morning.
(B) From what I heard, they really didn't like it.
(C) Let's try some different bread.

31. You've prepared the documents, haven't you?
(A) By express mail.
(B) I thought we had more time.
(C) Yes, a pair of shoes.

PART 3

Questions 32-34 refer to the following conversation.

M: Good afternoon. I'm calling about ordering some uniforms for my tech company's soccer team.
W: OK. Do you have a design in mind? If not, you can use our Web site to view different styles, including colors and logos. Then you can submit your order through the site, too.
M: Oh, I'll just do that. But... we have a big tournament next month. Will the uniforms be ready by then?
W: I guarantee it. I can even have your order ready by the end of this week.

32. What are the speakers mainly discussing?
33. According to the woman, how should the man submit information?
34. What does the man say will happen next month?

Questions 35-37 refer to the following conversation with three speakers.

M1: It's time for me to buy a new bed. My current one is too old. Jasmine and Nathan, do you have any idea which brand I should look into?
W: Have you heard of Sandman Mattresses and Beds? I bought one of their beds for my guest room, and I love the special foam in its mattress – much more comfortable than other materials.
M2: Yeah, I agree. I bought a pillow from them that is made with the same foam. It was a 'buy two-get one free' deal, so I have an extra one that I'm not using.
M1: Oh, could I try it? I'd like to know how it feels.
M2: Sure.

35. What product is being discussed?
36. What does the woman like about the product?
37. What does Nathan agree to do?

Questions 38-40 refer to the following conversation.

W: Hello, I'm calling about some computer hardware I bought at your store recently. It's a Slim Speed graphics card. I finally installed it yesterday, but it isn't compatible with my computer. Could I trade it for another?

M: It shouldn't be a problem. When you come in, take it to the customer service desk. They can help you.
W: I'm worried I bought it too long ago, though. I think it has been more than two weeks, but I at least still have my receipt.
M: Well, we have a 30-day trade-in policy, so I'm sure it's okay. When you visit the store, just remember to bring your receipt.

38. What is the woman calling about?
39. What does the woman say she is worried about?
40. What does the man remind the woman to bring?

Questions 41-43 refer to the following conversation.

M: Congratulations on finishing the training program, Ms. Han. I hear you'll be joining the Art and Design Team on the sixth floor now. Are you excited?
W: I am. I've worked hard to get an advertising job like this, and I'm ready to be a part of the agency.
M: I'm sure you'll do great, and this is a promising start to a successful career. Do you know which project you'll be working on?
W: Yes. I'll be creating magazine ads for Huxley Motor Oil. In fact, I need to present some artwork to their representative on Friday. Would you give it a look before then?

41. Why does the man congratulate the woman?
42. Where do the speakers most likely work?
43. What will take place on Friday?

Questions 44-46 refer to the following conversation with three speakers.

W: Mitch, I need some help fixing the sound system in Theater C. The audio is coming through with a lot of static.
M1: I need to take over at the ticket booth, but a film in Theater A just finished, so...
W: Yeah, but you know we have a full schedule because of the film festival, and the next showing starts in 20 minutes.
M2: It's probably just because of a few old auxiliary cables.
M1: I bet that's it. Just try replacing them.
W: Where can I find new ones?
M2: I know we just received a shipment of them. Ask your shift manager; he should know.
W: I'll do that. Thanks.

44. What does the woman need help doing?
45. Why does Mitch say, "a film in Theater A just finished"?
46. What will the woman most likely do next?

Questions 47-49 refer to the following conversation.

M: Hello, this is William Tice, project manager at the Primm Natural Gas Company. I need to rent some heavy machinery from you so we can repair some supply pipes. I think we'll need a backhoe for digging.
W: Sure, we have plenty available. In fact, we just purchased a new one that's ready for rental. What dates would you like to use it?
M: September 12 and 13. That should be enough time to finish, even if we run into some problems on the job.
W: OK. I'll start drawing up the agreement. Oh, and could I get your driver's license number? We'll need it for insurance purposes.

47. Where does the man work?
48. What does the man want to do?
49. What does the woman ask the man to do?

Questions 50-52 refer to the following conversation.

M: Good evening, Ms. Jung. How are you enjoying your first day at our resort? Does the room meet your expectations?
W: Oh, it's really quite comfortable, but there is one problem. The personal safe in my room – I followed the instructions, but I couldn't get it to open.
M: Ah, that one has been malfunctioning lately. I'll have Philip from the front desk bring a new one to your room.
W: I'd appreciate it.
M: Oh, if you aren't busy right now, the sun is about to set. Why don't you take your camera down to the beach? You'll be able to get some great pictures.

50. What problem does the woman mention?
51. What will the man ask Philip to do?
52. What does the man suggest the woman do?

Questions 53-55 refer to the following conversation.

W: Brendan, I just looked at the movie posters you created for *The First Star*. They look great, but the posters that will go up around Seattle don't even feature the main actor, only the supporting cast. Why are they different from the rest?

M: Oh, I read in a magazine that a few members of the cast are from Seattle, so I thought I would feature them in one poster. I figured it would have a positive effect on the ticket sales in that area.

W: Hmm.. I didn't know that. Could I take a look at the article? If that strategy is effective, then I'll consider making it a part of the plan for future films. Next time, though, stick to the original design.

53. What question does the woman have about a promotional campaign?

54. Which department does the man most likely work in?

55. What does the woman ask to see?

Questions 56-58 refer to the following conversation.

M: Hello, Ms. Anderson. I'd like to talk to you about all of the service requests the IT Department has been receiving lately.

W: I heard you've been quite busy in the past few weeks. Can you handle them?

M: Yes, but we keep fixing easily preventable problems. Employees continue to download programs full of hidden viruses, and it's causing us to lose progress on other important projects.

W: Hmm.. we can't transfer anyone to your department like last time. But what if I were to give a presentation on Internet security procedures?

M: That should help. Do you need me to do anything?

W: Just get me a list of the programs they should avoid, and that should be enough.

56. What does the man say is a problem?

57. How does the woman propose solving the problem?

58. What does the woman ask the man to do?

Questions 59-61 refer to the following conversation.

M: Good morning, Ms. Wolfe.

W: Hello, Mr. Cardin. The Marketing Department would like an update on the new travel app's development. How's the progress on the hotel search engine? Does it work?

M: Actually, it's already running smoothly. We might even be finished by next month.

W: Wow! That wasn't what I was expecting. It will be nice to have it ready well before launch.

M: I know. I'm excited about it, too. We might even be able to release it earlier than expected.

W: Well, let me check the Marketing Team's plan. They already have an advertising schedule in mind, and they're supposed to send me a copy this afternoon.

59. What are the speakers mainly discussing?

60. What does the woman imply when she says, "Wow! That wasn't what I was expecting"?

61. What will the woman receive soon?

Questions 62-64 refer to the following conversation and Web site.

M: How's the menu for the Eco First vegetarian dinner coming along? The organizer would like to know the courses we're preparing.

W: I'm almost finished. I have several appetizers and a few main dishes planned, but I can't come up with enough variety for the entrées. The cooking sites I use all feature the same ingredients in their vegetarian recipes.

M: Do you use souper-chef.com? We just started a trial membership, so you can access their entire database. The site specializes in utilizing various unique ingredients, and it has a great variety of recipes in every category. I'm sure it will have what you need.

62. What project is the man working on?

63. Look at the graphic. Which category will the woman most likely search?

64. Why does the man recommend using recipes from souper-chef.com?

Questions 65-67 refer to the following conversation and sign.

W: Hi, Kevin. I want to thank you again for coming in to work the evening shift. I know you were really busy working this morning, too.
M: I need the extra hours, and I know the other kitchen staff members are feeling sick.
W: Well, I'm glad you're here. But... I noticed that you're wearing sneakers.
M: Oh, it started to rain while I was walking home this afternoon, so my work shoes got wet.
W: Well, I think we have an extra pair in the back that should fit you. Sorry, but it's important to wear shoes with proper grip in the kitchen, for your own safety.
M: I understand. I'll go and check.

65. What does the woman thank the man for?
66. What happened to the man this afternoon?
67. Look at the graphic. Which safety & hygiene rule are the speakers discussing?

Questions 68-70 refer to the following conversation and label template.

W: Adam, our new frozen burritos are becoming really popular, especially on university campuses. I think we should increase our advertising to students; it's a large and profitable market.
M: Well, let's push back our other deadlines and focus on promoting our burritos then.
W: OK. I'll make the changes to our work schedule.
M: Oh, and since you're here, I'm finishing up the label for the backside of the new flavor's wrapper. Take a look at this printout.
W: It looks neat. But... three minutes? It's the spicy chicken flavor, so three and a half minutes is the ideal cooking time.
M: Oh, yeah, I forgot. I'll fix it later.

68. What does the woman say they will need to do?
69. What does the man suggest?
70. Look at the graphic. Which section of the label will the man need to revise?

PART 4

Questions 71-73 refer to the following telephone message.

Good morning, Mr. Lutz. This is Christian Garner from Garner's Print Shop. I'm calling about the catalogues you want us to print for your new electronics shop. It's important that you pick the kind of paper you want us to use so we can finish your order. You want to mail them out before the grand opening, which you said is on March 3. That's only two weeks away. If you're concerned about the cost, you should use the price estimator on our Web site. That will give you an idea of how much each option would be. I'll talk to you soon.

71. What is the speaker calling about?
72. According to the speaker, what will take place on March 3?
73. What does the speaker say is available on a Web site?

Questions 74-76 refer to the following talk.

Hello, everyone, and welcome to your first orientation session at Pinnacle Software Studios. I'm sure you're all excited to start your new jobs, and I know we're happy to have you join our software development team. This morning, we'll go over your basic job responsibilities and benefits. But first, please take a moment to fill out a name tag, and feel free to write your preferred nickname if you have one. Finally, you'll have some time to explore our rather large campus, so you can pick up a floor map from the back of the room to make sure you don't get lost. You'll have some free time after lunch, which will be around noon.

74. What kind of company does the speaker work for?
75. What are the listeners asked to do first?
76. What does the speaker say is available in the back of the room?

Questions 77-79 refer to the following talk.

Good morning, everyone. Welcome to today's tour of Old Belleview Town. I'll be showing you around the beautiful old streets of Belleview this morning, and we'll be stopping off at various local businesses and markets along the way. Many of you have already asked me about the town's beginnings as a fishing port, but I'm afraid that's not my area of expertise. If you check the tour itinerary, you'll see that Ms. Dawson will discuss the town's history this afternoon. Now, the first thing we'll do this morning is enjoy some of the town's famous breakfast waffles and sausages at a nearby café. I'm sure you'll all be very impressed.

77. Who is the speaker most likely talking to?
78. What does the speaker mean when he says, "Ms. Dawson will discuss the town's history this afternoon"?
79. What will the listeners most likely do next?

Questions 80-82 refer to the following excerpt from a meeting.

I'm glad you could all make time in your busy schedules to come to this meeting. Again, I'm sorry for moving up the deadline for the next issue's articles. The Publishing Department just needs an earlier start to meet the higher demand. Anyway, we have something important to discuss. I've been studying the feedback from our subscribers lately, and there's a common complaint. Most readers find our Web site to be boring. And since a lot of people prefer to access our content via the Internet, I've decided to hire a Web developer who can improve our page. I'll post the position on Tuesday, so hopefully we can start interviews by next week.

80. What does the speaker apologize for?
81. According to the survey, what are customers dissatisfied with?
82. What will happen on Tuesday?

Questions 83-85 refer to the following news report.

For our top story tonight, the Bainbridge city council has voted to secure the funds for the construction of a brand new community center. This building will be available for numerous public events and house several sports facilities, including basketball and tennis courts. The driving force for the decision was to give youths in the area access to organized and safe activities. To that end, the council is working with Heads Up Development, a non-profit organization, to recruit skilled teachers and local talent who can coach sports teams and lead community classes. And if you have a request for the new community center, you can call Councilman Hines at his office to share your idea. Here's how you can reach him.

83. What is the news report mainly about?
84. According to the speaker, what will Heads Up Development do?
85. What are the listeners invited to do?

Questions 86-88 refer to the following telephone message.

Hi, Ms. Horatio. This is Peter Craft from Epic Recruiting. I'm glad you decided to contact me. With your upcoming expansion, I think you're making the smart choice to use our recruiting company to increase your workforce. You'll see that we're more effective and efficient than in-house hiring methods thanks to our wide-reaching network and finely tailored applicant algorithms. We guarantee to find the best workers for your company. In fact, we just did some follow-up research on Cross Water Manufacturing, who we recently worked with, and they're enjoying their highest employee retention rate ever. I'll be on vacation next week, but I hope we can arrange some plans before then.

86. What type of industry does the speaker work in?
87. Why does the speaker say, "they're enjoying their highest employee retention rate ever"?
88. What does the speaker say he will do next week?

Questions 89-91 refer to the following talk.

Destiny Athletic Company is delighted to introduce its newest footwear at this year's ALC Sportswear Convention: the Destiny Light 7 sneakers. These sneakers are an updated version of the Destiny Light 6 sneakers, and they're designed for use in all types of sports. When you insert your feet into the shoes, the laces will immediately tighten to provide maximum stability and comfort. This means that you don't need to spend time tying the laces yourself. Now, I'd like to show you how these sneakers work. So, please watch closely as I put a pair of them on.

89. What is the purpose of the talk?
90. What feature of the sneakers does the speaker mention?
91. What will the speaker most likely do next?

Questions 92-94 refer to the following telephone message.

Hello Eugene, it's Alexa. I apologize, but we'll have to reschedule our meeting this afternoon. The clients from Asia flew in a day earlier than we expected, so they'll require my full attention. However, I had some time this morning to read through your proposal for establishing an office on the West Coast. It looks like it would help us to stay in better contact with our overseas partners and improve company communications. But, the fact remains that the majority of our client base is situated in New York. We'll discuss it more later.

92. Why is the speaker canceling today's meeting?
93. According to the speaker, what was the listener's proposal about?
94. What does the speaker imply when she says, "We'll discuss it more later"?

Questions 95-97 refer to the following telephone message and parking directory.

Good morning, Mr. Burton. I'm glad we're finally meeting face-to-face tomorrow. The advertising sponsorship your company has proposed could be a very exciting and lucrative opportunity for the Lakeside Amusement Park. You know that our main offices are located within the park itself, so you'll need to know where to go when you get here. Oh, and of course, remember to pick up your visitor pass from the ticket booth. Now, since you're driving, you'll want to park in the lot closest to our offices. That way, you won't have to walk all over the park. So, find the Yellow Lot, and then come in through the first entrance of that lot. Our headquarters is right next to it.

95. What will most likely be discussed at the meeting?
96. What should the listener do at the ticket booth?
97. Look at the graphic. Which entrance is the speaker's office located at?

Questions 98-100 refer to the following excerpt from a meeting and chart.

Last on the agenda is a quick look at our recent customer survey about what our audience would like to see from the next video game in the Dragon Sword series. Now, we've already promised to improve the visuals from the last title. There were a lot of complaints, so these results aren't surprising. However, this 25% response wasn't expected. That's enough people that I think we should do something about it. So, to meet that goal, we've decided to hire more staff members. We'll start looking at applications this week, with interviews soon to follow.

98. Who most likely are the listeners?
99. Look at the graphic. Which category is the speaker concerned about?
100. What has the company decided to do?

TEST 4

TEST 5

정답

PART 1

1. (B) **2**. (D) **3**. (C) **4**. (B) **5**. (C) **6**. (A)

PART 2

7. (C) **8**. (B) **9**. (C) **10**. (B) **11**. (B) **12**. (A) **13**. (A) **14**. (C) **15**. (A) **16**. (A) **17**. (C) **18**. (A) **19**. (C)

20. (B) **21**. (A) **22**. (C) **23**. (B) **24**. (C) **25**. (A) **26**. (A) **27**. (A) **28**. (B) **29**. (B) **30**. (B) **31**. (C)

PART 3

32. (B) **33**. (D) **34**. (C) **35**. (C) **36**. (A) **37**. (A) **38**. (D) **39**. (D) **40**. (A) **41**. (B) **42**. (C) **43**. (D) **44**. (C)

45. (C) **46**. (B) **47**. (D) **48**. (C) **49**. (D) **50**. (B) **51**. (C) **52**. (A) **53**. (B) **54**. (C) **55**. (B) **56**. (B) **57**. (D)

58. (A) **59**. (B) **60**. (C) **61**. (D) **62**. (B) **63**. (D) **64**. (B) **65**. (A) **66**. (C) **67**. (B) **68**. (D) **69**. (B) **70**. (A)

PART 4

71. (B) **72**. (A) **73**. (D) **74**. (D) **75**. (C) **76**. (A) **77**. (A) **78**. (A) **79**. (D) **80**. (B) **81**. (A) **82**. (D) **83**. (C)

84. (B) **85**. (A) **86**. (D) **87**. (B) **88**. (C) **89**. (D) **90**. (B) **91**. (C) **92**. (D) **93**. (C) **94**. (D) **95**. (A) **96**. (D)

97. (B) **98**. (B) **99**. (C) **100**. (C)

PART 1

1. (A) She's searching in her bag.
(B) She's looking in a display case.
(C) She's paying for her purchase.
(D) She's displaying some jewelry.

2. (A) The people are rearranging some furniture.
(B) The counter has been cleared of objects.
(C) The woman is making some coffee.
(D) The man is leaning forward to touch a keyboard.

3. (A) A man is carrying a bucket.
(B) A man is washing a window.
(C) Water is being sprayed from a hose.
(D) A car is being driven on a highway.

4. (A) A truck is being parked in a garage.
(B) Some pedestrians are crossing the street.
(C) Road signs are being set up in an intersection.
(D) A traffic light is being installed.

5. (A) Some people are boarding a boat.
(B) A stone bridge is being built over a river.
(C) Some buildings are located on a hill.
(D) Trees are lined along the shore.

6. (A) Some artworks are hanging on the wall.
(B) Potted plants are growing on a balcony.
(C) Some clothes are being folded.
(D) Some pillows are being arranged on a sofa.

PART 2

7. Where can I find a delivery menu?
(A) About 30 minutes.
(B) Yes, please.
(C) In the break room.

8. When did you move into your new apartment?
(A) Right next to the shopping center.
(B) Last week during the holiday.
(C) It should be the same address.

9. Why are there balloons in the break room?
(A) The refrigerator is full.
(B) I'll pick up the supplies.
(C) Because of Robert's retirement party.

10. How can I get in touch with the hiring consultant?
(A) To request a consultation.
(B) Here's his e-mail address.
(C) Sometime next week.

11. It was a long book, wasn't it?
(A) The bookstore downtown.
(B) Yes, more than 800 pages.
(C) I can't find it.

12. Who's going to organize the investors' meeting?
(A) Owen Proust will.
(B) That will help a lot, thanks.
(C) No, I still have mine.

13. When does the new health club open?
(A) At the end of the month.
(B) Your next health checkup.
(C) On the corner of Tuft Street and Pike Avenue.

14. Do you know where I can find Melissa's office?
(A) It's an official document.
(B) To schedule a meeting.
(C) It's at the end of the hall.

15. Wasn't this report due yesterday?
(A) We needed more data.
(B) Fifteen pages long.
(C) No, you can keep it.

16. Let's go over the building designs tomorrow.
(A) We could just do it now.
(B) He decided to resign.
(C) My office is in that building.

17. Whose turn is it to buy lunch?
(A) Soup and a sandwich.
(B) In the cafeteria.
(C) I got it last time.

18. How should we arrange all of the chairs?
(A) Lauren will show us.
(B) On the lawn.
(C) Please take a seat.

19. Have you completed the machinery training yet?
(A) A training partner.
(B) No, they haven't arrived.
(C) My team doesn't need to do it.

20. Where will the awards dinner be next month?
(A) Every month.
(B) We have a few options.
(C) No, I haven't tried it.

21. Why don't we test the show with an older audience?
(A) That could work.
(B) The show comes on at 8.
(C) I'm expecting around 25.

22. What kind of e-book reader do you have?
(A) I have some time now.
(B) An online store.
(C) Are you interested in getting one?

23. Wouldn't you rather book a hotel near the airport?
(A) Flights start at $250.
(B) I'd like to see the city.
(C) Yes, the trip was fantastic.

24. You charged them for the express service, didn't you?
(A) In three to four days.
(B) That's a good deal.
(C) How much did they pay?

25. Would you like to add airport pickup service to your reservation?
(A) No, I can get a taxi.
(B) Checkout is at 11 o'clock.
(C) A king-size bed, please.

26. Would you like to try another size, or does this one fit?
(A) It fits perfectly, thanks.
(B) That will be $20.
(C) It's a nice jacket.

27. The bill is due on Tuesday.
(A) I thought it was on the 10th.
(B) They're in the mail.
(C) No, I'm really busy.

28. There's an overnight flight to Chicago available, right?
(A) 20 minutes from the station.
(B) Yes, it arrives at 6:30 A.M.
(C) Usually at a friend's apartment.

29. I can't seem to open the attachment.
(A) Yes, they're still open.
(B) Let me upload it online.
(C) We can't see from here.

30. How soon can you meet with the reporter?
(A) It's a sales report.
(B) I'm leaving now.
(C) Bring five copies with you.

31. Should I print copies of the flyer to hand out, or just send invitations via e-mail?

(A) Black and white is fine.

(B) A charity dinner and concert.

(C) Everyone uses social media nowadays.

PART 3

Questions 32-34 refer to the following conversation.

W: Hi, this is Tate Waste Management. How can I help you?

M: Good morning. I just opened a new restaurant on Grand Central Avenue. I need to find a reliable company to handle our waste, especially our used vegetable oil.

W: Of course. We already work with several other restaurants in the area. Our costs are determined by the quantity of waste and the frequency of pick-ups. Do you have this information?

M: Ah, I need to find that out. I'll just go and check how much oil we used yesterday, and then I'll call you back and let you know.

32. Where does the woman work?

33. Why is the man calling?

34. What will the man most likely do next?

Questions 35-37 refer to the following conversation.

W: In theater news, the new musical by Damian Caudill, *Tea Spoons*, has finally opened at the local Montgomery Theater. Cliff Wilson, the director, is here to tell us about the opening night. Mr. Wilson, thanks for coming.

M: The pleasure is mine. Actually, the opening night was quite difficult. For one thing, half of the lights on stage wouldn't turn on! The actors could barely see each other during the first act of the show.

W: Well, you still received some great reviews. Critics especially like the songs, so let's listen to the main track from the show. Afterward, Cliff Wilson can tell us about the lyrics.

35. What is the topic of the conversation?

36. What caused a problem?

37. What will the listeners hear next?

Questions 38-40 refer to the following conversation.

M: Hello. I'd like to buy two tickets for the aquarium.

W: OK. Just to let you know, the sea turtle exhibit is closed right now, but the other five areas are still open.
M: Oh, that's too bad. Turtles are my friend's favorite animal.
W: Ah, I'm sorry. But if it helps, the gift shop is giving away free t-shirts right now. The designs are on the wall behind me; you can choose either the shark or the sea turtle.
M: Hmm... We'll take one of each.
W: Great, just use these coupons at the gift shop then. Oh, and it's next to the Seaside Cafeteria. You should have lunch there; it has a great selection of delicious food to enjoy.

38. What does the man want to do?
39. What is the man asked to choose?
40. What does the woman suggest doing?

Questions 41-43 refer to the following conversation.

M: I'm so glad we started having musicians perform live when they appear on our radio show. I looked at our ratings for last week, and they were higher than ever.
W: Oh, fantastic. I don't like having to move all of the recording gear around the studio, but it seems to be paying off.
M: Yeah, I know. I think more bands are interested in appearing now, too. Have you seen the lineup for the Asheville Acoustic Festival? I have a flyer at home. A lot of good bands are playing.
W: I haven't, but some of them might like to be on the show.
M: Then I'll bring it with me tomorrow.

41. Where do the speakers most likely work?
42. What does the woman say she dislikes doing?
43. What does the man say he will bring to work tomorrow?

Questions 44-46 refer to the following conversation.

M: Oh, hi, Kelly. I thought you left a while ago. Do you need a ride home? It's raining pretty hard.
W: Do you mind? My car is still in the shop, and I can't wait for a bus in this weather.
M: Didn't your car break down last week? I thought it would be fixed by now.
W: Yeah, but a special part had to be shipped from overseas.
M: Oh, that's unfortunate. At least we live in the same part of town, so let me know if you still need help tomorrow too.
W: I really appreciate it. Let me buy you dinner as a way of saying thanks.

44. What does the man offer to do?
45. According to the man, what happened last week?
46. Why does the woman say, "a special part had to be shipped from overseas"?

Questions 47-49 refer to the following conversation with three speakers.

M1: Haejin and Josh, I appreciate your help with interviewing the applicants for the sports columnist position today. I needed multiple opinions, especially since we had such impressive candidates.
W: Yeah, I was surprised. Any one of them would be a great fit for our newspaper.
M2: True, but I think we all agree that we found the right person. Should we still have more interviews tomorrow?
M1: Hmm... we shouldn't waste anyone's time. Josh, would you call the other applicants and cancel their interviews as soon as possible?

47. Where do the speakers work?
48. What were the speakers surprised by?
49. What has Josh been asked to do next?

Questions 50-52 refer to the following conversation.

W: Good morning, Anders. You've been consulting with us about our financial situation for six months now. As the CEO, I'd like to know what you think about the state of the company.
M: Some departments needed to cut back on their spending when I first started, but now your accounts are balanced. I expect you'll start seeing more growth next quarter.
W: That's good to hear. As you know, there are only a couple of weeks left on our contract together. However, I'm very pleased with your work. Would you consider joining us as our new head of accounting?
M: Wow, I didn't expect that. I'll have to think about it.

50. Who most likely is the man?
51. What does the woman ask for?
52. What does the man receive?

Questions 53-55 refer to the following conversation.

W: Estevan, thanks for coming to discuss the landscaping at my resort. Everyone I spoke to highly recommended you.
M: I'm glad you contacted me. And yes, I've done a lot of landscaping work at other luxury hotels and resorts recently. Now, what don't you like about your existing layout?
W: Well, it's too complicated. The grounds crew has trouble maintaining all the different plants.
M: I see. I believe a simple design would be a good solution then. Minimalism and wide open spaces are in style right now, too.
W: That's what I was thinking. So how soon could you start?
M: I'll finish my current project with a downtown hotel in two weeks. Then I'll start on your plans.

53. Who is the man?
54. What problem does the woman mention?
55. What does the man say he will complete in two weeks?

Questions 56-58 refer to the following conversation with three speakers.

W: Hi, Bob, Joshua... I'm sorry, but the board members weren't too enthusiastic about the design you came up with for our new logo.
M1: Oh, that's a shame. We worked really hard on that.
M2: Yes, what exactly didn't they like about it?
W: Well, they thought that the combination of brown and black was rather unattractive. Do you think you can explain things to them?
M1: Yes! We can show them why those colors will seem modern and professional to our clients.
M2: Exactly. I'll start working on some presentation slides right away. Susie, do you think you can set up a meeting?
W: Sure, I'll deal with that now.

56. What are the speakers mainly discussing?
57. What problem does the woman mention?
58. What do the men agree to do?

Questions 59-61 refer to the following conversation.

W: Hi, Hugo. I wanted to let you know that everything is prepared for your visit to our Madrid office next Monday. People here can't stop talking about the plans for the company's new refrigerator model.
M: Thanks. I'm excited too, especially regarding one amazing feature.
W: Oh? Which one?
M: This model will use less energy than any other refrigerator on the market, saving our customers money while also being better for the environment.
W: Great! I can't wait to hear more about it. Also, there's an orchestra performance that evening, and we thought you'd like to attend.
M: Oh, my favorite soccer team is playing that night.
W: Ah, I understand. Well, until then!

59. What type of product is being discussed?
60. Which product feature is the man most proud of?
61. Why does the man say, "my favorite soccer team is playing that night"?

Questions 62-64 refer to the following conversation and sign.

W: Hmm... I need to go to this area, so I guess I owe you $12. Is that right?
M: Well, $12 is the normal rate. But... it is rush hour right now.
W: Oh, I didn't realize. Is that a problem?
M: Not at all, but there is an extra fee during this time since we'll be sitting in traffic for a while.
W: OK, I understand. Should I pay you in cash, or just send the money through the mobile application?
M: Either way is fine. But if you would, please remember to give me a good driver rating and positive feedback. It will help me get more customers.

62. Look at the graphic. Where is the woman going?
63. Why does the man say the trip will cost extra?
64. What does the man remind the woman to do?

Questions 65-67 refer to the following conversation and schedule.

W: Our flight isn't until the early evening, so I was thinking that we could take a tour of Olsen Grand Station today. You know, it was one of the largest train stations in the country.

M: Well, we haven't booked our spots in advance. Can we still get tickets?

W: I'm sure of it. We just need to keep in mind that our hotel checkout is at 2 P.M.

M: Oh yeah, we can make it back by then. I just brought up the Olsen Grand Station Web site on my laptop. Oh, this should be the perfect time – there are still four tickets available.

W: Great! Go ahead and buy them now.

65. What do the speakers plan to tour?
66. What does the woman remind the man about?
67. Look at the graphic. Which tour will the speakers buy tickets for?

Questions 68-70 refer to the following conversation and menu.

W: Oh, Ramone, thanks for coming in on short notice. I didn't expect our café to be so busy on a Tuesday morning.

M: There are a lot of people here. Maybe it's because of the conference being held down the street. Anyway, are we ready for the lunch rush?

W: Well, it usually starts around 11 o'clock. Oh, and someone forgot to put the cheese back in the refrigerator last night, so we can't use any of it. I'm going to change the menu so the customers will know that sandwich isn't available today.

M: You know what? I'll make my special sauce so we can offer an option other than cheese today.

68. Why is the woman surprised?
69 Look at the graphic. Which item will be removed from the menu?
70. What will the man probably do next?

PART 4

Questions 71-73 refer to the following telephone message.

Hi, Louise. This is Frank, the manager of the sports store. I'm calling because I'd like you to start your shift one hour early tomorrow morning. I'll be there to receive a large shipment of new ice hockey equipment, and I'd like you to create a display using the new merchandise before the store opens. I've also contacted Rachel, and she has agreed to come in. If you both work together, I'm sure you'll get the task finished before opening time. And I'll give you both tickets for the next basketball game at King Plaza. Please let me know if you're able to help. Thanks.

71. What kind of a business does the speaker manage?
72. Why should the listener come to work early tomorrow?
73. What does the speaker offer the listener?

Questions 74-76 refer to the following advertisement.

Are you looking for a healthy beverage that can help you lose weight and provide all the nutrients you'd normally get from a balanced meal? Then... Stop what you are doing! I'm here to tell you about the brand new range of Wonder Shakes, available in all major supermarkets and health stores. Wonder Shakes combine natural ingredients and fruit juice with a wide variety of vitamins and health supplements. We recommend that you drink one shake per day, instead of a regular meal. For a chance to win a free pack of our delicious milkshakes, visit our Web site at www.wondershakes.com.

74. What is being advertised?
75. What does the speaker mean when she says, "Stop what you are doing"?
76. According to the speaker, what can listeners do on a Web site?

Questions 77-79 refer to the following excerpt from a meeting.

I'd like to start this meeting with exciting news. August Studios has decided to present its game developers, everyone in this room, with a career-defining opportunity. The company has purchased a brand new digital design engine, and we'll be the first to use it. What makes this engine so advanced is its VR capability, meaning we can work on our projects, in real time, in virtual reality. This opens up all kinds of new possibilities. A representative will be here Friday to give us a demonstration. I can't wait to see what we can do.

77. Who most likely are the listeners?
78. According to the speaker, what aspect of the new software is particularly interesting?
79. What does the speaker say will happen on Friday?

Questions 80-82 refer to the following instructions.

Gather around, everyone. It should be a busy night tonight, so stay focused and try to push tonight's dinner special. It's a 9 ounce porterhouse steak served with garlic-roasted shrimp, a twice-baked potato and a side salad. We only have enough for 15 orders, so keep each other updated on how many you sell. Also, we really need to increase our dessert sales. I'd describe all the cakes we have available, but, well, this isn't your first night. And finally, you might've heard, but there's a change to the employee meal policy. Instead of a 50% discount per shift, your meal will now be entirely free.

80. What does the speaker ask the listeners to do?
81. What does the speaker imply when she says, "This isn't your first night"?
82. What does the speaker say about the employee meals?

Questions 83-85 refer to the following announcement.

Attention, ladies and gentlemen. We're pleased to announce a new program here at the Epsom National History Museum. We really care about youth education, so we would like you, our patrons, to consider registering your children for one of our new history classes, which will run every Saturday here at the museum. You can choose from five different classes, based on different age groups. All classes will be led by a knowledgeable expert on our national history. If you think your child might enjoy this learning experience, our museum curator Olivia Treadwell will be giving a detailed presentation on the program in fifteen minutes.

83. Why is a new program being started?
84. What are the listeners invited to do?
85. Who is Olivia Treadwell?

Questions 86-88 refer to the following excerpt from a meeting.

Good morning, everyone, and thanks for coming in today. As employees of the company's Human Resources Department, it is up to us to provide morale-improving, team-building activities that our staff members can look forward to. So let's see where we're at with this autumn's hiking trip. We've waited to have it later this year, and since the weather will be changing soon, we need to remind everyone to dress warmly for this trip. I'll send out a memo later this week. Now, we also have to choose the date, so take a look at these work calendars I'm handing out and let us know of any important deadlines that aren't included on it.

86. What is the talk mainly about?
87. According to the speaker, what will change soon?
88. What does the speaker want the listeners to do next?

Questions 89-91 refer to the following tour information.

OK, everyone. We'll park our tour van here, and then you'll have the next three hours to hike around the western area of the park at your leisure. You can follow a trail, go for a swim, or stay here and rest. If you're not sure of what to do, I always enjoy visiting Sumac Falls. So, whatever you do, remember that we'll meet again in three hours. We'll drive back to the park's visitor hall, and at 6 o'clock the director will give a short lecture about the biodiversity of the surrounding area. It's always interesting, so you'll definitely want to stick around for it.

89. Who most likely is the speaker?
90. Why does the speaker say, "I always enjoy visiting Sumac Falls"?
91. What is planned for 6 o'clock?

Questions 92-94 refer to the following broadcast.

This is Maxine with WTAP Nightly News. For tonight's main story, the new Nelsonville Music Festival continues to grow. As the festival organizers prepare the fairgrounds, it's been announced that seven more bands from around the country have joined the lineup. Attendance is expected to be even higher now. However, the opinions of locals remain split. Some are worried about all the extra people who will be staying in town for the festival, but others are looking forward to the extra business they'll be bringing and the live entertainment. I'm here at Athena Park where I'll ask some Nelsonville residents how they feel about the upcoming event.

92. What does the speaker say has recently been announced?
93. According to the speaker, what makes some people dislike the festival?
94. What will the speaker do next?

Questions 95-97 refer to the following recorded message and schedule.

Hi, Ye Sung, this is Claire. I just sent you a first draft of our upcoming performance schedule. I'd like to talk with you about doing an extra show on the 25th, possibly in the afternoon as a matinée. I'm overseeing a recording session tomorrow morning, but I have some time in the afternoon because my phone interview with WXR Classical Radio was canceled. It will only give me an hour, but it shouldn't take long to talk. Call me back if you're available.

95. What does the speaker want to discuss with the listener?
96. What does the speaker say she will lead tomorrow morning?
97. Look at the graphic. When will the speaker and the listener most likely meet?

Questions 98-100 refer to the following excerpt from a meeting and diagrams.

I'd like to start by thanking you all for volunteering to organize our annual community craft fair. This year's fair will include many well-known artists and craftspeople from our local area. Also, because it is being held in Leland Park, which is an easy location for most people to visit, we expect a larger attendance than we have ever received in the past. Now, we need to start erecting the vendor tents in Leland Park. We should arrange the tents in a way that allows people to easily walk through the park and see all of the vendors. So, when walking from the main gate, there should be one row of tents on the left side, and another row of tents on the right. Who wants to be in charge of setting up all these tents?

98. What kind of event is being organized?
99. Why is the speaker expecting attendance to be high?
100. Look at the graphic. Which arrangement will be used in Leland Park?

TEST 6

정답

PART 1

1. (B) **2**. (B) **3**. (C) **4**. (C) **5**. (D) **6**. (B)

PART 2

7. (B) **8**. (B) **9**. (C) **10**. (A) **11**. (A) **12**. (B) **13**. (C) **14**. (C) **15**. (A) **16**. (C) **17**. (A) **18**. (A) **19**. (C)
20. (A) **21**. (C) **22**. (C) **23**. (C) **24**. (A) **25**. (C) **26**. (A) **27**. (B) **28**. (B) **29**. (A) **30**. (B) **31**. (C)

PART 3

32. (A) **33**. (B) **34**. (B) **35**. (B) **36**. (B) **37**. (A) **38**. (B) **39**. (C) **40**. (B) **41**. (C) **42**. (A) **43**. (D) **44**. (C)
45. (D) **46**. (B) **47**. (C) **48**. (D) **49**. (B) **50**. (B) **51**. (B) **52**. (A) **53**. (D) **54**. (B) **55**. (D) **56**. (B) **57**. (A)
58. (D) **59**. (C) **60**. (A) **61**. (C) **62**. (B) **63**. (C) **64**. (A) **65**. (C) **66**. (A) **67**. (D) **68**. (B) **69**. (C) **70**. (A)

PART 4

71. (B) **72**. (A) **73**. (A) **74**. (B) **75**. (C) **76**. (B) **77**. (C) **78**. (A) **79**. (D) **80**. (C) **81**. (D) **82**. (D) **83**. (B)
84. (B) **85**. (A) **86**. (B) **87**. (A) **88**. (C) **89**. (C) **90**. (D) **91**. (B) **92**. (A) **93**. (B) **94**. (C) **95**. (B) **96**. (D)
97. (B) **98**. (A) **99**. (C) **100**. (D)

PART 1

1. (A) He's trying on a shirt.
(B) He's examining a piece of clothing.
(C) He's paying for a purchase.
(D) He's looking in a store window.

2. (A) They're walking toward a doorway.
(B) One of the women is pushing a wheelbarrow.
(C) One of the women is carrying a bag on her shoulder.
(D) They're working on a construction site.

3. (A) A woman is setting up a display area.
(B) A man is putting on an apron.
(C) A man is talking with a customer.
(D) A man is placing merchandise in a cart.

4. (A) Water is being poured into glasses.
(B) Some chairs have been stacked next to a table.
(C) A floral arrangement has been placed on a table.
(D) Some chairs are occupied.

5. (A) A woman is carrying shopping bags.
(B) Some people are fishing on a river bank.
(C) A man is getting into a building.
(D) Some people are walking on a bridge.

6. (A) A light fixture has been mounted on the wall.
(B) A cabinet has been stocked with binders.
(C) Chairs are being pushed under the desk.
(D) A computer is being plugged in.

PART 2

7. Where's a good spot for the electronics expo?
(A) It wasn't that good.
(B) Seoul would be ideal.
(C) A lot of new technology.

8. Why did Kevin arrive early this morning?
(A) At 8 o'clock.
(B) To help with the sales report.
(C) Yes, he left before I did.

9. Is the cafeteria going to have a rice cooker?
(A) She's not here today.
(B) No, it's my favorite food.
(C) Yes, two will be available.

10. How do you get to the clinic from here?
(A) It's just across the bridge.
(B) From 9 to 5.
(C) 24-hour medical service.

11. Could you please send an e-mail to the conference organizer?
(A) Okay, but what should it say?
(B) No, I just got it.
(C) Check the attachment.

12. Didn't you say Sarah was going to be moving to another department?
(A) The moving company was great.
(B) Yes, but not until the end of the year.
(C) We ran out already.

13. What did Ms. Monroe think about our strategy?
(A) The department manager.
(B) I wasn't aware of that.
(C) I'll speak with her after lunch.

14. Isn't it better to have more light in the studio?
(A) I already turned it off.
(B) No, this one's too heavy.
(C) I suppose you're right.

15. Who are we interviewing next for the opening in sales?
(A) We're finished.
(B) Where's the break room?
(C) To the HR director.

16. Why weren't our research findings published?
(A) A respected research journal.
(B) Later in September.
(C) They need some more work.

17. Has Ms. Moore been to the dentist yet?
(A) No, she canceled her appointment.
(B) It's a new one on Main Street.
(C) Please take a seat in the waiting room.

18. Would you like to come to the ball game with us?
(A) I already have plans.
(B) She's coming later this evening.
(C) No, it was a lot of fun.

19. Should we get a cake for the party, or do you prefer ice cream?
(A) I agree with you.
(B) At the bakery.
(C) A cake is better.

20. When should we turn in the grant proposal?
(A) The deadline's tomorrow.
(B) Turn left on Myer Street.
(C) The mailroom in the basement.

21. Could you help me move the tables for the meeting?
(A) Do you have enough copies?
(B) I met him last week.
(C) I can after I finish this.

22. May I speak with my colleague briefly?
(A) There isn't another copy.
(B) The third speaker is Mr. Lee.
(C) We don't have any more time.

23. The director wants everyone to be at the theater by 6.
(A) We'll let you know.
(B) About two hours long.
(C) I have a client meeting then.

24. Why did the sales team come to work late?
(A) I have no idea.
(B) You're early.
(C) She's working upstairs.

25. Mr. Pine has taught at the university for a long time, hasn't he?
(A) No, an assistant professor.
(B) Just a few more minutes.
(C) Yes, for about 25 years.

26. Which sandwich is the best at this diner?
(A) I've never been here before.
(B) Just down the road.
(C) No, it's the worst.

27. I'm updating the records that were in the cabinet.
(A) No, I'm almost finished.
(B) I'm not busy right now if you need some help.
(C) A cab would be expensive.

28. Is Mr. Pollock's flight still on schedule for this evening?
(A) Is there one without connections?
(B) It departed from Moscow on time.
(C) To meet with some investors.

29. You reserved the concert tickets, right?
(A) I won't be able to make it.
(B) What are the dinner specials?
(C) A rock band.

30. Do you want to report to the board of directors first, or should I?
(A) No, they haven't.
(B) I need a few more minutes.
(C) All eight board members.

31. How are the online services at Evergreen Bank?
(A) I let them know.
(B) Some people think so.
(C) They're fairly limited.

PART 3

Questions 32-34 refer to the following conversation.

W: Hi, Tyler. Can we talk about the rise in customer complaints we've been experiencing? Customers are waiting longer and longer on the phone when they call to talk about their cable service.
M: I know. It's been like this since we implemented the recent price increase. So many people are calling to ask why their bills are more expensive that my customer service team has just been overwhelmed.
W: I see. Would it help to send a letter to our customers explaining the change?
M: I don't think that's necessary. If we recorded a message that the callers could be automatically directed to, it would take care of the majority of the calls. Then we could focus on other issues.

32. What is the purpose of the conversation?
33. What department does the man work in?
34. What does the man suggest?

Questions 35-37 refer to the following conversation.

M: Good morning, Suki. Have you had breakfast yet? I'm going to try the hotel's breakfast buffet again, but the food really didn't impress me yesterday.
W: Well, there's a diner next to the hotel that might be better. It has a lot of options, and every meal comes with unlimited coffee.
M: Yeah, but... I might as well eat here since it's free. Maybe I just need to get to the buffet earlier in the morning when the food is still fresh.

35. What complaint does the man have about the breakfast service?
36. What does the woman suggest the man do?
37. Why does the man reject the woman's suggestion?

Questions 38-40 refer to the following conversation with three speakers.

W: Hi, Bobby. Hi, Steve. I won two tickets to see a baseball match between the Vipers and the Wallabies. Would you guys like to have them?

M1: Oh, I'm a huge fan of baseball. When's the game?
W: This Friday evening, at Lester Stadium.
M1: Steve, do you fancy it? We could go directly there after we leave the office.
M2: I'd love to, but I don't want to drive on a Friday evening. The traffic will be terrible. How about taking the subway instead?
M1: That sounds good to me.
W: That's settled then! The tickets were sent to me by e-mail, so I'll forward them to you now. You'll just need to print them out yourselves.

38. What type of event is being discussed?
39. What do the men decide to do?
40. What will the woman most likely do next?

Questions 41-43 refer to the following conversation.

W: Our annual holiday concerts with the Mohawk Valley Orchestra are coming up next month, and I want to make sure we're prepared. Did you submit the newspaper advertisement yet?
M: Oh, I actually need to make a few final changes to it. I promise I'll finish it by this afternoon.
W: OK, please do so. What else needs to be done?
M: Well, I just remembered that all of the shows sold out last year, and more people wanted tickets. We don't want that to happen again, do we?
W: Ah, that's right. Why don't we add one more performance on Saturday afternoon? I'm sure all of the members will agree to it.
M: Yeah, that's a good idea.

41. What are the speakers discussing?
42. What does the man say he will do this afternoon?
43. What does the woman suggest?

Questions 44-46 refer to the following conversation.

M: Hello, EunHye. I'm looking for a hotel to stay at during the conference, and I'm thinking about the Point Hotel on Summer Avenue. That's where you're staying, right?
W: Indeed. It has a gorgeous view of the city, and you can see the ocean from the higher floors, too.
M: So I've heard. The scenery is why I want to stay there. I called, and there are only large suites available still. I've asked some of the other workers in my department if they'd want to share a room with me.
W: That's a good idea. Oh, I'm planning to take a tour of some sights around the city Saturday morning, too. You're welcome to join me, especially if it's your first time there.

44. What feature does the woman mention about the Point Hotel?
45. What does the man say he has done?
46. What does the woman invite the man to do?

Questions 47-49 refer to the following conversation.

W1: Oh, hi, Lucinda. You're back from the real estate seminar! How was it?
W: I really enjoyed it, and all of the talks were helpful.
M: Really? I'd love to hear all about it.
W: Well, for example, a speaker named Natalie Romanov recommended that realtors like us read her book on building good relationships with clients. I think it might be a good idea.
M: Sure, we could try that. Building relationships with clients is a key part of our job here.
W: And the good thing is, all seminar attendees were given this voucher to get 25 percent off the book.
M: Great! I tell you what, why don't you go down to the bookstore on your lunch break and grab a copy?
W: I was thinking that I could do that now. My next appointment isn't for another couple of hours.

47. What type of business do the speakers work for?
48. What did Natalie Romanov suggest?
49. What does the woman say she will do?

Questions 50-52 refer to the following conversation.

W: Hey, Antoine, would you mind looking over the sales projections before our meeting with the prospective client?
M: I already checked them this morning. The figures looked pretty accurate, and I think the client will be impressed.
W: Great. It seems like we're ready for our business meeting then. After lunch, I'm going to make sure the conference room is prepared. Will I meet you there around 1?

TEST 6

M: Actually, I have some bad news. I don't think I'll be able to help you with the negotiations this afternoon. I've just been called to head office to deal with an important matter.
W: Oh, but... It's a crucial negotiation, and I just joined the firm.
M: I understand, but you're a better negotiator than I am. I'm sure you can manage fine by yourself.

50. What does the woman ask the man to do?
51. What does the woman plan to do today?
52. Why does the woman say, "I just joined the firm"?

Questions 53-55 refer to the following conversation with three speakers.

W: Sean and Thomas, I'm glad you're here. I've been meaning to ask about your trip to Miami.
M1: Hi, Maria. It was great. The designer showed us his entire clothing line, and he signed off on our distribution agreement.
W: Fantastic. And Thomas, this was your first trip with our company. How was it?
M2: I learned a lot, but we have so many stores around the northeast that I forgot to mention some of the smaller retail locations we have. I was lucky Sean was there to help.
W: Oh, don't worry about it. I'm working on a handbook that you can use next time. It will have a lot of information, including photos and addresses for all of our stores.
M2: Oh, great. Thanks, Maria.

53. Why did the men travel to Miami?
54. What problem does Thomas say he had?
55. According to the woman, what will be included in a handbook?

Questions 56-58 refer to the following conversation.

W: So, this is where we'll have our new studio. The wiring isn't finished yet, but it will be all ready for us to start recording the album in November.
M: I love it! It will be a good place for our band to practice, too.
W: Yeah, there's enough space for all of us and our gear.
M: But... I think there are some apartments next door.
W: That's right. I'll call the contractor later and see what he can do about adding some sound-dampening material to the walls so it won't be so loud.

56. What are the speakers planning to do in November?
57. What does the man mean when he says, "I think there are some apartments next door"?
58. What does the woman say she will do?

Questions 59-61 refer to the following conversation.

M: Hello, is this seat taken? I've been looking forward to seeing Walsh Motors' presentation all week.
W: It's available, and I'm excited, too. There are a lot of new developments in our field. This trade show has been fantastic.
M: I agree. Which company are you with?
W: StarPoint Navigation. I develop the software for our GPS systems.
M: Really? I'm with DuPree Auto. You know, we're actually looking for a new supplier for our vehicles' built-in GPS components.
W: This could be an exciting opportunity then. Here's my business card. Send me an e-mail with more details, and I'll get back to you about your options.

59. Where does the conversation most likely take place?
60. What does the woman's company sell?
61. How does the woman prefer to be contacted?

Questions 62-64 refer to the following conversation and invitation.

M: Hi, is this Kayla Briggs? My name is Rick Townsend. I'm calling to let you know that I plan to come to this year's Hands of Hope fundraising party.
W: Thanks, Rick. I'm glad you'll be joining us. Could you also let me know which meal you'd like?
M: Oh, of course. Umm... for one thing, I don't like seafood.
W: Sure. There are two other options: a three-bean casserole and lemon roasted chicken.
M: Ah... I really don't want the bean dish.

W: That settles it then. And don't forget, we'll have a courtesy valet service for the event, so feel free to drive here without having to worry about parking.

62. What kind of event is being held?
63. Look at the graphic. Which meal will the man have?
64. What does the woman encourage the man to do?

Questions 65-67 refer to the following conversation and fee chart.

W: Pardon me, sir. The next yoga class is starting soon. Are you signed up for it?
M: Yes, I already registered, but I seem to have forgotten my towel. Could I just rent one?
W: Sure, for a small price. All the fees, including towel rentals, are explained on the chart behind me.
M: I'll do that then. Let me get my wallet.
W: Oh, you can pay after the class so you're not late. Go ahead and go inside, and just leave your membership card with me.

65. What does the woman say will happen soon?
66. Look at the graphic. How much will the man have to pay?
67. What will the man most likely do next?

Questions 68-70 refer to the following conversation and signs.

M: Hi, my name is Tobias Wolfe. I saw a sign that said all visitors need to sign in here.
W: That's correct. May I ask your reason for visiting City Hall today?
M: Actually, I'd like to take a tour. I'm interested in historic buildings.
W: Is that so? We've had more visitors ever since the regional museum opened.
M: Oh, I was just there. Do you have any idea where I should start?
W: Here, take this brochure. It has some information about the building's history and shows you where the points of interest are. Let me know if you have any questions.

68. Look at the graphic. Which sign did the man refer to?
69. Why is the man at the city hall?
70. What does the woman give to the man?

PART 4

Questions 71-73 refer to the following telephone message.

Hello, Mr. Fitz. It's Daniel, your realtor. I have some bad news. It turns out that you won't be able to move into your office until next Wednesday, not on Monday as originally planned. The heating and ventilation system need some repairs, and the building's maintenance man still hasn't gotten to them. I'm sorry about that. Anyway, this also means that we'll need to meet again. I need you to sign a new lease since the dates will be different now. Let me know when you're available. Thanks.

71. According to the speaker, what is being delayed?
72. Why does the speaker apologize?
73. What does the speaker ask the listener to do?

Questions 74-76 refer to the following excerpt from a meeting.

And that should conclude a very productive meeting. I'm quite excited that our team has been put in charge of planning the agency's annual team-building trip, and we'll be able to do it at a fairly low cost, all things considered. After lunch, I'll start preparing the presentation that we'll give to the executive board. Once they approve our plans and funding, we can start reserving bus tickets and cabins for everyone. Oh, and speaking of which, please take a look at the campground's Web site. You can see all of the activities that are available, so then we can figure out the day-to-day itinerary.

74. What is the speaker helping to organize?
75. What does the speaker say she will do later today?
76. What does the speaker ask the listeners to do?

Questions 77-79 refer to the following telephone message.

Noah, this is Haley. It's about the city tour we are supposed to do with the designer who is visiting the agency this weekend. I'm really sorry, but something else came up, and you'll have to do it by yourself. I looked over the itinerary you planned, and it looks great. I e-mailed you the address of the café I was telling you about, too; I think you'll both enjoy it. If you need any other ideas, you have my cell phone number.

77. Who is visiting the agency this weekend?
78. What did the speaker send to the listener?
79. Why does the speaker say, "you have my cell phone number"?

Questions 80-82 refer to the following announcement.

Welcome, soccer fans, to Fairview Stadium. We're all excited for today's big game. However, some rain is expected for this afternoon, so I hope you brought an umbrella with you. If not, you can purchase one at any of our concession stands. In more exciting news, we will have a raffle contest today, and the winning ticket will be drawn after the first half of the game. The winner could go home today with a lot of extra money, so if you'd like to buy a ticket and enter, just ask one of the attendants working in each section.

80. Where is the announcement being made?
81. What problem does the speaker mention?
82. According to the speaker, why should the listeners talk with a staff member?

Questions 83-85 refer to the following instructions.

Welcome to the Hindell Building, where your new offices will be. First, we'll stop by the security desk to pick up your ID cards. And, remember, you and your employees will need them, especially since you're on the top floor. The elevators are equipped with scanners. Then, I'll show you a useful map of the area that includes popular transportation routes. Keep in mind, some bus routes have recently changed, so some are now better for morning commuters.

83. Who is the speaker talking to?
84. What does the speaker imply when she says, "The elevators are equipped with scanners"?
85. What does the speaker say has recently changed?

Questions 86-88 refer to the following telephone message.

Hello Alana, it's Ross. I know that you're on night shift duty this month on the assembly line, but we just received a huge request for 500 TMX brake pads that needs to go out as soon as possible. It would help me a lot if you could come in at noon and work the afternoon shift, too. I know it's asking a lot, but I would let you claim both shifts as overtime, which would result in a nice paycheck. Let me know right after you get this message. Thanks in advance.

86. Where does the speaker most likely work?
87. What problem does the speaker report?
88. What will the speaker allow the listener to do?

Questions 89-91 refer to the following excerpt from a meeting.

Welcome, everyone, to the weekly meeting here at our restaurant. Before we begin, I'd like to remind you to check your measurements for new uniforms and send them to the personnel manager by Wednesday. Now, let's start this meeting with some very pleasing news. We are fully booked tonight, for the first time in a few months. I'd like to thank you all for your hard work. Because of your efforts, our restaurant is becoming more and more popular. I had planned to issue you all a bonus payment, but our system is currently being updated, so check your bank accounts in a few days for an extra 100 dollars.

89. What does the speaker remind the listeners to do by Wednesday?
90. What good news does the speaker mention?
91. Why does the speaker say, "our system is currently being updated"?

Questions 92-94 refer to the following announcement.

Before we start, I know you are all tired from another long day in the office, so thank you for staying and working into the evening. It's necessary because we just found an error in our payroll program. And, as you know, paychecks need to go out tomorrow. So, until we fix the error, we need to go through and recalculate each paycheck ourselves. It will take a while, but as one way of saying thanks, I'll buy takeout for everybody this evening from Gino's. Just take a look at this menu and write down your order.

92. What does the speaker thank the listeners for?
93. In which division do the listeners most likely work?
94. What does the speaker say she will provide?

Questions 95-97 refer to the following telephone message and identification badge.

Hi. I'm leaving this message for the manager of the administration office, Georgina Travers. My name is David Wells, and I recently signed up for a six-month membership at Delaney Country Club. I spoke with you in your office yesterday afternoon. You gave me a membership card, but I just noticed that the assigned parking space number on the card is not the correct one. All the other details are fine, though. I'd appreciate it if you could call back whenever it's convenient for you. You can reach me at 555-8112.

95. Which department is the speaker calling?
96. Look at the graphic. What information does the speaker say is incorrect?
97. What does the speaker ask the listener to do?

Questions 98-100 refer to the following announcement and directory.

Welcome, shoppers, to Wire World Electronics! We'll be celebrating New Year's Day this month with fantastic deals throughout the store. For instance, right now we're having a sale on all of our computers, so check out that department to see how much you can save. Desktops, laptops, and even tablet devices have all had their prices dropped for this event! Also, stop by the new game console department to try out some of the most popular video games available. Finally, don't forget to visit our Web site to apply for a Wire World membership card to save even more money on your purchases.

98. Why is the sale being held?
99. Look at the graphic. Which floor is the sale on?
100. According to the speaker, what is available on a Web site?

TEST 7

정답

PART 1

1. (D) **2**. (A) **3**. (B) **4**. (B) **5**. (C) **6**. (B)

PART 2

7. (B) **8**. (C) **9**. (A) **10**. (C) **11**. (B) **12**. (A) **13**. (A) **14**. (B) **15**. (B) **16**. (B) **17**. (C) **18**. (B) **19**. (C)
20. (C) **21**. (B) **22**. (B) **23**. (B) **24**. (C) **25**. (B) **26**. (A) **27**. (A) **28**. (C) **29**. (B) **30**. (A) **31**. (C)

PART 3

32. (A) **33**. (D) **34**. (B) **35**. (A) **36**. (C) **37**. (C) **38**. (D) **39**. (B) **40**. (C) **41**. (C) **42**. (D) **43**. (A) **44**. (C)
45. (D) **46**. (B) **47**. (A) **48**. (D) **49**. (C) **50**. (B) **51**. (A) **52**. (C) **53**. (C) **54**. (C) **55**. (B) **56**. (C) **57**. (A)
58. (A) **59**. (C) **60**. (D) **61**. (B) **62**. (B) **63**. (C) **64**. (C) **65**. (B) **66**. (A) **67**. (C) **68**. (B) **69**. (A) **70**. (B)

PART 4

71. (C) **72**. (A) **73**. (A) **74**. (B) **75**. (C) **76**. (D) **77**. (B) **78**. (C) **79**. (B) **80**. (B) **81**. (D) **82**. (A) **83**. (B)
84. (D) **85**. (B) **86**. (C) **87**. (D) **88**. (B) **89**. (C) **90**. (B) **91**. (A) **92**. (B) **93**. (B) **94**. (C) **95**. (B) **96**. (A)
97. (A) **98**. (D) **99**. (A) **100**. (B)

PART 1

1. (A) A woman is entering a building.
(B) A woman is walking up some steps.
(C) A woman is carrying a suitcase.
(D) A woman is holding onto a railing.

2. (A) She's looking into a glass case.
(B) She's baking some cookies in an oven.
(C) She's holding a shopping bag.
(D) She's paying at a cash register.

3. (A) They are constructing a fence.
(B) One of the men is standing on a ladder.
(C) A storage area is being swept.
(D) One of the men is leaning against a wall.

4. (A) Some people are entering a supermarket.
(B) A vendor is selling merchandise to people.
(C) One of the men is paying for his purchase.
(D) One of the women is clearing off a table.

5. (A) Some buildings overlook a bridge.
(B) Some boats are tied to a dock.
(C) A bridge crosses over a river.
(D) Trees are being planted along a shore.

6. (A) People are passing through a doorway.
(B) People are admiring an artwork.
(C) People are hanging up a picture.
(D) People are sipping water from a mug.

PART 2

7. Where can I buy a good travel book?
(A) I used it a lot.
(B) You can try Ashley's Bookstore.
(C) The map was very detailed.

8. Would you like a glass of soda or some juice?
(A) Only sometimes.
(B) I didn't like it.
(C) Juice would be good.

9. When will the recreation area be available to our employees?
(A) Before the end of the year.
(B) A reservation for three.
(C) A television and massage chairs.

10. What time does your flight leave?
(A) No, it's too bright.
(B) Gate 42.
(C) Not until 6 P.M.

11. What kind of bike do you have?
(A) Just along the river.
(B) A mountain bike.
(C) More than 40 kilometers.

12. Would you mind wrapping this package?
(A) I'd be happy to.
(B) A box of equipment.
(C) No, it's not heavy.

13. I forgot to bring my wallet today.
(A) Oh, I can buy lunch.
(B) In the drawer.
(C) Thanks, it was on sale.

14. Can't Melissa lead the fitness class?
(A) Yes, I can order it for you.
(B) No, she's off that day.
(C) They already signed up.

15. Who's the lead designer for this project?
(A) The blueprint doesn't match.
(B) Mr. Thompson is handling it.
(C) In the lobby, I guess.

16. Can you recommend a good place to stay?
(A) No, it isn't open yet.
(B) I always go to my friend's apartment.
(C) $120 per night.

17. The copy machine is out of order, right?
(A) It's a scanner, too.
(B) Do you have any tea?
(C) I used it this morning.

18. Is there enough room in the back for my bag?
(A) A grey backpack.
(B) You'll have to hold it.
(C) She's in the living room.

19. Why are sneaker sales so high?
(A) That would be great.
(B) Check in the back.
(C) Because of the new advertisement.

20. Are you going to attend the conference in Seoul?
(A) It's in Conference Room B.
(B) Several major tech firms in Asia.
(C) I'm waiting for an update on our travel budget.

21. Why did you change the shipping address?
(A) By the 15th.
(B) We'll need it delivered to the work site.
(C) It's four sets, not three.

22. Shouldn't we hand out the report before the meeting?
(A) The reporter will be here soon.
(B) That's a good idea.
(C) It should be 15 pages long.

23. The charity's founder is giving a speech next month.
(A) Back in 1962.
(B) Is he making an announcement?
(C) He found it beneath the seat.

24. Where should I put my old monitor?
(A) We should all do that.
(B) By next Tuesday.
(C) Let the IT Department handle it.

25. Why wasn't the movie sequel ever released?
(A) Last November.
(B) The director quit.
(C) Yeah, let's see it together.

26. How are we going to fill a hundred more orders?
(A) By working on Saturday.
(B) The purchase was made online.
(C) The order form on the counter.

27. Who should I see about a refund?
(A) I'll get a manager.
(B) Only store credit.
(C) At any location.

28. How much has our market share increased this year?
(A) We started in February.
(B) Go to the one on Main Street.
(C) That data isn't ready yet.

29. Hasn't Patrick filled out the medical form yet?
(A) The box is full.
(B) He doesn't need to.
(C) At the hospital.

30. Can you come to the dinner with me?
(A) I already have plans.
(B) Sometime last week.
(C) He said it's somewhere downtown.

31. You read Ms. Bowman's latest novel, right?
(A) No, I leave tomorrow.
(B) I'd recommend that movie.
(C) Do you want to borrow it?

PART 3

Questions 32-34 refer to the following conversation.

M: Hello, this is Pandora Cable Company. What can I do for you today?
W: Hi. I just turned on my television to watch my favorite show, but I can't find the channel. Is it no longer provided through your cable service? I've always been able to get it before.
M: I'm sorry, ma'am. That channel is now a part of a premium package, and you still have basic service.
W: Well, I wish I had known.
M: I'm sorry, there should've been a notification. Here, I'll go ahead and give you a free sample month of the premium service. Then, call us back later if you'd like to change your subscription.

32. Why is the woman calling?
33. According to the man, what has recently changed?
34. What does the man offer to do?

Questions 35-37 refer to the following conversation.

W: There's another order already? Did a large party come in?
M: No, but we'll have more customers from now on because Owen's Diner across town closed this week. Now, we're the only burger place in the area.
W: Oh, I see. Well, if it's going to be this busy every day, we need to keep an eye on our stock of food. We might sell out.
M: I already thought of that. I placed an extra order from our supplier this morning.

35. Where are the speakers?
36. Why is the man expecting more customers than usual?
37. What does the man say he did?

Questions 38-40 refer to the following conversation with three speakers.

M: Let's see... How about you, Lily? How were sales for our new line of printers in August?
W1: Well, sales increased by 8%, which is great. However, this was mostly done in the domestic market.

TEST 7

M: Hmm... The plan is to become more competitive internationally. Elizabeth, why aren't we doing better abroad?

W2: I think we lack the staff to adequately represent our business overseas. We need to open an office in Europe that can better handle our printer sales.

M: I'm not sure we're able to make such a dramatic expansion. However, purchasing a smaller foreign company in our industry could help us achieve the same goal.

38. What product are the speakers discussing?
39. What does Elizabeth suggest?
40. What does the man propose?

Questions 41-43 refer to the following conversation.

M: Hello, Bethany. Is everything ready for the Simmons exhibition in the art gallery?

W: Actually, I just got off the phone with the artist. Apparently, he's decided to completely re-do the large sculpture we were planning to display in the main hall.

M: And... the opening night is still this Friday?

W: Yes, and that can't be changed. However, I'll message Ms. Wright in our public relations department to see if we can get the starting time delayed until later in the evening. We'll probably need an extra hour or two to set up that afternoon.

41. What are the speakers working on?
42. Why does the man say, "the opening night is still this Friday"?
43. What does the woman say she will do next?

Questions 44-46 refer to the following conversation.

W: Hello, Dylan. I know you've been working hard on the new microwave prototypes, but something has come up. We won't need them to be ready for a few more months.

M: Oh, ok. That's actually good news. May I ask why the deadline has changed?

W: Well, my department has decided to make several budget cuts, so the company can't fund as many projects simultaneously.

M: I see. I'll notify my teammates to let them know that we have extra time.

44. What does the woman notify the man about?
45. According to the woman, what recently happened in her department?
46. What does the man say he will do next?

Questions 47-49 refer to the following conversation.

W: Jerome, I want you to write a review of Tech Star's newest tablet computer. It's a budget model, but it supposedly still has a top-quality display.

M: Sure thing. You know, I worked at Tech Star briefly when I was still an engineer.

W: Yes, I'm aware. That's why I selected you for this task. And... I would like it to be ready to print in our next issue.

M: That comes out next week. I can do it, but it won't be as detailed as it could be.

W: Actually, I was thinking you could work on Saturday. You can take your time researching and writing, and then I'll let you take next Friday off.

47. What does the woman ask the man to create?
48. According to the woman, why was the man selected for the project?
49. What does the woman suggest the man do?

Questions 50-52 refer to the following conversation.

M: Sadie, I just spoke with Mr. Kellison. He wants us to add Italian-style brick oven pizza to our menu. Our competitors have introduced it, and it's selling really well. He thinks we'll lose a lot of customers if we don't follow the trend.

W: But, we would need to buy a special oven. It won't be cheap, and it will take a lot of space. I think we need to talk this over and make sure it's a realistic option.

M: Actually, a pizza shop in Albany is going out of business, and the owners are selling all of the kitchen appliances. We should go and see about buying their oven. I think we could negotiate a fair price with them.

50. What industry do the speakers work in?
51. What is the woman concerned about?
52. Why will the speakers go to Albany?

Questions 53-55 refer to the following conversation with three speakers.

M1: All right, everyone. We'll be working here at the Concord Business Tower for the next three hours. The bathrooms on each floor need to be cleaned, and the trash in the cafeteria needs to be sorted and taken out. I'll take care of that first.
M2: I'll start cleaning the windows on the sixth and seventh floors. Lisa, could you clean the ones on the eighth and ninth floors?
W: The client wants the conference hall's carpet shampooed.
M2: Oh, I forgot. I'll work fast and clean the windows on every floor.
M1: Great. Let's meet out front at 4 o'clock to pack up our supplies.
W: OK, I should be finished by then.

53. Where are the speakers?
54. Why does the woman say, "The client wants the conference hall's carpet shampooed"?
55. What do the speakers agree to do at 4 o'clock?

Questions 56-58 refer to the following conversation.

M: Hello, this is Tim from Sigma Stationery and Supplies. How can I help you?
W: I just bought a Renly S10 Wireless Printer from your store, but it isn't working correctly.
M: It's one of our most popular office appliances. What's wrong with it?
W: I'm a graphic artist, so I need to print my work in great detail, but it won't print in color. Obviously, I can't have all of my samples in black and white.
M: It should be easy to switch between the two. Are you sure the settings are correct from your computer?
W: Hmm... I can't seem to bring up that window.
M: Go ahead and turn your computer off and on. The software might need to finish installing.

56. Where does the man most likely work?
57. What problem does the woman mention about a printer?
58. What does the man tell the woman to do?

Questions 59-61 refer to the following conversation.

W: Hugh, did you take a look at the comments on the film festival Web page?
M: Yeah. A lot of contributors were upset about their late showing times. They wanted their premieres to be earlier in the evening.
W: Honestly, I don't think it was a big deal. The turnout this year was better than ever, even for the later films.
M: I agree, but a lot of attendees still left early, especially if they came with their children.
W: Well, that's true, but we specifically reserve daytime showings for more family-oriented material. All of the directors should understand that at least.
M: I get it, but maybe next year we should have one additional day of showings, just to ensure that everyone has a chance to see them.

59. According to the man, what did some people complain about?
60. Why does the woman say she is not concerned?
61. What does the man suggest?

Questions 62-64 refer to the following conversation and table.

M: Mary, I'm getting this order ready for shipping, but I think the customer gave us the wrong zip code for his address.
W: Actually, some of the codes in that area were recently changed because a few post offices closed.
M: Oh, I didn't know. Could you look up the new one?
W: Sure. What town is it?
M: Silver Pines.
W: OK. Use this zip code.
M: Thanks. And could you post the new codes in the office?
W: I can, but our online store will be updated soon to recognize them, so this shouldn't be a problem again.

62. What is the man having trouble with?
63. Look at the graphic. Which code should the man use?
64. What does the woman say will happen soon?

TEST 7

Questions 65-67 refer to the following conversation and promotional flyer.

M: Good morning, Ms. Watson. What can I do for you?
W: Hello, Willard. I want to remodel my living room, so I came in to buy some paint.
M: Well, it looks like you already picked out your colors. How many cans will you need?
W: I forgot to take measurements. Hmm.. I'll e-mail you a picture of the room. Then can you estimate how much I'll need?
M: I should be able to. By the way, did you see our flyer? There's a really good sale right now.
W: Oh, I see it now. Well, I did misplace my hammer. I'll just buy a new one.
M: Good idea! So, e-mail me that photo later, and I'll get your order ready for pickup by this afternoon.

65. What does the woman say she will send by e-mail?
66. Look at the graphic. Which items will the woman receive for free?
67. What does the man say he will do this afternoon?

Questions 68-70 refer to the following conversation and schedule.

M: Thanks for calling Highland Railways. What can I do for you?
W: Hello, I need to travel from Dundee to London tomorrow morning. I tried several times to call your ticket hotline at 555-7788, but I couldn't get through.
M: I'm sorry about that. For the ticket hotline, you now need to call 555-6655. We changed it last month. I can process your ticket request and payment now over the phone. What time are you planning to depart?
W: I don't mind what time I depart, as long as I arrive in London before noon. I have to get to a 12:30 interview at an art gallery in the city center.

68. Why does the man apologize?
69. Look at the graphic. What train will the woman most likely take?
70. What does the woman say she will do in London?

PART 4

Questions 71-73 refer to the following advertisement.

Attention, shoppers. Quick Stop is your one-stop destination for your day-to-day shopping. We carry everything you might need: delicious snacks, refreshing beverages, and a variety of household goods. And to provide you with even better service, we are starting a premium points program in April. The points you earn shopping with us can be used for extra savings at any of our stores in the country. You can keep track of these points with our mobile phone application, which you can download for free from our Web site.

71. What type of business is being advertised?
72. What will the listeners be able to do starting in April?
73. Why does the speaker invite the listeners to visit a Web site?

Questions 74-76 refer to the following introduction.

Good evening, everyone, and welcome to the unveiling of our newest operating system, Stellar 10X. After years in development, we're finally approaching a market-ready version. Now, I'll hand the mic off to Samuel Wentz, our lead developer on the platform, to walk you through all of the new features. Mr. Wentz has been at Ace Programming for eight years, and in that time he's helped us develop some of the most popular software used around the world. Mr. Wentz will talk to you about the design philosophies behind Stellar 10X, and afterward, please stick around to watch a short video clip we've prepared about the future of our company.

74. What is the purpose of the session?
75. Who is Mr. Wentz?
76. What will take place after Mr. Wentz's talk?

Questions 77-79 refer to the following talk.

Good afternoon. My name is Rafael, and I'm the concierge at the Hartford Inn. If you aren't aware, this is a unique hotel, so let me tell you about it. Every weekend, there's a play performed in our very own theater. The owner of the hotel, Lucas, is an experienced director who helps organize and direct every show. And lucky for you, there's a performance tonight of *The Dinner Guest*. It's a short, humorous play about a young doctor. I've seen it several times. So, please keep this option in mind as you make plans during your stay.

77. According to the speaker, what is special about the hotel?
78. Who is Lucas?
79. Why does the speaker say, "I've seen it several times"?

Questions 80-82 refer to the following excerpt from a meeting.

Before we start today's meeting, I'd like you all to meet Tony Chappitz, who has just joined our chapter of the Lion's Club. He has been active in other local charities over the past several years, and we're happy to have him join our ranks. Mr. Chappitz also just retired from his position as a quality assurance manager at Delco Industries, so he's eager to lend us some of his free time. After the meeting, I'll order some sandwiches from Del Mar's Deli so you can get to know him a bit better over lunch.

80. What is the main purpose of the talk?
81. What does the speaker say Tony Chappitz recently did?
82. What will the speaker do later today?

Questions 83-85 refer to the following telephone message.

Hi, this is Becky from sales. I was supposed to give a demonstration of our knives and cookware at this department store in Canton. Well, I got the supplies, drove out here, and set up all the equipment, expecting to meet the store representatives and start at 3 P.M. But... it's been about an hour now, and nobody has come. Since I'm here, I'll talk to some shoppers and promote our products. While I do that, could you double check that we have the right time and date?

83. Who is the speaker?
84. What does the company sell?
85. What does the speaker imply when she says, "nobody has come"?

Questions 86-88 refer to the following broadcast.

Thanks for tuning in to The Biz Cast. Today, Heather Park, a manager at an international architecture agency, is joining us to talk about some software she's used to help run such a large business. Namely, managing the payroll of employees spread across the globe and throughout different time zones proved to be a great challenge. But Ms. Park found the perfect software to help keep track of all the different accounts and make deposit payments on time. And remember, if you're listening and have a question you'd like to ask Ms. Park, just call in and we'll put you – and your great question – on the air!

86. What kind of business does Ms. Park manage?
87. What kind of software will Ms. Park discuss?
88. What are the listeners encouraged to do?

Questions 89-91 refer to the following excerpt from a meeting.

The last thing we need to discuss is *Evening Breeze*, the new novel by Jack Watson. We've all read the reviews. However, we still need to move enough copies to make a profit. I asked Paige to do some market research to find its best audience. According to her report, the book would be more popular with teenage readers rather than the 18-35 year olds it's currently being advertised to. We'll have to come up with a new strategy and discuss its shelf placement with retailers, but most importantly, I think we should give it a new title. So, does anyone have any good ideas?

89. What does the speaker mean when she says, "We've all read the reviews"?
90. What does Paige's report indicate?
91. What does the speaker ask the listeners to do?

Questions 92-94 refer to the following talk.

Thanks for coming, everyone. My name is Robert Chen, and I'll be showing you how to use the new Turner XP-40 projectors the company is having installed in each of the meeting rooms. The reason we bought this particular model is because each unit comes with replacement parts, so we'll be able to make any necessary repairs on our own. In addition, each one comes with a high-definition cable that we can use. This will make our presentation materials and videos much sharper and clearer.

92. What is the talk mainly about?
93. Why did the company choose the product?
94. What does the speaker say is offered with the product?

Questions 95-97 refer to the following announcement and ticket.

Good evening to all the Thunderclap fans out there! Just to let you know, a member of the opening act The Loose Cuffs has sprained his wrist, so they will not be able to perform. Instead, folk singer Eva Reilly will open. I know this might be a disappointment, but we'll be sure to schedule a make-up concert with them next month. We will post the information when we decide on a date. Please be aware that this change won't affect the start time. Also, don't forget tonight's special offer. Everyone with a valid ticket can get one free snack item from the concession stand. So enjoy your food and get ready for some great music!

95. According to the speaker, what has caused a problem?
96. Look at the graphic. According to the speaker, what piece of information on the ticket will change?
97. What does the speaker say the listeners can receive?

Questions 98-100 refer to the following telephone message and conference schedule.

Hi, this is Pete Campbell from Sterling and Partners. We spoke at the Advertising Today Conference last month. After your speech, I told you about a commercial my company was making for a clothing line for teenagers. I'm calling because I hope you can give us some feedback on whether you think it appeals to younger consumers. I know it's your specialty, so I've sent an e-mail with the latest version of the TV commercial attached. Could you watch it and let me know what you think? I'd appreciate it, and I'll pay you for your time.

98. What is the purpose of the call?
99. Look at the graphic. Who is the speaker calling?
100. What does the speaker ask the listener to do?

TEST 8

정답

PART 1

1. (B) **2**. (B) **3**. (D) **4**. (A) **5**. (D) **6**. (D)

PART 2

7. (A) **8**. (C) **9**. (C) **10**. (A) **11**. (C) **12**. (B) **13**. (C) **14**. (B) **15**. (B) **16**. (C) **17**. (B) **18**. (C) **19**. (A) **20**. (C) **21**. (C) **22**. (A) **23**. (C) **24**. (C) **25**. (B) **26**. (C) **27**. (B) **28**. (B) **29**. (A) **30**. (A) **31**. (B)

PART 3

32. (C) **33**. (D) **34**. (B) **35**. (B) **36**. (A) **37**. (D) **38**. (B) **39**. (C) **40**. (C) **41**. (C) **42**. (B) **43**. (D) **44**. (B) **45**. (B) **46**. (C) **47**. (B) **48**. (A) **49**. (B) **50**. (C) **51**. (C) **52**. (B) **53**. (B) **54**. (A) **55**. (D) **56**. (C) **57**. (B) **58**. (D) **59**. (A) **60**. (D) **61**. (B) **62**. (A) **63**. (B) **64**. (C) **65**. (C) **66**. (D) **67**. (D) **68**. (C) **69**. (B) **70**. (D)

PART 4

71. (A) **72**. (C) **73**. (B) **74**. (D) **75**. (B) **76**. (B) **77**. (B) **78**. (A) **79**. (D) **80**. (D) **81**. (C) **82**. (A) **83**. (B) **84**. (A) **85**. (C) **86**. (B) **87**. (D) **88**. (B) **89**. (B) **90**. (C) **91**. (C) **92**. (C) **93**. (B) **94**. (A) **95**. (C) **96**. (D) **97**. (D) **98**. (C) **99**. (D) **100**. (D)

PART 1

1. (A) A man is tying his apron.
(B) A man is preparing some food.
(C) Some vegetables are on display.
(D) Some customers are being served.

2. (A) She's putting on a pair of glasses.
(B) She's working at a machine.
(C) She's looking at some clothing.
(D) She's rolling her sleeves up.

3. (A) One of the women is holding a stack of papers.
(B) One of the women is writing on a notepad.
(C) They're seated next to each other.
(D) They're examining some documents.

4. (A) Some people are seated at a table.
(B) Some people are having a snack outdoors.
(C) One of the women is reaching for her phone.
(D) One of the women is taking off her jacket.

5. (A) Some price tags are being printed.
(B) Some shopping bags have been left on the floor.
(C) Some clothes are being folded.
(D) Some clothes have been arranged for display.

6. (A) Park maintenance work is being carried out.
(B) Some trees are being trimmed.
(C) Leaves are being swept out of the road.
(D) Trees line a walkway.

PART 2

7. Where is the pharmaceuticals convention this year?
(A) I heard that it's in London.
(B) There's a pharmacy nearby.
(C) At the end of November.

8. Would you like to order one of today's specials?
(A) Please order them by date.
(B) At the vegetable market.
(C) I was just going to get a drink.

9. Why did you take the third floor office?
(A) To the break room.
(B) An official document.
(C) Because it's quieter here.

10. Which meeting room is being used?
(A) The one on the third floor.
(B) A laptop and projector.
(C) I'll show you how.

11. When are you booking a venue?
(A) For the year-end banquet.
(B) Because it's not spacious enough.
(C) Sometime today.

12. There's a package for you at the reception desk.
(A) Within three business days.
(B) Oh, thanks for telling me.
(C) Turn left when you exit the elevator.

13. How old is this public library?
(A) At least 10,000 books.
(B) I was born in 1975.
(C) It's been here for five decades.

14. Who portrayed the queen in that TV show you mentioned?
(A) Yes, it's shown every Monday and Friday.
(B) The award-winning actress, Linda Hughes.
(C) But most of the other actors were very good.

15. How much does it cost to reserve the banquet hall at your hotel?
(A) It holds up to 250 people.
(B) About $700.
(C) You can do that through our Web site.

16. Didn't you see a movie last night?
(A) We'll go at 6:15.
(B) Turn on the light, please.
(C) I was too tired.

17. Why was the Ralston Street branch of Burger Heaven closed this weekend?
(A) On Saturdays and Sundays.
(B) They're renovating the interior.
(C) It has an extensive menu.

18. Are the inspectors planning to check the assembly line?
(A) They're not hard to assemble.
(B) A manufacturing facility.
(C) It's already been looked at.

19. We have to postpone the trip until next weekend.
(A) I made other plans.
(B) He went to the post office.
(C) Where did you go?

20. This phone comes with earphones, doesn't it?
(A) You can call me anytime.
(B) I'm afraid I won't be able to come.
(C) Yes, there's a set in the box.

21. You'll send me the modified blueprint, right?
(A) Construction begins on the 3rd.
(B) He designed the new City Hall.
(C) Yes, but I'll need a few days.

22. Haven't you already rented a car for our business trip?
(A) Not yet, I'll get one today.
(B) An apartment near the river.
(C) Four days in Shanghai.

23. Do we need four or five hotel rooms for the company trip?
(A) It was a really enjoyable trip.
(B) A hotel next to the beach.
(C) I think four will be enough.

24. Who should I contact about cleaning our offices?
(A) No, he hasn't done it yet.
(B) On the third and fourth floors.
(C) Mary recommended a firm.

25. Are we setting off for the train station at 8 o'clock or 9 o'clock?
(A) No, it still hasn't arrived.
(B) Our train is at 9:05.
(C) Try changing the settings.

26. Where are the cartridges of printer toner?
(A) From the office supply store.
(B) Some printouts for my presentation.
(C) Didn't Luis buy some more?

27. I need to get a new file cabinet to organize all of these application forms.
(A) Isn't that organization one of our clients?
(B) I have a spare one you can use.
(C) No, I didn't apply for the position.

28. Do you accept cash?
(A) George accepted the shipment.
(B) No, we need a credit card payment.
(C) Yes, I found an ATM nearby.

29. Can you forward me the e-mail from head office?
(A) Sure, give me a few minutes.
(B) A memo about policy changes.
(C) The address is on the Web site.

30. Are you having difficulty opening your window, too?
(A) I just called the maintenance team.
(B) It's very hot outside today, isn't it?
(C) Yes, you should close it before you leave.

31. How do you plan to promote your services?
(A) He was promoted to sales manager.
(B) Mostly through social media.
(C) Yes, that's my plan.

PART 3

Questions 32-34 refer to the following conversation.

W: Mario, I just tried to get some office supplies from the store room, but the door seems to be stuck. I couldn't get into the room.
M: Oh, that's strange. Did you try pulling it hard? It can be quite stiff.
W: Yes, and I even asked Gareth to help me, but neither of us had any success.
M: Hmm... Well, would you mind calling the Maintenance Department and asking them to come up to fix it? We'll need to get in there for supplies throughout the day.
W: No problem. But, I need printer toner right now. What should I do?
M: Marriott Supplies is located just across the street from our office. Just buy some for now and I'll make sure you're reimbursed later.

32. What is the woman trying to do?
33. What does the man tell the woman to do?
34. What does the man say about Marriott Supplies?

Questions 35-37 refer to the following conversation.

M: I saw an advertisement for your restaurant in a local paper, and I'm interested in holding a company dinner there. Can you give me some more information?
W: My pleasure. When you hold a corporate event at Raffles Restaurant, your group will be seated in one of our beautiful private dining rooms. You'll be given a choice of three set menus, each of which includes five courses. And none of our rivals can match our very reasonable prices.
M: That sounds great. I'm actually recruiting several new employees in October, so I'm planning to welcome them by taking them all out for dinner.

35. How did the man hear about Raffles Restaurant?
36. According to the woman, what makes Raffles Restaurant different from its competitors?
37 What will the man do in October?

Questions 38-40 refer to the following conversation with three speakers.

M1: Thanks for coming in today, Ms. Tracy. We've finished drawing up plans for your new location, and the contractor, Mr. Tucker, is here too if you have any other requests.
W: It's nice to finally meet you both. I can't wait for my restaurant to move into its new location. We really need the extra kitchen space.
M2: You also mentioned having a terrace for outside dining?
W: Yes, as long as it's possible to use some of the parking lot area.
M2: That shouldn't be a problem at all.
W: Wonderful, but will it add much time to the work schedule? I need to be operating by August. That's when the county fair is, and the restaurant makes a lot of money during that time.

38. According to the woman, why is the restaurant moving to a new location?
39. What addition has the woman requested?
40. According to the woman, why must the work be completed in August?

Questions 41-43 refer to the following conversation.

W: Hello, Richard. I didn't expect to see you here. What kind of book are you looking for?
M: Hey, Anita. I'm actually looking for a book on software development. It has always been a goal of mine to create innovative computer programs.
W: That's interesting. Actually, I have a friend who works with computer programs. He's a programmer for a business software company. He'd maybe be able to recommend the most useful books to you. Would you like me to give him a call?
M: Wow, that would be nice. But I don't mind asking him myself. I might include several other questions as well. Do you think he'd mind if you gave me his e-mail address?
W: I doubt it. I'll text it to you later today.

41. What goal does the man have?
42. What does the woman offer to do for the man?
43. What information does the man ask for?

Questions 44-46 refer to the following conversation.

W: Anthony, are the preparations for the company excursion going well?
M: Yes, they are, Ms. Jenner. All flights and accommodations are booked, and now I'm finalizing the activity schedule for our employees.
W: Great. As I mentioned earlier, one of the activities will be a hike on Mount Randall. And... I know the mountain well, so I'd like to be in charge of the hiking group.
M: I'm sure the staff will be happy that you're leading them. Which day do you think would be best for that?
W: I think we should do that on the Friday. The mountain can get far too crowded on weekends.
M: Hmm... I had scheduled a scuba diving lesson for then, but I can change that to Saturday.

44. What are the speakers discussing?
45. What would the woman like to do?
46. What does the man say he will do?

Questions 47-49 refer to the following conversation.

W: Hello, Connor, I called you to talk about the market research feedback we received about our company's office chairs.
M: Oh, hi Bethany. I hope the focus group enjoyed the product.
W: Actually, much of the feedback was quite negative. I think changing the design of the product made it less comfortable.
M: Hmm... isn't it too late to do anything about that now?
W: No, I think it would be in our best interests to go back to the original design we had before the recent changes. We had no complaints from the previous focus group.
M: I suppose you're right. I'll pass on the message to the design team and they can create some new prototypes for testing.

47. What type of product are the speakers discussing?
48. According to the woman, what information was disappointing?
49. What does the woman suggest doing?

Questions 50-52 refer to the following conversation.

M: I'm glad you were able to come in today, Ms. Harvey.
W: Wow! Your store looks so modern and neat. I thought you just did online sales.
M: We did, but we've only recently opened this location. Anyway, let's get started. You can see for yourself what other products we specialize in, and I hope that after today, you'll agree to sell your candles through our store.
W: Well, I would like to be able to focus on creating new scents. But since it's just me, I really won't be able to fill large orders. Do you move high quantities of your other clients' products?
M: Actually, they're similar to you - selling limited numbers of hand-made goods at higher prices.

50. Why is the woman surprised?
51. Why does the woman meet with the man?
52. What does the man say about his clients?

Questions 53-55 refer to the following conversation.

W: Oh, hi Mark. I'm glad you're still here at the office. I was just looking at the strategy schedule for our Most Oats cereal commercial. Do you have some time?
M: It's already past 5:30. What's wrong?
W: Well, I found a mistake. It says our meeting with the CNS Network executives is on the 17th, but they already said they weren't available then. Haven't we rescheduled it?
M: You're right, but we had a quick meeting about it after lunch, and we decided that the 20th would work. Weren't you there for it?
W: Oh, sorry. I was out of the office for a dentist appointment.

53. What does the man imply when he says, "It's already past 5:30"?
54. What is the woman concerned about?
55. Why does the woman apologize?

Questions 56-58 refer to the following conversation with three speakers.

W: Hi, Andrew and Ivan. I was hoping to see you at this company-wide training workshop.
M1: It's nice to run into you, too, Andrea. We haven't seen you since the company trip to Bali last summer. Things have been pretty busy at our branch office.
W: Yeah, that's what I heard! Isn't your branch busy working on the upcoming global advertising campaign for our new range of cosmetics?
M2: That's right, and it's probably the biggest project we've ever worked on. It's going to include social media, magazines, and billboards worldwide.
W: Wow! I was responsible for all the market research for the new cosmetics. We got a lot of positive feedback from focus group members, so I'm sure the products will be a big hit.

56. Where are the speakers?
57. What project are the men working on?
58. What does the woman say she was in charge of?

Questions 59-61 refer to the following conversation.

W: Jonathan, our CEO, Mr. Molson, just sent me an e-mail. He's been evaluating our new mountain bike, and he's impressed with all the features. The only thing he isn't keen on is the bike frame. He thinks it should be white instead of grey.
M: Really? But wasn't he the one that suggested grey in the first place?
W: I believe so, but I guess he must've changed his mind for some reason. I spoke with the head of the design team, and he said it will take at least a week to repaint the bikes that are already assembled.
M: The project schedule says we should be completely finished by this Friday.
W: That's true. I'll reply to his e-mail now and make sure he knows that we'll need a few extra days.

59. What did Mr. Molson dislike about a bicycle frame?
60. Why does the man say, "The project schedule says we should be completely finished by this Friday"?
61. What does the woman say she will do?

Questions 62-64 refer to the following conversation and chart.

W: Hi, Trevor. How's the seminar schedule for the Technology & Innovation Conference going?
M: It's going slowly because I'm still waiting to hear back from some of the speakers I contacted. I'm really hoping that Paul Butler will agree to give a talk.
W: Oh, I just spoke with Paul Butler yesterday. He told me that he sent you an e-mail confirming that he would take the speaking slot right after Karen Singh.
M: Really? I guess it must've gone to my junk mail folder then. But that's good news. I'll add him to the schedule.
W: Good. I'm just on my way to the conference hall now to test that the microphones and speakers are working correctly. Let's talk more this afternoon.

62. Why is the man waiting to finish a seminar schedule?
63. Look at the graphic. When will Paul Butler give a talk?
64. Why is the woman going to an event space?

Questions 65-67 refer to the following conversation and invoice.

M: Hello, Ms. Parkinson. Are you here for the catalogs you asked us to print for your company?
W: Yes. And we really appreciate that you were able to print them so quickly. We're going to mail them out to all customers on our mailing list next week.
M: No problem. I hope they prove to be successful for your business. Here are the catalogs.
W: Thanks. Oh... I think you gave me one extra. We just ordered one hundred 10-page catalogs, but there seems to be one 20-page one here as well. Have I been charged for that one?
M: Oh, sorry, yes... I'm not sure how that happened. I'll refund that amount to you now, if you give me your credit card again. While I'm doing that, my colleague will carry these out to your car for you.
W: Thanks a lot.

65. What does the woman say she will do with the printed catalogs?
66. Look at the graphic. Which amount will be refunded to the woman?
67. What does the man say his colleague will do?

Questions 68-70 refer to the following conversation and parking layout.

M: Excuse me, this is my first week at the company, and I was told to come to the administration department to get a private parking space.
W: Oh, hello. You're the new director of marketing, right? It's nice to finally meet you. In order to assign you a parking space, I'll need your vehicle's license plate number.
M: Sure, it's K04-237. Do you need my employee number as well?
W: No, that's not necessary. I have all of your other details on the system here. Okay... We're all done here. I've given you the space that's directly across from our CEO's space. You won't be able to miss it.

68. What department does the woman work in?
69. What information does the woman ask for?
70. Look at the graphic. Which space has been assigned to the man?

TEST 8

PART 4

Questions 71-73 refer to the following telephone message.

Good morning, Mr. Grady. My name is Irene Fischer, and I work for Green Giant Groceries. This message is about the distribution agreement we made with your farm. I'm working on the delivery schedule right now. It will include the weekly deliveries we've previously discussed, and I'm trying to make them at times that are in line with your farm's production rate. It would be helpful to have an estimate of how large your weekly produce shipments will be, though. So, if you could, please let me know about that as soon as you can. Thanks, Mr. Grady.

71. Where does the listener work?
72. What is the speaker mainly discussing?
73. What does the speaker ask the listener to submit?

Questions 74-76 refer to the following talk.

Welcome to Harrington Art Museum. My name is Rupert, and I'll be your guide this morning. Our main exhibitions are on the first floor of the building. We also have some outdoor exhibits that you can enjoy in the grounds of the building. The weather should be clear all morning. Also, don't forget that we're running a competition this week. If you pick up a quiz sheet from the information desk and answer all of the questions correctly, you'll receive a voucher for $20 that can be redeemed in our gift shop.

74. Where most likely does the speaker work?
75. Why does the speaker say, "The weather should be clear all morning"?
76. What does the speaker say is happening this week?

Questions 77-79 refer to the following advertisement.

Listen up, everyone! The Carlson Street branch of Grady Home Furnishings is trying to make room for several new ranges of incoming stock. That means we need to hold a huge sale in order to shift our current items! The sale will begin this Saturday at 10 A.M. We'll be offering discounts on various items such as sofas, dining tables, and desks. If you visit our Web site at www.gradyhome.com, you can take a look at our full list of stock, including the special reduced prices. We hope to see you at our store this weekend!

77. What is the advertisement mainly about?
78. What type of business is being advertised?
79. According to the speaker, what can the listeners do on a Web site?

Questions 80-82 refer to the following excerpt from a meeting.

Hello, everyone. As you might have heard, Dr. Alberto Lorentz has decided to open up a new research department at the end of September. We will be hiring some new staff for the positions, and we'll mostly search for recent graduates through job-hunting Web sites. However, I would like to remind all of you that it is possible to transfer, if you'd like to. It's our policy to encourage staff to get experience and training in as many fields as possible. I believe this strengthens our company overall. So, there will be a presentation about Dr. Lorentz's plans next week. If you'd like to learn more, let your supervisor know that you're planning to be there.

80. What is Alberto Lorentz planning to do?
81. What company policy does the speaker mention?
82. According to the speaker, why should the listeners talk to a manager?

Questions 83-85 refer to the following talk.

I'm Omari Garrett, and I'll be showing you around the manufacturing plant here at Renfrew Furniture. I know that all of you are interested in viewing our facilities before you decide whether or not to invest in our firm. By becoming investors here, you'll be able to influence decisions made by the board of directors, in addition to receiving several benefits. As you walk around the facility today, please take the time to speak to our valued employees, who will be happy to explain work processes to you. But before we begin the tour, I'm going to introduce you to Mr. Craig Renfrew, who founded this company more than twenty years ago.

83. What is the purpose of the talk?
84. What does the woman recommend the listeners do?
85. What will the listeners do next?

Questions 86-88 refer to the following excerpt from a workshop.

Good morning everyone, and thanks for taking the time to attend this brief workshop.

Now, as you all know, the rest of the maintenance crew and I have been hard at work installing the new security doors on each floor of the office. So today, I'll explain how they can be accessed throughout the day. Now, some people think this is an unnecessary measure, but research shows that data-theft crimes are on the rise in our industry. By taking some extra steps, we can prevent some bad scenarios. Anyway, now I'll pass out the security cards you'll need to use between the hours of 7 A.M. and 7 P.M. to enter the office.

86. What department does the speaker work in?
87. What is the topic of the workshop?
88. What will the listeners do next?

Questions 89-91 refer to the following telephone message.

Hello, this is Barney Prentice, regional sales manager at Radical Clothing Designs. You called me last week about purchasing some of our customizable T-shirts, so I'm calling you back with some information. You mentioned that you want to buy them for all volunteers helping out at your town's annual craft fair. Well, if you order at least fifty of them, we will waive the shipping fee on your order. I think you said that your event is happening this weekend. In that case, please get in touch to let me know what you want printed on the T-shirts. We don't have many orders to fill this week.

89. What is the speaker calling about?
90. What does the speaker offer the listener?
91. What does the speaker imply when he says, "We don't have many orders to fill this week"?

Questions 92-94 refer to the following broadcast.

Welcome, listeners. You're tuned in to my show, Cooking With Lydia. I'm Lydia Ryder, owner of a successful restaurant, and a chef for more than thirty years. I'm here with more tips on cooking for beginners. Today, I want to tell you how to create an impressive meal when hosting a dinner party at your home. Now, hosting a dinner party can be rather expensive. But it is possible to keep the cost of a dinner party low, if you follow a few simple guidelines. And keeping costs at a minimum does not mean that you need to use low-quality ingredients. Now, I'll give you my top five tips for planning a successful yet inexpensive meal that will amaze your guests.

92. Why is the speaker qualified to host the show?
93. Why does the speaker say, "hosting a dinner party can be rather expensive"?
94. What will the speaker most likely do next?

Questions 95-97 refer to the following announcement and pictures.

Good afternoon, passengers. Welcome aboard Bus 553 headed for East Newbigging. Now that we are on our way, feel free to get up and use the restroom at the back of the bus if necessary. Otherwise, please remain seated and keep your seatbelt fastened. We'll be passing through several old towns today, so you'll be able to see a few historic landmarks from the bus windows. Right now, we're passing the famous Burnside Fountain, which was built in the 17th century. You can find more information about the fountain and the other landmarks on the tourist map in the seat pocket in front of you. Enjoy the ride.

95. What does the speaker say that passengers are now permitted to do?
96. Look at the graphic. Where most likely is the bus now?
97. According to the speaker, how can the listeners get more information?

Questions 98-100 refer to the following excerpt from a meeting and graph.

Good morning, everyone, and thanks for making time in your schedule for this executive meeting for the Halliday Broadcasting Company. As we've been discussing, we need to acquire a new show to support our fall primetime line-up, and we've been exploring four options in particular. First, although it scored well with the test audience, Second Chance Hospital is just too expensive to produce. Furthermore, we've decided that we already have enough game shows on our channel. That leaves us with one candidate, and the $20 million expected production cost will work within our budget. The show's creator, Robert Oras, has joined us today, and he'll walk us through the filming schedule he hopes to follow. If it fits our plan, then our decision should be finalized.

98. Who most likely are the listeners?
99. Look at the graphic. Which show will most likely be acquired?
100. What will Robert Oras talk about next?

TEST 8

TEST 9

정답

PART 1

1. (C) **2**. (C) **3**. (C) **4**. (A) **5**. (B) **6**. (A)

PART 2

7. (C) **8**. (A) **9**. (B) **10**. (B) **11**. (A) **12**. (B) **13**. (C) **14**. (C) **15**. (A) **16**. (B) **17**. (A) **18**. (A) **19**. (B)
20. (B) **21**. (B) **22**. (C) **23**. (A) **24**. (A) **25**. (A) **26**. (C) **27**. (B) **28**. (C) **29**. (C) **30**. (A) **31**. (A)

PART 3

32. (D) **33**. (A) **34**. (D) **35**. (B) **36**. (D) **37**. (C) **38**. (D) **39**. (A) **40**. (B) **41**. (C) **42**. (D) **43**. (D) **44**. (A)
45. (C) **46**. (A) **47**. (D) **48**. (C) **49**. (B) **50**. (A) **51**. (A) **52**. (C) **53**. (D) **54**. (D) **55**. (B) **56**. (B) **57**. (A)
58. (A) **59**. (A) **60**. (B) **61**. (C) **62**. (B) **63**. (D) **64**. (C) **65**. (B) **66**. (D) **67**. (D) **68**. (D) **69**. (D) **70**. (A)

PART 4

71. (D) **72**. (B) **73**. (B) **74**. (B) **75**. (B) **76**. (C) **77**. (A) **78**. (B) **79**. (D) **80**. (B) **81**. (C) **82**. (C) **83**. (C)
84. (C) **85**. (D) **86**. (D) **87**. (D) **88**. (B) **89**. (A) **90**. (C) **91**. (B) **92**. (C) **93**. (B) **94**. (B) **95**. (B) **96**. (B)
97. (D) **98**. (A) **99**. (B) **100**. (C)

PART 1

1. (A) He is repairing a walkway.
(B) He is parking his bicycle near a curb.
(C) He is crossing a road.
(D) He is walking toward a doorway.

2. (A) They are examining items in a store.
(B) They are putting away their bags.
(C) They are facing each other.
(D) They are waiting to make a purchase.

3. (A) She is looking into a microscope.
(B) She is removing her safety goggles.
(C) She is wearing protective gloves.
(D) She is pouring water into glasses.

4. (A) Various fresh items are on display.
(B) A cart has been loaded with merchandise.
(C) Fruits are being stocked on the shelf.
(D) Price tags are being attached to the produce.

5. (A) The chairs are stacked in a corner.
(B) Reading materials are spread out on a table.
(C) A laptop is being stored on a bookshelf.
(D) A table is being polished.

6. (A) Rows of potted plants are hanging in a greenhouse.
(B) A man is spraying water from a hose in a garden.
(C) Several tools are being used for gardening.
(D) A worker is spreading soil in a gardening area.

PART 2

7. What time is the next presentation?
(A) In Hall C.
(B) It's by Natalya Hesch.
(C) It's at 1 P.M.

8. Where should I put these decorations for the holiday party?
(A) Anywhere in the break room.
(B) Some posters and lights.
(C) A few people can't come.

9. Why did you return your new camera?
(A) I'm going on vacation next week.
(B) The battery wouldn't charge.
(C) The electronics store downtown.

10. Can I bring you the lunch menu?
(A) A ten dollar special.
(B) No, I already ate.
(C) I can't come in today.

11. When are you supposed to leave for Australia?
(A) Not until Friday afternoon.
(B) For a conference.
(C) With a friend.

12. How much do you pay for your parking spot?
(A) It's near the entrance.
(B) Only 25 dollars a month.
(C) Not in a while.

13. What should I include in the meeting minutes?
(A) We'll discuss the sales report later.
(B) Sorry, I misplaced them.
(C) I know Michelle used to take them.

14. Have you met Ms. Lopez, the event planner?
(A) A charity fundraiser.
(B) Two other caterers.
(C) Oh, I haven't had the chance.

15. Do you want me to help you fill out the application?
(A) Yes, some parts are unclear.
(B) We're not currently hiring.
(C) Has anyone helped you?

16. I just started baking the cake that we're preparing for the celebration.
(A) A couple of forks, and a knife.
(B) Should I remove it after it's finished?
(C) I'm not sure, maybe chocolate.

17. Was it Antonio or Rebecca who reviewed the presentation slides?
(A) I think it was the intern.
(B) It has a view of the city.
(C) A lucrative investment.

18. You'll finish the press release by this afternoon, won't you?
(A) Yes, but it might be shorter than expected.
(B) They need to make a good impression.
(C) Three different newspapers.

19. Which building is Hector staying in at the resort?
(A) Let's stay here a while.
(B) He hasn't checked in yet.
(C) On Boardwalk Avenue.

20. Will the student volunteers be wearing name tags?
(A) Great, we need some more help.
(B) Is that necessary?
(C) It's spelled with an 'e'.

21. Are you paying by cash, or do you want to use a credit card?
(A) That will be 75 dollars.
(B) Cash, please.
(C) A low interest rate.

22. Would you be interested in speaking at the awards dinner?
(A) It was a fantastic meal.
(B) The manager told me so.
(C) I'll have to check my schedule.

23. The packaging redesign is due tomorrow, isn't it?
(A) No, we got an extension.
(B) Four packages of supplies.
(C) Yes, I like it, too.

24. Who'll be the host of the new talk show?
(A) Jimmy Yates has expressed interest.
(B) It premieres on May 20.
(C) Check the stage lighting.

25. Why can't I open this document?
(A) I'll print a copy for you.
(B) It's on the desk.
(C) An expense report.

26. How much would it cost to renovate this property?
(A) Rent is 800 dollars per month.
(B) The vacant building on Jones Street.
(C) What work do you want to do?

27. Who's going to restock the Electronics Department?
(A) Near the back of the store.
(B) I did it last time.
(C) A two-bedroom apartment.

28. Kendrick wants us to finish the magazine advertisement by tomorrow.
(A) It was an interesting article.
(B) I canceled my subscription.
(C) But we haven't started yet.

29. Weren't the walls repainted over the weekend?
(A) I might see a movie.
(B) From the hardware store.
(C) They must not have finished.

30. Does anyone have time to make a delivery?
(A) Rory isn't busy.
(B) It's half past three.
(C) Two large pizzas.

31. We need to hire a programmer to maintain our Web site.
(A) Alex has a background in it.
(B) When does the program finish?
(C) I forgot the password.

PART 3

Questions 32-34 refer to the following conversation.

W: Centerville Fitness Center, how may I help you?
M: Hi, I'm calling to reserve one of your tennis courts for Saturday. I'm organizing a tournament that will last... three or four hours.
W: Sure thing. There are a lot of openings that day, but... it's supposed to rain in the afternoon, so you might want to schedule it in the morning since it will last several hours. Will that be OK with you?
M: I'm sure everyone will be fine with it. So, let's start at 8 A.M. I'll come earlier to rent some gear.
W: Great. Oh, and you should know that this Saturday we're hosting a complimentary, healthy lunch, so you can enjoy that after you finish.

32. What are the speakers mainly discussing?
33. What does the woman warn the man about?
34. According to the woman, what is scheduled for Saturday afternoon?

Questions 35-37 refer to the following conversation with three speakers.

M: Hi, Nancy. Hi, Alison. I'm glad I bumped into you both. I'm looking for two staff members who can work at the Birmingham branch next week.
W1: I'd be happy to do that. How about you, Alison?
W2: Well, it's more than fifty miles from my house to Birmingham. That's quite a long way to travel every day.
M: Oh, it's only for two days of training workshops, and the company will be happy to cover your gas expenses.
W2: In that case...sure, sign me up. Perhaps Nancy and I could even travel together.
W1: Great! That sounds good to me!

35. What are the speakers mainly discussing?
36. What is Alison concerned about?
37. What will the company provide to the women?

Questions 38-40 refer to the following conversation.

M: Wilma, you were in charge of the market research study for our new digital camera, right? I heard the participants in the study really liked the prototype they tested out.
W: That's right. All of the group members especially liked that the camera is very light, so it's easy to carry around day-to-day.
M: How much do you think it will retail for once it's launched?
W: I heard that it will cost somewhere between $250 and $280.
M: That's not bad. But we need to make sure it doesn't cost more than our competitors' models. Let's bring that up when we meet with the marketing team after lunch today.

38. What type of product is being discussed?
39. What did the market research group like about the product?
40. What will the speakers most likely do this afternoon?

Questions 41-43 refer to the following conversation.

W: Hello, I'm calling about the Pegasus 300 treadmill that you're selling. I noticed an advertisement online this morning. Is it still available?
M: Hi, yes, it is! I'm leaving my current apartment this weekend, and my new one is a lot smaller. I just won't have enough space for it.
W: That's a shame. I'm definitely interested in buying it, but would you mind holding on to it for a few days? I'd like to take a look at it later this week.
M: Well, I've had calls all morning. And as I mentioned in the ad, I'd like to find a buyer before Friday.
W: Oh, I understand. In that case, I'll try to go over to your place this afternoon. Would you mind giving me your address?

41. What is the man selling?
42. What will the man do this weekend?
43. What does the man imply when he says, "I've had calls all morning"?

Questions 44-46 refer to the following conversation.

W: Hi, Tarik. Did you know that the advertising team is looking for someone who can help improve our Web site? I might volunteer.
M: Well, you are quite talented in Web design. The freelance work you did for some local businesses looked professional.
W: Thank you! It would also give me a chance to work with other departments in the office, and I love doing that. It really makes me feel like an important part of the company.
M: I think you should go for it.
W: Yeah, I will. I'll talk to Mr. Price in Advertising right now.
M: Good luck, and let me know what he's like. He's new here, and I haven't spoken with him yet.

44. What are the speakers mainly discussing?
45. What does the woman say she enjoys doing?
46. What does the man say about Mr. Price?

Questions 47-49 refer to the following conversation.

W: Good morning. I'm interested in renting out one of your studios to record some music for a commercial I'm making next month. The last time I came here, Harvey Crank assisted with the controls.
M: Actually, Mr. Crank left the company and found his own studio. However, our new audio technician, Penelope Cage, has years of experience and could assist you for a fraction of the price.
W: Well, I'd really prefer to work with Mr. Crank again. Is there any way that you could help us get in touch with him?
M: It's against our company's policy to give out that kind of information. However, you should take a few minutes to give Ms. Cage's work a listen. She produced the background music for some of the catchiest commercials on the air today.

47. What is the purpose of the woman's visit?
48. Why is the woman unable to work with Mr. Crank?
49. What does the man suggest the woman do?

Questions 50-52 refer to the following conversation.

M: Marisa, I've been thinking about your suggestion to collaborate with Holden Construction on the shopping mall project. I think we should go for it.

W: I'm glad you agree! Actually, I've already drafted a proposal. The first thing we'll need to do is arrange a meeting with Holden Corporation's management.
M: Hmm... I've never worked with anyone at that firm before. Who would be the best person to speak with about a potential joint venture?
W: Well, Kevin worked at Holden Construction. I'm sure he'd know.
M: That's a good point. Let's invite him for lunch and come up with an effective negotiation strategy.

50. What are the speakers mainly discussing?
51. What does the woman imply when she says, "Kevin worked at Holden Construction"?
52. What does the man suggest?

Questions 53-55 refer to the following conversation with three speakers.

W1: This meeting will go over the progress on our newest video game. It won't be released until November, but we need to release a trailer soon. How are we looking, Hans?
M: Fantastic. The animations have been finalized and the graphics look great. However, we're way over budget, so I asked Zoe from Accounting to give us an update.
W2: Hans is right. But if we can cut back on spending until next quarter, then we should be able to secure more funds, especially if the product looks promising.
W1: I'll talk to the board of directors. In the meantime, slow down development, Hans, and see if you can push back the next deadline by a month or so.

53. What are the speakers talking about?
54. What problem does the man mention?
55. What is the man asked to do?

Questions 56-58 refer to the following conversation.

W: Chef Fieri? Do you recall our discussion about contracting with a food delivery service? I just found out about a small start-up that specializes in delivering meals to nearby customers.
M: Oh, good. Do you know how quickly they guarantee the arrival? I don't want our customers to receive cold food.
W: They advertise taking 30 minutes or less, so I think they're a great match for us. They have ten drivers on staff who drive motorbikes so they can cut through the city traffic.
M: Well, I'll keep it in mind. Oh, and look them up online. Maybe their users have left positive comments about them.

56. Where do the speakers most likely work?
57. What does the man ask about?
58. What does the man tell the woman to do?

Questions 59-61 refer to the following conversation.

M: Hello. I just realized that I left the office without sending an important e-mail. I can do it on my phone while I shop for groceries, as long as there's WiFi available here.
W: I'm sorry, sir, but we don't have any in the store. The manager thinks it helps keep the employees off their phones while working.
M: Oh.. I see. Well, do you know any place nearby where I could go to get a wireless connection?
W: There's a café right across the street that I always use during my breaks. You'll need to order a drink, and then the barista will give you the password.

59. What problem does the man mention?
60. Where are the speakers?
61. What does the woman suggest the man do?

Questions 62-64 refer to the following conversation and list.

M: Hello, I'm here for an interview with Mr. Joseph Mulder on the fifth floor. Can you tell me where the elevator is?
W: Of course. You just need to go around this corner. I think you'd better hurry... Mr. Mulder normally takes his lunch break at noon.
M: Yes, I'm behind schedule. I had engine trouble on the way here and had to drop my car off at the auto shop.
W: Oh, that's too bad! Here, take this... you'll need to show this visitor's card to the security guard at the elevator.
M: Okay, got it. Thanks for your help.

62. Look at the graphic. Which company does Mr. Mulder most likely work for?

63. Why is the man running late?
64. What does the woman give to the man?

Questions 65-67 refer to the following conversation and floor plan.

W: Hi, my name is Diana Smith, and I've booked a court at your sports center for 3 P.M. today. I was just wondering if it's possible to borrow some extra badminton rackets for my friends.
M: Yes, you can do that. Actually, the court you booked is right next to the storage closet, so you can grab some extra rackets from there. It'll be $5 per racket.
W: Great! My friends don't play badminton often, so they don't have their own gear.
M: Well, how about coming along to our beginners' sessions on Saturday mornings? We have an excellent instructor.
W: Hmm… I'll mention it to my friends and let you know later. Thanks!

65. Why is the woman calling?
66. Look at the graphic. Which badminton court has the woman reserved?
67. What does the man suggest?

Questions 68-70 refer to the following conversation and receipt.

M: Hi, I'm one of the lawyers at Boyle & Partners on the third floor. When I stopped by here for office supplies this morning, I think I was overcharged.
W: Oh, I'm sorry to hear that. What do you think you shouldn't have been charged for?
M: Well, I checked the receipt, and it seems I was charged for the envelopes. But, according to your current special offer, these should've been free. I'm hoping you'll give me a refund for those.
W: Yes, of course. I'm afraid we just hired new staff, and I guess one of them made a mistake when calculating your total. I'll make sure it never happens again.

68. Where does the man work?
69. What problem does the woman mention?
70. Look at the graphic. What amount will be refunded to the man?

PART 4

Questions 71-73 refer to the following telephone message.

Hello, Ms. Ruby. This is Scott from EverBeauty Cosmetics calling to let you know that the lotion you wanted, Silky Plus, has just been restocked. You can come in any time this week to get it, or we can ship it to you if that would be more convenient. Just call me back with your address. Oh, and don't forget that you only paid half of the total cost when you placed your order, so you'll have to complete the payment either in person or over our Web site.

71. Why does the speaker call the listener?
72. What can the listener request?
73. What does the speaker remind the listener about?

Questions 74-76 refer to the following telephone message.

Good morning. This is Peter Lemansky in the Quality Assurance Department. I'm in the warehouse and there seems to be a problem with one of the forklift trucks. I can turn it on and lift boxes, but I can't drive it anywhere. It was working fine yesterday, so I do not really know what the problem could be. I need this to be taken care of before lunch. There is a large shipment of merchandise that must be shipped out by 3 o'clock, and I still have to inspect the items and reload them by that time. Please let me know when you can have this looked at. The sooner, the better. Thanks.

74. What department does the speaker work in?
75. What does the speaker need help with?
76. Why does the problem have to be solved soon?

Questions 77-79 refer to the following excerpt from a meeting.

I'd like to welcome everyone to today's meeting. First of all, everyone should be reminded that next month, our company will begin allowing children aged thirteen to seventeen to open bank accounts with us. However, anyone of this age who would like to open an account must have a parent present who is already one of our customers. So the first thing you need to do is ask the adult to prove that they have an account with our bank. Changing the subject, we also have some great news. Recent customer surveys have shown that our clients are incredibly pleased about receiving such great financial recommendations from us. I'd like to congratulate you for paying such careful attention to both the market and the needs of our clientele.

77. According to the speaker, what is scheduled to happen next month?
78. What are employees asked to verify?
79. Why have some customers praised the bank recently?

Questions 80-82 refer to the following announcement.

On behalf of all retailers here at the Pontiac Mall, I hope you are having an enjoyable shopping experience today. Please take a moment to learn about our brand new membership program. By signing up to become a member, you can receive notifications about upcoming sales events and special performances at the mall. You'll also collect rewards points that can be redeemed for free products at the end of each month. Just go to the information desk on the second floor and fill out a membership form. That's all it takes! And don't forget to check our Web site for weekly discount vouchers that you can print out and use at our stores.

80. Where is the announcement being made?
81. What does the speaker imply when she says, "That's all it takes"?
82. Why are listeners encouraged to visit a Web site?

Questions 83-85 refer to the following excerpt from a meeting.

As you've all heard, our law firm has been selected to represent the Bank of New Mexico. It's a huge client, and we'll be handling all their legal issues, from tax code requirements to land acquisition deals for their upcoming expansions. It will be a lot of hard work and we want our best people working with them, so we will be conducting performance reviews. The partners will interview and observe all of the associate attorneys, so please send an e-mail to me by the end of the week detailing your work schedule for the month. We'll make arrangements from there.

83. What kind of business do the listeners most likely work for?
84. What news does the speaker share with the listeners?
85. What does the speaker ask the listeners to submit by the end of the week?

Questions 86-88 refer to the following excerpt from a meeting.

Last on the agenda is the valet parking that we will soon begin offering at Gaston Grill and Bistro. Several other top-end restaurants in the area offer valet services, and they also have higher scores than us with the Michigan Restaurant Board. We hope that adding this service will ultimately help us attain a better rating this year. Now, please take a look at this map that has been marked with available parking garages in the neighborhood we can rent. Let's decide which location will be best for us.

86. What is being discussed?
87. What is Gaston Grill and Bistro hoping to do?
88. What are the listeners asked to review?

Questions 89-91 refer to the following broadcast.

Now, let's see what's coming up next week in Belle Valley. Starting Saturday, the Monroe High School marching band will begin making deliveries for its annual hanging flower sale, which happens to coincide with Mother's Day. If you'd like to receive a beautiful basket of begonias or petunias, be sure to get the band your order by Wednesday afternoon. The Old Rail Festival will also start on Thursday evening at the historic Depot Park. Live performances and cooking contests are planned, but keep up-to-date with the event's social media page since frequent showers are expected. Next, we'll check in on some big news in sports.

89. What is the broadcast mainly about?
90. What are the listeners reminded to do by Wednesday afternoon?
91. What does the speaker imply when he says, "frequent showers are expected"?

Questions 92-94 refer to the following advertisement.

If you like to try new things that have several nutritional benefits, try Golden Foods' new range of bird's nest soup. Most Western consumers are unfamiliar with the health benefits of the soup, but trust me when I tell you that it can help cleanse your body and give you smoother skin. This product has never before been sold by local retailers, but thanks to our direct connection with Chinese suppliers, we can import the soup and sell it to our local customers at reasonable prices. Chinese people have been enjoying its benefits for thousands of years, and... Millions can't be wrong! Come on down to our store today for a free sample!

92. What is being advertised?
93. What does the speaker say is special about the product?
94. What does the speaker imply when she says, "Millions can't be wrong"?

Questions 95-97 refer to the following announcement and sign.

Good morning, and welcome to this year's Watersports Rowing Expo on the Allegheny River. First, I'd like to acknowledge Reynold's Boating and Tours for supplying the life jackets for all the rowers. I also need to announce a couple of changes. In previous years, we have had four events, but this year there will only be three. The one-kilometer race has been canceled due to a lack of participation. But don't worry; there will still be plenty to watch. And don't forget, you can share any photos you take today on our event's social media page. You can find the address on the back of your tickets.

95. What is Reynold's Boating and Tours providing?
96. Look at the graphic. Which race is canceled?
97. What are the participants reminded to do?

Questions 98-100 refer to the following excerpt from a meeting and chart.

As we discussed last week, we're implementing a new company-wide waste-reduction initiative. Last week, we combined the Marketing and Advertising Departments in an effort to reduce paper usage for memos and notices. We've seen some improvement, but we really need to work hard to achieve our goal of a 50 percent reduction. This week, I posted the chart with ideal limits for each department. In my department, we will be limited to 3,000 sheets of paper per month, which will be difficult, but possible. We'll review the results of these waste-reducing measures at the next meeting.

98. What is the speaker mainly discussing?
99. What does the speaker say happened last week?
100. Look at the graphic. In which department does the speaker work?

TEST 10

정답

PART 1

1. (B) **2**. (C) **3**. (C) **4**. (A) **5**. (D) **6**. (C)

PART 2

7. (B) **8**. (A) **9**. (C) **10**. (B) **11**. (A) **12**. (B) **13**. (B) **14**. (B) **15**. (C) **16**. (B) **17**. (A) **18**. (B) **19**. (C) **20**. (A)
21. (C) **22**. (C) **23**. (B) **24**. (B) **25**. (B) **26**. (A) **27**. (B) **28**. (B) **29**. (C) **30**. (A) **31**. (C)

PART 3

32. (B) **33**. (C) **34**. (B) **35**. (C) **36**. (A) **37**. (D) **38**. (D) **39**. (C) **40**. (D) **41**. (C) **42**. (B) **43**. (C) **44**. (C) **45**. (B)
46. (D) **47**. (D) **48**. (A) **49**. (A) **50**. (C) **51**. (D) **52**. (C) **53**. (C) **54**. (D) **55**. (C) **56**. (B) **57**. (B) **58**. (D) **59**. (A)
60. (B) **61**. (C) **62**. (C) **63**. (C) **64**. (C) **65**. (D) **66**. (C) **67**. (D) **68**. (A) **69**. (D) **70**. (C)

PART 4

71. (B) **72**. (B) **73**. (B) **74**. (B) **75**. (C) **76**. (D) **77**. (D) **78**. (B) **79**. (B) **80**. (A) **81**. (B) **82**. (D) **83**. (C) **84**. (C)
85. (D) **86**. (A) **87**. (B) **88**. (A) **89**. (B) **90**. (C) **91**. (B) **92**. (A) **93**. (B) **94**. (B) **95**. (C) **96**. (B) **97**. (B) **98**. (D)
99. (D) **100**. (A)

PART 1

1. (A) A man is working at a table.
(B) A man is holding a piece of furniture.
(C) Books have been put on shelves.
(D) A table is being placed in the corner.

2. (A) He's checking his telephone.
(B) He's packing some equipment.
(C) He's working with some tools.
(D) He's cleaning his workstation.

3. (A) A wall is being painted in the room.
(B) A man is giving some papers to people.
(C) A small group has gathered in a seating area.
(D) Some people are looking at a monitor.

4. (A) Boxes are arranged on the shelves.
(B) A man is putting on a safety helmet.
(C) Employees are setting up a booth.
(D) A man is driving a vehicle on the road.

5. (A) Tables are stacked on top of each other.
(B) Some dishes have been placed on the floor.
(C) Water is being poured into the glasses.
(D) A light fixture is hanging above the table.

6. (A) The woman is showing exhibits to visitors.
(B) The man is arranging some objects on a table.
(C) The man is pointing to one of the displayed items.
(D) Some shelves are being assembled.

PART 2

7. What happened to our staff dinner?
(A) Throughout the evening.
(B) It was postponed a week.
(C) It is, to be honest.

8. When is the new version available?
(A) Next Friday.
(B) The programmers.
(C) In the desk drawer.

9. Which would you suggest, a newspaper advertisement or a TV commercial?
(A) I would, really.
(B) In the studio.
(C) Neither, actually.

10. Where does the highway from the beach lead?
(A) Every two hours.
(B) To downtown.
(C) Well, it might.

11. Why is the department hiring more people?
(A) Because it's expanding.
(B) I'm not retiring soon.
(C) An updated résumé.

12. We need to purchase some new office desks.
(A) It's about three feet long.
(B) For which departments?
(C) You look pretty comfortable.

13. Who authorized the loan program?
(A) Yes, I've read it.
(B) Somebody from Operations.
(C) When you upload it.

14. You attended the convention last week, didn't you?
(A) I'll modify it soon.
(B) No, I was working.
(C) Yes, I can't wait to go there.

15. Where should I park the van?
(A) It's next to the storage closet.
(B) I just bought one.
(C) There are spaces in the basement.

16. Would you like to organize the event?
(A) No, let's hold it tonight.
(B) I'd be happy to.
(C) Look at the schedule.

17. When should we schedule the factory inspection?
(A) How about next month?
(B) The safety inspector might.
(C) Right around the corner.

18. Why was the product demonstration moved from the McManus Room?
(A) The shoppers purchased some.
(B) There weren't enough seats.
(C) Sure, let's go now.

19. Who was the man who just passed by?
(A) Jason won't walk there.
(B) In the parking garage.
(C) He is the vice president.

20. I'm going on a vacation next week.
(A) Thanks for notifying me.
(B) I went there this morning.
(C) Maybe to the beach.

21. How often should the meeting be held?
(A) She usually does.
(B) He wants to meet with us.
(C) At least twice a month.

22. Ms. Shapiro is taking a flight tomorrow, isn't she?
(A) It hasn't been filed.
(B) When did she arrive?
(C) Yes, around noon.

23. Do you know last month's sales figures?
(A) The director of sales.
(B) Look in this report.
(C) A drop in prices.

24. We'd better limit personal calls in the office.
(A) Yes, you should e-mail the client.
(B) I was considering that.
(C) He called ten minutes ago.

25. How did Susan figure out how to set up the stereo cables?
(A) They bought a couple of stereos.
(B) She learned from a video.
(C) The television isn't plugged in.

26. The subway's Blue Line has been shut down.
(A) Really? I rode it just the other day.
(B) I haven't reserved a seat yet.
(C) Get off at City Hall.

27. Don't you have the same kind of cell phone that Zoey has?
(A) I'd suggest a similar kind.
(B) I believe hers is newer.
(C) Haven't you called them?

28. The item will be ready by three if you can pick it up then.
(A) Yes, I have fixed a few.
(B) How about four, instead?
(C) No, I haven't picked up anything.

29. You would prefer that I present our proposal, right?
(A) Yes, she is very professional.
(B) No, they didn't propose it yet.
(C) If you think you're ready to.

30. Did you hear that the party will be held at seven?
(A) I hope I can get there on time.
(B) I didn't open the present yet.
(C) I arrived around eight.

31. Won't Maya show up at one?

(A) It was incredibly easy.

(B) She told me that you lost.

(C) That's what she said.

PART 3

Questions 32-34 refer to the following conversation.

M: Hello, I've been using your satellite television service and have been really impressed with your business. Unfortunately, many of my channels have had bad reception all day. I'm pretty worried because the soccer championship is on tonight. I need to get this taken care of so I can watch the game.

W: We'll take a look at it as soon as we can. A technician will stop by your home at some point this evening to fix it.

M: And do you think I could also get my service upgraded to high definition? I'd be happy to pay more. It would be wonderful to have a clearer picture for tonight.

W: Of course. You will need to transfer the setup fee immediately to have it done by tonight. It'll be $40, and there will be an additional $10 a month. The technician's visit is covered by your contract.

32. What does the man want to do?

33. What will happen this evening?

34. According to the woman, what will the man be charged for?

Questions 35-37 refer to the following conversation.

M: Hey, Nora. Do you plan on seeing the new documentary when it releases this Saturday?

W: The one about the revitalization of the waterfront in Auburn City? Definitely. Sage Cinema Weekly recommends that anyone interested in the history of the region should check it out.

M: I also read that it is a great study on how businesses can make positive contributions to poor areas. Unfortunately, all of the tickets have sold out for the weekend. I waited too long to buy one, and the film is only showing for one weekend.

W: You know what? The theater occasionally waits until the last minute and then releases some extra tickets for sale. I know the owner of the theater, and I can ask him if he intends to do that for this film.

35. What are the speakers mainly discussing?

36. What is the man's problem?

37. What does the woman offer to do?

Questions 38-40 refer to the following conversation with three speakers.

M: Hi, Debbie... Hi, Bella. How are the preparations going for the launch of our new restaurant this Friday?
W1: Great! Everything inside the restaurant is ready, so we spent a few hours this morning handing out flyers to shoppers in town.
W2: Yes, and it seems like a lot of them plan to attend our grand opening!
M: Let's hope so. Bella, can you get in touch with all of the staff we've hired and ask them to come in early on Friday? I'd like to speak to them before the first customers come in.
W1: No problem. I'll do that right away. Debbie, do you have their details?
W2: I do. Just give me a moment and I'll get the list of contact numbers for you.

38. What does the man say will happen on Friday?
39. What did the women do this morning?
40. What does the man ask Bella to do?

Questions 41-43 refer to the following conversation.

W: Have you heard about the apartment in Curry Grove that I've been assigned to design? It turns out that it will take a lot more time than originally planned. Would you be able to help me out?
M: Unfortunately, I'm not going to be able to. I'm supposed to train our new worker over the next two weeks, so I am not going to have time to do anything else. You can't do it all on your own?
W: I probably can, but it is a very important project. I'm hoping to get it done by the deadline for sure. I really want to finish this work on time.
M: Then, you should tell Mr. Cortez and see if you can get help from him. He's a very generous coworker, so I think he would be happy to help you a bit if you can't do it on your own.

41. Who most likely are the speakers?
42. Why is the man unable to help the woman?
43. What does the man suggest the woman do?

Questions 44-46 refer to the following conversation.

W: Carlos, before the end of the week, I need your opinion on whether we should sign a contract with Blash Collective or Lotus Plantation. I am a little anxious that we still do not know who will be providing us with the coffee beans for our restaurant.
M: My team has just finished analyzing the benefits of each company. I'll look it over this afternoon, and hand in my final report to you first thing tomorrow so you can make the final decision.
W: That would be great. If we don't sign a deal with a supplier soon, we may have to delay the planned March opening of our special coffee service.

44. What is the woman concerned about?
45. What does the man say he will do?
46. What is scheduled to happen in March?

Questions 47-49 refer to the following conversation with three speakers.

W: Hello, I'm just checking out of Room 501, but I can't find my watch anywhere. Has anyone found it and handed it in?
M1: I'm afraid I just started my shift a moment ago. Let me check with my colleague. Jason, has anyone handed in a watch this morning?
M2: I'm afraid not. Do you have any idea where you may have left it, ma'am?
W: I guess I could've put it down near the pool area. The problem is that I'm in a rush right now to catch a bus. Could you ask around and try to locate it for me?
M1: Certainly. I'll talk with the staff at the pool area and ask if they found it.
M2: And I'll check with housekeeping. We'll be sure to give you a call if it turns up.

47. Where is the conversation taking place?
48. What problem does the woman mention?
49. What do the men agree to do?

Questions 50-52 refer to the following conversation.

M: Donna, did the building manager e-mail you the layout for the main ballroom in McIntosh Hall? I read up on it and it seems like it would be the perfect place to hold our company's anniversary celebration.

It's the only room available with a view of the river.

W: Yesterday, I tried to talk to her about the room dimensions and maximum capacity, but she was out of her office.

M: Why don't you just drop by the building so you can check it out yourself? I'd hate for someone else to book it before us if you think it's suitable.

50. What is the man interested in doing?
51. What did the woman want to get?
52. What does the man suggest the woman do?

Questions 53-55 refer to the following conversation.

M: Did you hear that the board has chosen a replacement for Mr. Harris?

W: Finally! Mr. Harris retired almost two months ago. So, who is going to be our new CEO?

M: They picked Mr. Cowell, the current head of international marketing. He'll officially start as CEO at the beginning of next month.

W: Oh, good for him! He's certainly experienced, and he has good leadership skills. Let's go down to the coffee shop and buy him a gift card as a way of saying congratulations.

53. What does the woman imply when she says, "Finally"?
54. What does the man say about Mr. Cowell?
55. What will the speakers do next?

Questions 56-58 refer to the following conversation.

W: Hey, Marvin. Is it true that headquarters has approved giving everyone a ten percent pay increase? What would cause them to do that?

M: Well, the profits for last year were much higher than expected, and, according to the company's policy, a portion of increased revenue should go to the workers. So, they thought a substantial pay raise would be possible.

W: That makes sense, and it should help the business stay strong. The company's success has caused a lot of our employees to be sought out by other companies, so this will make workers more likely to stay here. Will the pay raises take effect next month?

M: Actually, the company will ask everyone to renegotiate a new deal soon because most workers usually only get a five percent pay increase per year.

56. Why is the company making changes to workers' salaries?
57. What is an additional result of the pay change?
58. What will happen soon?

Questions 59-61 refer to the following conversation.

W: Martin, do you think you'd be able to do me a favor this afternoon? I just found out I'll need to leave the bank at around noon.

M: Sure. But how come you need to leave so early today?

W: I just got a call from headquarters. They want me to go there to train some new workers for the branch that's opening in July.

M: Ah, I see. What can I help you with?

W: Well, I was planning on contacting the applicants for the customer service jobs at our branch. I need to let them know that the interview room has been changed.

M: Leave it to me. I have some free time after lunch today.

59. Where do the speakers work?
60. Why has the woman been asked to visit headquarters?
61. What does the man mean when he says, "Leave it to me"?

Questions 62-64 refer to the following conversation and list.

M: Good morning. One of your employees attempted to deliver a package to my home address yesterday, but I was out at the time. The note he left said I could collect it here.

W: That's correct, sir. But, in addition to the note, I'll need to see your driver's license or health insurance card to verify your name.

M: Oh, really? I left my wallet in my car, and I'm parked a few blocks from here. Is it really necessary?

W: Well, in that case, you'll need to speak directly with my manager, Ms. Anders. Please hold on while I go and find her.

M: No problem. I'll wait right here.

62. What is the man trying to do?
63. What does the woman ask for?
64. Look at the graphic. What branch does the woman work at?

Questions 65-67 refer to the following conversation and building layout.

M: Here you are, ma'am. One ticket for the 2:15 train to Norwich. That will be 12 pounds, please.
W: Thanks. There you are. Oh, I was wondering… I didn't have time to grab lunch on my way here to the station. Does my train have a dining car?
M: I'm afraid not. But you'll be able to buy some light snacks and beverages once you get on the train.
W: Well, I guess that'll be fine. I don't have much time anyway. Can you tell me which platform I need to go to for my train?
M: Sure. It's the one just over there where the information center is. And you'd better hurry – your train is leaving in a few minutes.

65. Who most likely is the man?
66. What does the woman ask about?
67. Look at the graphic. Which platform will the woman go to next?

Questions 68-70 refer to the following conversation and schedule.

M: Judith, I just wanted to thank you for all your help. All of the flyers and posters you made for this year's Burnaby Jazz Festival look amazing.
W: No problem! I was delighted that you asked me to get involved! I really hope that this year's event proves to be a big success.
M: Well, I just heard that a reporter from *Gold Soundz* magazine is here to write a review of all the concert performers, so that's exciting!
W: It sure is! Do you have any time to meet up sometime this afternoon?
M: Sure. Let's meet at the main stage at the end of Catriona Salford's set. Then we can watch the next musician together.

68. Who most likely are the speakers?
69. What does the man mention about the jazz festival?
70. Look at the graphic. When will the speakers probably meet?

PART 4

Questions 71-73 refer to the following telephone message.

Good morning. My name is Alonzo Farnsworth, and I'm the customer service manager of *Architects Weekly*. This call is in regard to your payment for the month of June. When I received your check this morning, I noticed that you paid ten dollars less than you should have. You were supposed to pay us thirty-five dollars for our standard magazine subscription. We require that you pay the rest so we can process your order. Our next issue is scheduled to be sent out next week. Unfortunately, unless we receive the rest of your payment today, I will be forced to suspend your order tomorrow.

71. Where does the speaker most likely work?
72. What problem is reported?
73. What does the speaker say he might do tomorrow?

Questions 74-76 refer to the following excerpt from a meeting.

We are pleased to announce that, to celebrate the merger of the Peerless Foundation and the Knope Group, we plan to introduce a new logo. Our board has decided to have a contest so our employees can participate and help generate better ideas. Any of you who are interested should submit your design in person to Ms. Perkins in the Human Resources Department. The last day for turning in a design will be on September 10, and then the official new logo will be unveiled on September 20, when we open our new combined offices.

74. What is the purpose of the contest?
75. According to the speaker, why should workers go to the Human Resources Department?
76. What will take place on September 20?

Questions 77-79 refer to the following advertisement.

Tired of driving miles away to find good tools and equipment? Then you should come to the grand opening of Zanzibar's Mill. From next Monday, you can find the widest selection of hardware, such as tools, paints, and building materials, at Zanzibar's Mill. What's even better is that you can become a Zanzibar store member, which gives you special discounts, with just a few clicks on our Web site. For our grand opening, we will have a sales event named 'Night Madness.' On the day of the opening, we will be open for twenty-four hours straight, and then we will begin our normal 9 A.M. to 10 P.M. hours from the following day.

77. What kind of business is being advertised?
78. When is the store's grand opening?
79. How can customers become a member?

Questions 80-82 refer to the following news report.

It's everyone's favorite time of year again! The annual HBC Music Festival will take place this weekend at venues located around the popular neighborhood. Each year, the festival attracts talented musicians who play at a variety of stages and cafés, so be sure to check out the Web site for an event map with all the show locations. The most talked about event will be at the Boston Club. Twilight Zone, who has recently become famous across the nation, will be performing there at 9 P.M. Get there around dinner time to enjoy some great food and other fantastic shows and, most importantly, because the Boston Club has a limited capacity.

80. What information should the listeners look for on a Web site?
81. Why is the event at the Boston Club expected to be popular?
82. Why does the speaker say, "the Boston Club has limited capacity"?

Questions 83-85 refer to the following telephone message.

Good morning. My name is Ray Venky. I visited your Web site last week and ordered some posters for promoting a concert I'm organizing. This morning, I received an e-mail informing me that they've been printed and sent out to me, but I just realized I forgot to order the leaflets that share the same design as the posters. I need to have these materials delivered without delay as the concert takes place next weekend. I'd be willing to come down to your printing location in person to collect them if that's what it takes to get them quickly. Please call me at my office at 555-1197. Thank you.

83. What problem has the caller discovered?
84. What event is scheduled for next weekend?
85. What does the caller offer to do?

Questions 86-88 refer to the following talk.

On behalf of the board here at Magni Chemicals, I'd like to express our gratitude to each and every one of you for your hard work this year. As our sales force, you have met and exceeded all of the targets we set for you at the beginning of the year. As a result, our profits are higher than we could have anticipated. To show our appreciation, we will be giving each of you a $200 bonus this month. We wish we could offer more. But, please understand that we need to keep an eye on our budget for next year. Now, I'd like to show you a clip of our new product ranges that you'll be selling next year. Please look this way.

86. Who most likely are the listeners?
87. What does the speaker mean when she says, "We wish we could offer more"?
88. What will the listeners probably do next?

Questions 89-91 refer to the following talk.

Good afternoon, everyone. I can't tell you how honored I am to win the Westbrook Humanitarian Prize here at the Midwest Philanthropy Awards. I'd like to thank the event organizers for giving this incredible prize to me. As you saw in the introductory video, I have contributed millions of dollars to organizations all over the world. Even though this helped me earn recognition, the most important part of my philanthropic efforts has been going to many areas myself and helping out the poor. I've helped to build houses, install plumbing, hand out food, and more. For my next project, I will concentrate on helping the towns hit by the latest hurricanes. Let me tell you about how these natural disasters can make it so difficult for communities to recover.

89. Where most likely are the listeners?
90. According to the speaker, what has been the most important aspect of his work?
91. What will the speaker probably talk about next?

Questions 92-94 refer to the following radio broadcast.

Good morning, listeners. I'm Grace Lee, and I'm here with your local news. This weekend is an exciting one for local residents because the annual town soccer tournament will be held in Marigold Park on Saturday. Teams from many local businesses will participate, and all proceeds from ticket sales will be distributed among local charitable foundations. This will be the first time that Marigold Park has been used for a public event since the city council had it landscaped last month. The event is expected to begin at 9 A.M., but...that has yet to be confirmed. I'll bring you more details as soon as I find out.

92. What is the speaker mainly discussing?
93. What did the city council do last month?
94. What does the speaker mean when she says, "that has yet to be confirmed"?

Questions 95-97 refer to the following talk and list.

Next up, we're going to take a look at some of the most successful movies that were shown throughout July. Now, as regular listeners of this show will know, I don't often go to the cinema, but I must admit that there were some excellent films out this summer. For example, the emotional drama *Dreams of Flight* was the month's most profitable movie, closely followed by the new Brad Ford movie in second place. Further down the list, *Eastern Winds* has taken a respectable $24 million, despite only being out for one week so far. This is partly due to all the praise it has received from popular film magazines and Web sites.

95. Who most likely is the speaker?
96. Look at the graphic. How much money did Brad Ford's new movie make in July?
97. What does the speaker say about Eastern Winds?

Questions 98-100 refer to the following telephone message and map.

Hello, this is Caelan Waddell calling regarding the work you'll be carrying out in my yard this weekend. First, I've decided that I'd rather have roses planted instead of tulips. Also, I agree about the patio – I'll go with the Riker paving slabs you suggested. Before I leave the house on Saturday, I'll write down some extra things I'd like you to do, and I'll leave the note on the picnic table in my back yard. Oh, and just a reminder... To get to my place, you need to come in through the West Gate of the housing development. Then take your first left. Thanks, and let me know if you have any questions.

98. Why is the speaker calling?
99. What does the speaker say he will do on Saturday?
100. Look at the graphic. Which neighborhood is the speaker's house located in?

TEST 10

TEST 11

정답

PART 1

1. (B) **2**. (B) **3**. (D) **4**. (A) **5**. (B) **6**. (B)

PART 2

7. (B) **8**. (A) **9**. (C) **10**. (A) **11**. (A) **12**. (B) **13**. (B) **14**. (C) **15**. (A) **16**. (B) **17**. (A) **18**. (B) **19**. (B)
20. (A) **21**. (C) **22**. (C) **23**. (A) **24**. (A) **25**. (C) **26**. (A) **27**. (C) **28**. (C) **29**. (C) **30**. (C) **31**. (B)

PART 3

32. (B) **33**. (A) **34**. (D) **35**. (B) **36**. (A) **37**. (A) **38**. (C) **39**. (A) **40**. (B) **41**. (A) **42**. (D) **43**. (C) **44**. (C)
45. (C) **46**. (C) **47**. (D) **48**. (A) **49**. (C) **50**. (B) **51**. (A) **52**. (C) **53**. (B) **54**. (D) **55**. (C) **56**. (A) **57**. (B)
58. (D) **59**. (A) **60**. (C) **61**. (D) **62**. (D) **63**. (C) **64**. (B) **65**. (C) **66**. (C) **67**. (D) **68**. (C) **69**. (D) **70**. (C)

PART 4

71. (B) **72**. (D) **73**. (D) **74**. (B) **75**. (A) **76**. (D) **77**. (D) **78**. (B) **79**. (B) **80**. (A) **81**. (A) **82**. (D) **83**. (B)
84. (D) **85**. (D) **86**. (D) **87**. (B) **88**. (C) **89**. (D) **90**. (B) **91**. (B) **92**. (D) **93**. (B) **94**. (A) **95**. (A) **96**. (C)
97. (B) **98**. (B) **99**. (B) **100**. (A)

PART 1

1. (A) He is fixing a fence.
(B) He is standing on a ladder.
(C) He is stepping onto a stage.
(D) He is washing a paintbrush.

2. (A) Some tires are being replaced.
(B) Some people are beside a parked car.
(C) They are purchasing suitcases.
(D) They are waiting in line to check in.

3. (A) The tables have been set for dinner.
(B) Chairs have been stacked in a corner.
(C) Some plants are being watered.
(D) Potted flowers have been set on tables.

4. (A) Some people are sitting near a vehicle.
(B) A man is driving a truck down the street.
(C) Some people are setting up chairs.
(D) A woman is cutting down some trees.

5. (A) Some people are using computers.
(B) Some people are waiting at a counter.
(C) Some people are shaking hands.
(D) Some people are walking in the same direction.

6. (A) Some trees surround a parking lot.
(B) Some materials have been piled on the ground.
(C) Supplies are being unloaded from a truck.
(D) Workers are moving some building equipment.

PART 2

7. Who's the new security guard in the east wing?
(A) It's down the hallway to the left.
(B) That would be Arnold Whitehead.
(C) To watch the warehouse.

8. Where is the nearest hardware store?
(A) Just around the corner.
(B) To repair a bookshelf.
(C) A construction worker.

9. When will the software be installed?
(A) No, in the electronics store.
(B) It's a simple installation.
(C) It was set up before lunch.

10. Are you applying for the supervisory position?
(A) No, I'm not qualified.
(B) I'm not sure he will.
(C) She applied for a loan.

11. The second floor renovation will be finished soon, right?
(A) In a few days.
(B) A brand new floor.
(C) She wasn't very busy.

12. Who's responsible for travel reimbursements?
(A) It's on the next page.
(B) I'm not sure but I'll check.
(C) I'm going on a trip overseas.

13. Isn't the highway restricted due to construction?
(A) Marvin revised the contract.
(B) No, they completed it last week.
(C) My boss is very strict about doing it.

14. Mr. Johnson called to say he just sent the proposal.
(A) That's what I proposed.
(B) I didn't return his call.
(C) Well, let's check it out.

15. Where will they take the client before the exhibition?
(A) To the research laboratory.
(B) About the new line of washing machines.
(C) Following the commercial's debut.

16. Which batteries does this radio use?
(A) Every two or three months.
(B) The ones in my drawer.
(C) I'm buying a new TV.

17. Would you rather order the leather chairs or the vinyl chairs?
(A) The vinyl ones are much cheaper.
(B) Around a hundred dollars.
(C) Yes, we received them.

18. Perhaps we should decorate the lobby.
(A) It might be for the ceremony.
(B) Sure. Let's get started.
(C) No, Mr. Foster created it.

19. Where can we find restaurants that serve Korean food?
(A) He lived in Seoul for many years.
(B) Harriet can point some out.
(C) They are resting in the lounge.

20. Why aren't we still manufacturing the phones?
(A) There was an issue with them.
(B) No, I'm not busy.
(C) I bought a new one.

21. When did Angelica get hired?
(A) It was a terrific interview.
(B) In the Accounting Department.
(C) Not too long ago.

22. I need someone to accompany me to the conference.
(A) No, she didn't.
(B) A technology company.
(C) I could lend you a hand.

23. Won't the branch opening boost profits?
(A) Well, it might not.
(B) They extended the opening hours.
(C) Yes, if you would like to.

24. How are you getting to the convention?
(A) By subway.
(B) The first two speeches.
(C) That wasn't my intention.

25. Would you prefer a seat in the front row, or on the balcony?
(A) I'm feeling down.
(B) Move a little to the right.
(C) Up in front, I guess.

26. There are rumors that Ms. Higuchi is retiring.
(A) Seriously? I don't believe it.
(B) The rooms seem very spacious.
(C) Yes, she's hiring an assistant.

27. Why hasn't the train arrived yet?
(A) Let's meet at the station.
(B) One more hour.
(C) There was a delay.

28. How did you like the hotel?
(A) Close to the airport.
(B) No, only once or twice.
(C) It wasn't very comfortable.

29. Won't it cost too much to renovate the bathroom?
(A) It should be in the kitchen.
(B) Yes, she said that she might.
(C) Only if we change the flooring.

30. I was shocked to see your full page ad in the newspaper.
(A) No, thank you. I'm already full.
(B) I watch the nightly news on Channel 13.
(C) That way we'll get more publicity.

31. Should we go directly to the airport or stop for some lunch first?

(A) It's a direct flight.

(B) I don't mind.

(C) Yes, that's correct.

PART 3

Questions 32-34 refer to the following conversation.

M: Susan, did you go to the press conference yesterday? Ms. Walken mentioned you by name, but nobody could find you.

W: Unfortunately, I didn't. I was originally scheduled to discuss the benefits of getting seasonal passes for our spring line of plays, but I couldn't make it. I tried to get back to the theater after a meeting with some investors, but I got stuck in traffic.

M: That's too bad. There were plenty of reporters there. I read a very enthusiastic article in this morning's paper, too. You should go to my office and pick up my copy.

32. What event did the woman miss?

33. Why did the woman miss the event?

34. What does the man suggest the woman do?

Questions 35-37 refer to the following conversation.

M: Hi, Lillian. I'm having an issue setting up this printer. Whenever I try to print something, this red light keeps flashing. I'm pretty sure that everything is plugged in properly.

W: Oh, I think you were at lunch when the delivery man dropped it off. He noted that your computer needs to have special software downloaded in order to make it compatible. It won't work unless you do that.

M: OK, I see. I did find this disk in the box, but I have no idea how to install it properly. Should I call someone from the IT Department?

W: I don't think so. I remember seeing an instruction manual when you removed the printer from the box. Maybe you should check to see if you can find it in there.

35. What is the man having problems with?

36. What happened while the man was on his lunch break?

37. What does the woman tell the man to do?

Questions 38-40 refer to the following conversation with three speakers.

M: We need to organize a dinner for Mark in the Accounting Department. He's turning forty next week.

W1: Great idea! But, he's not in Accounting anymore. He moved to the General Affairs Department last week.

M: Oh, that's right! Anyway, do either of you have any ideas for a fairly cheap place where we could host a party?

W2: Hmm... How about King Lobster on the corner of 12th and Bergdorf? It gets great reviews.

M: I thought of that, but unfortunately, it went out of business recently.

W1: Then why don't Lauren and I contact some local places and check how much their dishes cost?

W2: Yes, we'll try to find somewhere relatively cheap and get back to you later.

38. What are the speakers mainly discussing?
39. What problem does the man mention?
40. What do the women intend to do?

Questions 41-43 refer to the following conversation.

M: Hello, Tamika. I'm really impressed with your suggestions for the menu. It's so important to keep thinking up exciting new choices ever since our location was featured in that newspaper article.

W: I know. Now customers expect us to constantly come up with different pizza options. And it's been so busy here lately that I don't know how we will possibly be able to meet the demand once we unveil this bigger new menu.

M: I've been thinking a lot about that. Do you think it would be a good idea to purchase a new oven? We have plenty of space and it would allow us to keep up with all of the orders.

41. Where do the speakers most likely work?
42. What are the speakers discussing?
43. What does the man suggest doing?

Questions 44-46 refer to the following conversation.

W: Robert, would you mind pulling over at the corner? I want to jump out and grab a coffee and a bagel from the Artisan Café.

M: Are you sure that's a good idea? Your interview at Polaris Construction starts at 10 A.M. And that coffee shop is always so busy.

W: Only between 8 and 9. It should be empty right now.

M: If you're sure, then. And, if we are stopping anyway, I might as well come in and get something for myself.

44. Where is the conversation taking place?
45. What will the woman do this morning?
46. What does the woman imply when she says, "It should be empty right now"?

Questions 47-49 refer to the following conversation.

W: Good evening, Mr. Lomas. This is Eve Dickey, your advisor from Cartel Consulting. I was calling to discuss our findings concerning your company's proposal to acquire Redwater Industries.

M: Excellent. I was expecting your call. We've really been struggling with this decision so we were interested in what you had to say. We were wondering in particular if it would be worth it, since their factories seem to be less productive than most others in the industry.

W: We also pinpointed that as a potential problem. However, we think with a few minor changes you can drastically improve them. If you can give us a little time to put something together, we'll come to your office next week and present our recommendations to you in person. Then you can make your final decision.

47. What is the conversation mainly about?
48. What are the speakers worried about?
49. What does the woman say she will do next week?

Questions 50-52 refer to the following conversation with three speakers.

M1: Ms. Harmon, we don't have any more films showing tonight, and Steve and I have already cleaned the auditoriums. Would you mind if we head off fifteen minutes early?

M2: Yes, there's a big concert downtown tonight, and although we aren't going, we're worried about how busy the streets will be. It might take a while to get home.

W: Oh, that's no problem at all. But, Philip, would you mind quickly changing the posters in the foyer? We need to put the new ones up.

M1: Okay. They're in the main office, right?

W: That's right. Just on top of the file cabinets.

M2: I'll go and get those and lend you a hand, Philip. We'll get it done faster doing it together.

50. Where do the speakers most likely work?
51. Why do the men want to leave work early?
52. What does the woman ask Philip to do?

Questions 53-55 refer to the following conversation.

M: Martha, the restaurant won't be closing for another three hours, but there's barely any salad dressing or bread sticks left. We'd better watch our levels.
W: I've already told the chef about it. He said that he already noticed the shortages yesterday.
M: Oh, really? Well, I wish he had told me about it. If he had spoken to me, I could've replenished our supplies today.
W: I mentioned that to him. Well, what are we going to do for the rest of the evening?
M: I guess I should go to our other branch to borrow the items we need. I should be back within 45 minutes.

53. What does the man mean when he says, "We'd better watch our levels"?
54. What has caused a problem?
55. What will the man probably do next?

Questions 56-58 refer to the following conversation.

M: We'll have to make some changes to next month's company newsletter. I've just heard that Steven Cobb, the founder and CEO of Polyzon Corporation, will be visiting our city. He is scheduled to give a lecture at Laverne University.
W: Oh, this will be of great interest to everyone at our company. Mr. Cobb has done so much for the field of electronics, especially the sizable amounts of money he has invested in promising start-up firms.
M: That's why I'd like you to find out more about his lecture by getting in touch with the Public Affairs Department at the university. I've already tried to contact Mr. Cobb directly, but I have yet to hear anything back from him or his staff. I'm sure our employees would like to read about the event in the newsletter and find out how to get tickets.

56. What are the speakers discussing?
57. What has Mr. Cobb done for the field of electronics?
58. What does the man ask the woman to do?

Questions 59-61 refer to the following conversation.

M: Hi, Athena. It looks like you've already discovered that our new computers have arrived. What do you think of them?
W: I'm checking out a movie I downloaded and it looks amazing on this monitor. I'd really like to purchase a new one for my home computer, so this model might be perfect for me.
M: Actually, when our company bought these computers, they sent extra coupons for all of their electronics, including monitors. It would save you thirty percent off the retail value. I could give you one of them if you wanted.
W: That sounds wonderful. I've wanted a new computer monitor for a few months now, but they are all so expensive. Maybe I'll finally be able to get one with this discount.

59. What are the speakers mainly discussing?
60. What does the man offer to do?
61. What is the woman's problem?

Questions 62-64 refer to the following conversation and poster.

W: Hi, I'm here to pick up the posters for the Willard County Airshow. Are they ready yet?
M: Yes, we just finished printing them. Here you are. That'll be $50, please.
W: Hold on a moment. I'm sorry, but there's a mistake. Kids actually get into the event for free!
M: Oh, dear! I'm not sure how that happened. I'll take care of that straight away. Would you mind coming back in a couple of hours?
W: No, that's okay. I have some other supplies to buy for the event anyway. Shall I just pay when I come back then?
M: Yes, and I'm really sorry for the inconvenience.

62. Who most likely is the man?
63. Look at the graphic. What information on the poster should be changed?
64. What will the woman probably do next?

TEST 11

Questions 65-67 refer to the following conversation and list.

M: Harriet, is the conference room all set up for our meeting with the clients this afternoon?
W: Everything is ready, except there's a problem that I guess we both forgot about.
M: Oh, what's that?
W: Did you forget that the TV in that room broke down a few days ago?
M: Ah, of course. We'll need one to present our data to the clients. I'll rush out and buy a new one at lunchtime.
W: Make sure you get one with a bright display and high resolution. We'll want to present our graphs clearly.
M: Definitely. I'll get a Psion Full HD TV, and I'll make sure that it's the biggest one they have.

65. What are the speakers preparing for?
66. What is the woman concerned about?
67. Look at the graphic. Which television will the man most likely buy?

Questions 68-70 refer to the following conversation and screenshot.

M: Do you have a minute, Rachel? I wanted to test out this new program, but I can't open it on my computer. I e-mailed you a download link for it.
W: Oh, I was wondering what that was. I'll start the download now.
M: Thanks. If it's effective, I'm going to recommend it to everyone at the meeting today. Will you be there?
W: No, I'm not a part of that team project. The manager wants me to stay focused on our international clients.

68. Look at the graphic. What is the name of the man speaking?
69. How will the woman help the man?
70. Why will the woman be absent from a meeting?

PART 4

Questions 71-73 refer to the following telephone message.

Hello, I'm calling for Grant Noriega. My name is Heidi Thames, the superintendent for the Stansfield Tower Apartments. I just read your message regarding the visit from our maintenance worker, Jimmy Moreland. Apparently, he finished the installation of your new washing machine, but forgot to complete the repair of your air conditioner. He is out of town for the evening, but I will give him a call first thing in the morning to have him stop by your apartment again. Each apartment has different air conditioner units, so I need you to call me back with the make and model number so we can be sure that we will be able to repair it right away. I apologize for any inconvenience.

71. What is the speaker calling about?
72. What does the speaker say she will do tomorrow?
73. What is the listener asked to do?

Questions 74-76 refer to the following announcement.

As the CEO of Welker Industries, I am delighted to be able to tell you that, as of next month, we will be shooting our own TV commercials for all of our products. We have just finished building a studio in our headquarters in Detroit, and the first shoot is scheduled for August 13. This will allow us to take advantage of the talents of some of our gifted young public relations staff. By creating our videos here, we can make our commercials as we are developing products, so we can start our advertising campaigns just as our products are released.

74. What will be made in the new facility?
75. According to the speaker, where will the new facility be?
76 According to the speaker, what is an advantage of the new facility?

Questions 77-79 refer to the following instructions.

A lot of our guests are complaining about lost reservations, so I think some of you have been entering their room requests into the system incorrectly. So, let's quickly review how to confirm reservations using our Web site. Now, first of all, be sure to log in as an employee. This will let you view and alter our schedule. Then, select the dates the guest requested and add the room details in the text box at the right corner of the window. If everyone does this correctly, we should have fewer errors. If you continue having problems, Sean will be in later.

77. Where most likely are the listeners?
78. What are the speaker's instructions mainly about?
79. What does the speaker imply when she says, "Sean will be in later"?

Questions 80-82 refer to the following tour information.

As part of your orientation at Flexo Fitness Center, you'll be taught how to use our brand-new running machines. Each Travelex 500 treadmill is equipped with a 3.8-horsepower motor and can reach a top speed of 19 kilometers per hour. That's 2 kilometers per hour more than our old machines, which were equipped with less powerful 3.5-horsepower motors. In a moment, we'll enter the main gym, and our most experienced fitness instructor, Mr. Kang, will demonstrate how the machine works and explain the different pre-installed exercise programs. Afterwards, I'll show you the free weights area and give you some safety tips.

80. Who most likely are the listeners?
81. How are the new machines better than the previous ones?
82. What will Mr. Kang do?

Questions 83-85 refer to the following telephone message.

Hello, Mr. Crowley. This is Rebecca Moffat calling from Onyx Interiors. Thanks for confirming all the details in the renovation plan I sent to you yesterday, and for sending the initial down payment for the work. With all of that taken care of, we're finally ready to go! My team and I will arrive at your home at 55 Valley Road at 8:30 on Monday morning and begin preparations for the remodeling. We'll get all the painting done during the first week and move on to the carpeting, curtains, and furnishings the following week. Don't forget to take a look at the carpet samples I gave you, and then let me know your preference when I see you. Thanks.

83. Where does the speaker most likely work?
84. Why does the speaker say, "We're finally ready to go"?
85. What is the listener reminded to do?

Questions 86-88 refer to the following telephone message.

Hi, this is Jackson Smith, the branch manager of Fitz Financial. Yesterday, the PX5400 copy machine I ordered arrived at our office. However, the instruction manual wasn't sent with it, and it's a rather complicated machine. I checked your Web site to see if there was one I could download, but when I checked the "Manuals" page, it wasn't there. I think the fastest way to resolve this would be for you to just send an e-mail with the attached document. Please send it to jsmith@fitz.com. We have a lot of printing to do, so please respond soon.

86. What is the purpose of the message?
87. What does the speaker say about the Web site?
88. What does the speaker request?

TEST 11

Questions 89-91 refer to the following excerpt from a meeting.

Thanks for coming in early, everyone. Before the restaurant opens tonight, I need to talk to you about the rise in complaints we've received from diners. I've heard that some servers have been bringing customers the wrong dishes, and some kitchen staff have been failing to prepare food correctly. This just won't do. To address this issue, starting next week, I'll be carrying out regular performance evaluations on all staff. If you have any questions about your job duties, please feel free to ask me at any time. Now, let's make sure the dining area and kitchen are spotless before the first customers arrive.

89. What is the speaker mainly discussing?
90. What does the speaker mean when she says, "This just won't do"?
91. What will the listeners do next?

Questions 92-94 refer to the following telephone message.

Good morning. Is this the office of Victor Cruz? This is Lisa Mason from the Purchasing Department at Malgalo Foods. I'm contacting you because your company has been supplying us with the tomatoes for our pasta since we were founded. However, there's a chance that we will have to cancel our contract because we want to switch to all organic vegetables in April. I understand that you have begun producing organic tomatoes as well, and I'd be interested in hearing more about them. I'll let you know how much we'd be interested in ordering. I would also like to know roughly how much this would cost in total. I would appreciate it if you could give me this information by e-mailing me at the usual address. Thanks.

92. What department does the speaker work in?
93. What is scheduled to happen in April?
94. What does the speaker ask the listener to do?

Questions 95-97 refer to the following telephone message and list.

Hello, this is Troy Barnes calling. I've been a customer of yours for 12 months and have really enjoyed your cable TV, Internet and phone services. I'd like to sign up for a further 12 months, so I was hoping I could just do that over the phone. Please make sure that my package continues to include the Golden Years movie option. I've been really impressed with the number of classic films I've been able to watch thanks to that feature. I currently pay $24.99 each month, and I assume I can continue receiving the same service at the same rate. Please call me back to confirm. Thanks.

95. What is the main purpose of the message?
96. What is the speaker most pleased with?
97. Look at the graphic. Which package does the speaker currently have?

Questions 98-100 refer to the following excerpt from a meeting and chart.

I'd like to start this meeting by taking a look at the data for new subscribers last month. As the founder of the firm, I'm very pleased with the figures, especially considering our closest rival launched several new magazines in February. *Prime Fitness* is once again our most popular magazine, with more than three thousand new subscribers signing up for a 12-month subscription in March. This is partly due to the complimentary water bottle and gym towel we offered to new subscribers. Only one of our magazines failed to attract more than two thousand subscribers in March. Let's take a look at some strategies we can use to try to boost that publication's appeal.

98. Who most likely is the speaker?
99. According to the speaker, what happened in March?
100. Look at the graphic. Which magazine will the speaker discuss next?

TEST 12

TEST 12

정답

PART 1

1. (C) **2**. (B) **3**. (B) **4**. (D) **5**. (D) **6**. (C)

PART 2

7. (C) **8**. (B) **9**. (C) **10**. (A) **11**. (C) **12**. (A) **13**. (B) **14**. (A) **15**. (B) **16**. (A) **17**. (C) **18**. (B) **19**. (B)
20. (C) **21**. (C) **22**. (A) **23**. (C) **24**. (B) **25**. (B) **26**. (B) **27**. (C) **28**. (C) **29**. (A) **30**. (C) **31**. (B)

PART 3

32. (A) **33**. (C) **34**. (C) **35**. (B) **36**. (D) **37**. (A) **38**. (B) **39**. (D) **40**. (A) **41**. (C) **42**. (B) **43**. (D) **44**. (B)
45. (D) **46**. (A) **47**. (C) **48**. (B) **49**. (A) **50**. (D) **51**. (D) **52**. (A) **53**. (A) **54**. (D) **55**. (C) **56**. (C) **57**. (D)
58. (C) **59**. (A) **60**. (B) **61**. (C) **62**. (D) **63**. (C) **64**. (D) **65**. (A) **66**. (A) **67**. (C) **68**. (C) **69**. (D) **70**. (B)

PART 4

71. (C) **72**. (C) **73**. (D) **74**. (B) **75**. (C) **76**. (D) **77**. (C) **78**. (A) **79**. (D) **80**. (B) **81**. (C) **82**. (A) **83**. (D)
84. (D) **85**. (D) **86**. (A) **87**. (B) **88**. (D) **89**. (B) **90**. (D) **91**. (A) **92**. (C) **93**. (B) **94**. (C) **95**. (C) **96**. (C)
97. (B) **98**. (D) **99**. (B) **100**. (C)

PART 1

1. (A) He is putting on his hat.
(B) He is preparing some food.
(C) He is washing his hands.
(D) He is clearing away some utensils.

2. (A) They're looking out the window.
(B) A man is addressing a group.
(C) A woman is arranging items on the table.
(D) A man is handing out papers.

3. (A) People are standing on the balconies.
(B) Some of the blinds have been raised.
(C) Some windows are being washed.
(D) The balconies overlook the park.

4. (A) Passengers are boarding a yacht.
(B) A man is talking on his cell phone.
(C) Boats are being tied to the dock.
(D) A man is standing near the water.

5. (A) Office supplies are spread out on the desks.
(B) A computer monitor is being turned on.
(C) Workstations are separated by glass partitions.
(D) Plants have been arranged in an office.

6. (A) Pedestrians have gathered to watch a performance.
(B) Some people are walking under a bridge.
(C) A clock is on the exterior of the building.
(D) People are chatting at an outdoor café.

PART 2

7. When should we schedule the appointment?
(A) In Mr. Slaughter's office.
(B) It isn't occupied.
(C) How does eleven sound?

8. Who is demonstrating our new air purifier this weekend?
(A) At the convention center.
(B) The public relations team.
(C) Yes, at the very end.

9. Where did Harold put the file this morning?
(A) To show the client.
(B) I wrote it yesterday evening.
(C) On top of the cabinet.

10. How was the presentation rehearsal last night?
(A) There were too many mistakes.
(B) Yes, with the wall projector.
(C) He's feeling sick.

11. Joel is taking you to the airport, isn't he?
(A) He got a really great deal.
(B) The flight is about four hours.
(C) No, he had to change his plans.

12. What was the meeting about?
(A) Menu options.
(B) I'm pretty sure.
(C) He brought a few.

13. Which room contains the cleaning supplies?
(A) But I ordered some new ones.
(B) The second one on the left.
(C) No, it's drying.

14. The plants need to be watered before we leave.
(A) Andre told me that he'd do it.
(B) I'd like to reserve some.
(C) No, I left one in my office.

15. Could you show me how to work the control panel?
(A) Not very often.
(B) It might take a little while.
(C) It was my pleasure.

16. Would you update the inventory on the Web site this afternoon?
(A) Unfortunately, I have other obligations.
(B) Did she arrive this morning?
(C) Yes, if they are invited.

17. Why were so many cameras installed in our store?
(A) An electronic malfunction.
(B) I can't operate any of them.
(C) So nobody will steal our merchandise.

18. Who will be the new manager of the Publishing Department?
(A) On the twelfth floor.
(B) I believe it's Wesley Elizondo.
(C) I'll schedule it for 4.

19. How many guest speakers will be at the convention?
(A) The first one is at five thirty.
(B) Let me look at the schedule.
(C) You'll have to convince me.

20. Aren't you driving to the seminar tomorrow?
(A) He took a taxi.
(B) It's about office management.
(C) I thought it was next Friday.

21. Would you prefer to listen to the radio or watch TV?
(A) I'll turn it up.
(B) We left them on the counter.
(C) I don't mind either.

22. How did you feel about the speech?
(A) It was so inspiring.
(B) He showed up in time.
(C) At the Grand Pavilion.

23. Can I make some recommendations about your trip?
(A) It will last for around ten days.
(B) I'm thinking of taking a flight.
(C) I always appreciate your advice.

24. How much food do we need to order?
(A) Two more signatures.
(B) That depends on the attendance.
(C) For the most part.

25. I thought this suit included a free tie.
(A) Put it on for the ceremony.
(B) No, that's sold separately.
(C) Aren't they still in production?

26. Why don't you take out an ad in the paper?
(A) Maybe you could try the classified section.
(B) I was thinking of putting one online.
(C) Around one or two pages.

27. Could Alex stop by my office, or is he in a meeting?
(A) He was officially hired.
(B) It's on my desk.
(C) Oh, he just took off.

28. The new restaurant on 3rd Street has some of the worst service in town.
(A) I haven't rested all evening.
(B) The boiled lobster with lemon sauce.
(C) I know, but the food is incredible.

29. You still haven't fixed the air conditioner, have you?
(A) No, I'll try to this afternoon.
(B) I'm washing them now.
(C) I haven't seen the picture.

30. Why did Betty Parkinson appear on the talk show?
(A) No, she's from New York.
(B) In the main studio.
(C) To promote her new film.

31. The head office requires that you hand in a doctor's notice for sick days.

(A) No, she's visiting the dentist.

(B) Is that a recent rule change?

(C) A two o'clock appointment.

PART 3

Questions 32-34 refer to the following conversation.

M: Hello, I'm Albert Mcbride from Boxhead Auto Repair. The flower shop owner phoned me saying that a vehicle needs to be repaired.

W: I'm the owner. Thanks for coming down here so quickly. I'm so glad that you're here. Our delivery man was about to take the car to deliver some roses to a client when the engine stopped working. We have four more deliveries to make this evening, and the engine won't even start now.

M: That could be a few things. Could you get the keys for me? I want to look under the hood and see if the wires are connected properly.

32. Where does the conversation most likely take place?

33. What is the problem?

34. What does the man say he will do next?

Questions 35-37 refer to the following conversation with three speakers.

M: Good morning, Miranda. This is our new sales representative, Priyanka Kapoor.

W1: Welcome to the company.

W2: Thank you.

M: The entire sales team will have lunch together to greet her. But I thought you'd like to meet her earlier since she'll be taking over a lot of your duties. So I thought you could get started on her training, Miranda.

W1: Oh, of course. Are you free today, Priyanka?

W2: Well, I have orientation all morning.

W1: I have a meeting soon anyways. How about this afternoon?

W2: That will work. Could you bring some examples of your weekly reports so I can see what they're like?

35. In which department do the speakers work?

36. What does the man suggest that the women do?

37. What does Priyanka Kapoor ask for?

Questions 38-40 refer to the following conversation.

M: Wow, your menu is really amazing. My uncle told me I should check out your restaurant. He said that this place is wonderful for people who do not eat meat, and he was right.

W: Yes, we pride ourselves on having a diverse menu that caters to a wide variety of people. And it's about to get better. Next month we will start receiving our produce from Marigold Farm, which is known for having the freshest and most delicious fruits and vegetables in the area. Have you decided what you want to eat?

M: I'll have the broccoli pasta with fennel. Oh, but I'm allergic to wheat.

W: That shouldn't be a problem. I'll make sure that the pasta noodles aren't made with wheat.

38. Why was the restaurant recommended to the man?
39. What does the woman say is happening next month?
40. What will the woman most likely do next?

Questions 41-43 refer to the following conversation.

M: Good afternoon. This is Cosimo Ruben from the Ruben Group. I'm calling to confirm my company's online order for thirty of your cars. I was also hoping they could be delivered by next week.

W: Terrific. Let me just verify this on our network. Okay, it looks like everything is in order. By the way, if you're going to continue purchasing so many vehicles from us, I'd recommend signing up for a corporate member's account for huge discounts.

M: Oh, if I did that now, could I get the cost of this purchase reduced?

W: Well, I can't authorize that on my own. Let me have my supervisor call you back to discuss your options.

41. Why is the man calling the woman?
42. What does the woman suggest?
43. What does the woman offer to do?

Questions 44-46 refer to the following conversation with three speakers.

M1: Are you both excited about the charity tennis tournament this weekend?

M2: Yes, it should be a lot of fun, and we should be able to raise a lot of money for the local children's hospital.

W: I hope so. How do you plan on getting to the tennis courts in Kings Park?

M1: I think I'll just take the subway there. Traffic can be pretty bad on the weekends, and it might be hard to find a parking space. Right, Desmond?

M2: Well, there are usually plenty of spots on Rickard Avenue, and that's just a 5-minute walk from the courts.

W: Hmm... I'll probably drive then. So, do you guys want to meet for breakfast before the event begins?

M1: Sure. We need to be at the park by 9:30 A.M., so let's meet one hour before that.

44. What is the main topic of the conversation?
45. What does Desmond mention about Rickard Avenue?
46. What does the woman suggest?

Questions 47-49 refer to the following conversation.

W: Hi, this is Tricia Hayes, and I would like some information about my reservation for April 10. My coworker just informed me that our room isn't available now, but I haven't heard anything about it. Shouldn't I have been notified?

M: I apologize, but I did call the number on the account. I must've spoken with your secretary. But anyways, it seems that we were unable to accept your credit card. And as for the room you requested, it was booked by another party during the delay. Would you like me to book another one for you?

W: I actually don't have the time at the moment. I need to leave the office now if I'm ever going to beat this rush hour traffic. I'll call back once I get home, and we'll resolve this issue.

47. According to the man, what was the company unable to do?
48. What does the man offer to do for the woman?
49. Why does the woman need to leave soon?

Questions 50-52 refer to the following conversation.

M: Claire, I just overheard that you'll be on the local news to promote next week's fundraiser. That will really help us out. When will it air?

W: I'll be on the Wednesday morning show. And, actually, I would really appreciate it if you would do it with me. You are the event organizer, after all.

TEST 12

M: Oh, I wish I could, but I'll be out of town on Wednesday visiting some of our biggest donors. I'd be happy to go over some talking points with you before then, though.

50. What is the woman doing on Wednesday?
51. Why does the woman say, "You are the event organizer, after all"?
52. What does the man need to do on Wednesday?

Questions 53-55 refer to the following conversation.

W: Robert, can you make thirty copies of the poster highlighting our plan to expand overseas? I want them to be prominently displayed in each of our local branches by next Monday, so it's crucial to send them out today.
M: Well, I talked to the head of our printing department earlier, and he said that the ink would take at least twenty-four hours to dry, so we wouldn't be able to send them out today.
W: Oh, no. Maybe we should have them printed at a professional printing shop. They may have the capability to finish the posters today. Plus, most of them usually have delivery services as well.

53. What does the woman mention about the posters?
54. What problem does the man report?
55. What does the woman recommend doing?

Questions 56-58 refer to the following conversation.

M: Hello. I have a sore shoulder from playing basketball, and I wanted to try a new brand of heat therapy patches called Estus Recovery. Do you carry it at this pharmacy?
W: We do! That item is right over here.
M: There it is. But... I've never used it before.
W: Oh, it's very simple. Just follow the instructions on the packaging. It's all right here.
M: It looks easy enough. Also, I would like to print some pictures from a family picnic.
W: I'm guessing you took them with your smart phone? If so, you can use our photo kiosk located next to the checkout counter. I can show you how to use it.
M: Sure, if you wouldn't mind.

56. Where most likely are the speakers?
57. What does the man mean when he says, "I've never used it before"?
58. Where will the speakers most likely go next?

Questions 59-61 refer to the following conversation.

M: I'm so glad that you decided to submit an application and some writing examples to us, Ms. Florence. I was really astonished by how beautifully written your articles were. You have such a unique perspective on a variety of topics. May I ask you why you want to work here, though? The publication you currently work for is so much more successful.
W: To be honest, I'm getting a little frustrated by the direction they are moving in. They used to confront important issues, but they are increasingly covering more trivial matters like fashion and the lives of celebrities.
M: Well, we would like to appeal to a more sophisticated audience, especially with regard to global matters. In fact, we hope that you would be willing to fly to Europe or Asia fairly often to do in-depth research.

59. What about the woman impressed the man?
60. Why does the woman say she is interested in the job?
61. According to the man, what does the job require?

Questions 62-64 refer to the following conversation and coupon.

M: Thanks for calling Zane's Office Supplies customer service. What can I do for you?
W: Hi, I would like to buy some A4 paper from your online store with a coupon I received for having a membership.
M: Oh, sure. That's for the delivery order discount? What's the total cost of the paper you're buying?
W: It's 15 reams, so... $75. However, when I check out, it won't accept the discount. It stays at $75.
M: You know, I don't think the promotion was programmed correctly into the online store. Let me speak with our Web designer, and then I'll call you back.
W: OK. I'll talk to you soon.

62. What is the woman trying to buy?
63. Look at the graphic. Which discount should the

woman receive?

64. What does the man offer to do?

Questions 65-67 refer to the following conversation and poster.

W: I can't wait to start working on the advertisements for the new restaurant that just opened.
M: Me, too. The owner was very friendly, and it seems like he wants something creative and new for the ads. I already have some great ideas for the commercial.
W: Yeah, it should be a lot of fun. But, for now, I'm ready for the weekend. Do you have any plans?
M: I'm going to check out the literature festival at the university.
W: Oh, I will, too. Every year, I go on the first day because that's when poets come to speak. Charles Kinney is giving a lecture this year.
M: Really? He's one of my favorite poets. I'm sure he'll give an excellent talk.

65. What project will the speakers be working on?
66. Look at the graphic. Which date will the woman attend the festival?
67. Who is Charles Kinney?

Questions 68-70 refer to the following conversation and list.

M: Okay, Ms. Hodge, we've organized your hotel room and car rental. The last thing we need to do is finalize your flight ticket. You just need a one-way ticket, right?
W: That's right. I'd like a seat on Corsair Airways Flight CA 56. I already checked the tickets online, and I'd like the one that costs $5,200.
M: No problem... I'll get that booked for you straight away. Do you have any special requirements?
W: Actually, yes. Please make sure that I get a vegetarian meal. And, I'd prefer a seat next to a window.

68. Where is the conversation most likely taking place?
69. Look at the graphic. What type of ticket does the woman purchase?
70. What special request does the woman make?

PART 4

Questions 71-73 refer to the following talk.

Welcome back. I'm pleased that everyone could attend today's business writing workshop. For the first 20 minutes, you will each write a business letter. After everyone is finished, we will hear from Richard Bowers, who will explain common mistakes that people make while writing. You will then have a chance to read your letter again and check for mistakes you may have made. You should also remember that, next week, we will be starting our research reports, so you need to have an idea for a topic when you show up. If you have trouble thinking of one, you should look on our Web site for a list of ideas.

71. What will listeners most likely do when they finish writing?
72. What does the speaker remind listeners about?
73. What does the speaker say can be found on a Web site?

Questions 74-76 refer to the following announcement.

Before you leave, I have one final reminder. As I mentioned last week, it is the firm's annual Career Day next Sunday. Like previous years, we'll be providing lots of product demonstrations and giving talks about career opportunities within our company. We still need volunteers to operate information kiosks in each of our departments, and you can sign up to help out with that by sending an e-mail to Clint Howe in the personnel office. We hope to recruit more new staff this year than ever before. Oh, and don't forget that I'd like you all to come in 30 minutes earlier than usual on Monday so that we can clean up any remaining event materials in our offices.

74. What kind of event is being discussed?
75. According to the speaker, what can listeners do by e-mail?
76. Why should listeners arrive early on Monday?

Questions 77-79 refer to the following radio broadcast.

You're listening to Food Heaven on Radio WRSP, and next I'd like to bring you a quick review of a new restaurant called Mandalay. I was lucky enough to attend its big opening night last night, and it was a fun event, with several local celebrities in attendance. The interior of the restaurant is beautiful, but when it comes to the food, well... I've had better. Perhaps things will improve over the next few weeks. I must admit, however, that the prices were reasonable and the service was excellent. Now, for those of you who prefer to eat at home, stay tuned, because I'll be back in a moment with some advice on making the perfect steaks.

77. What is the speaker mainly discussing?
78. What does the speaker mean when she says, "I've had better"?
79. What will the speaker talk about next?

Questions 80-82 refer to the following telephone message.

Good afternoon, Ms. Livingston. This is Tyler McFarlane calling you back. I'm really excited that you agreed to hire me at Cielo Industries' Marketing Department. I know that we agreed in principle to all the terms of the contract, but now I'm having second thoughts. I've decided that I would like a five percent salary increase over the figure that we previously settled on. Another potential employer came back to me with a much improved offer, so I feel like it'd be in my best interest to ask for more money. I have not signed anything with them yet, but I'll call you tomorrow and let you know by what date I will need you to make your decision. Thanks for your patience, and I'll talk to you soon.

80. Who most likely is the message for?
81. Why is the speaker calling?
82. What does the speaker say he will do tomorrow?

Questions 83-85 refer to the following introduction.

Good morning, everyone. I gathered you here because I'd like to formally introduce you all to Dr. Ferrier, who will primarily be treating patients here on Ward 21. Now, remember... It's his first day. He won't know where we keep some of our equipment or how we fill out certain paperwork, so he'll need to rely on all of you until he gets settled in. Also, we'll be having a welcome dinner at Mario's Bistro at 7 P.M. next Tuesday, and all workers from Ward 21 are encouraged to attend. I hope to see all of you there.

83. Where is the talk taking place?
84. Why does the speaker say, "It's his first day"?
85. According to the speaker, what will happen on Tuesday?

Questions 86-88 refer to the following excerpt from a meeting.

I'd like to welcome everybody to today's meeting. The main item on today's agenda is the implementation of our new preparation policy for the kitchen. By now, I am sure that everyone has heard of our difficulties keeping up with customers' orders because it takes so long to prepare many of our salads and appetizers. Therefore, we will occasionally prepare certain menu items before leaving at the end of the day, which will make serving them much easier the following day and let us focus on our main entrées. Unfortunately, this means that each of you will have to work a little bit longer than normal on certain nights. Your station leaders will notify you when you are expected to perform this duty. Next, I would like to speak about how we will be preparing each of these items.

86. Who most likely is the speaker?
87. What problem does the speaker mention?
88. What are the station leaders expected to do?

Questions 89-91 refer to the following excerpt from a speech.

Hello, everyone. I'm so excited to be giving a reading here in Southampton for the first time ever. I've received a lot of e-mails from people requesting that I stop off here during my tour, so I'm glad I have this opportunity. *Principles of the Premises* is the first book I've published in a few years, and I really hope that you enjoy it. After my reading, I'd like to discuss effective ways to resurface the exteriors of real estate using cheap, simple methods. A lot of people don't realize that it's actually quite easy to improve not just how a property looks, but how much it is worth. Also, if you sign up for my mailing list, information about some of the discussion topics will be sent directly to you. Okay, then. Let's get started.

89. What has the speaker recently done?
90. What does the speaker want to discuss?
91. What does the speaker encourage listeners to do?

Questions 92-94 refer to the following telephone message.

Hi, Geraldine. I'm just calling to let you know the plan for Barcelona this week. Again, I'm very pleased that you offered to join me on this trip. I'm going to appreciate your help when I'm preparing for my talk at the engineering conference on Friday. Anyway, here's the plan... We'll be arriving in Barcelona on Thursday evening and then checking into the Plaza Hotel. After my talk the next day, we'll go for dinner with some of our colleagues based in Europe. I know you wanted to visit some of Barcelona's famous cathedrals on Saturday, but... our flight is at 12. Hopefully, you'll have another opportunity in the future. Let's talk more tomorrow.

92. Why is the speaker calling?
93. What will the speaker do on Friday?
94. What does the speaker mean when she says, "our flight is at 12"?

Questions 95-97 refer to the following telephone message and list.

Hello, this is Dan Stevens calling from the administration office at Topeka National Park. I received your message regarding your upcoming trip to the park, and I'm calling to confirm that I've reserved the cabin with 3 bathrooms and 5 bedrooms for you and your group. I've also spoken to Martin Cosgrove, our climbing instructor, and signed you up for his advanced classes at Ridgeback Mountain. Please don't forget that you'll need to pay a security deposit when you arrive at the park on Saturday morning. This will be returned to you at the end of your trip, as long as no damage occurs to the cabin.

95. Who most likely is the speaker?
96. Look at the graphic. Which cabin has been reserved for the listener?
97. What should the listener do on Saturday?

Questions 98-100 refer to the following talk and diagram.

Before the restaurant opens today, I'd like to discuss some health and safety issues. Several employees have reported burns and other injuries when cleaning our grill at the end of a work shift. If you are following the guidelines correctly, you should not be experiencing any problems. However, to lower the chance of burns from occurring, I'd like to amend one of the steps involved in cleaning the grill. Starting from today, you'll need to wait 15 minutes after turning off the grill. Now, in case anyone has forgotten the other steps, I'm going to show you all one more time how to clean the grill properly. Please follow me to the kitchen.

98. What is the purpose of the talk?
99. Look at the graphic. Which step does the speaker want to change?
100. What will probably happen next?

TEST 13

정답

PART 1

1. (A) **2**. (C) **3**. (C) **4**. (D) **5**. (B) **6**. (D)

PART 2

7. (B) **8**. (A) **9**. (C) **10**. (C) **11**. (C) **12**. (A) **13**. (B) **14**. (B) **15**. (A) **16**. (B) **17**. (C) **18**. (C) **19**. (B)
20. (C) **21**. (B) **22**. (C) **23**. (C) **24**. (C) **25**. (A) **26**. (B) **27**. (A) **28**. (C) **29**. (C) **30**. (A) **31**. (C)

PART 3

32. (C) **33**. (B) **34**. (C) **35**. (C) **36**. (A) **37**. (B) **38**. (C) **39**. (C) **40**. (D) **41**. (C) **42**. (D) **43**. (A) **44**. (C)
45. (A) **46**. (C) **47**. (C) **48**. (C) **49**. (D) **50**. (A) **51**. (B) **52**. (D) **53**. (D) **54**. (B) **55**. (D) **56**. (A) **57**. (A)
58. (C) **59**. (B) **60**. (A) **61**. (C) **62**. (C) **63**. (C) **64**. (C) **65**. (D) **66**. (B) **67**. (C) **68**. (B) **69**. (C) **70**. (D)

PART 4

71. (B) **72**. (C) **73**. (D) **74**. (D) **75**. (A) **76**. (B) **77**. (C) **78**. (C) **79**. (B) **80**. (A) **81**. (B) **82**. (B) **83**. (A)
84. (A) **85**. (D) **86**. (A) **87**. (D) **88**. (B) **89**. (B) **90**. (D) **91**. (A) **92**. (B) **93**. (A) **94**. (D) **95**. (B) **96**. (D)
97. (B) **98**. (D) **99**. (C) **100**. (B)

PART 1

1. (A) She's typing on a computer.
(B) She's lifting a machine off the desk.
(C) She's posing for a photo.
(D) She's drinking from a cup of water.

2. (A) A man is hanging some tools on the wall.
(B) All the equipment has been removed from the site.
(C) A man is using a tool on some wood.
(D) Some equipment has been laid out on the counter.

3. (A) A man is adjusting his glasses.
(B) Servers are waiting on a customer.
(C) They are clearing snow off the ground.
(D) One of the men is putting away a shovel.

4. (A) Workers are watering trees in a park.
(B) People are relaxing around the fountain.
(C) Tourists are taking a group picture.
(D) Water is flowing out of the fountain.

5. (A) The man is pouring some water.
(B) A table is being set for a meal.
(C) All the chairs are occupied.
(D) The woman is taking notes.

6. (A) A railing is being installed on a stairway.
(B) The buildings overlook a waterfall.
(C) Trees line either side of the pathway.
(D) A path leads to a building.

PART 2

7. Where are the batteries I bought the other day?
(A) It's good for two days.
(B) We used them up already.
(C) Yes, it's much better.

8. Who is going to run the new retail location?
(A) It hasn't been confirmed yet.
(B) It will be a clothing store.
(C) Over on 42nd Avenue.

9. When is the annual shareholders meeting?
(A) In the conference room.
(B) No, we had it last year.
(C) On the first day of October.

10. Is the band bringing its own instruments?
(A) They'll be here soon.
(B) Put them down on the stage.
(C) No, we have to provide them.

11. Where did you hear that the shipment would be delayed?
(A) By more than three days.
(B) It was sent from Atlanta.
(C) We received an e-mail this morning.

12. How often do they publish the company newsletter?
(A) Every two months.
(B) For a week.
(C) I subscribed to the paper.

13. Hasn't Jerome Smith worked here longer than you?
(A) I'll start work in October.
(B) By more than two years.
(C) No, he hasn't found a job.

14. Don't you need directions to the hotel?
(A) He's the director.
(B) I've been there before.
(C) A two-night reservation.

15. When will the production of the new car model begin?
(A) Sometime in the spring.
(B) For two years.
(C) At the Montecito plant.

16. Which bus goes to the Lisbon Music Hall?
(A) About a mile.
(B) Number 302 stops there.
(C) Yes, we hold many large events.

17. You are not going to be around this Wednesday, are you?
(A) Yes, it's just around the corner.
(B) That sounds good to me.
(C) No, I have an expo to go to.

18. Donna is the best candidate for the internship, isn't she?
(A) Yes, she sent out the applications.
(B) At least twenty candidates.
(C) I think Carol is more qualified.

19. Who did Charles attend the conference with?
(A) Actually, I went there by myself.
(B) A couple of the salespeople.
(C) Yes, he attended last week.

20. Did she know about the printing deadline?
(A) Yes, around 30 copies.
(B) I got an extension.
(C) No, I forgot to update her.

21. What was the reason for the promotional event being unsuccessful?
(A) Yes, it was very successful.
(B) It was poorly advertised.
(C) I was promoted last week.

22. How long have you been on hold?
(A) We can hold items for 2 days.
(B) Longer, if you like.
(C) At least twenty minutes.

23. Will you be able to review these figures or should I just go over them myself?
(A) I'll go with you.
(B) I was quite surprised by the view.
(C) I'm actually done with them.

24. Let's ask the general affairs office about the new policy.
(A) That's today's date.
(B) To lease an apartment.
(C) I tried to call them earlier.

25. Your boss will give you a 5% raise, won't he?
(A) I think he's considering it.
(B) No, our sales rose by 10%.
(C) He's leaving at 6.

26. Has he been in charge of overseas sales for many years?
(A) Yes, he plans to study abroad.
(B) No, he mostly handles domestic sales.
(C) It hasn't been discussed.

27. George negotiated a higher wage with the firm.
(A) He deserves it.
(B) We need to hire more staff.
(C) A competitive salary.

28. Mr. Potter transferred to the head office, right?
(A) The bus has been delayed.
(B) At the Chicago branch.
(C) As far as I know, yes.

29. Do you know where I can find a stapler?
(A) There are more staples in the drawer.
(B) Yes, I'm still looking.
(C) Check with Mr. Hopkins.

30. This new laptop computer is so powerful and it weighs only 8 pounds.
(A) It must have cost a lot.
(B) Your diet must be working.
(C) That's a great price.

31. Why does Richard want to apply for a position that no one is interested in?

(A) Yes, we've received several applications.

(B) To buy some office appliances.

(C) I guess he just wants to try something different.

PART 3

Questions 32-34 refer to the following conversation.

M: This has been an interesting tour. I've really enjoyed seeing all the state-of-the-art facilities in our new plant. Now I should get back to the office and report to the director.

W: Aren't you going to go to lunch with us? There's a nice restaurant right across from the factory.

M: I'm sorry, but now that I have seen the plant I have some recommendations for the director about the building and machinery.

W: Well, I guess you should let him know right away since we will commence operations at the plant from next month.

32. Where are the speakers?
33. What will the man do now?
34. What will happen next month?

Questions 35-37 refer to the following conversation.

M: Hello. My name is Peter Waters. I received your telephone message about a problem with your computer. How can I help you?

W: Oh, thanks for getting back to me so fast. The problem is that I accidentally spilled water on the keyboard and now it won't work.

M: Well, it might be possible to rectify the problem quite easily, although it might require some replacement parts. Could you bring it in to our service center downtown and let me have a look at it?

W: Sure, that sounds great. But I'm new to this city and don't really know my way around yet. Can you please explain the best way to get to your business? I live in the Clarksdale neighborhood.

35. What is wrong with the woman's computer?
36. What does the man suggest the woman do?
37. What does the woman want to know?

Questions 38-40 refer to the following conversation with three speakers.

W1: I'd like to thank both of you for all your help with putting up the decorations in the office. I think the Christmas party is going to be a lot of fun this year.

M: It was our pleasure. I'm pretty shocked that the company gave us so much money for this year's party.
W2: Me, too. What are we going to spend it all on?
W1: Well, I'm glad you asked, Isabel. I'd like you to start looking for a band that could play music at the event. Try to book one with lots of experience.

38. What have the speakers been doing?
39. What is the man surprised about?
40. What has Isabel been asked to do next?

Questions 41-43 refer to the following conversation.

W: Hi, Mark. Can you tell me how much your monthly phone bill usually is? My phone bills have been outrageously high these past few months. The latest one is over $200.
M: Really? Mine are usually around $50. If you get a telephone membership card, you receive 100 free minutes of calls.
W: I didn't know that! I think I should definitely go out and get one right now. Do you know where I can go to get one?
M: You can get one at any of your mobile phone company's business locations. Actually, there's one just around the corner. Let's go there together and I can show you how to do it.

41. What is the woman concerned about?
42. What does the man suggest the woman do?
43. What will the woman probably do next?

Questions 44-46 refer to the following conversation.

M: Margaret, would you like to do some sightseeing when you're in Toronto next week?
W: I normally would, but I just won't have enough time. My sculpture exhibition is scheduled to finish on Thursday and I will have to be back in Chicago by Friday morning.
M: That's too bad. I really wanted to take you to a few of my favorite places.
W: I will have more time when I return in December. I'll be in town for around ten days and I'll just be visiting some of my colleagues, so perhaps we can meet up then.

44. Why is the woman going to Toronto next week?
45. What did the man intend to do?
46. What does the woman suggest to the man?

Questions 47-49 refer to the following conversation.

M: Hi, Nicole. I was thinking that I'd like to make March 28 the first day of the sale so that we can take advantage of the holiday weekend.
W: Unfortunately, I don't think we can start it until April 2. The problem is that none of our advertisements will appear in the newspapers until that date.
M: Well, that means we're going to miss one of the busiest shopping weekends of the year.
W: You're probably right, but if we start selling before the advertisements begin, then we won't be able to make the best of the sale. Let's see what Carol in Marketing thinks. She might come up with a good solution.

47. What are the speakers discussing?
48. What does the woman say will happen on April 2?
49. What will the speakers probably do next?

Questions 50-52 refer to the following conversation.

W: I'm looking for the third volume of the *Detective Steve Smart* series. Do you have it here?
M: Ah, the title of that one is *The Mystery of the Golden Idol.* I'm afraid we're sold out right now.
W: Can I place an order to have a copy shipped here? I'd like to give it to my husband for his birthday.
M: Sure, you can leave half the book price as a deposit and pay the balance when you pick up the book. It will arrive in about a week.

50. Where is this conversation most likely taking place?
51. What does the woman want to do?
52. What does the man suggest that the woman do?

Questions 53-55 refer to the following conversation.

M: I just heard that the company president wants us to make several changes to the product packaging designs we submitted yesterday.
W: Oh, okay. How about getting together after lunch tomorrow to work on them?
M: What's wrong with today? We don't have any other urgent work to finish, and the conference room is free at 2 P.M.
W: I suppose you're right. Should I bring some of the alternative designs that we worked on?
M: Yes. And would you mind sending them to me right now by e-mail? I'd like to start working on them.
W: No problem. Just give me a couple of minutes.

53. What have the speakers been working on?
54. What does the man mean when he says, "What's wrong with today"?
55. What will the woman probably do next?

Questions 56-58 refer to the following conversation.

W: Hello, I'm one of the new staff members here at the department store. My supervisor advised me to report to the personnel office to get an extra work uniform, but I'm not sure how to get there. Can you tell me where it is?
M: Oh, this store is massive, isn't it? I think I should tell the personnel manager to include a map of the building in the employee handbook. Anyway, you will find the personnel office up on the third floor adjacent to the staff meeting room.
W: Okay, thanks. Oh, I left my employee access card in my locker. Will I need it in order to go up to the third floor?
M: Actually, you will. But, if you hold on for just a moment, I'll bring you a temporary access card so that you can gain entry to that part of the building.

56. Why does the woman want to go to the personnel office?
57. What does the man say about the employee handbook?
58. What will the man get for the woman?

Questions 59-61 refer to the following conversation.

M: Hello, I'd like two tickets to see the play called *Midwinter Fire* on September 25.
W: Okay, but do you have cash? I'm sorry, but our credit card reader has malfunctioned, and we won't have a new one until tomorrow.
M: Oh, well, that means I'll need to come back again tomorrow unless I can borrow some cash from a friend here in town.
W: There's no need to rush. The tickets only just went on sale, and we don't expect the event to sell out fast.
M: In that case, I'll just come back in the morning. Thanks!

59. What type of event does the man want to attend?
60. Why does the woman apologize?
61. What does the woman imply when she says, "There's no need to rush"?

Questions 62-64 refer to the following conversation and list.

M: Patricia, I'm growing a little concerned about the rising number of complaints here at Midvale Bank.
W: I know what you mean. In fact, I'm going through a list of customer complaints we received yesterday and calling them to apologize. The last customer I spoke to was really upset.
M: Oh, really? What was the problem?
W: According to our homepage, our branch is open until 6 P.M. on Fridays. Well, he turned up at that time and found that we were closed.
M: Well, I'm not surprised he was upset. Please make sure that the closing time on our site is changed to 5:30, like it should be.
W: Okay, I'll get right on it.

62. Where do the speakers work?
63. Look at the graphic. Which customer is being discussed?
64. What does the man ask the woman to do?

TEST 13

Questions 65-67 refer to the following conversation and chart.

W: Mr. Peacock, I thought you might like to see the figures for our Web site traffic over the past six months. We've seen a fairly steady increase since you opened the business in January.

M: Thanks, Katy. Hmm... It looks like we saw a sharp rise in visitors when the IT team redesigned the Web site and added the new features.

W: Yes, that was the first time that we ever received more than 15,000 visitors.

M: I see. Well, these are very pleasing results. But we need to make sure that our Web traffic continues to increase. We'll soon be launching our online ad campaign, and we want as many people as possible to see it.

65. Who most likely is the man?

66. Look at the graphic. When did the company redesign its Web site?

67. According to the man, what does the company intend to do?

Questions 68-70 refer to the following conversation and weather forecast.

M: Annie, how are all our preparations going for the concert to celebrate our city's 500th birthday? We only have a few days left.

W: I think we're all set! The stage is being built outside City Hall, and we're expecting thousands of people to show up, despite the cold temperatures.

M: That's great! But I'm a little concerned about the forecast. It's calling for snow on the day of the event.

W: Hmm... I guess we should have a back-up plan in case the weather is too bad. Why don't you call City Hall and see if they have an auditorium we can use for the event, just in case we need to move it indoors?

M: Okay. It's worth a try.

68. What type of event are the speakers preparing for?

69. Look at the graphic. On what date is the event scheduled to take place?

70. What does the woman suggest?

PART 4

Questions 71-73 refer to the following recorded message.

This is Anna, from The Belt Buckle. Two of the three items that you ordered last week have arrived, but I'm afraid there's a problem. The warehouse sent a green sweater instead of a red one. There's no problem with your pants. The black leather high-heel boots that you ordered should arrive in a couple of days. They're being sent from our Denver warehouse, which is farther away, so the shipping time takes longer. Please either call us or come in to let us know whether or not you want to keep the sweater. I've reordered the color that you wanted anyway, so it's up to you. Thank you.

71. What is the problem with the customer's sweater?

72. Why are the boots arriving later than expected?

73. What does the speaker request that the listener do?

Questions 74-76 refer to the following talk.

Thank you all for coming this evening. Each employee at this company has contributed to its success, but we are here tonight to thank one person in particular who has helped greatly during the past year. Christine Espinoza opened our overseas sales division in March, and since then it has brought in more than 3 million dollars of profit for the company. That is why we're giving her the Employee of the Year award. Please join me in welcoming Ms. Espinoza to the stage.

74. What is the purpose of the talk?

75. What was mentioned about the overseas sales division?

76. What contribution has Christine Espinoza made to the company?

Questions 77-79 refer to the following announcement.

Attention, ladies and gentlemen. I'm sorry to interrupt today's baseball game, but there's a matter that must be dealt with urgently. We need the owner of the blue sedan, license plate R56T 6HW, to move the vehicle immediately. Your car is blocking the service entrance to the stadium, and it is currently impossible for other vehicles to enter or leave the building. We know that the parking signs can be a little confusing. So, don't worry – there's no penalty. When you come outside, one of our workers will meet you at your vehicle and direct you to the nearest available free parking space. Once again, everyone, I'm sorry for the interruption.

77. Where is the announcement being made?
78. What problem does the speaker mention?
79. Why does the speaker say, "there's no penalty"?

Questions 80-82 refer to the following advertisement.

Have you ever wanted to go somewhere quiet to enjoy a cup of coffee or tea, only to find all of the coffee houses in your area play loud music? Smooth Java, Seattle's newest coffee lounge, plays soft jazz, classical, and new age music, all at a pleasantly low volume. We offer more than thirty beverages and our pastries are all baked in-house. Besides that, we're initiating a car-ordering service from next month. If you call us at least 20 minutes in advance, we'll prepare your order and deliver it right to your car when you arrive.

80. What does the speaker mention about Smooth Java?
81. According to the speaker, what food can customers order at Smooth Java?
82. What will Smooth Java do from next month?

Questions 83-85 refer to the following talk.

I've completed my review of Spander Corporation's operations, and I'd like to start off by going over the main points. The main problem I observed was with the sharing of information. A lot of time is spent reading irrelevant e-mails or taking part in overly long meetings, and there is also important information which is not shared with everyone. Accordingly, I have two key recommendations. First, I suggest appointing an employee to ensure that information is shared efficiently between departments. Second, I recommend putting some guidelines in place regarding internal e-mails and meetings within the office.

83. What is the purpose of the talk?
84. According to the speaker, what needs to be improved?
85. What does the speaker suggest?

Questions 86-88 refer to the following advertisement.

There has never been a better time to purchase your own home. Interest rates are at an all-time low. Houses by the thousands are being built in every state. Mountain Realty wants to help you find the home you've always dreamed of. We have more than two hundred properties on our books right now, all waiting for the perfect family to move in. Come in today to look at our catalogs and schedule a visit to your future house. Or, you can visit our Web site and view the houses as if you were there by taking our top quality simulation tour.

86. According to the speaker, why is now a good time to purchase a home?
87. What are listeners recommended to do?
88. What can listeners do on Mountain Realty's Web site?

Questions 89-91 refer to the following excerpt from a meeting.

One last thing: I really appreciate everyone coming in to learn about our new shipping procedures and routes over the weekend. Because you all came in to work on a Saturday, we'll be ready to get back to work immediately after moving into our new offices next week in Atlanta. I know our company is expanding quite quickly, and even more new employees will be joining us soon, but don't worry. I visited the new location again recently, and there's a lot of room.

89. Why does the speaker thank the listeners?
90. According to the speaker, what is scheduled for next week?
91. What does the speaker imply when she says, "there's a lot of room"?

Questions 92-94 refer to the following news report.

This is Todd Wentworth with your Conifer Valley afternoon news update. Fast food enthusiasts are already lining up for the grand opening of Gilbert's Burgers this Saturday. The franchise has become increasingly popular thanks in part to the gigantic serving sizes it has become known for through numerous viral videos. The restaurant will officially open at 11 A.M., accompanied by a speech from the CEO and a wide selection of free samples for the hungry crowd. If you're traveling along Burt Avenue at the time, then expect to find more traffic than usual. Local officials even expect an increase in tourism in Conifer Valley, as there are only three locations in the Midwest.

92. What is the talk mainly about?
93. What does the speaker mention about Burt Avenue?
94. What does the speaker imply when he says, "there are only three locations in the Midwest"?

Questions 95-97 refer to the following talk and diagram.

Welcome, everyone. On behalf of Green Fields Ice Cream, I'd like to tell you it's a great pleasure to have you here today. As you know, we are hoping that you decide to invest in our firm once you've sampled our products and toured our factory. You'll also watch a presentation about our plan to open retail locations throughout Europe next year. Now, before the tour begins, I'd like to introduce you to one of our new Tropical Medley range of flavors. This particular flavor was very popular with focus group members, achieving an approval rating of 95 percent. Please take a moment to enjoy it before we move on.

95. Who are the listeners?
96. According to the speaker, what does the company intend to do next year?
97. Look at the graphic. What type of ice cream does the speaker give to the listeners?

Questions 98-100 refer to the following telephone message and flyer.

Hello, this is Kenneth Starling calling. I stayed at the Carlton Hotel in December, and I just noticed on my credit card statement that I was overcharged for my stay. According to the flyer I received that describes the special offer for that month, I should only have been charged for four nights. However, it seems as though I've been charged for every night that I stayed. Please get back to me at your earliest possible convenience to discuss this matter. I look forward to receiving your call. Thanks.

98. Why is the speaker calling?
99. Look at the graphic. For how many days did the speaker probably stay at the hotel?
100. What is the listener asked to do?

TEST 14

정답

PART 1

1. (D) **2**. (A) **3**. (A) **4**. (C) **5**. (B) **6**. (D)

PART 2

7. (C) **8**. (A) **9**. (C) **10**. (C) **11**. (A) **12**. (B) **13**. (A) **14**. (A) **15**. (C) **16**. (B) **17**. (C) **18**. (B) **19**. (B)
20. (A) **21**. (C) **22**. (A) **23**. (C) **24**. (B) **25**. (B) **26**. (C) **27**. (B) **28**. (A) **29**. (C) **30**. (A) **31**. (A)

PART 3

32. (B) **33**. (B) **34**. (D) **35**. (C) **36**. (C) **37**. (B) **38**. (C) **39**. (B) **40**. (A) **41**. (A) **42**. (B) **43**. (B) **44**. (D)
45. (A) **46**. (C) **47**. (D) **48**. (C) **49**. (C) **50**. (C) **51**. (C) **52**. (A) **53**. (D) **54**. (A) **55**. (D) **56**. (D) **57**. (A)
58. (B) **59**. (D) **60**. (C) **61**. (C) **62**. (A) **63**. (C) **64**. (D) **65**. (B) **66**. (D) **67**. (B) **68**. (D) **69**. (C) **70**. (C)

PART 4

71. (C) **72**. (D) **73**. (C) **74**. (D) **75**. (B) **76**. (C) **77**. (B) **78**. (C) **79**. (A) **80**. (B) **81**. (B) **82**. (B) **83**. (A)
84. (C) **85**. (C) **86**. (B) **87**. (D) **88**. (A) **89**. (C) **90**. (A) **91**. (D) **92**. (C) **93**. (B) **94**. (A) **95**. (C) **96**. (D)
97. (B) **98**. (D) **99**. (B) **100**. (B)

PART 1

1. (A) A woman is planting some trees.
(B) A woman is arranging some potted plants.
(C) There is a wheelbarrow behind the woman.
(D) Some plants are being sprinkled with water.

2. (A) They are performing repairs individually.
(B) They are adjusting a workbench.
(C) They are putting away some work tools.
(D) They are riding bicycles together.

3. (A) Garments are being displayed on racks.
(B) A man is repairing a light fixture.
(C) Boxes are being stacked on a cart.
(D) Some merchandise is being packaged.

4. (A) Some people are sitting by the shore.
(B) Some logs are piled by the water's edge.
(C) A path runs alongside the lake.
(D) A man is trimming some bushes.

5. (A) One of the men is checking his phone.
(B) One of the men is leaning over a vehicle.
(C) A car has been lifted for repairs.
(D) They're selling merchandise at a street market.

6. (A) Some workers are climbing a ladder.
(B) A cart is being loaded with bricks.
(C) A wheelbarrow is being pushed to the worksite.
(D) Scaffolding has been put up in front of the building.

PART 2

7. What was the weather like in Chicago?
(A) It depends on which airline I use.
(B) I'm not sure whether it did.
(C) It rained the entire time.

8. Should we go for dinner now?
(A) I still have a thing or two to get done.
(B) He contacted us this morning.
(C) Well, how about Tuesday?

9. Who was at the banquet?
(A) More people were invited this year.
(B) We expected Garcia to come.
(C) Here's the list of attendees.

10. He's the new head of finance, isn't he?
(A) The company's headquarters.
(B) Yes, I just reviewed your finance report.
(C) You mean the man with the bow tie?

11. The delegates will be arriving any minute now.
(A) We'd better get ready to greet them.
(B) Whenever you like.
(C) It's due at five this afternoon.

12. When did you buy that car?
(A) Not until next month.
(B) It actually belongs to my company.
(C) At the dealership downtown.

13. How much paper should I order?
(A) Three boxes should do.
(B) Fifty-nine dollars in total.
(C) Please check with me first.

14. Did that package ever make it to the Paris branch?
(A) I was told they received it.
(B) Yes, they're all ready to be shipped.
(C) I wonder how much they weighed.

15. Whose laptop is that on the table?
(A) Mr. Jacobs booked a table for 4.
(B) Mostly for visitors to the store.
(C) The client must have left it by accident.

16. I'm having trouble with my car.
(A) That'd be a breakthrough.
(B) Why not take it to the shop?
(C) Do you know when it ended?

17. Where do you want this stack of books?
(A) At least 100, I think.
(B) Can you do it for me by Friday?
(C) Let me make some room.

18. How long have the technicians been working on the problem?
(A) About a week ago.
(B) It hasn't been very long at all.
(C) During the next three days.

19. Do you have time to review the proposal now or would you prefer to do it later?
(A) If you don't mind, thanks.
(B) Let me get something to eat first.
(C) It would be quite noisy in there.

20. Aren't you finished using this computer?
(A) I'm nearly done with it.
(B) It should be the latest model.
(C) Let me show you how.

21. Who told you to put a hold on the order of supplies?
(A) My secretary put them in order.
(B) Well, let's postpone it until Friday.
(C) The manager said we had enough of everything.

22. Where can I see today's lunch menu?
(A) It's posted on our Web site.
(B) Probably at noon.
(C) I'll have the soup of the day.

23. Ms. Huang will be back to work soon, won't she?
(A) From 9 A.M. to 5 P.M.
(B) She said she'll get it back to us tomorrow.
(C) The date hasn't been decided yet.

24. When is the award winner going to be announced?
(A) It arrives at 5 o'clock.
(B) During the year-end reception.
(C) At the municipal auditorium.

25. What if I want to end the lease agreement early?
(A) We'll end up rushing to finish on time.
(B) You may have to pay an extra fee.
(C) The first one leaves this morning.

26. Is there any way to have these charts ready for tomorrow's meeting?
(A) Why don't you prepare for your speech?
(B) He should be there by ten.
(C) I suppose so, if I work late.

27. You haven't seen the updated list of suppliers, have you?
(A) I think I saw him downstairs.
(B) It's still being compiled.
(C) We're running low on supplies.

28. Why aren't more customers subscribing to our new online service?
(A) It seems that the menu is difficult to use.
(B) It's quite time-consuming for us.
(C) You can register on our Web site.

29. Could you give the visitors a tour of our production facility?
(A) Our plant was understaffed.
(B) Productivity is on the rise.
(C) Sure. Where are they?

30. This tie doesn't match my suit for the party.
(A) Wear the other one.
(B) They're our new partners.
(C) In the corporate ballroom.

31. Has the meeting been rescheduled for Tuesday or Thursday?
(A) I'm not sure, but I can find out.
(B) Let me know what you decide.
(C) Could we do it both ways?

PART 3

Questions 32-34 refer to the following conversation.

M: Hello. I have a suit I'd like to have dry cleaned, but I'm checking out tomorrow morning. Can your cleaning service take care of it that quickly?
W: It normally takes up to 48 hours for a suit, but we have an in-house express service, which costs an extra five dollars. If we get the suit before noon, we can have it ready for you by 8 P.M.
M: I definitely need it for my meeting tomorrow, so I don't mind paying more.
W: Okay, I'll send someone up to collect the suit now. May I have your room number?

32. Why is the man calling?
33. What does the woman say about the express service?
34. What does the woman offer to do?

Questions 35-37 refer to the following conversation with three speakers.

W1: Eddie, have you finished cooking all of the dishes for the client's wedding reception?
M: Yes, everything is done and ready to go. Emma is just about to drive everything over to the banquet hall.
W2: That's right... I'm just loading up the truck. I should be ready to go in about ten minutes.
W1: Great work, guys. Are you going to take the expressway?
W2: Yes, that's the plan. I think it's the quickest way.
M: Oh, I wouldn't do that, if I were you. When I used it this morning, there were traffic jams due to road maintenance. You'd be quicker going along Marina Road.

35. What type of business do the speakers most likely work for?
36. What does Emma say she will do?
37. What does the man recommend?

Questions 38-40 refer to the following conversation.

W: Jim, I've heard that you're giving the opening speech at next month's conference. Are you looking forward to it?

M: Actually, I'm rather nervous. I've never been very confident addressing a large audience, and I heard that they're expecting over 300 participants this year.
W: I used to feel the same way about speaking to large groups as well, but I bought an excellent book on the subject by David Reese. It really helped me a lot. If you're working tomorrow, I can bring it in for you.
M: Actually, I will be out inspecting the plant all day. If you leave the book on my desk, I'll take a look at it when I'm back in the office on the following day. Thanks, I need all the help I can get.

38. What are the speakers discussing?
39. Who most likely is David Reese?
40. What will the man do tomorrow?

Questions 41-43 refer to the following conversation.

W: Mr. Olson, there's no Betafix cereal left. This is the second month in a row that we've run out before getting the next shipment.
M: It's certainly been selling very well since the manufacturer lowered its prices.
W: Yes, lots of customers have been asking for it. I told the cashiers to suggest other brands, but maybe we should put in a bigger order next month.
M: That's a great idea. I'd hate to lose business to other stores because of this. I'll tell the purchasing manager to order larger quantities of the cereal.

41. What problem is mentioned?
42. What does the woman recommend?
43. What is the man's concern?

Questions 44-46 refer to the following conversation with three speakers.

W: Rupert, Harry... we have a problem on Aisle 5. A customer has dropped a carton of eggs and I need you to clean up the mess before somebody slips.
M1: No problem. I'll grab the mop from the storeroom. What should Harry do?
W: Please place a sign next to the spillage warning customers that the floor is slippery.
M2: Got it. Can I get one of those from the store room?
W: That's right. Rupert will show you where everything is. And don't forget that the store will shut at 6 tonight instead of 7, so you'll need to finish all of your other tasks quickly.

44. Where most likely do the speakers work?
45. What does the woman ask Harry to do?
46. What reminder does the woman give to the men?

Questions 47-49 refer to the following conversation.

M: Hi, Wendy. I heard that your department's bid for the Wapshot project was accepted. Well done.
W: Thanks. To be honest, though, I'm a little concerned about our ability to finish the work on time. Our department has won a lot of new contracts lately, so everyone has a very hectic schedule, especially since Ron retired.
M: We're pretty busy in the Accounting Department these days as well. We're getting the annual expense report ready for the board meeting next week. But after that, I could spare one or two staff members if you need help.

47. What is the woman worried about?
48. What has the woman's department done recently?
49. What does the man offer to do?

Questions 50-52 refer to the following conversation.

M: Diana, I'm really struggling to sell the 2-bedroom apartment down by the waterfront. I think the owner's asking price is just too high.
W: Yes, I guess property prices are soaring at the waterfront because of the new cinema that's being built there.
M: Right, and that's only the beginning. The council has mentioned a brand new sports complex and swimming pool, too.
W: Wow! It's certainly gonna be a desirable neighborhood.
M: Definitely. Oh, that reminds me... I have a couple of other apartments there that I need to add to our online listings. I'll catch up with you later.

50. Who most likely are the speakers?

51. What does the man mean when he says, "that's only the beginning"?
52. What will the man probably do next?

Questions 53-55 refer to the following conversation.

W1: These floral arrangements aren't creating the right kind of visual impact because the tables are just too big by comparison. What should we do? We don't have much time before the reception starts.
W2: I was sure we'd ordered enough flowers, but you're right. We'll need to get more to fill out the centerpieces. How about plates? We have enough for all of the attendees, don't we?
W1: Yes, we have ample dinnerware, but we could use a few extra chairs. Could you get about ten more in case any unexpected guests show up at the function?
W2: Sure. I'll go ask the front desk staff if we can borrow some from the hotel. In the meantime, Bob is headed to the restaurant to pick up the appetizers and main courses right now. I'll give him a call and ask him to drop by the florist on his way back.

53. Who most likely are the speakers?
54. What problem is mentioned by the speakers?
55. What is Bob currently doing?

Questions 56-58 refer to the following conversation.

M: Elizabeth, I'm afraid that our AccountTec software is already out-of-date.
W: Really? We just launched the current edition a few months ago. What's the problem?
M: I just looked at Gigasoft's new EZBooks software, which was released last week. It's the same price as our AccountTec software, but it has many more advanced features and is much more powerful. It looks like it'll soon be outselling us in the market.
W: Even if we start work on a new version immediately, it's going to take at least six months to develop. Well, after I finish reviewing the sales data, I'll talk to the supervisor and ask what we can do about it.

56. What kind of company do the speakers work for?
57. What is mentioned about the EZBooks software?
58. What will the woman most likely do next?

Questions 59-61 refer to the following conversation.

M: Christina, are you interested in going to see the new Mark Holland film at the cinema tonight?
W: Sure, Chris. I'd love to. Do we need to get tickets in advance?
M: Well, I was going to book them online using my phone, but my battery has died. Can I use yours?
W: Go right ahead. The code is 6-7-2-3.
M: Thanks. Let's see... Oh, it seems like there are no seats left for this evening's showing.
W: That's a shame. Well, how about going this weekend instead? I don't have any plans.
M: That's fine with me. I'll just stop by the box office tomorrow to get us some seats.

59. What do the speakers want to do?
60. What does the woman mean when she says, "Go right ahead"?
61. What problem does the man mention?

Questions 62-64 refer to the following conversation and sign.

M: Hello, you've reached the IT Department. What can I do for you?
W: Hi, I just started working in the west wing of the facility. However, I'm having difficulty using the keycard scanner when I arrive for work, so I always need to ask someone else to open the door for me.
M: Oh, that's strange. I guess there must be a problem with your card. If you'd like to stop by my department sometime today, I can issue a new one to you. Would you mind giving me your name and work location in advance?
W: Sure. I'm Greta Nisbet, and I work in the Biochemistry lab. I'll stop by your department after lunch. Thanks for your help!

62. What does the woman ask for help with?
63. Why does the man suggest the woman visit his department?
64. Look at the graphic. Which laboratory does the woman work in?

Questions 65-67 refer to the following conversation and weather information.

W: Todd, you must be getting excited about your trip to Nessus Island! How does the weather forecast look?
M: It's not too bad. Luckily, I get there the day after a big thunderstorm, and then I have some sunny days to enjoy.
W: Great! So, do you have a lot of things planned during your vacation?
M: Not really. I mostly plan to relax on the beach and get a sun tan.
W: Well, it will certainly be a lot more relaxing than being here in the office! How long will you be gone?
M: Just seven days. I'll be back in time for our monthly management meeting on the 23rd.

65. Look at the graphic. When will the man arrive on Nessus Island?
66. What activity is the man looking forward to?
67. How long will the man be on vacation?

Questions 68-70 refer to the following conversation and list.

W: Thank you for calling Derry Tours. How can I help you today?
M: Hi, this is Jon Lanegan. I called yesterday to book four spots on one of your tours this weekend. But, due to a family emergency, we won't be able to participate.
W: Oh, I'm sorry to hear that. Can you please remind me which tour you signed up for?
M: Umm... it was the one that visits the castle in the morning, followed by the walk along the waterfront. And then a trip to the market at night.
W: Ah, yes, I've found your booking. To issue a refund, I'll need the number of the card you used to pay for the tour.
M: Sure. It's 4435-3210-6784. Thank you.

68. Why is the man calling?
69. Look at the graphic. Which tour did the man sign up for?
70. What information does the woman ask for?

PART 4

Questions 71-73 refer to the following telephone message.

Hi, Josh. This is Valerie. I'm calling about the brochure that you asked me to send to the printers. I've been looking it over, and there seem to be several errors. First, the brochure lists the price of our J-50 portable heater as 78 dollars, but the company Web site has it listed as 68 dollars. Also, I believe the picture above the HS-35 ceiling fan listing is actually a photo of the HS-40. Finally, the brochure has a listing for the A-70 air conditioner, but that model was discontinued last year. Obviously, I will hold off on sending in the brochure until I hear back from you, so please call me as soon as you get this.

71. What item's listing has an incorrect photograph?
72. What does the speaker say about the A-70 model?
73. According to the message, what is the speaker going to do now?

Questions 74-76 refer to the following talk.

Thanks for attending this unveiling of the new smartphone by Lexx Electronics, the Polaris 4. My name is Elizabeth Munro, and I was the head of the design team for this new model. It's my great honor to be able to show you all of the phone's innovative features, such as its amazing 3D display. You won't believe it! We expect this new model to exceed sales of our current best-seller, the Polaris 3, by the end of this year. And, to celebrate its launch, we're going to give each of you a coupon that entitles you to receive $100 off the retail price of a new Polaris 4 smartphone.

74. Where is the talk taking place?
75. What does the speaker mean when he says, "You won't believe it"?
76. What will the listeners receive?

Questions 77-79 refer to the following talk.

Well, everyone, that concludes your Smiling Cow cheese factory experience. Now, get ready for something truly special. On the other side of the door, you'll find more than 50 varieties of cheese produced on site. You're welcome to taste whatever you like, and, of course, purchase some to take home with you. On your way out, you'll pass by the pasture. Please be sure to offer some grass to our cows. They've worked hard to bring you this delicious cheese!

77. Where is the talk taking place?
78. What will take place next?
79. What are listeners encouraged to do before they leave?

Questions 80-82 refer to the following excerpt from a meeting.

I have one final announcement before we conclude today's meeting. Our CEO has accepted my suggestion that all of us in Customer Service be given our own personal office. Our department manager, Ms. Bucher, explained to the CEO how this change could help us enhance our reputation in terms of meeting the demands of our customers. Consequently, the Marketing Department will develop a commercial in which our customers throw huge parties to celebrate how hospitable we are. Offices will be apportioned on a first-come, first-served basis, so to select which one you want, grab a request form from Ms. Bucher's office as soon as you can.

80. What will the company give the listeners?
81. Who most likely are the listeners?
82. According to the speaker, why should listeners go to Ms. Bucher's office?

Questions 83-85 refer to the following radio broadcast.

Welcome to Entertainment Talk. Tonight we'll be speaking to members of the famous Attam Family. The Attam Family has performed at the Mackenzie Auditorium every summer, but this year the concert will not feature the voice of Batima Attam. It will instead be a guitar recital by her brothers. The music is taken from their upcoming album *Dance Without Words*. The brothers will speak on tonight's show about this album and about guitarists who have inspired them. Later, they will answer your questions and play three of the tunes from the new album right here in the studio. But first we'll talk to actor-turned-director Molly Hanson about her recent movie.

83. Who most likely is Batima Attam?
84. What does the speaker say about the brothers?
85. What will listeners most likely hear next?

Questions 86-88 refer to the following talk.

Thanks for coming to this workshop on public speaking. The park owner has recruited me to help you become more entertaining and adaptable tour guides. Basically, the better the job you do, the better the guests will feel about their visit. First, we will discuss jokes and stories you can tell during the tour to make your guests laugh and feel comfortable. Then, we'll role play through some possible difficult situations that you might face. Throughout the workshop, we'll be quite active, especially as we practice our scripts. That's why we didn't schedule a meal break. However, I was told there are snacks available in the lobby.

86. Who most likely are the listeners?
87. What is the purpose of the talk?
88. What does the speaker imply when he says, "there are snacks available in the lobby"?

Questions 89-91 refer to the following talk.

I appreciate everyone finding the time to participate in this computer training workshop. Before you leave, please take a few moments to complete the comment cards included inside your package of course materials. Your input will be very beneficial in helping us refine our teaching techniques for the course. I'd also like to inform you of a seminar that will be introduced this fall. It is a full-day seminar entitled "Advanced Corporate Strategies". It covers all the practical tips needed to accomplish your business objectives. You can read about all the other workshops and training seminars available to company staff in the document I'm going to pass out now.

89. Who most likely is the speaker?
90. What are the listeners asked to do?
91. What will the speaker most likely do next?

Questions 92-94 refer to the following talk.

Welcome, everyone, to your first day at Trident Manufacturing. My name is Dave Sparks, and I'm the HR manager here at the factory. I'll be giving you a tour of the building here this morning, and I'll also be providing you with information about our company's wide range of products as well as its goals over the next decade. At noon, we'll take a break for lunch. We have a staff cafeteria, but there are also some coffee shops and restaurants nearby. You have several options. At 2 P.M., you'll all be sent to your respective departments, where you'll be introduced to your direct supervisors. I hope you all have an enjoyable day.

92. Who are the listeners?
93. What does the speaker mean when he says, "You have several options"?
94. What will the listeners do this afternoon?

Questions 95-97 refer to the following talk and list.

Before we start our hike today, I need to remind you about some guidelines you need to follow when hiking through Deer Horn National Park. First of all, please do not drop any litter anywhere. Not only does this ruin the park's natural appearance, but it also poses a danger to local wildlife. Also, visitors are not permitted to remove any local plants from the park without written permission from the rangers' office. Finally, please be careful when walking along the trail. Some of the ground is a little damp, and I don't want anyone to slip and fall. Now, let's get going. This is the easiest trail in the park, so we should be back within a few hours.

95. What is the main purpose of the talk?
96. What does the woman warn the listeners about?
97. Look at the graphic. Which trail will the listeners see today?

Questions 98-100 refer to the following excerpt from a meeting and diagram.

I've called this department meeting because a staff member informed me that our bins are not being emptied. That employee was unhappy because it makes our workplace look very untidy and unprofessional. I have to agree! I came down to check the bins early this morning, and I was disappointed to see that most of them were almost full. In fact, I had to empty the green one myself because it was overflowing. To ensure that these bins are being emptied regularly, I'm going to post this emptying schedule next to them. Please take a moment to check it.

98. What is the speaker mainly discussing?
99. Look at the graphic. Which bin did the speaker empty earlier?
100. What will the speaker do next?

TEST 15

정답

PART 1

1. (D) **2**. (C) **3**. (B) **4**. (B) **5**. (B) **6**. (D)

PART 2

7. (A) **8**. (B) **9**. (C) **10**. (C) **11**. (C) **12**. (A) **13**. (A) **14**. (A) **15**. (B) **16**. (A) **17**. (A) **18**. (C) **19**. (B)
20. (C) **21**. (A) **22**. (B) **23**. (A) **24**. (B) **25**. (B) **26**. (B) **27**. (A) **28**. (C) **29**. (A) **30**. (B) **31**. (C)

PART 3

32. (D) **33**. (B) **34**. (B) **35**. (D) **36**. (C) **37**. (B) **38**. (A) **39**. (D) **40**. (A) **41**. (C) **42**. (C) **43**. (A) **44**. (D)
45. (C) **46**. (D) **47**. (B) **48**. (C) **49**. (D) **50**. (B) **51**. (A) **52**. (D) **53**. (D) **54**. (B) **55**. (C) **56**. (C) **57**. (C)
58. (D) **59**. (C) **60**. (D) **61**. (B) **62**. (C) **63**. (D) **64**. (B) **65**. (B) **66**. (D) **67**. (A) **68**. (C) **69**. (D) **70**. (D)

PART 4

71. (D) **72**. (A) **73**. (B) **74**. (C) **75**. (D) **76**. (B) **77**. (B) **78**. (A) **79**. (C) **80**. (D) **81**. (C) **82**. (A) **83**. (C)
84. (D) **85**. (A) **86**. (D) **87**. (C) **88**. (A) **89**. (D) **90**. (C) **91**. (B) **92**. (C) **93**. (D) **94**. (A) **95**. (C) **96**. (A)
97. (D) **98**. (D) **99**. (B) **100**. (C)

PART 1

1. (A) She is talking to a passenger.
(B) She is sitting in an outdoor café.
(C) She is looking at the map.
(D) She is holding the steering wheel.

2. (A) Passengers are eating some snacks.
(B) A man is waving a flag on a boat.
(C) Some people are enjoying a boat ride.
(D) Water has been sprinkled on the floor.

3. (A) They are setting up some chairs.
(B) They have placed their belongings beside them.
(C) Both of them are lying on the ground.
(D) They're seated next to each other.

4. (A) Handrails are being installed in the stairwell.
(B) Shadows are being cast on the sidewalk.
(C) Some people are sitting outside at a coffee shop.
(D) Parking areas are separated by some trees.

5. (A) Passengers are waiting to get on a boat.
(B) The scenery is reflected on the surface of the water.
(C) A bridge spans over a body of water.
(D) A lighthouse is located near the shoreline.

6. (A) Some people are waiting in line.
(B) A walkway is being constructed.
(C) The driveway is being paved.
(D) The structure has a peaked roof.

PART 2

7. Who is the assistant to the Chief Executive Officer?
(A) Mr. Harbaugh.
(B) She made an executive decision.
(C) Yes, I'd be happy to help.

8. What is that program on the monitor?
(A) On the left of the screen.
(B) A file I'm editing.
(C) I'll turn it on in a minute.

9. Which of those jackets is Jennifer's?
(A) She bought a jacket yesterday.
(B) No, it's not hers.
(C) The long black one.

10. Do you feel like loaning me that magazine after you're done?
(A) Yes, I'll e-mail it to her.
(B) No, I just memorized it.
(C) Sure, it's no problem.

11. Would you like to go to a movie this evening?
(A) Mostly just horror films.
(B) I thought it was really funny.
(C) Sorry, I already have plans.

12. When is the work shift schedule due?
(A) By 3 P.M. this Friday.
(B) For the part-time employees.
(C) The warehouse.

13. Do you have more batteries or should I get some from the shop?
(A) I will just recharge the device.
(B) I'm shutting it down now.
(C) At the shop around the corner.

14. Which job are you applying for?
(A) Director of sales.
(B) She's applying online.
(C) No, next time.

15. How can I get in touch with you on weekends?
(A) Yes, every Saturday.
(B) By text message.
(C) That's fine.

16. I can't believe it has already been a year since our grand opening.
(A) Time really flies, doesn't it?
(B) We made our biggest profit last month.
(C) I'd rather you keep them closed.

17. What would you like to drink with your meal?
(A) I'll just have a glass of water.
(B) Let's order some dessert.
(C) Yes, I drink coffee every morning.

18. There aren't any more buses downtown tonight, are there?
(A) Take a left and walk straight.
(B) Only three more stops.
(C) Not until the morning.

19. How much did your new car cost?
(A) Yes, it did cost a lot.
(B) Twice the price of the old one.
(C) By making monthly payments.

20. Aren't you flying to Singapore next week?
(A) Business class seats.
(B) On a travel Web site.
(C) No, I had to cancel.

21. Who updates the inventory for our online shopping mall?
(A) The webmaster, I guess.
(B) He was hired only two months ago.
(C) We accept all major credit cards.

22. Should I read this list of projects aloud?
(A) Yes, you're allowed to leave.
(B) No, we each have a copy.
(C) Sarah will make a great leader.

23. Where did you learn bookkeeping?
(A) Actually, I taught myself.
(B) There were a few matters to attend to.
(C) About a year ago.

24. I need a word with you about the Henderson contract.
(A) Try calling his cell phone.
(B) Is anything the matter with it?
(C) You can leave it on his desk.

25. Has next year's budget been discussed yet?
(A) No, I can't afford that.
(B) Yes, at yesterday's meeting.
(C) Forward the details to me.

26. Would you like black and white or color copies?
(A) It's a nice poster.
(B) Is the price different?
(C) There's a wide range.

27. Can we attract more gym members?
(A) Sure, if we advertise online.
(B) We can track it for you.
(C) I don't remember, either.

28. When can I expect to hear your decision?
(A) That's better than I thought.
(B) Yes, I heard the same thing.
(C) Within a few days.

29. Our ovens weren't turned on in time to serve breakfast right away.
(A) Should we open on time anyway?
(B) Yes, every day at exactly 9 A.M.
(C) A mushroom omelet with a side of bacon.

30. How can we be certain that employees read the memo?

(A) We reviewed the invoice.

(B) Post it on the bulletin board.

(C) You should memorize the password.

31. It'll be easier to understand if you put the figures beside each column.

(A) It's actually too heavy to move.

(B) I thought they were very understanding.

(C) I need more space on the page.

PART 3

Questions 32-34 refer to the following conversation.

W: Hey, Tsusuka. It's been such a long time since you left our office for your new position. What's it like being at a major publishing company?

M: Well, I'm usually busy meeting so many famous authors, but I'm really satisfied with my work.

W: That sounds incredible. I'm actually looking for something new and interesting to read because I'm going on a vacation in a few weeks. Do you have any ideas about what I can get?

M: Hmm, well, I can't think of anything right now. Let me think about it for a bit, and I'll send you a list of books I think you'd like.

32. Where does the man work?

33. What does the man say about his current position?

34. What does the man offer to do for the woman?

Questions 35-37 refer to the following conversation with three speakers.

M: Hi, Ursula...Hi, Charlotte. Did you hear that Amy Sutherland will be signing copies of her new novel at Watermark Books next Wednesday? I know you're both big fans.

W1: Oh, really? I would love to go and get my copy signed.

W2: Me, too! What time does it begin on Wednesday?

M: It starts at 5 P.M. The problem is that our manager hasn't finalized next week's schedule yet, so we don't know what time we will be able to leave.

W1: Hmm... Charlotte, why don't we go and speak to her now and request to finish by 4?

W2: Great idea. I think she's in her office.

35. What is the main topic of the conversation?

36. What problem does the man mention?

37. What will the women probably do next?

Questions 38-40 refer to the following conversation.

M: I'm looking forward to getting together with you for lunch tomorrow to discuss possible new exhibits for our museum. The only problem is that I heard it's incredibly difficult to get lunch reservations at Bastian's Bistro.

TEST 15

It is always packed around that time.

W: I heard that, too. Actually, I contacted the restaurant manager for seats a few minutes ago and she said that they are fully booked all week for lunch.

M: Well, I know that their business slows down in the evening, so would you prefer to just meet for dinner?

38. What are the speakers planning to talk about tomorrow?
39. Why did the woman contact the restaurant?
40. What does the man suggest?

Questions 41-43 refer to the following conversation with three speakers.

W1: Welcome to Cedar Lakes Campgrounds. I'm the camp director, and this is Martha, the owner. You're interested in holding your company retreat here?

M: I am. I work for Firefly Electronics, and I'm in charge of organizing our annual teambuilding retreat in July for over one hundred employees.

W2: Well, as you can see, it's a beautiful campground, and we have ample lodging available if you intend for it to be an overnight stay.

M: Yes, it's gorgeous here – very scenic. What kind of activities could we plan for everyone to participate in?

W1: There are numerous hiking trails, and the lake can be used for water sports.

W2: And keep in mind, we have free parking if your employees choose to drive themselves.

41. What type of event is being planned?
42. What does the man ask about?
43. What does the venue offer for free?

Questions 44-46 refer to the following conversation.

M: Hello, I assume you are Ms. Alduin? I'm Marcellus Pike from Marpike Industries. I'm sorry for being a little early, but I thought it would be better to come as soon as possible to check what furniture you'd like to recommend for my office.

W: Oh, yes. Good morning. I'm glad to meet you. Here, you can see firsthand the style of furniture we specialize in. Our chairs, sofas, and tables are considered by critics to be the best available in the area.

M: Would you say that they mainly enjoy the look of your furniture?

W: Not really. They are more impressed that we specialize in simple, practical designs using various recycled materials.

44. Why is the man at the shop?
45. What does the woman's shop sell?
46. Why does the woman mention the recycled materials?

Questions 47-49 refer to the following conversation.

M: Gloria, how are things going at your new apartment? Are you settled in?

W: Yes, I just have a few more things to buy, and then I'll be all set.

M: Great! What kind of things are you looking for?

W: Well, I'd really like to get a new Typhoon dishwasher. I'm hoping I can get one for around $500.

M: For a brand new one? You'll be lucky!

W: Oh, well... that's all I have left to spend. Perhaps I'll need to wait and save up a little more.

M: Why don't you try a Whizz dishwasher instead? They're pretty comparable to the Typhoon models in terms of performance, but much more affordable.

W: Hmm... I'll look into it. Thanks.

47. What is the woman planning to purchase?
48. What does the man imply when he says, "You'll be lucky"?
49. What does the man recommend the woman do?

Questions 50-52 refer to the following conversation.

W: Hey, Oliver. I have some bad news. It appears that yesterday was the expiration date for the corporate credit card issued to our department.

M: Are we going to have a new one by Friday? I'm responsible for purchasing all of the food for the staff party, and it'll cost too much for me to pay for it by myself.

W: I doubt it. I'll need to talk to the credit card company and have them send us a new one. Even if I have them rush the delivery, it probably won't arrive for a few days.

M: Maybe I could talk to the manager at the place I ordered from last time and see if he would allow us to pay next week.

50. What is the problem?
51. Why is the man concerned?
52. What does the man say he will do?

Questions 53-55 refer to the following conversation.

W: Hello, is this Mr. Jerome Jenkins, the president of Jenkins Industries? This is Esmeralda Metcalf from Occam Employment Connections, calling to administer this year's survey about our services.
M: Actually, many employees that you send to my company do not really seem to have enough experience to be working here. I spend a lot of time giving them extra training. How could I ensure that we are assigned better workers?
W: Well, Mr. Jenkins, we try to make sure that everyone we assign is as qualified as possible. In fact, I have given everyone who has applied to our employment agency proficiency exams to make sure they can handle whichever jobs we assign them.

53. Why is the woman calling?
54. What is the man's problem?
55. What does the woman say she did?

Questions 56-58 refer to the following conversation.

W: Well, it has been our busiest day of the year, and I think all of our employees have performed well.
M: Absolutely! We sold more extra value meals than ever before, and nobody waited too long for their food.
W: That's great! I think we should start letting some of our staff go home. Who has been here the longest today?
M: Well, Pedro has been here since 6 A.M.
W: Okay, let him know the good news. And then please remind our customers that we will be closing in around ten minutes.
M: No problem.

56. Where do the speakers work?
57. What does the man imply when he says, "Pedro has been here since 6 A.M."?
58. What does the woman ask the man to do?

Questions 59-61 refer to the following conversation.

M: Good morning. I'm here to check if you would be able to cater an event on August 12. My company will be hosting a party in the Orchid Building at 5:30 P.M.
W: Of course we can. We have a variety of menu options to choose from that we could serve on that day. Would you also like to have a wine service?
M: Well, the event will have two separate parts. There will only be employees in attendance until 7 o'clock, with family members joining after that. Is it possible to have a wine service available even if there are children at the event?
W: That should be OK. But if children are present, you are asked to pay a small fee so we can hand out wristbands to tell the underage guests apart from the adults.

59. Where most likely does the woman work?
60. What will happen at 7 o'clock on August 12?
61. According to the woman, what are the wristbands for?

Questions 62-64 refer to the following conversation and schedule.

W: Jason, I tried to reserve the meeting room for our client presentation, but it seems that Allan Ripley has already booked the room when we need it.
M: Oh, that's too bad. Well, how about giving our presentation in the IT lounge instead? It's normally empty around that time.
W: I'd rather do it in the meeting room, as it has all the equipment we planned to use. I could try to call Allan and ask him to give us his time slot. What do you think?
M: It's worth a try. His extension is three-zero-one.

62. Look at the graphic. When does the woman want to use the meeting room?
63. What does the man suggest?
64. What will the woman probably do next?

Questions 65-67 refer to the following conversation and list.

M: Hi, this is Kenneth calling. I just got a message that you stopped by my office earlier today. I believe you wanted to meet with me sometime this week.

W: That's right. I'd like to get your advice on the blueprint I'm creating for the new hospital in Greenhaven. I'm having a bit of trouble designing the entrance lobby and reception area.

M: Oh, I'd love to help, but I'm afraid my schedule is full all week. Would you be able to send me the document by e-mail? Then I can reply to you with some notes.

W: Sure, that would be a big help.

65. Look at the graphic. What is the name of the woman the man is calling?
66. What is the woman currently working on?
67. What does the man suggest the woman do?

Questions 68-70 refer to the following conversation and list.

W: Richard, hold on a moment. I think we should buy some souvenirs for our coworkers before we get on our flight. I noticed a few duty free shops not far from our gate.

M: Hmm... Okay. But, we'd better hurry. Our plane will be taking off at 7:45, and we don't want to be late for the boarding call.

W: Don't worry... We still have plenty of time. We're in row twenty-five, so we'll be two of the last passengers to board the plane.

68. What are the speakers mainly discussing?
69. Why is the man concerned?
70. Look at the graphic. What boarding group do the speakers belong to?

PART 4

Questions 71-73 refer to the following introduction.

Welcome back, everyone. You're listening to WKRP Radio and I am your host, Hari Schultz. Next, I'd like to welcome Molly Singer to the studio. Many of you are probably familiar with Ms. Singer from her popular cable television show, House Guru, in which Ms. Singer helps people to decorate their homes and make each room stylish and attractive. What you might not be aware of, though, is that Ms. Singer first got interested in interior design when she began writing a magazine column offering general household tips. Today, she's going to tell us her top three tips for how to conserve heat and energy at home this winter. Now, it is my pleasure to welcome Molly Singer.

71. Who is Molly Singer?
72. What does the speaker say about the television show, House Guru?
73. What will Molly Singer discuss today?

Questions 74-76 refer to the following message.

Good afternoon. This is Jeremy Blake from Pebbles Appliances. I am calling about our conversation the other day regarding our air conditioners. If you would still like our new model, you should act quickly as there are only a few left. Sadly, though, we would not be able to deliver it before the weekend. If you think you can wait until next Monday, our delivery truck will be returned from the auto mechanics shop by then and ready to go. Please let me know if you would like to order one so I can write a note to our sales staff later today stating that you are eligible for free delivery. Whenever you are ready, please call us back at 555-6788. Thank you.

74. What problem does the speaker mention?
75. According to the speaker, what will happen on Monday?
76. What does the speaker say he will do today?

Questions 77-79 refer to the following excerpt from a meeting.

The last thing to discuss at this week's meeting is the CEO's decision to change the overtime rate. Starting next month, if you work overtime, you'll only be paid at a time-and-a-half rate, not the typical double time rate. The company has been forced to modify this policy because it is going through a particularly difficult financial period. Earnings have been getting lower and lower over the past six months, so this type of action is unavoidable. Just like you, I'm not happy about this news. In fact, I visited headquarters to try to persuade the CEO to change his mind, but... it's too late.

77. What is the speaker mainly discussing?
78. What does the speaker mention about the company?
79. What does the speaker mean when he says, "it's too late"?

Questions 80-82 refer to the following talk.

With computer technology advancing at an incredible pace, many of you freelance computer programmers believe you need to frequently purchase new equipment in order to remain competitive. This can be a needless expense, as many of you probably aren't using your existing computers and networks as efficiently as you could be. Before spending a fortune on new systems, it's worth looking at what you have now. Internal memory can be upgraded for just a small amount of money, and by regularly checking developers' Web sites for software updates, you can ensure that you always have the most recent version of your essential software.

80. Who most likely are the listeners?
81. According to the speaker, what are many people doing?
82. What does the speaker say is available at a reasonable price?

Questions 83-85 refer to the following talk.

Before we get started this morning, I have some exciting news to share. As you all know, ever since we launched our local commercial, we've received a lot of new clients at our beauty salon. However, some of them are already displeased. Three weeks is a long time to wait for an appointment. Because of this, I've decided to open an additional location in the city center. The rent will start next month, so we'll be able to see more clients. Of course, we will need to also hire additional staff, so later this afternoon, I would ask that some of you help me review recent applications.

83. Why does the speaker say, "Three weeks is a long time to wait for an appointment"?
84. What does the speaker say will happen next month?
85. What does the speaker ask for help with?

Questions 86-88 refer to the following telephone message.

Hello, this is Rick from Carpet King Wholesale. I just spoke with our representative at the manufacturing factory, and it turns out that the carpeting you ordered for your lobby has been recalled and is no longer available. I still have a list of the other options you were looking at, though you'll need to make a decision quickly if we want to stay on schedule. How about I stop by your office tomorrow and we can discuss your other choices? Thank you for your understanding.

86. Where does the speaker most likely work?
87. What problem does the speaker report?
88. What does the speaker offer to do?

Questions 89-91 refer to the following talk.

Hello, everyone. My name is Vic Pounder, the tour director here at Pudge's Chocolate Factory. I'm glad that you all have decided to take part in today's tour of the facility. We'll use the first couple of minutes to talk about what we will do today before moving on to actually seeing the facility at work. To begin with, everyone will receive their guest cards and gift packets. After that, we'll all take a look around the building. Then, we will be headed for the Popple Room, where we will be met by Pudge's spokesperson, Penelope Prudhomme. She will show you a short video and take questions about it. Finally, we will move on to the Pudge Cafeteria, where everyone can sample some of our finest products.

89. What is the main purpose of the talk?
90. Where does the speaker work?
91. What does the speaker say the spokesperson will do?

Questions 92-94 refer to the following talk.

Gather around, shoppers. Let me tell you all about the new and amazing blender from Dillon Electronics. This versatile device can be used to make delicious fruit smoothies and wholesome soups, and it comes with a five-year money-back warranty! As you can see, it has been elegantly designed, and thanks to our advanced sound-dampening technology, you'll barely know it's there! The three specially-angled blades easily cut through all foods and even ice. To prove it, I'll make some frozen strawberry smoothie right now. Pay attention, everyone!

92. What type of product is the speaker promoting?
93. What does the speaker mean when she says, "you'll barely know it's there"?
94. What will the speaker do next?

Questions 95-97 refer to the following talk and diagram.

Good morning, everyone. As you know, this is the last time I'll be teaching you here at Alton Community Center. So, I'd like to give you a chance to meet your new teacher, Steve Jensen. Steve will be running your beginners classes starting from next Saturday. He has a lot of experience as a swimming coach, and he has even won awards for competing in national swimming competitions. As I previously mentioned, I'm planning to open a sports store in the city center next month, so I hope I see some of you from time to time. I'll stock a wide variety of swimming gear. Now, I'll let Steve say a few words.

95. What is the main purpose of the talk?
96. Look at the graphic. Which lane will the listeners use?
97. What will the speaker do next month?

Questions 98-100 refer to the following announcement and sign.

As employees of Hanley's Department Store, you'll be delighted to hear that the company will implement a special staff incentive plan from today onward. What that means is that the employees who manage to sell the most clothing items and jewelry in our department will be rewarded with gift certificates and cash bonuses, based on their performance. In order to keep track of each individual's sales performance, I need you to record each sale, and hand in a full sales report to me at the end of each shift. Those who are eligible for a reward will be informed at the end of each month.

98. What is being announced?
99. Look at the graphic. Where most likely do the listeners work?
100. What are the listeners required to do at the end of each work shift?

TOEIC 점수 환산표 [LC]

맞은 개수 (틀린 개수)	LC 점수	맞은 개수 (틀린 개수)	LC 점수	맞은 개수 (틀린 개수)	LC 점수
100 (0)	495	**66 (–34)**	275–285	**32 (–68)**	100–110
99 (–1)	495	**65 (–35)**	270–280	**31 (–69)**	95–105
98 (–2)	495	**64 (–36)**	265–275	**30 (–70)**	95–105
97 (–3)	495	**63 (–37)**	260–270	**29 (–71)**	90–100
96 (–4)	490–495	**62 (–38)**	255–265	**28 (–72)**	85–95
95 (–5)	485–490	**61 (–39)**	250–260	**27 (–73)**	85–95
94 (–6)	475–485	**60 (–40)**	245–255	**26 (–74)**	80–90
93 (–7)	470–480	**59 (–41)**	240–250	**25 (–75)**	75–85
92 (–8)	465–475	**58 (–42)**	235–245	**24 (–76)**	70–80
91 (–9)	465–475	**57 (–43)**	230–240	**23 (–77)**	65–75
90 (–10)	455–465	**56 (–44)**	225–235	**22 (–78)**	60–70
89 (–11)	445–455	**55 (–45)**	220–230	**21 (–79)**	55–65
88 (–12)	435–445	**54 (–46)**	215–225	**20 (–80)**	55–65
87 (–13)	425–435	**53 (–47)**	210–220	**19 (–81)**	50–60
86 (–14)	415–425	**52 (–48)**	205–215	**18 (–82)**	50–60
85 (–15)	405–415	**51 (–49)**	200–210	**17 (–83)**	45–55
84 (–16)	395–405	**50 (–50)**	195–205	**16 (–84)**	40–50
83 (–17)	385–395	**49 (–51)**	190–200	**15 (–85)**	35–45
82 (–18)	375–385	**48 (–52)**	185–195	**14 (–86)**	35–45
81 (–19)	365–375	**47 (–53)**	180–190	**13 (–87)**	30–40
80 (–20)	360–370	**46 (–54)**	170–180	**12 (–88)**	30–40
79 (–21)	355–365	**45 (–55)**	165–175	**11 (–89)**	25–35
78 (–22)	350–360	**44 (–56)**	160–170	**10 (–90)**	25–35
77 (–23)	345–355	**43 (–57)**	155–165	**9 (–91)**	20–30
76 (–24)	335–345	**42 (–58)**	150–160	**8 (–92)**	20–30
75 (–25)	325–335	**41 (–59)**	145–155	**7 (–93)**	15–25
74 (–26)	320–330	**40 (–60)**	140–150	**6 (–94)**	10–20
73 (–27)	315–325	**39 (–61)**	135–145	**5 (–95)**	5–10
72 (–28)	310–320	**38 (–62)**	130–140	**4 (–96)**	5–10
71 (–29)	305–315	**37 (–63)**	125–135	**3 (–97)**	5
70 (–30)	300–310	**36 (–64)**	120–130	**2 (–98)**	5
69 (–31)	295–305	**35 (–65)**	115–125	**1 (–99)**	5
68 (–32)	285–295	**34 (–66)**	110–120	**0 (–100)**	5
67 (–33)	280–290	**33 (–67)**	105–115		

ANSWER SHEET

모의고사 답안지입니다.
절취하여 실제 시험처럼
마킹하면서 풀어보세요.

답안지가 더 필요할 경우
시원스쿨랩(lab.siwonschool.com)
홈페이지의 교재 자료실에서
다운로드 받아 사용하세요.

ANSWER SHEET

시원스쿨 LAB

이름		테스트 회차		날짜	

LISTENING COMPREHENSION (PART 1~4)

NO	ANSWER A B C D	NO	ANSWER A B C D	NO	ANSWER A B C D	NO	ANSWER A B C D	NO	ANSWER A B C D
1	ⓐ ⓑ ⓒ ⓓ	21	ⓐ ⓑ ⓒ	41	ⓐ ⓑ ⓒ ⓓ	61	ⓐ ⓑ ⓒ ⓓ	81	ⓐ ⓑ ⓒ ⓓ
2	ⓐ ⓑ ⓒ ⓓ	22	ⓐ ⓑ ⓒ	42	ⓐ ⓑ ⓒ ⓓ	62	ⓐ ⓑ ⓒ ⓓ	82	ⓐ ⓑ ⓒ ⓓ
3	ⓐ ⓑ ⓒ ⓓ	23	ⓐ ⓑ ⓒ	43	ⓐ ⓑ ⓒ ⓓ	63	ⓐ ⓑ ⓒ ⓓ	83	ⓐ ⓑ ⓒ ⓓ
4	ⓐ ⓑ ⓒ ⓓ	24	ⓐ ⓑ ⓒ	44	ⓐ ⓑ ⓒ ⓓ	64	ⓐ ⓑ ⓒ ⓓ	84	ⓐ ⓑ ⓒ ⓓ
5	ⓐ ⓑ ⓒ ⓓ	25	ⓐ ⓑ ⓒ	45	ⓐ ⓑ ⓒ ⓓ	65	ⓐ ⓑ ⓒ ⓓ	85	ⓐ ⓑ ⓒ ⓓ
6	ⓐ ⓑ ⓒ ⓓ	26	ⓐ ⓑ ⓒ	46	ⓐ ⓑ ⓒ ⓓ	66	ⓐ ⓑ ⓒ ⓓ	86	ⓐ ⓑ ⓒ ⓓ
7	ⓐ ⓑ ⓒ	27	ⓐ ⓑ ⓒ	47	ⓐ ⓑ ⓒ ⓓ	67	ⓐ ⓑ ⓒ ⓓ	87	ⓐ ⓑ ⓒ ⓓ
8	ⓐ ⓑ ⓒ	28	ⓐ ⓑ ⓒ	48	ⓐ ⓑ ⓒ ⓓ	68	ⓐ ⓑ ⓒ ⓓ	88	ⓐ ⓑ ⓒ ⓓ
9	ⓐ ⓑ ⓒ	29	ⓐ ⓑ ⓒ	49	ⓐ ⓑ ⓒ ⓓ	69	ⓐ ⓑ ⓒ ⓓ	89	ⓐ ⓑ ⓒ ⓓ
10	ⓐ ⓑ ⓒ	30	ⓐ ⓑ ⓒ	50	ⓐ ⓑ ⓒ ⓓ	70	ⓐ ⓑ ⓒ ⓓ	90	ⓐ ⓑ ⓒ ⓓ
11	ⓐ ⓑ ⓒ	31	ⓐ ⓑ ⓒ	51	ⓐ ⓑ ⓒ ⓓ	71	ⓐ ⓑ ⓒ ⓓ	91	ⓐ ⓑ ⓒ ⓓ
12	ⓐ ⓑ ⓒ	32	ⓐ ⓑ ⓒ ⓓ	52	ⓐ ⓑ ⓒ ⓓ	72	ⓐ ⓑ ⓒ ⓓ	92	ⓐ ⓑ ⓒ ⓓ
13	ⓐ ⓑ ⓒ	33	ⓐ ⓑ ⓒ ⓓ	53	ⓐ ⓑ ⓒ ⓓ	73	ⓐ ⓑ ⓒ ⓓ	93	ⓐ ⓑ ⓒ ⓓ
14	ⓐ ⓑ ⓒ	34	ⓐ ⓑ ⓒ ⓓ	54	ⓐ ⓑ ⓒ ⓓ	74	ⓐ ⓑ ⓒ ⓓ	94	ⓐ ⓑ ⓒ ⓓ
15	ⓐ ⓑ ⓒ	35	ⓐ ⓑ ⓒ ⓓ	55	ⓐ ⓑ ⓒ ⓓ	75	ⓐ ⓑ ⓒ ⓓ	95	ⓐ ⓑ ⓒ ⓓ
16	ⓐ ⓑ ⓒ	36	ⓐ ⓑ ⓒ ⓓ	56	ⓐ ⓑ ⓒ ⓓ	76	ⓐ ⓑ ⓒ ⓓ	96	ⓐ ⓑ ⓒ ⓓ
17	ⓐ ⓑ ⓒ	37	ⓐ ⓑ ⓒ ⓓ	57	ⓐ ⓑ ⓒ ⓓ	77	ⓐ ⓑ ⓒ ⓓ	97	ⓐ ⓑ ⓒ ⓓ
18	ⓐ ⓑ ⓒ	38	ⓐ ⓑ ⓒ ⓓ	58	ⓐ ⓑ ⓒ ⓓ	78	ⓐ ⓑ ⓒ ⓓ	98	ⓐ ⓑ ⓒ ⓓ
19	ⓐ ⓑ ⓒ	39	ⓐ ⓑ ⓒ ⓓ	59	ⓐ ⓑ ⓒ ⓓ	79	ⓐ ⓑ ⓒ ⓓ	99	ⓐ ⓑ ⓒ ⓓ
20	ⓐ ⓑ ⓒ	40	ⓐ ⓑ ⓒ ⓓ	60	ⓐ ⓑ ⓒ ⓓ	80	ⓐ ⓑ ⓒ ⓓ	100	ⓐ ⓑ ⓒ ⓓ

READING COMPREHENSION (PART 5~7)

NO	ANSWER A B C D	NO	ANSWER A B C D	NO	ANSWER A B C D	NO	ANSWER A B C D	NO	ANSWER A B C D
101	ⓐ ⓑ ⓒ ⓓ	121	ⓐ ⓑ ⓒ ⓓ	141	ⓐ ⓑ ⓒ ⓓ	161	ⓐ ⓑ ⓒ ⓓ	181	ⓐ ⓑ ⓒ ⓓ
102	ⓐ ⓑ ⓒ ⓓ	122	ⓐ ⓑ ⓒ ⓓ	142	ⓐ ⓑ ⓒ ⓓ	162	ⓐ ⓑ ⓒ ⓓ	182	ⓐ ⓑ ⓒ ⓓ
103	ⓐ ⓑ ⓒ ⓓ	123	ⓐ ⓑ ⓒ ⓓ	143	ⓐ ⓑ ⓒ ⓓ	163	ⓐ ⓑ ⓒ ⓓ	183	ⓐ ⓑ ⓒ ⓓ
104	ⓐ ⓑ ⓒ ⓓ	124	ⓐ ⓑ ⓒ ⓓ	144	ⓐ ⓑ ⓒ ⓓ	164	ⓐ ⓑ ⓒ ⓓ	184	ⓐ ⓑ ⓒ ⓓ
105	ⓐ ⓑ ⓒ ⓓ	125	ⓐ ⓑ ⓒ ⓓ	145	ⓐ ⓑ ⓒ ⓓ	165	ⓐ ⓑ ⓒ ⓓ	185	ⓐ ⓑ ⓒ ⓓ
106	ⓐ ⓑ ⓒ ⓓ	126	ⓐ ⓑ ⓒ ⓓ	146	ⓐ ⓑ ⓒ ⓓ	166	ⓐ ⓑ ⓒ ⓓ	186	ⓐ ⓑ ⓒ ⓓ
107	ⓐ ⓑ ⓒ ⓓ	127	ⓐ ⓑ ⓒ ⓓ	147	ⓐ ⓑ ⓒ ⓓ	167	ⓐ ⓑ ⓒ ⓓ	187	ⓐ ⓑ ⓒ ⓓ
108	ⓐ ⓑ ⓒ ⓓ	128	ⓐ ⓑ ⓒ ⓓ	148	ⓐ ⓑ ⓒ ⓓ	168	ⓐ ⓑ ⓒ ⓓ	188	ⓐ ⓑ ⓒ ⓓ
109	ⓐ ⓑ ⓒ ⓓ	129	ⓐ ⓑ ⓒ ⓓ	149	ⓐ ⓑ ⓒ ⓓ	169	ⓐ ⓑ ⓒ ⓓ	189	ⓐ ⓑ ⓒ ⓓ
110	ⓐ ⓑ ⓒ ⓓ	130	ⓐ ⓑ ⓒ ⓓ	150	ⓐ ⓑ ⓒ ⓓ	170	ⓐ ⓑ ⓒ ⓓ	190	ⓐ ⓑ ⓒ ⓓ
111	ⓐ ⓑ ⓒ ⓓ	131	ⓐ ⓑ ⓒ ⓓ	151	ⓐ ⓑ ⓒ ⓓ	171	ⓐ ⓑ ⓒ ⓓ	191	ⓐ ⓑ ⓒ ⓓ
112	ⓐ ⓑ ⓒ ⓓ	132	ⓐ ⓑ ⓒ ⓓ	152	ⓐ ⓑ ⓒ ⓓ	172	ⓐ ⓑ ⓒ ⓓ	192	ⓐ ⓑ ⓒ ⓓ
113	ⓐ ⓑ ⓒ ⓓ	133	ⓐ ⓑ ⓒ ⓓ	153	ⓐ ⓑ ⓒ ⓓ	173	ⓐ ⓑ ⓒ ⓓ	193	ⓐ ⓑ ⓒ ⓓ
114	ⓐ ⓑ ⓒ ⓓ	134	ⓐ ⓑ ⓒ ⓓ	154	ⓐ ⓑ ⓒ ⓓ	174	ⓐ ⓑ ⓒ ⓓ	194	ⓐ ⓑ ⓒ ⓓ
115	ⓐ ⓑ ⓒ ⓓ	135	ⓐ ⓑ ⓒ ⓓ	155	ⓐ ⓑ ⓒ ⓓ	175	ⓐ ⓑ ⓒ ⓓ	195	ⓐ ⓑ ⓒ ⓓ
116	ⓐ ⓑ ⓒ ⓓ	136	ⓐ ⓑ ⓒ ⓓ	156	ⓐ ⓑ ⓒ ⓓ	176	ⓐ ⓑ ⓒ ⓓ	196	ⓐ ⓑ ⓒ ⓓ
117	ⓐ ⓑ ⓒ ⓓ	137	ⓐ ⓑ ⓒ ⓓ	157	ⓐ ⓑ ⓒ ⓓ	177	ⓐ ⓑ ⓒ ⓓ	197	ⓐ ⓑ ⓒ ⓓ
118	ⓐ ⓑ ⓒ ⓓ	138	ⓐ ⓑ ⓒ ⓓ	158	ⓐ ⓑ ⓒ ⓓ	178	ⓐ ⓑ ⓒ ⓓ	198	ⓐ ⓑ ⓒ ⓓ
119	ⓐ ⓑ ⓒ ⓓ	139	ⓐ ⓑ ⓒ ⓓ	159	ⓐ ⓑ ⓒ ⓓ	179	ⓐ ⓑ ⓒ ⓓ	199	ⓐ ⓑ ⓒ ⓓ
120	ⓐ ⓑ ⓒ ⓓ	140	ⓐ ⓑ ⓒ ⓓ	160	ⓐ ⓑ ⓒ ⓓ	180	ⓐ ⓑ ⓒ ⓓ	200	ⓐ ⓑ ⓒ ⓓ

ANSWER SHEET

시원스쿨 LAB

이름		테스트 회차		날짜	

LISTENING COMPREHENSION (PART 1~4)

NO	ANSWER A B C D	NO	ANSWER A B C D	NO	ANSWER A B C D	NO	ANSWER A B C D	NO	ANSWER A B C D
1	ⓐ ⓑ ⓒ ⓓ	21	ⓐ ⓑ ⓒ	41	ⓐ ⓑ ⓒ ⓓ	61	ⓐ ⓑ ⓒ ⓓ	81	ⓐ ⓑ ⓒ ⓓ
2	ⓐ ⓑ ⓒ ⓓ	22	ⓐ ⓑ ⓒ	42	ⓐ ⓑ ⓒ ⓓ	62	ⓐ ⓑ ⓒ ⓓ	82	ⓐ ⓑ ⓒ ⓓ
3	ⓐ ⓑ ⓒ ⓓ	23	ⓐ ⓑ ⓒ	43	ⓐ ⓑ ⓒ ⓓ	63	ⓐ ⓑ ⓒ ⓓ	83	ⓐ ⓑ ⓒ ⓓ
4	ⓐ ⓑ ⓒ ⓓ	24	ⓐ ⓑ ⓒ	44	ⓐ ⓑ ⓒ ⓓ	64	ⓐ ⓑ ⓒ ⓓ	84	ⓐ ⓑ ⓒ ⓓ
5	ⓐ ⓑ ⓒ ⓓ	25	ⓐ ⓑ ⓒ	45	ⓐ ⓑ ⓒ ⓓ	65	ⓐ ⓑ ⓒ ⓓ	85	ⓐ ⓑ ⓒ ⓓ
6	ⓐ ⓑ ⓒ ⓓ	26	ⓐ ⓑ ⓒ	46	ⓐ ⓑ ⓒ ⓓ	66	ⓐ ⓑ ⓒ ⓓ	86	ⓐ ⓑ ⓒ ⓓ
7	ⓐ ⓑ ⓒ	27	ⓐ ⓑ ⓒ	47	ⓐ ⓑ ⓒ ⓓ	67	ⓐ ⓑ ⓒ ⓓ	87	ⓐ ⓑ ⓒ ⓓ
8	ⓐ ⓑ ⓒ	28	ⓐ ⓑ ⓒ	48	ⓐ ⓑ ⓒ ⓓ	68	ⓐ ⓑ ⓒ ⓓ	88	ⓐ ⓑ ⓒ ⓓ
9	ⓐ ⓑ ⓒ	29	ⓐ ⓑ ⓒ	49	ⓐ ⓑ ⓒ ⓓ	69	ⓐ ⓑ ⓒ ⓓ	89	ⓐ ⓑ ⓒ ⓓ
10	ⓐ ⓑ ⓒ	30	ⓐ ⓑ ⓒ	50	ⓐ ⓑ ⓒ ⓓ	70	ⓐ ⓑ ⓒ ⓓ	90	ⓐ ⓑ ⓒ ⓓ
11	ⓐ ⓑ ⓒ	31	ⓐ ⓑ ⓒ	51	ⓐ ⓑ ⓒ ⓓ	71	ⓐ ⓑ ⓒ ⓓ	91	ⓐ ⓑ ⓒ ⓓ
12	ⓐ ⓑ ⓒ	32	ⓐ ⓑ ⓒ ⓓ	52	ⓐ ⓑ ⓒ ⓓ	72	ⓐ ⓑ ⓒ ⓓ	92	ⓐ ⓑ ⓒ ⓓ
13	ⓐ ⓑ ⓒ	33	ⓐ ⓑ ⓒ ⓓ	53	ⓐ ⓑ ⓒ ⓓ	73	ⓐ ⓑ ⓒ ⓓ	93	ⓐ ⓑ ⓒ ⓓ
14	ⓐ ⓑ ⓒ	34	ⓐ ⓑ ⓒ ⓓ	54	ⓐ ⓑ ⓒ ⓓ	74	ⓐ ⓑ ⓒ ⓓ	94	ⓐ ⓑ ⓒ ⓓ
15	ⓐ ⓑ ⓒ	35	ⓐ ⓑ ⓒ ⓓ	55	ⓐ ⓑ ⓒ ⓓ	75	ⓐ ⓑ ⓒ ⓓ	95	ⓐ ⓑ ⓒ ⓓ
16	ⓐ ⓑ ⓒ	36	ⓐ ⓑ ⓒ ⓓ	56	ⓐ ⓑ ⓒ ⓓ	76	ⓐ ⓑ ⓒ ⓓ	96	ⓐ ⓑ ⓒ ⓓ
17	ⓐ ⓑ ⓒ	37	ⓐ ⓑ ⓒ ⓓ	57	ⓐ ⓑ ⓒ ⓓ	77	ⓐ ⓑ ⓒ ⓓ	97	ⓐ ⓑ ⓒ ⓓ
18	ⓐ ⓑ ⓒ	38	ⓐ ⓑ ⓒ ⓓ	58	ⓐ ⓑ ⓒ ⓓ	78	ⓐ ⓑ ⓒ ⓓ	98	ⓐ ⓑ ⓒ ⓓ
19	ⓐ ⓑ ⓒ	39	ⓐ ⓑ ⓒ ⓓ	59	ⓐ ⓑ ⓒ ⓓ	79	ⓐ ⓑ ⓒ ⓓ	99	ⓐ ⓑ ⓒ ⓓ
20	ⓐ ⓑ ⓒ	40	ⓐ ⓑ ⓒ ⓓ	60	ⓐ ⓑ ⓒ ⓓ	80	ⓐ ⓑ ⓒ ⓓ	100	ⓐ ⓑ ⓒ ⓓ

READING COMPREHENSION (PART 5~7)

NO	ANSWER A B C D	NO	ANSWER A B C D	NO	ANSWER A B C D	NO	ANSWER A B C D	NO	ANSWER A B C D
101	ⓐ ⓑ ⓒ ⓓ	121	ⓐ ⓑ ⓒ ⓓ	141	ⓐ ⓑ ⓒ ⓓ	161	ⓐ ⓑ ⓒ ⓓ	181	ⓐ ⓑ ⓒ ⓓ
102	ⓐ ⓑ ⓒ ⓓ	122	ⓐ ⓑ ⓒ ⓓ	142	ⓐ ⓑ ⓒ ⓓ	162	ⓐ ⓑ ⓒ ⓓ	182	ⓐ ⓑ ⓒ ⓓ
103	ⓐ ⓑ ⓒ ⓓ	123	ⓐ ⓑ ⓒ ⓓ	143	ⓐ ⓑ ⓒ ⓓ	163	ⓐ ⓑ ⓒ ⓓ	183	ⓐ ⓑ ⓒ ⓓ
104	ⓐ ⓑ ⓒ ⓓ	124	ⓐ ⓑ ⓒ ⓓ	144	ⓐ ⓑ ⓒ ⓓ	164	ⓐ ⓑ ⓒ ⓓ	184	ⓐ ⓑ ⓒ ⓓ
105	ⓐ ⓑ ⓒ ⓓ	125	ⓐ ⓑ ⓒ ⓓ	145	ⓐ ⓑ ⓒ ⓓ	165	ⓐ ⓑ ⓒ ⓓ	185	ⓐ ⓑ ⓒ ⓓ
106	ⓐ ⓑ ⓒ ⓓ	126	ⓐ ⓑ ⓒ ⓓ	146	ⓐ ⓑ ⓒ ⓓ	166	ⓐ ⓑ ⓒ ⓓ	186	ⓐ ⓑ ⓒ ⓓ
107	ⓐ ⓑ ⓒ ⓓ	127	ⓐ ⓑ ⓒ ⓓ	147	ⓐ ⓑ ⓒ ⓓ	167	ⓐ ⓑ ⓒ ⓓ	187	ⓐ ⓑ ⓒ ⓓ
108	ⓐ ⓑ ⓒ ⓓ	128	ⓐ ⓑ ⓒ ⓓ	148	ⓐ ⓑ ⓒ ⓓ	168	ⓐ ⓑ ⓒ ⓓ	188	ⓐ ⓑ ⓒ ⓓ
109	ⓐ ⓑ ⓒ ⓓ	129	ⓐ ⓑ ⓒ ⓓ	149	ⓐ ⓑ ⓒ ⓓ	169	ⓐ ⓑ ⓒ ⓓ	189	ⓐ ⓑ ⓒ ⓓ
110	ⓐ ⓑ ⓒ ⓓ	130	ⓐ ⓑ ⓒ ⓓ	150	ⓐ ⓑ ⓒ ⓓ	170	ⓐ ⓑ ⓒ ⓓ	190	ⓐ ⓑ ⓒ ⓓ
111	ⓐ ⓑ ⓒ ⓓ	131	ⓐ ⓑ ⓒ ⓓ	151	ⓐ ⓑ ⓒ ⓓ	171	ⓐ ⓑ ⓒ ⓓ	191	ⓐ ⓑ ⓒ ⓓ
112	ⓐ ⓑ ⓒ ⓓ	132	ⓐ ⓑ ⓒ ⓓ	152	ⓐ ⓑ ⓒ ⓓ	172	ⓐ ⓑ ⓒ ⓓ	192	ⓐ ⓑ ⓒ ⓓ
113	ⓐ ⓑ ⓒ ⓓ	133	ⓐ ⓑ ⓒ ⓓ	153	ⓐ ⓑ ⓒ ⓓ	173	ⓐ ⓑ ⓒ ⓓ	193	ⓐ ⓑ ⓒ ⓓ
114	ⓐ ⓑ ⓒ ⓓ	134	ⓐ ⓑ ⓒ ⓓ	154	ⓐ ⓑ ⓒ ⓓ	174	ⓐ ⓑ ⓒ ⓓ	194	ⓐ ⓑ ⓒ ⓓ
115	ⓐ ⓑ ⓒ ⓓ	135	ⓐ ⓑ ⓒ ⓓ	155	ⓐ ⓑ ⓒ ⓓ	175	ⓐ ⓑ ⓒ ⓓ	195	ⓐ ⓑ ⓒ ⓓ
116	ⓐ ⓑ ⓒ ⓓ	136	ⓐ ⓑ ⓒ ⓓ	156	ⓐ ⓑ ⓒ ⓓ	176	ⓐ ⓑ ⓒ ⓓ	196	ⓐ ⓑ ⓒ ⓓ
117	ⓐ ⓑ ⓒ ⓓ	137	ⓐ ⓑ ⓒ ⓓ	157	ⓐ ⓑ ⓒ ⓓ	177	ⓐ ⓑ ⓒ ⓓ	197	ⓐ ⓑ ⓒ ⓓ
118	ⓐ ⓑ ⓒ ⓓ	138	ⓐ ⓑ ⓒ ⓓ	158	ⓐ ⓑ ⓒ ⓓ	178	ⓐ ⓑ ⓒ ⓓ	198	ⓐ ⓑ ⓒ ⓓ
119	ⓐ ⓑ ⓒ ⓓ	139	ⓐ ⓑ ⓒ ⓓ	159	ⓐ ⓑ ⓒ ⓓ	179	ⓐ ⓑ ⓒ ⓓ	199	ⓐ ⓑ ⓒ ⓓ
120	ⓐ ⓑ ⓒ ⓓ	140	ⓐ ⓑ ⓒ ⓓ	160	ⓐ ⓑ ⓒ ⓓ	180	ⓐ ⓑ ⓒ ⓓ	200	ⓐ ⓑ ⓒ ⓓ

ANSWER SHEET

시원스쿨 LAB

이름		테스트 회차		날짜	

LISTENING COMPREHENSION (PART 1~4)

NO	ANSWER A B C D	NO	ANSWER A B C D	NO	ANSWER A B C D	NO	ANSWER A B C D	NO	ANSWER A B C D
1	ⓐ ⓑ ⓒ ⓓ	21	ⓐ ⓑ ⓒ	41	ⓐ ⓑ ⓒ ⓓ	61	ⓐ ⓑ ⓒ ⓓ	81	ⓐ ⓑ ⓒ ⓓ
2	ⓐ ⓑ ⓒ ⓓ	22	ⓐ ⓑ ⓒ	42	ⓐ ⓑ ⓒ ⓓ	62	ⓐ ⓑ ⓒ ⓓ	82	ⓐ ⓑ ⓒ ⓓ
3	ⓐ ⓑ ⓒ ⓓ	23	ⓐ ⓑ ⓒ	43	ⓐ ⓑ ⓒ ⓓ	63	ⓐ ⓑ ⓒ ⓓ	83	ⓐ ⓑ ⓒ ⓓ
4	ⓐ ⓑ ⓒ ⓓ	24	ⓐ ⓑ ⓒ	44	ⓐ ⓑ ⓒ ⓓ	64	ⓐ ⓑ ⓒ ⓓ	84	ⓐ ⓑ ⓒ ⓓ
5	ⓐ ⓑ ⓒ ⓓ	25	ⓐ ⓑ ⓒ	45	ⓐ ⓑ ⓒ ⓓ	65	ⓐ ⓑ ⓒ ⓓ	85	ⓐ ⓑ ⓒ ⓓ
6	ⓐ ⓑ ⓒ ⓓ	26	ⓐ ⓑ ⓒ	46	ⓐ ⓑ ⓒ ⓓ	66	ⓐ ⓑ ⓒ ⓓ	86	ⓐ ⓑ ⓒ ⓓ
7	ⓐ ⓑ ⓒ	27	ⓐ ⓑ ⓒ	47	ⓐ ⓑ ⓒ ⓓ	67	ⓐ ⓑ ⓒ ⓓ	87	ⓐ ⓑ ⓒ ⓓ
8	ⓐ ⓑ ⓒ	28	ⓐ ⓑ ⓒ	48	ⓐ ⓑ ⓒ ⓓ	68	ⓐ ⓑ ⓒ ⓓ	88	ⓐ ⓑ ⓒ ⓓ
9	ⓐ ⓑ ⓒ	29	ⓐ ⓑ ⓒ	49	ⓐ ⓑ ⓒ ⓓ	69	ⓐ ⓑ ⓒ ⓓ	89	ⓐ ⓑ ⓒ ⓓ
10	ⓐ ⓑ ⓒ	30	ⓐ ⓑ ⓒ	50	ⓐ ⓑ ⓒ ⓓ	70	ⓐ ⓑ ⓒ ⓓ	90	ⓐ ⓑ ⓒ ⓓ
11	ⓐ ⓑ ⓒ	31	ⓐ ⓑ ⓒ	51	ⓐ ⓑ ⓒ ⓓ	71	ⓐ ⓑ ⓒ ⓓ	91	ⓐ ⓑ ⓒ ⓓ
12	ⓐ ⓑ ⓒ	32	ⓐ ⓑ ⓒ ⓓ	52	ⓐ ⓑ ⓒ ⓓ	72	ⓐ ⓑ ⓒ ⓓ	92	ⓐ ⓑ ⓒ ⓓ
13	ⓐ ⓑ ⓒ	33	ⓐ ⓑ ⓒ ⓓ	53	ⓐ ⓑ ⓒ ⓓ	73	ⓐ ⓑ ⓒ ⓓ	93	ⓐ ⓑ ⓒ ⓓ
14	ⓐ ⓑ ⓒ	34	ⓐ ⓑ ⓒ ⓓ	54	ⓐ ⓑ ⓒ ⓓ	74	ⓐ ⓑ ⓒ ⓓ	94	ⓐ ⓑ ⓒ ⓓ
15	ⓐ ⓑ ⓒ	35	ⓐ ⓑ ⓒ ⓓ	55	ⓐ ⓑ ⓒ ⓓ	75	ⓐ ⓑ ⓒ ⓓ	95	ⓐ ⓑ ⓒ ⓓ
16	ⓐ ⓑ ⓒ	36	ⓐ ⓑ ⓒ ⓓ	56	ⓐ ⓑ ⓒ ⓓ	76	ⓐ ⓑ ⓒ ⓓ	96	ⓐ ⓑ ⓒ ⓓ
17	ⓐ ⓑ ⓒ	37	ⓐ ⓑ ⓒ ⓓ	57	ⓐ ⓑ ⓒ ⓓ	77	ⓐ ⓑ ⓒ ⓓ	97	ⓐ ⓑ ⓒ ⓓ
18	ⓐ ⓑ ⓒ	38	ⓐ ⓑ ⓒ ⓓ	58	ⓐ ⓑ ⓒ ⓓ	78	ⓐ ⓑ ⓒ ⓓ	98	ⓐ ⓑ ⓒ ⓓ
19	ⓐ ⓑ ⓒ	39	ⓐ ⓑ ⓒ ⓓ	59	ⓐ ⓑ ⓒ ⓓ	79	ⓐ ⓑ ⓒ ⓓ	99	ⓐ ⓑ ⓒ ⓓ
20	ⓐ ⓑ ⓒ	40	ⓐ ⓑ ⓒ ⓓ	60	ⓐ ⓑ ⓒ ⓓ	80	ⓐ ⓑ ⓒ ⓓ	100	ⓐ ⓑ ⓒ ⓓ

READING COMPREHENSION (PART 5~7)

NO	ANSWER A B C D	NO	ANSWER A B C D	NO	ANSWER A B C D	NO	ANSWER A B C D	NO	ANSWER A B C D
101	ⓐ ⓑ ⓒ ⓓ	121	ⓐ ⓑ ⓒ ⓓ	141	ⓐ ⓑ ⓒ ⓓ	161	ⓐ ⓑ ⓒ ⓓ	181	ⓐ ⓑ ⓒ ⓓ
102	ⓐ ⓑ ⓒ ⓓ	122	ⓐ ⓑ ⓒ ⓓ	142	ⓐ ⓑ ⓒ ⓓ	162	ⓐ ⓑ ⓒ ⓓ	182	ⓐ ⓑ ⓒ ⓓ
103	ⓐ ⓑ ⓒ ⓓ	123	ⓐ ⓑ ⓒ ⓓ	143	ⓐ ⓑ ⓒ ⓓ	163	ⓐ ⓑ ⓒ ⓓ	183	ⓐ ⓑ ⓒ ⓓ
104	ⓐ ⓑ ⓒ ⓓ	124	ⓐ ⓑ ⓒ ⓓ	144	ⓐ ⓑ ⓒ ⓓ	164	ⓐ ⓑ ⓒ ⓓ	184	ⓐ ⓑ ⓒ ⓓ
105	ⓐ ⓑ ⓒ ⓓ	125	ⓐ ⓑ ⓒ ⓓ	145	ⓐ ⓑ ⓒ ⓓ	165	ⓐ ⓑ ⓒ ⓓ	185	ⓐ ⓑ ⓒ ⓓ
106	ⓐ ⓑ ⓒ ⓓ	126	ⓐ ⓑ ⓒ ⓓ	146	ⓐ ⓑ ⓒ ⓓ	166	ⓐ ⓑ ⓒ ⓓ	186	ⓐ ⓑ ⓒ ⓓ
107	ⓐ ⓑ ⓒ ⓓ	127	ⓐ ⓑ ⓒ ⓓ	147	ⓐ ⓑ ⓒ ⓓ	167	ⓐ ⓑ ⓒ ⓓ	187	ⓐ ⓑ ⓒ ⓓ
108	ⓐ ⓑ ⓒ ⓓ	128	ⓐ ⓑ ⓒ ⓓ	148	ⓐ ⓑ ⓒ ⓓ	168	ⓐ ⓑ ⓒ ⓓ	188	ⓐ ⓑ ⓒ ⓓ
109	ⓐ ⓑ ⓒ ⓓ	129	ⓐ ⓑ ⓒ ⓓ	149	ⓐ ⓑ ⓒ ⓓ	169	ⓐ ⓑ ⓒ ⓓ	189	ⓐ ⓑ ⓒ ⓓ
110	ⓐ ⓑ ⓒ ⓓ	130	ⓐ ⓑ ⓒ ⓓ	150	ⓐ ⓑ ⓒ ⓓ	170	ⓐ ⓑ ⓒ ⓓ	190	ⓐ ⓑ ⓒ ⓓ
111	ⓐ ⓑ ⓒ ⓓ	131	ⓐ ⓑ ⓒ ⓓ	151	ⓐ ⓑ ⓒ ⓓ	171	ⓐ ⓑ ⓒ ⓓ	191	ⓐ ⓑ ⓒ ⓓ
112	ⓐ ⓑ ⓒ ⓓ	132	ⓐ ⓑ ⓒ ⓓ	152	ⓐ ⓑ ⓒ ⓓ	172	ⓐ ⓑ ⓒ ⓓ	192	ⓐ ⓑ ⓒ ⓓ
113	ⓐ ⓑ ⓒ ⓓ	133	ⓐ ⓑ ⓒ ⓓ	153	ⓐ ⓑ ⓒ ⓓ	173	ⓐ ⓑ ⓒ ⓓ	193	ⓐ ⓑ ⓒ ⓓ
114	ⓐ ⓑ ⓒ ⓓ	134	ⓐ ⓑ ⓒ ⓓ	154	ⓐ ⓑ ⓒ ⓓ	174	ⓐ ⓑ ⓒ ⓓ	194	ⓐ ⓑ ⓒ ⓓ
115	ⓐ ⓑ ⓒ ⓓ	135	ⓐ ⓑ ⓒ ⓓ	155	ⓐ ⓑ ⓒ ⓓ	175	ⓐ ⓑ ⓒ ⓓ	195	ⓐ ⓑ ⓒ ⓓ
116	ⓐ ⓑ ⓒ ⓓ	136	ⓐ ⓑ ⓒ ⓓ	156	ⓐ ⓑ ⓒ ⓓ	176	ⓐ ⓑ ⓒ ⓓ	196	ⓐ ⓑ ⓒ ⓓ
117	ⓐ ⓑ ⓒ ⓓ	137	ⓐ ⓑ ⓒ ⓓ	157	ⓐ ⓑ ⓒ ⓓ	177	ⓐ ⓑ ⓒ ⓓ	197	ⓐ ⓑ ⓒ ⓓ
118	ⓐ ⓑ ⓒ ⓓ	138	ⓐ ⓑ ⓒ ⓓ	158	ⓐ ⓑ ⓒ ⓓ	178	ⓐ ⓑ ⓒ ⓓ	198	ⓐ ⓑ ⓒ ⓓ
119	ⓐ ⓑ ⓒ ⓓ	139	ⓐ ⓑ ⓒ ⓓ	159	ⓐ ⓑ ⓒ ⓓ	179	ⓐ ⓑ ⓒ ⓓ	199	ⓐ ⓑ ⓒ ⓓ
120	ⓐ ⓑ ⓒ ⓓ	140	ⓐ ⓑ ⓒ ⓓ	160	ⓐ ⓑ ⓒ ⓓ	180	ⓐ ⓑ ⓒ ⓓ	200	ⓐ ⓑ ⓒ ⓓ

ANSWER SHEET

시원스쿨 LAB

이름		테스트 회차		날짜	

LISTENING COMPREHENSION (PART 1~4)

NO	ANSWER A B C D	NO	ANSWER A B C D	NO	ANSWER A B C D	NO	ANSWER A B C D	NO	ANSWER A B C D
1	ⓐ ⓑ ⓒ ⓓ	21	ⓐ ⓑ ⓒ	41	ⓐ ⓑ ⓒ ⓓ	61	ⓐ ⓑ ⓒ ⓓ	81	ⓐ ⓑ ⓒ ⓓ
2	ⓐ ⓑ ⓒ ⓓ	22	ⓐ ⓑ ⓒ	42	ⓐ ⓑ ⓒ ⓓ	62	ⓐ ⓑ ⓒ ⓓ	82	ⓐ ⓑ ⓒ ⓓ
3	ⓐ ⓑ ⓒ ⓓ	23	ⓐ ⓑ ⓒ	43	ⓐ ⓑ ⓒ ⓓ	63	ⓐ ⓑ ⓒ ⓓ	83	ⓐ ⓑ ⓒ ⓓ
4	ⓐ ⓑ ⓒ ⓓ	24	ⓐ ⓑ ⓒ	44	ⓐ ⓑ ⓒ ⓓ	64	ⓐ ⓑ ⓒ ⓓ	84	ⓐ ⓑ ⓒ ⓓ
5	ⓐ ⓑ ⓒ ⓓ	25	ⓐ ⓑ ⓒ	45	ⓐ ⓑ ⓒ ⓓ	65	ⓐ ⓑ ⓒ ⓓ	85	ⓐ ⓑ ⓒ ⓓ
6	ⓐ ⓑ ⓒ ⓓ	26	ⓐ ⓑ ⓒ	46	ⓐ ⓑ ⓒ ⓓ	66	ⓐ ⓑ ⓒ ⓓ	86	ⓐ ⓑ ⓒ ⓓ
7	ⓐ ⓑ ⓒ	27	ⓐ ⓑ ⓒ	47	ⓐ ⓑ ⓒ ⓓ	67	ⓐ ⓑ ⓒ ⓓ	87	ⓐ ⓑ ⓒ ⓓ
8	ⓐ ⓑ ⓒ	28	ⓐ ⓑ ⓒ	48	ⓐ ⓑ ⓒ ⓓ	68	ⓐ ⓑ ⓒ ⓓ	88	ⓐ ⓑ ⓒ ⓓ
9	ⓐ ⓑ ⓒ	29	ⓐ ⓑ ⓒ	49	ⓐ ⓑ ⓒ ⓓ	69	ⓐ ⓑ ⓒ ⓓ	89	ⓐ ⓑ ⓒ ⓓ
10	ⓐ ⓑ ⓒ	30	ⓐ ⓑ ⓒ	50	ⓐ ⓑ ⓒ ⓓ	70	ⓐ ⓑ ⓒ ⓓ	90	ⓐ ⓑ ⓒ ⓓ
11	ⓐ ⓑ ⓒ	31	ⓐ ⓑ ⓒ	51	ⓐ ⓑ ⓒ ⓓ	71	ⓐ ⓑ ⓒ ⓓ	91	ⓐ ⓑ ⓒ ⓓ
12	ⓐ ⓑ ⓒ	32	ⓐ ⓑ ⓒ ⓓ	52	ⓐ ⓑ ⓒ ⓓ	72	ⓐ ⓑ ⓒ ⓓ	92	ⓐ ⓑ ⓒ ⓓ
13	ⓐ ⓑ ⓒ	33	ⓐ ⓑ ⓒ ⓓ	53	ⓐ ⓑ ⓒ ⓓ	73	ⓐ ⓑ ⓒ ⓓ	93	ⓐ ⓑ ⓒ ⓓ
14	ⓐ ⓑ ⓒ	34	ⓐ ⓑ ⓒ ⓓ	54	ⓐ ⓑ ⓒ ⓓ	74	ⓐ ⓑ ⓒ ⓓ	94	ⓐ ⓑ ⓒ ⓓ
15	ⓐ ⓑ ⓒ	35	ⓐ ⓑ ⓒ ⓓ	55	ⓐ ⓑ ⓒ ⓓ	75	ⓐ ⓑ ⓒ ⓓ	95	ⓐ ⓑ ⓒ ⓓ
16	ⓐ ⓑ ⓒ	36	ⓐ ⓑ ⓒ ⓓ	56	ⓐ ⓑ ⓒ ⓓ	76	ⓐ ⓑ ⓒ ⓓ	96	ⓐ ⓑ ⓒ ⓓ
17	ⓐ ⓑ ⓒ	37	ⓐ ⓑ ⓒ ⓓ	57	ⓐ ⓑ ⓒ ⓓ	77	ⓐ ⓑ ⓒ ⓓ	97	ⓐ ⓑ ⓒ ⓓ
18	ⓐ ⓑ ⓒ	38	ⓐ ⓑ ⓒ ⓓ	58	ⓐ ⓑ ⓒ ⓓ	78	ⓐ ⓑ ⓒ ⓓ	98	ⓐ ⓑ ⓒ ⓓ
19	ⓐ ⓑ ⓒ	39	ⓐ ⓑ ⓒ ⓓ	59	ⓐ ⓑ ⓒ ⓓ	79	ⓐ ⓑ ⓒ ⓓ	99	ⓐ ⓑ ⓒ ⓓ
20	ⓐ ⓑ ⓒ	40	ⓐ ⓑ ⓒ ⓓ	60	ⓐ ⓑ ⓒ ⓓ	80	ⓐ ⓑ ⓒ ⓓ	100	ⓐ ⓑ ⓒ ⓓ

READING COMPREHENSION (PART 5~7)

NO	ANSWER A B C D	NO	ANSWER A B C D	NO	ANSWER A B C D	NO	ANSWER A B C D	NO	ANSWER A B C D
101	ⓐ ⓑ ⓒ ⓓ	121	ⓐ ⓑ ⓒ ⓓ	141	ⓐ ⓑ ⓒ ⓓ	161	ⓐ ⓑ ⓒ ⓓ	181	ⓐ ⓑ ⓒ ⓓ
102	ⓐ ⓑ ⓒ ⓓ	122	ⓐ ⓑ ⓒ ⓓ	142	ⓐ ⓑ ⓒ ⓓ	162	ⓐ ⓑ ⓒ ⓓ	182	ⓐ ⓑ ⓒ ⓓ
103	ⓐ ⓑ ⓒ ⓓ	123	ⓐ ⓑ ⓒ ⓓ	143	ⓐ ⓑ ⓒ ⓓ	163	ⓐ ⓑ ⓒ ⓓ	183	ⓐ ⓑ ⓒ ⓓ
104	ⓐ ⓑ ⓒ ⓓ	124	ⓐ ⓑ ⓒ ⓓ	144	ⓐ ⓑ ⓒ ⓓ	164	ⓐ ⓑ ⓒ ⓓ	184	ⓐ ⓑ ⓒ ⓓ
105	ⓐ ⓑ ⓒ ⓓ	125	ⓐ ⓑ ⓒ ⓓ	145	ⓐ ⓑ ⓒ ⓓ	165	ⓐ ⓑ ⓒ ⓓ	185	ⓐ ⓑ ⓒ ⓓ
106	ⓐ ⓑ ⓒ ⓓ	126	ⓐ ⓑ ⓒ ⓓ	146	ⓐ ⓑ ⓒ ⓓ	166	ⓐ ⓑ ⓒ ⓓ	186	ⓐ ⓑ ⓒ ⓓ
107	ⓐ ⓑ ⓒ ⓓ	127	ⓐ ⓑ ⓒ ⓓ	147	ⓐ ⓑ ⓒ ⓓ	167	ⓐ ⓑ ⓒ ⓓ	187	ⓐ ⓑ ⓒ ⓓ
108	ⓐ ⓑ ⓒ ⓓ	128	ⓐ ⓑ ⓒ ⓓ	148	ⓐ ⓑ ⓒ ⓓ	168	ⓐ ⓑ ⓒ ⓓ	188	ⓐ ⓑ ⓒ ⓓ
109	ⓐ ⓑ ⓒ ⓓ	129	ⓐ ⓑ ⓒ ⓓ	149	ⓐ ⓑ ⓒ ⓓ	169	ⓐ ⓑ ⓒ ⓓ	189	ⓐ ⓑ ⓒ ⓓ
110	ⓐ ⓑ ⓒ ⓓ	130	ⓐ ⓑ ⓒ ⓓ	150	ⓐ ⓑ ⓒ ⓓ	170	ⓐ ⓑ ⓒ ⓓ	190	ⓐ ⓑ ⓒ ⓓ
111	ⓐ ⓑ ⓒ ⓓ	131	ⓐ ⓑ ⓒ ⓓ	151	ⓐ ⓑ ⓒ ⓓ	171	ⓐ ⓑ ⓒ ⓓ	191	ⓐ ⓑ ⓒ ⓓ
112	ⓐ ⓑ ⓒ ⓓ	132	ⓐ ⓑ ⓒ ⓓ	152	ⓐ ⓑ ⓒ ⓓ	172	ⓐ ⓑ ⓒ ⓓ	192	ⓐ ⓑ ⓒ ⓓ
113	ⓐ ⓑ ⓒ ⓓ	133	ⓐ ⓑ ⓒ ⓓ	153	ⓐ ⓑ ⓒ ⓓ	173	ⓐ ⓑ ⓒ ⓓ	193	ⓐ ⓑ ⓒ ⓓ
114	ⓐ ⓑ ⓒ ⓓ	134	ⓐ ⓑ ⓒ ⓓ	154	ⓐ ⓑ ⓒ ⓓ	174	ⓐ ⓑ ⓒ ⓓ	194	ⓐ ⓑ ⓒ ⓓ
115	ⓐ ⓑ ⓒ ⓓ	135	ⓐ ⓑ ⓒ ⓓ	155	ⓐ ⓑ ⓒ ⓓ	175	ⓐ ⓑ ⓒ ⓓ	195	ⓐ ⓑ ⓒ ⓓ
116	ⓐ ⓑ ⓒ ⓓ	136	ⓐ ⓑ ⓒ ⓓ	156	ⓐ ⓑ ⓒ ⓓ	176	ⓐ ⓑ ⓒ ⓓ	196	ⓐ ⓑ ⓒ ⓓ
117	ⓐ ⓑ ⓒ ⓓ	137	ⓐ ⓑ ⓒ ⓓ	157	ⓐ ⓑ ⓒ ⓓ	177	ⓐ ⓑ ⓒ ⓓ	197	ⓐ ⓑ ⓒ ⓓ
118	ⓐ ⓑ ⓒ ⓓ	138	ⓐ ⓑ ⓒ ⓓ	158	ⓐ ⓑ ⓒ ⓓ	178	ⓐ ⓑ ⓒ ⓓ	198	ⓐ ⓑ ⓒ ⓓ
119	ⓐ ⓑ ⓒ ⓓ	139	ⓐ ⓑ ⓒ ⓓ	159	ⓐ ⓑ ⓒ ⓓ	179	ⓐ ⓑ ⓒ ⓓ	199	ⓐ ⓑ ⓒ ⓓ
120	ⓐ ⓑ ⓒ ⓓ	140	ⓐ ⓑ ⓒ ⓓ	160	ⓐ ⓑ ⓒ ⓓ	180	ⓐ ⓑ ⓒ ⓓ	200	ⓐ ⓑ ⓒ ⓓ

ANSWER SHEET

시원스쿨LAB

이름		테스트 회차		날짜	

LISTENING COMPREHENSION (PART 1~4)

NO	ANSWER A B C D	NO	ANSWER A B C D	NO	ANSWER A B C D	NO	ANSWER A B C D	NO	ANSWER A B C D
1	ⓐ ⓑ ⓒ ⓓ	21	ⓐ ⓑ ⓒ	41	ⓐ ⓑ ⓒ ⓓ	61	ⓐ ⓑ ⓒ ⓓ	81	ⓐ ⓑ ⓒ ⓓ
2	ⓐ ⓑ ⓒ ⓓ	22	ⓐ ⓑ ⓒ	42	ⓐ ⓑ ⓒ ⓓ	62	ⓐ ⓑ ⓒ ⓓ	82	ⓐ ⓑ ⓒ ⓓ
3	ⓐ ⓑ ⓒ ⓓ	23	ⓐ ⓑ ⓒ	43	ⓐ ⓑ ⓒ ⓓ	63	ⓐ ⓑ ⓒ ⓓ	83	ⓐ ⓑ ⓒ ⓓ
4	ⓐ ⓑ ⓒ ⓓ	24	ⓐ ⓑ ⓒ	44	ⓐ ⓑ ⓒ ⓓ	64	ⓐ ⓑ ⓒ ⓓ	84	ⓐ ⓑ ⓒ ⓓ
5	ⓐ ⓑ ⓒ ⓓ	25	ⓐ ⓑ ⓒ	45	ⓐ ⓑ ⓒ ⓓ	65	ⓐ ⓑ ⓒ ⓓ	85	ⓐ ⓑ ⓒ ⓓ
6	ⓐ ⓑ ⓒ ⓓ	26	ⓐ ⓑ ⓒ	46	ⓐ ⓑ ⓒ ⓓ	66	ⓐ ⓑ ⓒ ⓓ	86	ⓐ ⓑ ⓒ ⓓ
7	ⓐ ⓑ ⓒ	27	ⓐ ⓑ ⓒ	47	ⓐ ⓑ ⓒ ⓓ	67	ⓐ ⓑ ⓒ ⓓ	87	ⓐ ⓑ ⓒ ⓓ
8	ⓐ ⓑ ⓒ	28	ⓐ ⓑ ⓒ	48	ⓐ ⓑ ⓒ ⓓ	68	ⓐ ⓑ ⓒ ⓓ	88	ⓐ ⓑ ⓒ ⓓ
9	ⓐ ⓑ ⓒ	29	ⓐ ⓑ ⓒ	49	ⓐ ⓑ ⓒ ⓓ	69	ⓐ ⓑ ⓒ ⓓ	89	ⓐ ⓑ ⓒ ⓓ
10	ⓐ ⓑ ⓒ	30	ⓐ ⓑ ⓒ	50	ⓐ ⓑ ⓒ ⓓ	70	ⓐ ⓑ ⓒ ⓓ	90	ⓐ ⓑ ⓒ ⓓ
11	ⓐ ⓑ ⓒ	31	ⓐ ⓑ ⓒ	51	ⓐ ⓑ ⓒ ⓓ	71	ⓐ ⓑ ⓒ ⓓ	91	ⓐ ⓑ ⓒ ⓓ
12	ⓐ ⓑ ⓒ	32	ⓐ ⓑ ⓒ ⓓ	52	ⓐ ⓑ ⓒ ⓓ	72	ⓐ ⓑ ⓒ ⓓ	92	ⓐ ⓑ ⓒ ⓓ
13	ⓐ ⓑ ⓒ	33	ⓐ ⓑ ⓒ ⓓ	53	ⓐ ⓑ ⓒ ⓓ	73	ⓐ ⓑ ⓒ ⓓ	93	ⓐ ⓑ ⓒ ⓓ
14	ⓐ ⓑ ⓒ	34	ⓐ ⓑ ⓒ ⓓ	54	ⓐ ⓑ ⓒ ⓓ	74	ⓐ ⓑ ⓒ ⓓ	94	ⓐ ⓑ ⓒ ⓓ
15	ⓐ ⓑ ⓒ	35	ⓐ ⓑ ⓒ ⓓ	55	ⓐ ⓑ ⓒ ⓓ	75	ⓐ ⓑ ⓒ ⓓ	95	ⓐ ⓑ ⓒ ⓓ
16	ⓐ ⓑ ⓒ	36	ⓐ ⓑ ⓒ ⓓ	56	ⓐ ⓑ ⓒ ⓓ	76	ⓐ ⓑ ⓒ ⓓ	96	ⓐ ⓑ ⓒ ⓓ
17	ⓐ ⓑ ⓒ	37	ⓐ ⓑ ⓒ ⓓ	57	ⓐ ⓑ ⓒ ⓓ	77	ⓐ ⓑ ⓒ ⓓ	97	ⓐ ⓑ ⓒ ⓓ
18	ⓐ ⓑ ⓒ	38	ⓐ ⓑ ⓒ ⓓ	58	ⓐ ⓑ ⓒ ⓓ	78	ⓐ ⓑ ⓒ ⓓ	98	ⓐ ⓑ ⓒ ⓓ
19	ⓐ ⓑ ⓒ	39	ⓐ ⓑ ⓒ ⓓ	59	ⓐ ⓑ ⓒ ⓓ	79	ⓐ ⓑ ⓒ ⓓ	99	ⓐ ⓑ ⓒ ⓓ
20	ⓐ ⓑ ⓒ	40	ⓐ ⓑ ⓒ ⓓ	60	ⓐ ⓑ ⓒ ⓓ	80	ⓐ ⓑ ⓒ ⓓ	100	ⓐ ⓑ ⓒ ⓓ

READING COMPREHENSION (PART 5~7)

NO	ANSWER A B C D	NO	ANSWER A B C D	NO	ANSWER A B C D	NO	ANSWER A B C D	NO	ANSWER A B C D
101	ⓐ ⓑ ⓒ ⓓ	121	ⓐ ⓑ ⓒ ⓓ	141	ⓐ ⓑ ⓒ ⓓ	161	ⓐ ⓑ ⓒ ⓓ	181	ⓐ ⓑ ⓒ ⓓ
102	ⓐ ⓑ ⓒ ⓓ	122	ⓐ ⓑ ⓒ ⓓ	142	ⓐ ⓑ ⓒ ⓓ	162	ⓐ ⓑ ⓒ ⓓ	182	ⓐ ⓑ ⓒ ⓓ
103	ⓐ ⓑ ⓒ ⓓ	123	ⓐ ⓑ ⓒ ⓓ	143	ⓐ ⓑ ⓒ ⓓ	163	ⓐ ⓑ ⓒ ⓓ	183	ⓐ ⓑ ⓒ ⓓ
104	ⓐ ⓑ ⓒ ⓓ	124	ⓐ ⓑ ⓒ ⓓ	144	ⓐ ⓑ ⓒ ⓓ	164	ⓐ ⓑ ⓒ ⓓ	184	ⓐ ⓑ ⓒ ⓓ
105	ⓐ ⓑ ⓒ ⓓ	125	ⓐ ⓑ ⓒ ⓓ	145	ⓐ ⓑ ⓒ ⓓ	165	ⓐ ⓑ ⓒ ⓓ	185	ⓐ ⓑ ⓒ ⓓ
106	ⓐ ⓑ ⓒ ⓓ	126	ⓐ ⓑ ⓒ ⓓ	146	ⓐ ⓑ ⓒ ⓓ	166	ⓐ ⓑ ⓒ ⓓ	186	ⓐ ⓑ ⓒ ⓓ
107	ⓐ ⓑ ⓒ ⓓ	127	ⓐ ⓑ ⓒ ⓓ	147	ⓐ ⓑ ⓒ ⓓ	167	ⓐ ⓑ ⓒ ⓓ	187	ⓐ ⓑ ⓒ ⓓ
108	ⓐ ⓑ ⓒ ⓓ	128	ⓐ ⓑ ⓒ ⓓ	148	ⓐ ⓑ ⓒ ⓓ	168	ⓐ ⓑ ⓒ ⓓ	188	ⓐ ⓑ ⓒ ⓓ
109	ⓐ ⓑ ⓒ ⓓ	129	ⓐ ⓑ ⓒ ⓓ	149	ⓐ ⓑ ⓒ ⓓ	169	ⓐ ⓑ ⓒ ⓓ	189	ⓐ ⓑ ⓒ ⓓ
110	ⓐ ⓑ ⓒ ⓓ	130	ⓐ ⓑ ⓒ ⓓ	150	ⓐ ⓑ ⓒ ⓓ	170	ⓐ ⓑ ⓒ ⓓ	190	ⓐ ⓑ ⓒ ⓓ
111	ⓐ ⓑ ⓒ ⓓ	131	ⓐ ⓑ ⓒ ⓓ	151	ⓐ ⓑ ⓒ ⓓ	171	ⓐ ⓑ ⓒ ⓓ	191	ⓐ ⓑ ⓒ ⓓ
112	ⓐ ⓑ ⓒ ⓓ	132	ⓐ ⓑ ⓒ ⓓ	152	ⓐ ⓑ ⓒ ⓓ	172	ⓐ ⓑ ⓒ ⓓ	192	ⓐ ⓑ ⓒ ⓓ
113	ⓐ ⓑ ⓒ ⓓ	133	ⓐ ⓑ ⓒ ⓓ	153	ⓐ ⓑ ⓒ ⓓ	173	ⓐ ⓑ ⓒ ⓓ	193	ⓐ ⓑ ⓒ ⓓ
114	ⓐ ⓑ ⓒ ⓓ	134	ⓐ ⓑ ⓒ ⓓ	154	ⓐ ⓑ ⓒ ⓓ	174	ⓐ ⓑ ⓒ ⓓ	194	ⓐ ⓑ ⓒ ⓓ
115	ⓐ ⓑ ⓒ ⓓ	135	ⓐ ⓑ ⓒ ⓓ	155	ⓐ ⓑ ⓒ ⓓ	175	ⓐ ⓑ ⓒ ⓓ	195	ⓐ ⓑ ⓒ ⓓ
116	ⓐ ⓑ ⓒ ⓓ	136	ⓐ ⓑ ⓒ ⓓ	156	ⓐ ⓑ ⓒ ⓓ	176	ⓐ ⓑ ⓒ ⓓ	196	ⓐ ⓑ ⓒ ⓓ
117	ⓐ ⓑ ⓒ ⓓ	137	ⓐ ⓑ ⓒ ⓓ	157	ⓐ ⓑ ⓒ ⓓ	177	ⓐ ⓑ ⓒ ⓓ	197	ⓐ ⓑ ⓒ ⓓ
118	ⓐ ⓑ ⓒ ⓓ	138	ⓐ ⓑ ⓒ ⓓ	158	ⓐ ⓑ ⓒ ⓓ	178	ⓐ ⓑ ⓒ ⓓ	198	ⓐ ⓑ ⓒ ⓓ
119	ⓐ ⓑ ⓒ ⓓ	139	ⓐ ⓑ ⓒ ⓓ	159	ⓐ ⓑ ⓒ ⓓ	179	ⓐ ⓑ ⓒ ⓓ	199	ⓐ ⓑ ⓒ ⓓ
120	ⓐ ⓑ ⓒ ⓓ	140	ⓐ ⓑ ⓒ ⓓ	160	ⓐ ⓑ ⓒ ⓓ	180	ⓐ ⓑ ⓒ ⓓ	200	ⓐ ⓑ ⓒ ⓓ

ANSWER SHEET

시원스쿨 LAB

이름		테스트 회차		날짜	

LISTENING COMPREHENSION (PART 1~4)

NO	ANSWER				NO	ANSWER				NO	ANSWER				NO	ANSWER				NO	ANSWER			
	A	B	C	D		A	B	C	D		A	B	C	D		A	B	C	D		A	B	C	D
1	ⓐ	ⓑ	ⓒ	ⓓ	21	ⓐ	ⓑ	ⓒ		41	ⓐ	ⓑ	ⓒ	ⓓ	61	ⓐ	ⓑ	ⓒ	ⓓ	81	ⓐ	ⓑ	ⓒ	ⓓ
2	ⓐ	ⓑ	ⓒ	ⓓ	22	ⓐ	ⓑ	ⓒ		42	ⓐ	ⓑ	ⓒ	ⓓ	62	ⓐ	ⓑ	ⓒ	ⓓ	82	ⓐ	ⓑ	ⓒ	ⓓ
3	ⓐ	ⓑ	ⓒ	ⓓ	23	ⓐ	ⓑ	ⓒ		43	ⓐ	ⓑ	ⓒ	ⓓ	63	ⓐ	ⓑ	ⓒ	ⓓ	83	ⓐ	ⓑ	ⓒ	ⓓ
4	ⓐ	ⓑ	ⓒ	ⓓ	24	ⓐ	ⓑ	ⓒ		44	ⓐ	ⓑ	ⓒ	ⓓ	64	ⓐ	ⓑ	ⓒ	ⓓ	84	ⓐ	ⓑ	ⓒ	ⓓ
5	ⓐ	ⓑ	ⓒ	ⓓ	25	ⓐ	ⓑ	ⓒ		45	ⓐ	ⓑ	ⓒ	ⓓ	65	ⓐ	ⓑ	ⓒ	ⓓ	85	ⓐ	ⓑ	ⓒ	ⓓ
6	ⓐ	ⓑ	ⓒ	ⓓ	26	ⓐ	ⓑ	ⓒ		46	ⓐ	ⓑ	ⓒ	ⓓ	66	ⓐ	ⓑ	ⓒ	ⓓ	86	ⓐ	ⓑ	ⓒ	ⓓ
7	ⓐ	ⓑ	ⓒ		27	ⓐ	ⓑ	ⓒ		47	ⓐ	ⓑ	ⓒ	ⓓ	67	ⓐ	ⓑ	ⓒ	ⓓ	87	ⓐ	ⓑ	ⓒ	ⓓ
8	ⓐ	ⓑ	ⓒ		28	ⓐ	ⓑ	ⓒ		48	ⓐ	ⓑ	ⓒ	ⓓ	68	ⓐ	ⓑ	ⓒ	ⓓ	88	ⓐ	ⓑ	ⓒ	ⓓ
9	ⓐ	ⓑ	ⓒ		29	ⓐ	ⓑ	ⓒ		49	ⓐ	ⓑ	ⓒ	ⓓ	69	ⓐ	ⓑ	ⓒ	ⓓ	89	ⓐ	ⓑ	ⓒ	ⓓ
10	ⓐ	ⓑ	ⓒ		30	ⓐ	ⓑ	ⓒ		50	ⓐ	ⓑ	ⓒ	ⓓ	70	ⓐ	ⓑ	ⓒ	ⓓ	90	ⓐ	ⓑ	ⓒ	ⓓ
11	ⓐ	ⓑ	ⓒ		31	ⓐ	ⓑ	ⓒ		51	ⓐ	ⓑ	ⓒ	ⓓ	71	ⓐ	ⓑ	ⓒ	ⓓ	91	ⓐ	ⓑ	ⓒ	ⓓ
12	ⓐ	ⓑ	ⓒ		32	ⓐ	ⓑ	ⓒ	ⓓ	52	ⓐ	ⓑ	ⓒ	ⓓ	72	ⓐ	ⓑ	ⓒ	ⓓ	92	ⓐ	ⓑ	ⓒ	ⓓ
13	ⓐ	ⓑ	ⓒ		33	ⓐ	ⓑ	ⓒ	ⓓ	53	ⓐ	ⓑ	ⓒ	ⓓ	73	ⓐ	ⓑ	ⓒ	ⓓ	93	ⓐ	ⓑ	ⓒ	ⓓ
14	ⓐ	ⓑ	ⓒ		34	ⓐ	ⓑ	ⓒ	ⓓ	54	ⓐ	ⓑ	ⓒ	ⓓ	74	ⓐ	ⓑ	ⓒ	ⓓ	94	ⓐ	ⓑ	ⓒ	ⓓ
15	ⓐ	ⓑ	ⓒ		35	ⓐ	ⓑ	ⓒ	ⓓ	55	ⓐ	ⓑ	ⓒ	ⓓ	75	ⓐ	ⓑ	ⓒ	ⓓ	95	ⓐ	ⓑ	ⓒ	ⓓ
16	ⓐ	ⓑ	ⓒ		36	ⓐ	ⓑ	ⓒ	ⓓ	56	ⓐ	ⓑ	ⓒ	ⓓ	76	ⓐ	ⓑ	ⓒ	ⓓ	96	ⓐ	ⓑ	ⓒ	ⓓ
17	ⓐ	ⓑ	ⓒ		37	ⓐ	ⓑ	ⓒ	ⓓ	57	ⓐ	ⓑ	ⓒ	ⓓ	77	ⓐ	ⓑ	ⓒ	ⓓ	97	ⓐ	ⓑ	ⓒ	ⓓ
18	ⓐ	ⓑ	ⓒ		38	ⓐ	ⓑ	ⓒ	ⓓ	58	ⓐ	ⓑ	ⓒ	ⓓ	78	ⓐ	ⓑ	ⓒ	ⓓ	98	ⓐ	ⓑ	ⓒ	ⓓ
19	ⓐ	ⓑ	ⓒ		39	ⓐ	ⓑ	ⓒ	ⓓ	59	ⓐ	ⓑ	ⓒ	ⓓ	79	ⓐ	ⓑ	ⓒ	ⓓ	99	ⓐ	ⓑ	ⓒ	ⓓ
20	ⓐ	ⓑ	ⓒ		40	ⓐ	ⓑ	ⓒ	ⓓ	60	ⓐ	ⓑ	ⓒ	ⓓ	80	ⓐ	ⓑ	ⓒ	ⓓ	100	ⓐ	ⓑ	ⓒ	ⓓ

READING COMPREHENSION (PART 5~7)

NO	ANSWER				NO	ANSWER				NO	ANSWER				NO	ANSWER				NO	ANSWER			
	A	B	C	D		A	B	C	D		A	B	C	D		A	B	C	D		A	B	C	D
101	ⓐ	ⓑ	ⓒ	ⓓ	121	ⓐ	ⓑ	ⓒ	ⓓ	141	ⓐ	ⓑ	ⓒ	ⓓ	161	ⓐ	ⓑ	ⓒ	ⓓ	181	ⓐ	ⓑ	ⓒ	ⓓ
102	ⓐ	ⓑ	ⓒ	ⓓ	122	ⓐ	ⓑ	ⓒ	ⓓ	142	ⓐ	ⓑ	ⓒ	ⓓ	162	ⓐ	ⓑ	ⓒ	ⓓ	182	ⓐ	ⓑ	ⓒ	ⓓ
103	ⓐ	ⓑ	ⓒ	ⓓ	123	ⓐ	ⓑ	ⓒ	ⓓ	143	ⓐ	ⓑ	ⓒ	ⓓ	163	ⓐ	ⓑ	ⓒ	ⓓ	183	ⓐ	ⓑ	ⓒ	ⓓ
104	ⓐ	ⓑ	ⓒ	ⓓ	124	ⓐ	ⓑ	ⓒ	ⓓ	144	ⓐ	ⓑ	ⓒ	ⓓ	164	ⓐ	ⓑ	ⓒ	ⓓ	184	ⓐ	ⓑ	ⓒ	ⓓ
105	ⓐ	ⓑ	ⓒ	ⓓ	125	ⓐ	ⓑ	ⓒ	ⓓ	145	ⓐ	ⓑ	ⓒ	ⓓ	165	ⓐ	ⓑ	ⓒ	ⓓ	185	ⓐ	ⓑ	ⓒ	ⓓ
106	ⓐ	ⓑ	ⓒ	ⓓ	126	ⓐ	ⓑ	ⓒ	ⓓ	146	ⓐ	ⓑ	ⓒ	ⓓ	166	ⓐ	ⓑ	ⓒ	ⓓ	186	ⓐ	ⓑ	ⓒ	ⓓ
107	ⓐ	ⓑ	ⓒ	ⓓ	127	ⓐ	ⓑ	ⓒ	ⓓ	147	ⓐ	ⓑ	ⓒ	ⓓ	167	ⓐ	ⓑ	ⓒ	ⓓ	187	ⓐ	ⓑ	ⓒ	ⓓ
108	ⓐ	ⓑ	ⓒ	ⓓ	128	ⓐ	ⓑ	ⓒ	ⓓ	148	ⓐ	ⓑ	ⓒ	ⓓ	168	ⓐ	ⓑ	ⓒ	ⓓ	188	ⓐ	ⓑ	ⓒ	ⓓ
109	ⓐ	ⓑ	ⓒ	ⓓ	129	ⓐ	ⓑ	ⓒ	ⓓ	149	ⓐ	ⓑ	ⓒ	ⓓ	169	ⓐ	ⓑ	ⓒ	ⓓ	189	ⓐ	ⓑ	ⓒ	ⓓ
110	ⓐ	ⓑ	ⓒ	ⓓ	130	ⓐ	ⓑ	ⓒ	ⓓ	150	ⓐ	ⓑ	ⓒ	ⓓ	170	ⓐ	ⓑ	ⓒ	ⓓ	190	ⓐ	ⓑ	ⓒ	ⓓ
111	ⓐ	ⓑ	ⓒ	ⓓ	131	ⓐ	ⓑ	ⓒ	ⓓ	151	ⓐ	ⓑ	ⓒ	ⓓ	171	ⓐ	ⓑ	ⓒ	ⓓ	191	ⓐ	ⓑ	ⓒ	ⓓ
112	ⓐ	ⓑ	ⓒ	ⓓ	132	ⓐ	ⓑ	ⓒ	ⓓ	152	ⓐ	ⓑ	ⓒ	ⓓ	172	ⓐ	ⓑ	ⓒ	ⓓ	192	ⓐ	ⓑ	ⓒ	ⓓ
113	ⓐ	ⓑ	ⓒ	ⓓ	133	ⓐ	ⓑ	ⓒ	ⓓ	153	ⓐ	ⓑ	ⓒ	ⓓ	173	ⓐ	ⓑ	ⓒ	ⓓ	193	ⓐ	ⓑ	ⓒ	ⓓ
114	ⓐ	ⓑ	ⓒ	ⓓ	134	ⓐ	ⓑ	ⓒ	ⓓ	154	ⓐ	ⓑ	ⓒ	ⓓ	174	ⓐ	ⓑ	ⓒ	ⓓ	194	ⓐ	ⓑ	ⓒ	ⓓ
115	ⓐ	ⓑ	ⓒ	ⓓ	135	ⓐ	ⓑ	ⓒ	ⓓ	155	ⓐ	ⓑ	ⓒ	ⓓ	175	ⓐ	ⓑ	ⓒ	ⓓ	195	ⓐ	ⓑ	ⓒ	ⓓ
116	ⓐ	ⓑ	ⓒ	ⓓ	136	ⓐ	ⓑ	ⓒ	ⓓ	156	ⓐ	ⓑ	ⓒ	ⓓ	176	ⓐ	ⓑ	ⓒ	ⓓ	196	ⓐ	ⓑ	ⓒ	ⓓ
117	ⓐ	ⓑ	ⓒ	ⓓ	137	ⓐ	ⓑ	ⓒ	ⓓ	157	ⓐ	ⓑ	ⓒ	ⓓ	177	ⓐ	ⓑ	ⓒ	ⓓ	197	ⓐ	ⓑ	ⓒ	ⓓ
118	ⓐ	ⓑ	ⓒ	ⓓ	138	ⓐ	ⓑ	ⓒ	ⓓ	158	ⓐ	ⓑ	ⓒ	ⓓ	178	ⓐ	ⓑ	ⓒ	ⓓ	198	ⓐ	ⓑ	ⓒ	ⓓ
119	ⓐ	ⓑ	ⓒ	ⓓ	139	ⓐ	ⓑ	ⓒ	ⓓ	159	ⓐ	ⓑ	ⓒ	ⓓ	179	ⓐ	ⓑ	ⓒ	ⓓ	199	ⓐ	ⓑ	ⓒ	ⓓ
120	ⓐ	ⓑ	ⓒ	ⓓ	140	ⓐ	ⓑ	ⓒ	ⓓ	160	ⓐ	ⓑ	ⓒ	ⓓ	180	ⓐ	ⓑ	ⓒ	ⓓ	200	ⓐ	ⓑ	ⓒ	ⓓ

ANSWER SHEET

시원스쿨 LAB

이름		테스트 회차		날짜	

LISTENING COMPREHENSION (PART 1~4)										READING COMPREHENSION (PART 5~7)									
NO	ANSWER A B C D	NO	ANSWER A B C D	NO	ANSWER A B C D	NO	ANSWER A B C D	NO	ANSWER A B C D	NO	ANSWER A B C D	NO	ANSWER A B C D	NO	ANSWER A B C D	NO	ANSWER A B C D	NO	ANSWER A B C D
1	ⓐ ⓑ ⓒ ⓓ	21	ⓐ ⓑ ⓒ	41	ⓐ ⓑ ⓒ ⓓ	61	ⓐ ⓑ ⓒ ⓓ	81	ⓐ ⓑ ⓒ ⓓ	101	ⓐ ⓑ ⓒ ⓓ	121	ⓐ ⓑ ⓒ ⓓ	141	ⓐ ⓑ ⓒ ⓓ	161	ⓐ ⓑ ⓒ ⓓ	181	ⓐ ⓑ ⓒ ⓓ
2	ⓐ ⓑ ⓒ ⓓ	22	ⓐ ⓑ ⓒ	42	ⓐ ⓑ ⓒ ⓓ	62	ⓐ ⓑ ⓒ ⓓ	82	ⓐ ⓑ ⓒ ⓓ	102	ⓐ ⓑ ⓒ ⓓ	122	ⓐ ⓑ ⓒ ⓓ	142	ⓐ ⓑ ⓒ ⓓ	162	ⓐ ⓑ ⓒ ⓓ	182	ⓐ ⓑ ⓒ ⓓ
3	ⓐ ⓑ ⓒ ⓓ	23	ⓐ ⓑ ⓒ	43	ⓐ ⓑ ⓒ ⓓ	63	ⓐ ⓑ ⓒ ⓓ	83	ⓐ ⓑ ⓒ ⓓ	103	ⓐ ⓑ ⓒ ⓓ	123	ⓐ ⓑ ⓒ ⓓ	143	ⓐ ⓑ ⓒ ⓓ	163	ⓐ ⓑ ⓒ ⓓ	183	ⓐ ⓑ ⓒ ⓓ
4	ⓐ ⓑ ⓒ ⓓ	24	ⓐ ⓑ ⓒ	44	ⓐ ⓑ ⓒ ⓓ	64	ⓐ ⓑ ⓒ ⓓ	84	ⓐ ⓑ ⓒ ⓓ	104	ⓐ ⓑ ⓒ ⓓ	124	ⓐ ⓑ ⓒ ⓓ	144	ⓐ ⓑ ⓒ ⓓ	164	ⓐ ⓑ ⓒ ⓓ	184	ⓐ ⓑ ⓒ ⓓ
5	ⓐ ⓑ ⓒ ⓓ	25	ⓐ ⓑ ⓒ	45	ⓐ ⓑ ⓒ ⓓ	65	ⓐ ⓑ ⓒ ⓓ	85	ⓐ ⓑ ⓒ ⓓ	105	ⓐ ⓑ ⓒ ⓓ	125	ⓐ ⓑ ⓒ ⓓ	145	ⓐ ⓑ ⓒ ⓓ	165	ⓐ ⓑ ⓒ ⓓ	185	ⓐ ⓑ ⓒ ⓓ
6	ⓐ ⓑ ⓒ ⓓ	26	ⓐ ⓑ ⓒ	46	ⓐ ⓑ ⓒ ⓓ	66	ⓐ ⓑ ⓒ ⓓ	86	ⓐ ⓑ ⓒ ⓓ	106	ⓐ ⓑ ⓒ ⓓ	126	ⓐ ⓑ ⓒ ⓓ	146	ⓐ ⓑ ⓒ ⓓ	166	ⓐ ⓑ ⓒ ⓓ	186	ⓐ ⓑ ⓒ ⓓ
7	ⓐ ⓑ ⓒ	27	ⓐ ⓑ ⓒ	47	ⓐ ⓑ ⓒ ⓓ	67	ⓐ ⓑ ⓒ ⓓ	87	ⓐ ⓑ ⓒ ⓓ	107	ⓐ ⓑ ⓒ ⓓ	127	ⓐ ⓑ ⓒ ⓓ	147	ⓐ ⓑ ⓒ ⓓ	167	ⓐ ⓑ ⓒ ⓓ	187	ⓐ ⓑ ⓒ ⓓ
8	ⓐ ⓑ ⓒ	28	ⓐ ⓑ ⓒ	48	ⓐ ⓑ ⓒ ⓓ	68	ⓐ ⓑ ⓒ ⓓ	88	ⓐ ⓑ ⓒ ⓓ	108	ⓐ ⓑ ⓒ ⓓ	128	ⓐ ⓑ ⓒ ⓓ	148	ⓐ ⓑ ⓒ ⓓ	168	ⓐ ⓑ ⓒ ⓓ	188	ⓐ ⓑ ⓒ ⓓ
9	ⓐ ⓑ ⓒ	29	ⓐ ⓑ ⓒ	49	ⓐ ⓑ ⓒ ⓓ	69	ⓐ ⓑ ⓒ ⓓ	89	ⓐ ⓑ ⓒ ⓓ	109	ⓐ ⓑ ⓒ ⓓ	129	ⓐ ⓑ ⓒ ⓓ	149	ⓐ ⓑ ⓒ ⓓ	169	ⓐ ⓑ ⓒ ⓓ	189	ⓐ ⓑ ⓒ ⓓ
10	ⓐ ⓑ ⓒ	30	ⓐ ⓑ ⓒ	50	ⓐ ⓑ ⓒ ⓓ	70	ⓐ ⓑ ⓒ ⓓ	90	ⓐ ⓑ ⓒ ⓓ	110	ⓐ ⓑ ⓒ ⓓ	130	ⓐ ⓑ ⓒ ⓓ	150	ⓐ ⓑ ⓒ ⓓ	170	ⓐ ⓑ ⓒ ⓓ	190	ⓐ ⓑ ⓒ ⓓ
11	ⓐ ⓑ ⓒ	31	ⓐ ⓑ ⓒ	51	ⓐ ⓑ ⓒ ⓓ	71	ⓐ ⓑ ⓒ ⓓ	91	ⓐ ⓑ ⓒ ⓓ	111	ⓐ ⓑ ⓒ ⓓ	131	ⓐ ⓑ ⓒ ⓓ	151	ⓐ ⓑ ⓒ ⓓ	171	ⓐ ⓑ ⓒ ⓓ	191	ⓐ ⓑ ⓒ ⓓ
12	ⓐ ⓑ ⓒ	32	ⓐ ⓑ ⓒ ⓓ	52	ⓐ ⓑ ⓒ ⓓ	72	ⓐ ⓑ ⓒ ⓓ	92	ⓐ ⓑ ⓒ ⓓ	112	ⓐ ⓑ ⓒ ⓓ	132	ⓐ ⓑ ⓒ ⓓ	152	ⓐ ⓑ ⓒ ⓓ	172	ⓐ ⓑ ⓒ ⓓ	192	ⓐ ⓑ ⓒ ⓓ
13	ⓐ ⓑ ⓒ	33	ⓐ ⓑ ⓒ ⓓ	53	ⓐ ⓑ ⓒ ⓓ	73	ⓐ ⓑ ⓒ ⓓ	93	ⓐ ⓑ ⓒ ⓓ	113	ⓐ ⓑ ⓒ ⓓ	133	ⓐ ⓑ ⓒ ⓓ	153	ⓐ ⓑ ⓒ ⓓ	173	ⓐ ⓑ ⓒ ⓓ	193	ⓐ ⓑ ⓒ ⓓ
14	ⓐ ⓑ ⓒ	34	ⓐ ⓑ ⓒ ⓓ	54	ⓐ ⓑ ⓒ ⓓ	74	ⓐ ⓑ ⓒ ⓓ	94	ⓐ ⓑ ⓒ ⓓ	114	ⓐ ⓑ ⓒ ⓓ	134	ⓐ ⓑ ⓒ ⓓ	154	ⓐ ⓑ ⓒ ⓓ	174	ⓐ ⓑ ⓒ ⓓ	194	ⓐ ⓑ ⓒ ⓓ
15	ⓐ ⓑ ⓒ	35	ⓐ ⓑ ⓒ ⓓ	55	ⓐ ⓑ ⓒ ⓓ	75	ⓐ ⓑ ⓒ ⓓ	95	ⓐ ⓑ ⓒ ⓓ	115	ⓐ ⓑ ⓒ ⓓ	135	ⓐ ⓑ ⓒ ⓓ	155	ⓐ ⓑ ⓒ ⓓ	175	ⓐ ⓑ ⓒ ⓓ	195	ⓐ ⓑ ⓒ ⓓ
16	ⓐ ⓑ ⓒ	36	ⓐ ⓑ ⓒ ⓓ	56	ⓐ ⓑ ⓒ ⓓ	76	ⓐ ⓑ ⓒ ⓓ	96	ⓐ ⓑ ⓒ ⓓ	116	ⓐ ⓑ ⓒ ⓓ	136	ⓐ ⓑ ⓒ ⓓ	156	ⓐ ⓑ ⓒ ⓓ	176	ⓐ ⓑ ⓒ ⓓ	196	ⓐ ⓑ ⓒ ⓓ
17	ⓐ ⓑ ⓒ	37	ⓐ ⓑ ⓒ ⓓ	57	ⓐ ⓑ ⓒ ⓓ	77	ⓐ ⓑ ⓒ ⓓ	97	ⓐ ⓑ ⓒ ⓓ	117	ⓐ ⓑ ⓒ ⓓ	137	ⓐ ⓑ ⓒ ⓓ	157	ⓐ ⓑ ⓒ ⓓ	177	ⓐ ⓑ ⓒ ⓓ	197	ⓐ ⓑ ⓒ ⓓ
18	ⓐ ⓑ ⓒ	38	ⓐ ⓑ ⓒ ⓓ	58	ⓐ ⓑ ⓒ ⓓ	78	ⓐ ⓑ ⓒ ⓓ	98	ⓐ ⓑ ⓒ ⓓ	118	ⓐ ⓑ ⓒ ⓓ	138	ⓐ ⓑ ⓒ ⓓ	158	ⓐ ⓑ ⓒ ⓓ	178	ⓐ ⓑ ⓒ ⓓ	198	ⓐ ⓑ ⓒ ⓓ
19	ⓐ ⓑ ⓒ	39	ⓐ ⓑ ⓒ ⓓ	59	ⓐ ⓑ ⓒ ⓓ	79	ⓐ ⓑ ⓒ ⓓ	99	ⓐ ⓑ ⓒ ⓓ	119	ⓐ ⓑ ⓒ ⓓ	139	ⓐ ⓑ ⓒ ⓓ	159	ⓐ ⓑ ⓒ ⓓ	179	ⓐ ⓑ ⓒ ⓓ	199	ⓐ ⓑ ⓒ ⓓ
20	ⓐ ⓑ ⓒ	40	ⓐ ⓑ ⓒ ⓓ	60	ⓐ ⓑ ⓒ ⓓ	80	ⓐ ⓑ ⓒ ⓓ	100	ⓐ ⓑ ⓒ ⓓ	120	ⓐ ⓑ ⓒ ⓓ	140	ⓐ ⓑ ⓒ ⓓ	160	ⓐ ⓑ ⓒ ⓓ	180	ⓐ ⓑ ⓒ ⓓ	200	ⓐ ⓑ ⓒ ⓓ

ANSWER SHEET

시원스쿨 LAB

이름		테스트 회차		날짜	

LISTENING COMPREHENSION (PART 1~4)										READING COMPREHENSION (PART 5~7)									
NO	ANSWER A B C D	NO	ANSWER A B C D	NO	ANSWER A B C D	NO	ANSWER A B C D	NO	ANSWER A B C D	NO	ANSWER A B C D	NO	ANSWER A B C D	NO	ANSWER A B C D	NO	ANSWER A B C D	NO	ANSWER A B C D
1	ⓐ ⓑ ⓒ ⓓ	21	ⓐ ⓑ ⓒ	41	ⓐ ⓑ ⓒ ⓓ	61	ⓐ ⓑ ⓒ ⓓ	81	ⓐ ⓑ ⓒ ⓓ	101	ⓐ ⓑ ⓒ ⓓ	121	ⓐ ⓑ ⓒ ⓓ	141	ⓐ ⓑ ⓒ ⓓ	161	ⓐ ⓑ ⓒ ⓓ	181	ⓐ ⓑ ⓒ ⓓ
2	ⓐ ⓑ ⓒ ⓓ	22	ⓐ ⓑ ⓒ	42	ⓐ ⓑ ⓒ ⓓ	62	ⓐ ⓑ ⓒ ⓓ	82	ⓐ ⓑ ⓒ ⓓ	102	ⓐ ⓑ ⓒ ⓓ	122	ⓐ ⓑ ⓒ ⓓ	142	ⓐ ⓑ ⓒ ⓓ	162	ⓐ ⓑ ⓒ ⓓ	182	ⓐ ⓑ ⓒ ⓓ
3	ⓐ ⓑ ⓒ ⓓ	23	ⓐ ⓑ ⓒ	43	ⓐ ⓑ ⓒ ⓓ	63	ⓐ ⓑ ⓒ ⓓ	83	ⓐ ⓑ ⓒ ⓓ	103	ⓐ ⓑ ⓒ ⓓ	123	ⓐ ⓑ ⓒ ⓓ	143	ⓐ ⓑ ⓒ ⓓ	163	ⓐ ⓑ ⓒ ⓓ	183	ⓐ ⓑ ⓒ ⓓ
4	ⓐ ⓑ ⓒ ⓓ	24	ⓐ ⓑ ⓒ	44	ⓐ ⓑ ⓒ ⓓ	64	ⓐ ⓑ ⓒ ⓓ	84	ⓐ ⓑ ⓒ ⓓ	104	ⓐ ⓑ ⓒ ⓓ	124	ⓐ ⓑ ⓒ ⓓ	144	ⓐ ⓑ ⓒ ⓓ	164	ⓐ ⓑ ⓒ ⓓ	184	ⓐ ⓑ ⓒ ⓓ
5	ⓐ ⓑ ⓒ ⓓ	25	ⓐ ⓑ ⓒ	45	ⓐ ⓑ ⓒ ⓓ	65	ⓐ ⓑ ⓒ ⓓ	85	ⓐ ⓑ ⓒ ⓓ	105	ⓐ ⓑ ⓒ ⓓ	125	ⓐ ⓑ ⓒ ⓓ	145	ⓐ ⓑ ⓒ ⓓ	165	ⓐ ⓑ ⓒ ⓓ	185	ⓐ ⓑ ⓒ ⓓ
6	ⓐ ⓑ ⓒ ⓓ	26	ⓐ ⓑ ⓒ	46	ⓐ ⓑ ⓒ ⓓ	66	ⓐ ⓑ ⓒ ⓓ	86	ⓐ ⓑ ⓒ ⓓ	106	ⓐ ⓑ ⓒ ⓓ	126	ⓐ ⓑ ⓒ ⓓ	146	ⓐ ⓑ ⓒ ⓓ	166	ⓐ ⓑ ⓒ ⓓ	186	ⓐ ⓑ ⓒ ⓓ
7	ⓐ ⓑ ⓒ	27	ⓐ ⓑ ⓒ	47	ⓐ ⓑ ⓒ ⓓ	67	ⓐ ⓑ ⓒ ⓓ	87	ⓐ ⓑ ⓒ ⓓ	107	ⓐ ⓑ ⓒ ⓓ	127	ⓐ ⓑ ⓒ ⓓ	147	ⓐ ⓑ ⓒ ⓓ	167	ⓐ ⓑ ⓒ ⓓ	187	ⓐ ⓑ ⓒ ⓓ
8	ⓐ ⓑ ⓒ	28	ⓐ ⓑ ⓒ	48	ⓐ ⓑ ⓒ ⓓ	68	ⓐ ⓑ ⓒ ⓓ	88	ⓐ ⓑ ⓒ ⓓ	108	ⓐ ⓑ ⓒ ⓓ	128	ⓐ ⓑ ⓒ ⓓ	148	ⓐ ⓑ ⓒ ⓓ	168	ⓐ ⓑ ⓒ ⓓ	188	ⓐ ⓑ ⓒ ⓓ
9	ⓐ ⓑ ⓒ	29	ⓐ ⓑ ⓒ	49	ⓐ ⓑ ⓒ ⓓ	69	ⓐ ⓑ ⓒ ⓓ	89	ⓐ ⓑ ⓒ ⓓ	109	ⓐ ⓑ ⓒ ⓓ	129	ⓐ ⓑ ⓒ ⓓ	149	ⓐ ⓑ ⓒ ⓓ	169	ⓐ ⓑ ⓒ ⓓ	189	ⓐ ⓑ ⓒ ⓓ
10	ⓐ ⓑ ⓒ	30	ⓐ ⓑ ⓒ	50	ⓐ ⓑ ⓒ ⓓ	70	ⓐ ⓑ ⓒ ⓓ	90	ⓐ ⓑ ⓒ ⓓ	110	ⓐ ⓑ ⓒ ⓓ	130	ⓐ ⓑ ⓒ ⓓ	150	ⓐ ⓑ ⓒ ⓓ	170	ⓐ ⓑ ⓒ ⓓ	190	ⓐ ⓑ ⓒ ⓓ
11	ⓐ ⓑ ⓒ	31	ⓐ ⓑ ⓒ	51	ⓐ ⓑ ⓒ ⓓ	71	ⓐ ⓑ ⓒ ⓓ	91	ⓐ ⓑ ⓒ ⓓ	111	ⓐ ⓑ ⓒ ⓓ	131	ⓐ ⓑ ⓒ ⓓ	151	ⓐ ⓑ ⓒ ⓓ	171	ⓐ ⓑ ⓒ ⓓ	191	ⓐ ⓑ ⓒ ⓓ
12	ⓐ ⓑ ⓒ	32	ⓐ ⓑ ⓒ ⓓ	52	ⓐ ⓑ ⓒ ⓓ	72	ⓐ ⓑ ⓒ ⓓ	92	ⓐ ⓑ ⓒ ⓓ	112	ⓐ ⓑ ⓒ ⓓ	132	ⓐ ⓑ ⓒ ⓓ	152	ⓐ ⓑ ⓒ ⓓ	172	ⓐ ⓑ ⓒ ⓓ	192	ⓐ ⓑ ⓒ ⓓ
13	ⓐ ⓑ ⓒ	33	ⓐ ⓑ ⓒ ⓓ	53	ⓐ ⓑ ⓒ ⓓ	73	ⓐ ⓑ ⓒ ⓓ	93	ⓐ ⓑ ⓒ ⓓ	113	ⓐ ⓑ ⓒ ⓓ	133	ⓐ ⓑ ⓒ ⓓ	153	ⓐ ⓑ ⓒ ⓓ	173	ⓐ ⓑ ⓒ ⓓ	193	ⓐ ⓑ ⓒ ⓓ
14	ⓐ ⓑ ⓒ	34	ⓐ ⓑ ⓒ ⓓ	54	ⓐ ⓑ ⓒ ⓓ	74	ⓐ ⓑ ⓒ ⓓ	94	ⓐ ⓑ ⓒ ⓓ	114	ⓐ ⓑ ⓒ ⓓ	134	ⓐ ⓑ ⓒ ⓓ	154	ⓐ ⓑ ⓒ ⓓ	174	ⓐ ⓑ ⓒ ⓓ	194	ⓐ ⓑ ⓒ ⓓ
15	ⓐ ⓑ ⓒ	35	ⓐ ⓑ ⓒ ⓓ	55	ⓐ ⓑ ⓒ ⓓ	75	ⓐ ⓑ ⓒ ⓓ	95	ⓐ ⓑ ⓒ ⓓ	115	ⓐ ⓑ ⓒ ⓓ	135	ⓐ ⓑ ⓒ ⓓ	155	ⓐ ⓑ ⓒ ⓓ	175	ⓐ ⓑ ⓒ ⓓ	195	ⓐ ⓑ ⓒ ⓓ
16	ⓐ ⓑ ⓒ	36	ⓐ ⓑ ⓒ ⓓ	56	ⓐ ⓑ ⓒ ⓓ	76	ⓐ ⓑ ⓒ ⓓ	96	ⓐ ⓑ ⓒ ⓓ	116	ⓐ ⓑ ⓒ ⓓ	136	ⓐ ⓑ ⓒ ⓓ	156	ⓐ ⓑ ⓒ ⓓ	176	ⓐ ⓑ ⓒ ⓓ	196	ⓐ ⓑ ⓒ ⓓ
17	ⓐ ⓑ ⓒ	37	ⓐ ⓑ ⓒ ⓓ	57	ⓐ ⓑ ⓒ ⓓ	77	ⓐ ⓑ ⓒ ⓓ	97	ⓐ ⓑ ⓒ ⓓ	117	ⓐ ⓑ ⓒ ⓓ	137	ⓐ ⓑ ⓒ ⓓ	157	ⓐ ⓑ ⓒ ⓓ	177	ⓐ ⓑ ⓒ ⓓ	197	ⓐ ⓑ ⓒ ⓓ
18	ⓐ ⓑ ⓒ	38	ⓐ ⓑ ⓒ ⓓ	58	ⓐ ⓑ ⓒ ⓓ	78	ⓐ ⓑ ⓒ ⓓ	98	ⓐ ⓑ ⓒ ⓓ	118	ⓐ ⓑ ⓒ ⓓ	138	ⓐ ⓑ ⓒ ⓓ	158	ⓐ ⓑ ⓒ ⓓ	178	ⓐ ⓑ ⓒ ⓓ	198	ⓐ ⓑ ⓒ ⓓ
19	ⓐ ⓑ ⓒ	39	ⓐ ⓑ ⓒ ⓓ	59	ⓐ ⓑ ⓒ ⓓ	79	ⓐ ⓑ ⓒ ⓓ	99	ⓐ ⓑ ⓒ ⓓ	119	ⓐ ⓑ ⓒ ⓓ	139	ⓐ ⓑ ⓒ ⓓ	159	ⓐ ⓑ ⓒ ⓓ	179	ⓐ ⓑ ⓒ ⓓ	199	ⓐ ⓑ ⓒ ⓓ
20	ⓐ ⓑ ⓒ	40	ⓐ ⓑ ⓒ ⓓ	60	ⓐ ⓑ ⓒ ⓓ	80	ⓐ ⓑ ⓒ ⓓ	100	ⓐ ⓑ ⓒ ⓓ	120	ⓐ ⓑ ⓒ ⓓ	140	ⓐ ⓑ ⓒ ⓓ	160	ⓐ ⓑ ⓒ ⓓ	180	ⓐ ⓑ ⓒ ⓓ	200	ⓐ ⓑ ⓒ ⓓ

ANSWER SHEET

시원스쿨 LAB

이름		테스트 회차		날짜	

LISTENING COMPREHENSION (PART 1~4)

NO	ANSWER A B C D	NO	ANSWER A B C D	NO	ANSWER A B C D	NO	ANSWER A B C D	NO	ANSWER A B C D
1	ⓐ ⓑ ⓒ ⓓ	21	ⓐ ⓑ ⓒ	41	ⓐ ⓑ ⓒ ⓓ	61	ⓐ ⓑ ⓒ ⓓ	81	ⓐ ⓑ ⓒ ⓓ
2	ⓐ ⓑ ⓒ ⓓ	22	ⓐ ⓑ ⓒ	42	ⓐ ⓑ ⓒ ⓓ	62	ⓐ ⓑ ⓒ ⓓ	82	ⓐ ⓑ ⓒ ⓓ
3	ⓐ ⓑ ⓒ ⓓ	23	ⓐ ⓑ ⓒ	43	ⓐ ⓑ ⓒ ⓓ	63	ⓐ ⓑ ⓒ ⓓ	83	ⓐ ⓑ ⓒ ⓓ
4	ⓐ ⓑ ⓒ ⓓ	24	ⓐ ⓑ ⓒ	44	ⓐ ⓑ ⓒ ⓓ	64	ⓐ ⓑ ⓒ ⓓ	84	ⓐ ⓑ ⓒ ⓓ
5	ⓐ ⓑ ⓒ ⓓ	25	ⓐ ⓑ ⓒ	45	ⓐ ⓑ ⓒ ⓓ	65	ⓐ ⓑ ⓒ ⓓ	85	ⓐ ⓑ ⓒ ⓓ
6	ⓐ ⓑ ⓒ ⓓ	26	ⓐ ⓑ ⓒ	46	ⓐ ⓑ ⓒ ⓓ	66	ⓐ ⓑ ⓒ ⓓ	86	ⓐ ⓑ ⓒ ⓓ
7	ⓐ ⓑ ⓒ	27	ⓐ ⓑ ⓒ	47	ⓐ ⓑ ⓒ ⓓ	67	ⓐ ⓑ ⓒ ⓓ	87	ⓐ ⓑ ⓒ ⓓ
8	ⓐ ⓑ ⓒ	28	ⓐ ⓑ ⓒ	48	ⓐ ⓑ ⓒ ⓓ	68	ⓐ ⓑ ⓒ ⓓ	88	ⓐ ⓑ ⓒ ⓓ
9	ⓐ ⓑ ⓒ	29	ⓐ ⓑ ⓒ	49	ⓐ ⓑ ⓒ ⓓ	69	ⓐ ⓑ ⓒ ⓓ	89	ⓐ ⓑ ⓒ ⓓ
10	ⓐ ⓑ ⓒ	30	ⓐ ⓑ ⓒ	50	ⓐ ⓑ ⓒ ⓓ	70	ⓐ ⓑ ⓒ ⓓ	90	ⓐ ⓑ ⓒ ⓓ
11	ⓐ ⓑ ⓒ	31	ⓐ ⓑ ⓒ	51	ⓐ ⓑ ⓒ ⓓ	71	ⓐ ⓑ ⓒ ⓓ	91	ⓐ ⓑ ⓒ ⓓ
12	ⓐ ⓑ ⓒ	32	ⓐ ⓑ ⓒ ⓓ	52	ⓐ ⓑ ⓒ ⓓ	72	ⓐ ⓑ ⓒ ⓓ	92	ⓐ ⓑ ⓒ ⓓ
13	ⓐ ⓑ ⓒ	33	ⓐ ⓑ ⓒ ⓓ	53	ⓐ ⓑ ⓒ ⓓ	73	ⓐ ⓑ ⓒ ⓓ	93	ⓐ ⓑ ⓒ ⓓ
14	ⓐ ⓑ ⓒ	34	ⓐ ⓑ ⓒ ⓓ	54	ⓐ ⓑ ⓒ ⓓ	74	ⓐ ⓑ ⓒ ⓓ	94	ⓐ ⓑ ⓒ ⓓ
15	ⓐ ⓑ ⓒ	35	ⓐ ⓑ ⓒ ⓓ	55	ⓐ ⓑ ⓒ ⓓ	75	ⓐ ⓑ ⓒ ⓓ	95	ⓐ ⓑ ⓒ ⓓ
16	ⓐ ⓑ ⓒ	36	ⓐ ⓑ ⓒ ⓓ	56	ⓐ ⓑ ⓒ ⓓ	76	ⓐ ⓑ ⓒ ⓓ	96	ⓐ ⓑ ⓒ ⓓ
17	ⓐ ⓑ ⓒ	37	ⓐ ⓑ ⓒ ⓓ	57	ⓐ ⓑ ⓒ ⓓ	77	ⓐ ⓑ ⓒ ⓓ	97	ⓐ ⓑ ⓒ ⓓ
18	ⓐ ⓑ ⓒ	38	ⓐ ⓑ ⓒ ⓓ	58	ⓐ ⓑ ⓒ ⓓ	78	ⓐ ⓑ ⓒ ⓓ	98	ⓐ ⓑ ⓒ ⓓ
19	ⓐ ⓑ ⓒ	39	ⓐ ⓑ ⓒ ⓓ	59	ⓐ ⓑ ⓒ ⓓ	79	ⓐ ⓑ ⓒ ⓓ	99	ⓐ ⓑ ⓒ ⓓ
20	ⓐ ⓑ ⓒ	40	ⓐ ⓑ ⓒ ⓓ	60	ⓐ ⓑ ⓒ ⓓ	80	ⓐ ⓑ ⓒ ⓓ	100	ⓐ ⓑ ⓒ ⓓ

READING COMPREHENSION (PART 5~7)

NO	ANSWER A B C D	NO	ANSWER A B C D	NO	ANSWER A B C D	NO	ANSWER A B C D	NO	ANSWER A B C D
101	ⓐ ⓑ ⓒ ⓓ	121	ⓐ ⓑ ⓒ ⓓ	141	ⓐ ⓑ ⓒ ⓓ	161	ⓐ ⓑ ⓒ ⓓ	181	ⓐ ⓑ ⓒ ⓓ
102	ⓐ ⓑ ⓒ ⓓ	122	ⓐ ⓑ ⓒ ⓓ	142	ⓐ ⓑ ⓒ ⓓ	162	ⓐ ⓑ ⓒ ⓓ	182	ⓐ ⓑ ⓒ ⓓ
103	ⓐ ⓑ ⓒ ⓓ	123	ⓐ ⓑ ⓒ ⓓ	143	ⓐ ⓑ ⓒ ⓓ	163	ⓐ ⓑ ⓒ ⓓ	183	ⓐ ⓑ ⓒ ⓓ
104	ⓐ ⓑ ⓒ ⓓ	124	ⓐ ⓑ ⓒ ⓓ	144	ⓐ ⓑ ⓒ ⓓ	164	ⓐ ⓑ ⓒ ⓓ	184	ⓐ ⓑ ⓒ ⓓ
105	ⓐ ⓑ ⓒ ⓓ	125	ⓐ ⓑ ⓒ ⓓ	145	ⓐ ⓑ ⓒ ⓓ	165	ⓐ ⓑ ⓒ ⓓ	185	ⓐ ⓑ ⓒ ⓓ
106	ⓐ ⓑ ⓒ ⓓ	126	ⓐ ⓑ ⓒ ⓓ	146	ⓐ ⓑ ⓒ ⓓ	166	ⓐ ⓑ ⓒ ⓓ	186	ⓐ ⓑ ⓒ ⓓ
107	ⓐ ⓑ ⓒ ⓓ	127	ⓐ ⓑ ⓒ ⓓ	147	ⓐ ⓑ ⓒ ⓓ	167	ⓐ ⓑ ⓒ ⓓ	187	ⓐ ⓑ ⓒ ⓓ
108	ⓐ ⓑ ⓒ ⓓ	128	ⓐ ⓑ ⓒ ⓓ	148	ⓐ ⓑ ⓒ ⓓ	168	ⓐ ⓑ ⓒ ⓓ	188	ⓐ ⓑ ⓒ ⓓ
109	ⓐ ⓑ ⓒ ⓓ	129	ⓐ ⓑ ⓒ ⓓ	149	ⓐ ⓑ ⓒ ⓓ	169	ⓐ ⓑ ⓒ ⓓ	189	ⓐ ⓑ ⓒ ⓓ
110	ⓐ ⓑ ⓒ ⓓ	130	ⓐ ⓑ ⓒ ⓓ	150	ⓐ ⓑ ⓒ ⓓ	170	ⓐ ⓑ ⓒ ⓓ	190	ⓐ ⓑ ⓒ ⓓ
111	ⓐ ⓑ ⓒ ⓓ	131	ⓐ ⓑ ⓒ ⓓ	151	ⓐ ⓑ ⓒ ⓓ	171	ⓐ ⓑ ⓒ ⓓ	191	ⓐ ⓑ ⓒ ⓓ
112	ⓐ ⓑ ⓒ ⓓ	132	ⓐ ⓑ ⓒ ⓓ	152	ⓐ ⓑ ⓒ ⓓ	172	ⓐ ⓑ ⓒ ⓓ	192	ⓐ ⓑ ⓒ ⓓ
113	ⓐ ⓑ ⓒ ⓓ	133	ⓐ ⓑ ⓒ ⓓ	153	ⓐ ⓑ ⓒ ⓓ	173	ⓐ ⓑ ⓒ ⓓ	193	ⓐ ⓑ ⓒ ⓓ
114	ⓐ ⓑ ⓒ ⓓ	134	ⓐ ⓑ ⓒ ⓓ	154	ⓐ ⓑ ⓒ ⓓ	174	ⓐ ⓑ ⓒ ⓓ	194	ⓐ ⓑ ⓒ ⓓ
115	ⓐ ⓑ ⓒ ⓓ	135	ⓐ ⓑ ⓒ ⓓ	155	ⓐ ⓑ ⓒ ⓓ	175	ⓐ ⓑ ⓒ ⓓ	195	ⓐ ⓑ ⓒ ⓓ
116	ⓐ ⓑ ⓒ ⓓ	136	ⓐ ⓑ ⓒ ⓓ	156	ⓐ ⓑ ⓒ ⓓ	176	ⓐ ⓑ ⓒ ⓓ	196	ⓐ ⓑ ⓒ ⓓ
117	ⓐ ⓑ ⓒ ⓓ	137	ⓐ ⓑ ⓒ ⓓ	157	ⓐ ⓑ ⓒ ⓓ	177	ⓐ ⓑ ⓒ ⓓ	197	ⓐ ⓑ ⓒ ⓓ
118	ⓐ ⓑ ⓒ ⓓ	138	ⓐ ⓑ ⓒ ⓓ	158	ⓐ ⓑ ⓒ ⓓ	178	ⓐ ⓑ ⓒ ⓓ	198	ⓐ ⓑ ⓒ ⓓ
119	ⓐ ⓑ ⓒ ⓓ	139	ⓐ ⓑ ⓒ ⓓ	159	ⓐ ⓑ ⓒ ⓓ	179	ⓐ ⓑ ⓒ ⓓ	199	ⓐ ⓑ ⓒ ⓓ
120	ⓐ ⓑ ⓒ ⓓ	140	ⓐ ⓑ ⓒ ⓓ	160	ⓐ ⓑ ⓒ ⓓ	180	ⓐ ⓑ ⓒ ⓓ	200	ⓐ ⓑ ⓒ ⓓ

ANSWER SHEET

시원스쿨LAB

이름		테스트 회차		날짜	

LISTENING COMPREHENSION (PART 1~4)

NO	ANSWER A B C D	NO	ANSWER A B C D	NO	ANSWER A B C D	NO	ANSWER A B C D	NO	ANSWER A B C D
1	ⓐ ⓑ ⓒ ⓓ	21	ⓐ ⓑ ⓒ	41	ⓐ ⓑ ⓒ ⓓ	61	ⓐ ⓑ ⓒ ⓓ	81	ⓐ ⓑ ⓒ ⓓ
2	ⓐ ⓑ ⓒ ⓓ	22	ⓐ ⓑ ⓒ	42	ⓐ ⓑ ⓒ ⓓ	62	ⓐ ⓑ ⓒ ⓓ	82	ⓐ ⓑ ⓒ ⓓ
3	ⓐ ⓑ ⓒ ⓓ	23	ⓐ ⓑ ⓒ	43	ⓐ ⓑ ⓒ ⓓ	63	ⓐ ⓑ ⓒ ⓓ	83	ⓐ ⓑ ⓒ ⓓ
4	ⓐ ⓑ ⓒ ⓓ	24	ⓐ ⓑ ⓒ	44	ⓐ ⓑ ⓒ ⓓ	64	ⓐ ⓑ ⓒ ⓓ	84	ⓐ ⓑ ⓒ ⓓ
5	ⓐ ⓑ ⓒ ⓓ	25	ⓐ ⓑ ⓒ	45	ⓐ ⓑ ⓒ ⓓ	65	ⓐ ⓑ ⓒ ⓓ	85	ⓐ ⓑ ⓒ ⓓ
6	ⓐ ⓑ ⓒ ⓓ	26	ⓐ ⓑ ⓒ	46	ⓐ ⓑ ⓒ ⓓ	66	ⓐ ⓑ ⓒ ⓓ	86	ⓐ ⓑ ⓒ ⓓ
7	ⓐ ⓑ ⓒ	27	ⓐ ⓑ ⓒ	47	ⓐ ⓑ ⓒ ⓓ	67	ⓐ ⓑ ⓒ ⓓ	87	ⓐ ⓑ ⓒ ⓓ
8	ⓐ ⓑ ⓒ	28	ⓐ ⓑ ⓒ	48	ⓐ ⓑ ⓒ ⓓ	68	ⓐ ⓑ ⓒ ⓓ	88	ⓐ ⓑ ⓒ ⓓ
9	ⓐ ⓑ ⓒ	29	ⓐ ⓑ ⓒ	49	ⓐ ⓑ ⓒ ⓓ	69	ⓐ ⓑ ⓒ ⓓ	89	ⓐ ⓑ ⓒ ⓓ
10	ⓐ ⓑ ⓒ	30	ⓐ ⓑ ⓒ	50	ⓐ ⓑ ⓒ ⓓ	70	ⓐ ⓑ ⓒ ⓓ	90	ⓐ ⓑ ⓒ ⓓ
11	ⓐ ⓑ ⓒ	31	ⓐ ⓑ ⓒ	51	ⓐ ⓑ ⓒ ⓓ	71	ⓐ ⓑ ⓒ ⓓ	91	ⓐ ⓑ ⓒ ⓓ
12	ⓐ ⓑ ⓒ	32	ⓐ ⓑ ⓒ ⓓ	52	ⓐ ⓑ ⓒ ⓓ	72	ⓐ ⓑ ⓒ ⓓ	92	ⓐ ⓑ ⓒ ⓓ
13	ⓐ ⓑ ⓒ	33	ⓐ ⓑ ⓒ ⓓ	53	ⓐ ⓑ ⓒ ⓓ	73	ⓐ ⓑ ⓒ ⓓ	93	ⓐ ⓑ ⓒ ⓓ
14	ⓐ ⓑ ⓒ	34	ⓐ ⓑ ⓒ ⓓ	54	ⓐ ⓑ ⓒ ⓓ	74	ⓐ ⓑ ⓒ ⓓ	94	ⓐ ⓑ ⓒ ⓓ
15	ⓐ ⓑ ⓒ	35	ⓐ ⓑ ⓒ ⓓ	55	ⓐ ⓑ ⓒ ⓓ	75	ⓐ ⓑ ⓒ ⓓ	95	ⓐ ⓑ ⓒ ⓓ
16	ⓐ ⓑ ⓒ	36	ⓐ ⓑ ⓒ ⓓ	56	ⓐ ⓑ ⓒ ⓓ	76	ⓐ ⓑ ⓒ ⓓ	96	ⓐ ⓑ ⓒ ⓓ
17	ⓐ ⓑ ⓒ	37	ⓐ ⓑ ⓒ ⓓ	57	ⓐ ⓑ ⓒ ⓓ	77	ⓐ ⓑ ⓒ ⓓ	97	ⓐ ⓑ ⓒ ⓓ
18	ⓐ ⓑ ⓒ	38	ⓐ ⓑ ⓒ ⓓ	58	ⓐ ⓑ ⓒ ⓓ	78	ⓐ ⓑ ⓒ ⓓ	98	ⓐ ⓑ ⓒ ⓓ
19	ⓐ ⓑ ⓒ	39	ⓐ ⓑ ⓒ ⓓ	59	ⓐ ⓑ ⓒ ⓓ	79	ⓐ ⓑ ⓒ ⓓ	99	ⓐ ⓑ ⓒ ⓓ
20	ⓐ ⓑ ⓒ	40	ⓐ ⓑ ⓒ ⓓ	60	ⓐ ⓑ ⓒ ⓓ	80	ⓐ ⓑ ⓒ ⓓ	100	ⓐ ⓑ ⓒ ⓓ

READING COMPREHENSION (PART 5~7)

NO	ANSWER A B C D	NO	ANSWER A B C D	NO	ANSWER A B C D	NO	ANSWER A B C D	NO	ANSWER A B C D
101	ⓐ ⓑ ⓒ ⓓ	121	ⓐ ⓑ ⓒ ⓓ	141	ⓐ ⓑ ⓒ ⓓ	161	ⓐ ⓑ ⓒ ⓓ	181	ⓐ ⓑ ⓒ ⓓ
102	ⓐ ⓑ ⓒ ⓓ	122	ⓐ ⓑ ⓒ ⓓ	142	ⓐ ⓑ ⓒ ⓓ	162	ⓐ ⓑ ⓒ ⓓ	182	ⓐ ⓑ ⓒ ⓓ
103	ⓐ ⓑ ⓒ ⓓ	123	ⓐ ⓑ ⓒ ⓓ	143	ⓐ ⓑ ⓒ ⓓ	163	ⓐ ⓑ ⓒ ⓓ	183	ⓐ ⓑ ⓒ ⓓ
104	ⓐ ⓑ ⓒ ⓓ	124	ⓐ ⓑ ⓒ ⓓ	144	ⓐ ⓑ ⓒ ⓓ	164	ⓐ ⓑ ⓒ ⓓ	184	ⓐ ⓑ ⓒ ⓓ
105	ⓐ ⓑ ⓒ ⓓ	125	ⓐ ⓑ ⓒ ⓓ	145	ⓐ ⓑ ⓒ ⓓ	165	ⓐ ⓑ ⓒ ⓓ	185	ⓐ ⓑ ⓒ ⓓ
106	ⓐ ⓑ ⓒ ⓓ	126	ⓐ ⓑ ⓒ ⓓ	146	ⓐ ⓑ ⓒ ⓓ	166	ⓐ ⓑ ⓒ ⓓ	186	ⓐ ⓑ ⓒ ⓓ
107	ⓐ ⓑ ⓒ ⓓ	127	ⓐ ⓑ ⓒ ⓓ	147	ⓐ ⓑ ⓒ ⓓ	167	ⓐ ⓑ ⓒ ⓓ	187	ⓐ ⓑ ⓒ ⓓ
108	ⓐ ⓑ ⓒ ⓓ	128	ⓐ ⓑ ⓒ ⓓ	148	ⓐ ⓑ ⓒ ⓓ	168	ⓐ ⓑ ⓒ ⓓ	188	ⓐ ⓑ ⓒ ⓓ
109	ⓐ ⓑ ⓒ ⓓ	129	ⓐ ⓑ ⓒ ⓓ	149	ⓐ ⓑ ⓒ ⓓ	169	ⓐ ⓑ ⓒ ⓓ	189	ⓐ ⓑ ⓒ ⓓ
110	ⓐ ⓑ ⓒ ⓓ	130	ⓐ ⓑ ⓒ ⓓ	150	ⓐ ⓑ ⓒ ⓓ	170	ⓐ ⓑ ⓒ ⓓ	190	ⓐ ⓑ ⓒ ⓓ
111	ⓐ ⓑ ⓒ ⓓ	131	ⓐ ⓑ ⓒ ⓓ	151	ⓐ ⓑ ⓒ ⓓ	171	ⓐ ⓑ ⓒ ⓓ	191	ⓐ ⓑ ⓒ ⓓ
112	ⓐ ⓑ ⓒ ⓓ	132	ⓐ ⓑ ⓒ ⓓ	152	ⓐ ⓑ ⓒ ⓓ	172	ⓐ ⓑ ⓒ ⓓ	192	ⓐ ⓑ ⓒ ⓓ
113	ⓐ ⓑ ⓒ ⓓ	133	ⓐ ⓑ ⓒ ⓓ	153	ⓐ ⓑ ⓒ ⓓ	173	ⓐ ⓑ ⓒ ⓓ	193	ⓐ ⓑ ⓒ ⓓ
114	ⓐ ⓑ ⓒ ⓓ	134	ⓐ ⓑ ⓒ ⓓ	154	ⓐ ⓑ ⓒ ⓓ	174	ⓐ ⓑ ⓒ ⓓ	194	ⓐ ⓑ ⓒ ⓓ
115	ⓐ ⓑ ⓒ ⓓ	135	ⓐ ⓑ ⓒ ⓓ	155	ⓐ ⓑ ⓒ ⓓ	175	ⓐ ⓑ ⓒ ⓓ	195	ⓐ ⓑ ⓒ ⓓ
116	ⓐ ⓑ ⓒ ⓓ	136	ⓐ ⓑ ⓒ ⓓ	156	ⓐ ⓑ ⓒ ⓓ	176	ⓐ ⓑ ⓒ ⓓ	196	ⓐ ⓑ ⓒ ⓓ
117	ⓐ ⓑ ⓒ ⓓ	137	ⓐ ⓑ ⓒ ⓓ	157	ⓐ ⓑ ⓒ ⓓ	177	ⓐ ⓑ ⓒ ⓓ	197	ⓐ ⓑ ⓒ ⓓ
118	ⓐ ⓑ ⓒ ⓓ	138	ⓐ ⓑ ⓒ ⓓ	158	ⓐ ⓑ ⓒ ⓓ	178	ⓐ ⓑ ⓒ ⓓ	198	ⓐ ⓑ ⓒ ⓓ
119	ⓐ ⓑ ⓒ ⓓ	139	ⓐ ⓑ ⓒ ⓓ	159	ⓐ ⓑ ⓒ ⓓ	179	ⓐ ⓑ ⓒ ⓓ	199	ⓐ ⓑ ⓒ ⓓ
120	ⓐ ⓑ ⓒ ⓓ	140	ⓐ ⓑ ⓒ ⓓ	160	ⓐ ⓑ ⓒ ⓓ	180	ⓐ ⓑ ⓒ ⓓ	200	ⓐ ⓑ ⓒ ⓓ

ANSWER SHEET

시원스쿨 LAB

이름		테스트 회차		날짜	

LISTENING COMPREHENSION (PART 1~4)										READING COMPREHENSION (PART 5~7)									
NO	ANSWER A B C D	NO	ANSWER A B C D	NO	ANSWER A B C D	NO	ANSWER A B C D	NO	ANSWER A B C D	NO	ANSWER A B C D	NO	ANSWER A B C D	NO	ANSWER A B C D	NO	ANSWER A B C D	NO	ANSWER A B C D
1	ⓐ ⓑ ⓒ ⓓ	21	ⓐ ⓑ ⓒ	41	ⓐ ⓑ ⓒ ⓓ	61	ⓐ ⓑ ⓒ ⓓ	81	ⓐ ⓑ ⓒ ⓓ	101	ⓐ ⓑ ⓒ ⓓ	121	ⓐ ⓑ ⓒ ⓓ	141	ⓐ ⓑ ⓒ ⓓ	161	ⓐ ⓑ ⓒ ⓓ	181	ⓐ ⓑ ⓒ ⓓ
2	ⓐ ⓑ ⓒ ⓓ	22	ⓐ ⓑ ⓒ	42	ⓐ ⓑ ⓒ ⓓ	62	ⓐ ⓑ ⓒ ⓓ	82	ⓐ ⓑ ⓒ ⓓ	102	ⓐ ⓑ ⓒ ⓓ	122	ⓐ ⓑ ⓒ ⓓ	142	ⓐ ⓑ ⓒ ⓓ	162	ⓐ ⓑ ⓒ ⓓ	182	ⓐ ⓑ ⓒ ⓓ
3	ⓐ ⓑ ⓒ ⓓ	23	ⓐ ⓑ ⓒ	43	ⓐ ⓑ ⓒ ⓓ	63	ⓐ ⓑ ⓒ ⓓ	83	ⓐ ⓑ ⓒ ⓓ	103	ⓐ ⓑ ⓒ ⓓ	123	ⓐ ⓑ ⓒ ⓓ	143	ⓐ ⓑ ⓒ ⓓ	163	ⓐ ⓑ ⓒ ⓓ	183	ⓐ ⓑ ⓒ ⓓ
4	ⓐ ⓑ ⓒ ⓓ	24	ⓐ ⓑ ⓒ	44	ⓐ ⓑ ⓒ ⓓ	64	ⓐ ⓑ ⓒ ⓓ	84	ⓐ ⓑ ⓒ ⓓ	104	ⓐ ⓑ ⓒ ⓓ	124	ⓐ ⓑ ⓒ ⓓ	144	ⓐ ⓑ ⓒ ⓓ	164	ⓐ ⓑ ⓒ ⓓ	184	ⓐ ⓑ ⓒ ⓓ
5	ⓐ ⓑ ⓒ ⓓ	25	ⓐ ⓑ ⓒ	45	ⓐ ⓑ ⓒ ⓓ	65	ⓐ ⓑ ⓒ ⓓ	85	ⓐ ⓑ ⓒ ⓓ	105	ⓐ ⓑ ⓒ ⓓ	125	ⓐ ⓑ ⓒ ⓓ	145	ⓐ ⓑ ⓒ ⓓ	165	ⓐ ⓑ ⓒ ⓓ	185	ⓐ ⓑ ⓒ ⓓ
6	ⓐ ⓑ ⓒ ⓓ	26	ⓐ ⓑ ⓒ	46	ⓐ ⓑ ⓒ ⓓ	66	ⓐ ⓑ ⓒ ⓓ	86	ⓐ ⓑ ⓒ ⓓ	106	ⓐ ⓑ ⓒ ⓓ	126	ⓐ ⓑ ⓒ ⓓ	146	ⓐ ⓑ ⓒ ⓓ	166	ⓐ ⓑ ⓒ ⓓ	186	ⓐ ⓑ ⓒ ⓓ
7	ⓐ ⓑ ⓒ	27	ⓐ ⓑ ⓒ	47	ⓐ ⓑ ⓒ ⓓ	67	ⓐ ⓑ ⓒ ⓓ	87	ⓐ ⓑ ⓒ ⓓ	107	ⓐ ⓑ ⓒ ⓓ	127	ⓐ ⓑ ⓒ ⓓ	147	ⓐ ⓑ ⓒ ⓓ	167	ⓐ ⓑ ⓒ ⓓ	187	ⓐ ⓑ ⓒ ⓓ
8	ⓐ ⓑ ⓒ	28	ⓐ ⓑ ⓒ	48	ⓐ ⓑ ⓒ ⓓ	68	ⓐ ⓑ ⓒ ⓓ	88	ⓐ ⓑ ⓒ ⓓ	108	ⓐ ⓑ ⓒ ⓓ	128	ⓐ ⓑ ⓒ ⓓ	148	ⓐ ⓑ ⓒ ⓓ	168	ⓐ ⓑ ⓒ ⓓ	188	ⓐ ⓑ ⓒ ⓓ
9	ⓐ ⓑ ⓒ	29	ⓐ ⓑ ⓒ	49	ⓐ ⓑ ⓒ ⓓ	69	ⓐ ⓑ ⓒ ⓓ	89	ⓐ ⓑ ⓒ ⓓ	109	ⓐ ⓑ ⓒ ⓓ	129	ⓐ ⓑ ⓒ ⓓ	149	ⓐ ⓑ ⓒ ⓓ	169	ⓐ ⓑ ⓒ ⓓ	189	ⓐ ⓑ ⓒ ⓓ
10	ⓐ ⓑ ⓒ	30	ⓐ ⓑ ⓒ	50	ⓐ ⓑ ⓒ ⓓ	70	ⓐ ⓑ ⓒ ⓓ	90	ⓐ ⓑ ⓒ ⓓ	110	ⓐ ⓑ ⓒ ⓓ	130	ⓐ ⓑ ⓒ ⓓ	150	ⓐ ⓑ ⓒ ⓓ	170	ⓐ ⓑ ⓒ ⓓ	190	ⓐ ⓑ ⓒ ⓓ
11	ⓐ ⓑ ⓒ	31	ⓐ ⓑ ⓒ	51	ⓐ ⓑ ⓒ ⓓ	71	ⓐ ⓑ ⓒ ⓓ	91	ⓐ ⓑ ⓒ ⓓ	111	ⓐ ⓑ ⓒ ⓓ	131	ⓐ ⓑ ⓒ ⓓ	151	ⓐ ⓑ ⓒ ⓓ	171	ⓐ ⓑ ⓒ ⓓ	191	ⓐ ⓑ ⓒ ⓓ
12	ⓐ ⓑ ⓒ	32	ⓐ ⓑ ⓒ ⓓ	52	ⓐ ⓑ ⓒ ⓓ	72	ⓐ ⓑ ⓒ ⓓ	92	ⓐ ⓑ ⓒ ⓓ	112	ⓐ ⓑ ⓒ ⓓ	132	ⓐ ⓑ ⓒ ⓓ	152	ⓐ ⓑ ⓒ ⓓ	172	ⓐ ⓑ ⓒ ⓓ	192	ⓐ ⓑ ⓒ ⓓ
13	ⓐ ⓑ ⓒ	33	ⓐ ⓑ ⓒ ⓓ	53	ⓐ ⓑ ⓒ ⓓ	73	ⓐ ⓑ ⓒ ⓓ	93	ⓐ ⓑ ⓒ ⓓ	113	ⓐ ⓑ ⓒ ⓓ	133	ⓐ ⓑ ⓒ ⓓ	153	ⓐ ⓑ ⓒ ⓓ	173	ⓐ ⓑ ⓒ ⓓ	193	ⓐ ⓑ ⓒ ⓓ
14	ⓐ ⓑ ⓒ	34	ⓐ ⓑ ⓒ ⓓ	54	ⓐ ⓑ ⓒ ⓓ	74	ⓐ ⓑ ⓒ ⓓ	94	ⓐ ⓑ ⓒ ⓓ	114	ⓐ ⓑ ⓒ ⓓ	134	ⓐ ⓑ ⓒ ⓓ	154	ⓐ ⓑ ⓒ ⓓ	174	ⓐ ⓑ ⓒ ⓓ	194	ⓐ ⓑ ⓒ ⓓ
15	ⓐ ⓑ ⓒ	35	ⓐ ⓑ ⓒ ⓓ	55	ⓐ ⓑ ⓒ ⓓ	75	ⓐ ⓑ ⓒ ⓓ	95	ⓐ ⓑ ⓒ ⓓ	115	ⓐ ⓑ ⓒ ⓓ	135	ⓐ ⓑ ⓒ ⓓ	155	ⓐ ⓑ ⓒ ⓓ	175	ⓐ ⓑ ⓒ ⓓ	195	ⓐ ⓑ ⓒ ⓓ
16	ⓐ ⓑ ⓒ	36	ⓐ ⓑ ⓒ ⓓ	56	ⓐ ⓑ ⓒ ⓓ	76	ⓐ ⓑ ⓒ ⓓ	96	ⓐ ⓑ ⓒ ⓓ	116	ⓐ ⓑ ⓒ ⓓ	136	ⓐ ⓑ ⓒ ⓓ	156	ⓐ ⓑ ⓒ ⓓ	176	ⓐ ⓑ ⓒ ⓓ	196	ⓐ ⓑ ⓒ ⓓ
17	ⓐ ⓑ ⓒ	37	ⓐ ⓑ ⓒ ⓓ	57	ⓐ ⓑ ⓒ ⓓ	77	ⓐ ⓑ ⓒ ⓓ	97	ⓐ ⓑ ⓒ ⓓ	117	ⓐ ⓑ ⓒ ⓓ	137	ⓐ ⓑ ⓒ ⓓ	157	ⓐ ⓑ ⓒ ⓓ	177	ⓐ ⓑ ⓒ ⓓ	197	ⓐ ⓑ ⓒ ⓓ
18	ⓐ ⓑ ⓒ	38	ⓐ ⓑ ⓒ ⓓ	58	ⓐ ⓑ ⓒ ⓓ	78	ⓐ ⓑ ⓒ ⓓ	98	ⓐ ⓑ ⓒ ⓓ	118	ⓐ ⓑ ⓒ ⓓ	138	ⓐ ⓑ ⓒ ⓓ	158	ⓐ ⓑ ⓒ ⓓ	178	ⓐ ⓑ ⓒ ⓓ	198	ⓐ ⓑ ⓒ ⓓ
19	ⓐ ⓑ ⓒ	39	ⓐ ⓑ ⓒ ⓓ	59	ⓐ ⓑ ⓒ ⓓ	79	ⓐ ⓑ ⓒ ⓓ	99	ⓐ ⓑ ⓒ ⓓ	119	ⓐ ⓑ ⓒ ⓓ	139	ⓐ ⓑ ⓒ ⓓ	159	ⓐ ⓑ ⓒ ⓓ	179	ⓐ ⓑ ⓒ ⓓ	199	ⓐ ⓑ ⓒ ⓓ
20	ⓐ ⓑ ⓒ	40	ⓐ ⓑ ⓒ ⓓ	60	ⓐ ⓑ ⓒ ⓓ	80	ⓐ ⓑ ⓒ ⓓ	100	ⓐ ⓑ ⓒ ⓓ	120	ⓐ ⓑ ⓒ ⓓ	140	ⓐ ⓑ ⓒ ⓓ	160	ⓐ ⓑ ⓒ ⓓ	180	ⓐ ⓑ ⓒ ⓓ	200	ⓐ ⓑ ⓒ ⓓ

ANSWER SHEET

시원스쿨 LAB

이름		테스트 회차		날짜	

LISTENING COMPREHENSION (PART 1~4)

NO	A	B	C	D	NO	A	B	C	D	NO	A	B	C	D	NO	A	B	C	D	NO	A	B	C	D
1	ⓐ	ⓑ	ⓒ	ⓓ	21	ⓐ	ⓑ	ⓒ		41	ⓐ	ⓑ	ⓒ	ⓓ	61	ⓐ	ⓑ	ⓒ	ⓓ	81	ⓐ	ⓑ	ⓒ	ⓓ
2	ⓐ	ⓑ	ⓒ	ⓓ	22	ⓐ	ⓑ	ⓒ		42	ⓐ	ⓑ	ⓒ	ⓓ	62	ⓐ	ⓑ	ⓒ	ⓓ	82	ⓐ	ⓑ	ⓒ	ⓓ
3	ⓐ	ⓑ	ⓒ	ⓓ	23	ⓐ	ⓑ	ⓒ		43	ⓐ	ⓑ	ⓒ	ⓓ	63	ⓐ	ⓑ	ⓒ	ⓓ	83	ⓐ	ⓑ	ⓒ	ⓓ
4	ⓐ	ⓑ	ⓒ	ⓓ	24	ⓐ	ⓑ	ⓒ		44	ⓐ	ⓑ	ⓒ	ⓓ	64	ⓐ	ⓑ	ⓒ	ⓓ	84	ⓐ	ⓑ	ⓒ	ⓓ
5	ⓐ	ⓑ	ⓒ	ⓓ	25	ⓐ	ⓑ	ⓒ		45	ⓐ	ⓑ	ⓒ	ⓓ	65	ⓐ	ⓑ	ⓒ	ⓓ	85	ⓐ	ⓑ	ⓒ	ⓓ
6	ⓐ	ⓑ	ⓒ	ⓓ	26	ⓐ	ⓑ	ⓒ		46	ⓐ	ⓑ	ⓒ	ⓓ	66	ⓐ	ⓑ	ⓒ	ⓓ	86	ⓐ	ⓑ	ⓒ	ⓓ
7	ⓐ	ⓑ	ⓒ		27	ⓐ	ⓑ	ⓒ		47	ⓐ	ⓑ	ⓒ	ⓓ	67	ⓐ	ⓑ	ⓒ	ⓓ	87	ⓐ	ⓑ	ⓒ	ⓓ
8	ⓐ	ⓑ	ⓒ		28	ⓐ	ⓑ	ⓒ		48	ⓐ	ⓑ	ⓒ	ⓓ	68	ⓐ	ⓑ	ⓒ	ⓓ	88	ⓐ	ⓑ	ⓒ	ⓓ
9	ⓐ	ⓑ	ⓒ		29	ⓐ	ⓑ	ⓒ		49	ⓐ	ⓑ	ⓒ	ⓓ	69	ⓐ	ⓑ	ⓒ	ⓓ	89	ⓐ	ⓑ	ⓒ	ⓓ
10	ⓐ	ⓑ	ⓒ		30	ⓐ	ⓑ	ⓒ		50	ⓐ	ⓑ	ⓒ	ⓓ	70	ⓐ	ⓑ	ⓒ	ⓓ	90	ⓐ	ⓑ	ⓒ	ⓓ
11	ⓐ	ⓑ	ⓒ		31	ⓐ	ⓑ	ⓒ		51	ⓐ	ⓑ	ⓒ	ⓓ	71	ⓐ	ⓑ	ⓒ	ⓓ	91	ⓐ	ⓑ	ⓒ	ⓓ
12	ⓐ	ⓑ	ⓒ		32	ⓐ	ⓑ	ⓒ	ⓓ	52	ⓐ	ⓑ	ⓒ	ⓓ	72	ⓐ	ⓑ	ⓒ	ⓓ	92	ⓐ	ⓑ	ⓒ	ⓓ
13	ⓐ	ⓑ	ⓒ		33	ⓐ	ⓑ	ⓒ	ⓓ	53	ⓐ	ⓑ	ⓒ	ⓓ	73	ⓐ	ⓑ	ⓒ	ⓓ	93	ⓐ	ⓑ	ⓒ	ⓓ
14	ⓐ	ⓑ	ⓒ		34	ⓐ	ⓑ	ⓒ	ⓓ	54	ⓐ	ⓑ	ⓒ	ⓓ	74	ⓐ	ⓑ	ⓒ	ⓓ	94	ⓐ	ⓑ	ⓒ	ⓓ
15	ⓐ	ⓑ	ⓒ		35	ⓐ	ⓑ	ⓒ	ⓓ	55	ⓐ	ⓑ	ⓒ	ⓓ	75	ⓐ	ⓑ	ⓒ	ⓓ	95	ⓐ	ⓑ	ⓒ	ⓓ
16	ⓐ	ⓑ	ⓒ		36	ⓐ	ⓑ	ⓒ	ⓓ	56	ⓐ	ⓑ	ⓒ	ⓓ	76	ⓐ	ⓑ	ⓒ	ⓓ	96	ⓐ	ⓑ	ⓒ	ⓓ
17	ⓐ	ⓑ	ⓒ		37	ⓐ	ⓑ	ⓒ	ⓓ	57	ⓐ	ⓑ	ⓒ	ⓓ	77	ⓐ	ⓑ	ⓒ	ⓓ	97	ⓐ	ⓑ	ⓒ	ⓓ
18	ⓐ	ⓑ	ⓒ		38	ⓐ	ⓑ	ⓒ	ⓓ	58	ⓐ	ⓑ	ⓒ	ⓓ	78	ⓐ	ⓑ	ⓒ	ⓓ	98	ⓐ	ⓑ	ⓒ	ⓓ
19	ⓐ	ⓑ	ⓒ		39	ⓐ	ⓑ	ⓒ	ⓓ	59	ⓐ	ⓑ	ⓒ	ⓓ	79	ⓐ	ⓑ	ⓒ	ⓓ	99	ⓐ	ⓑ	ⓒ	ⓓ
20	ⓐ	ⓑ	ⓒ		40	ⓐ	ⓑ	ⓒ	ⓓ	60	ⓐ	ⓑ	ⓒ	ⓓ	80	ⓐ	ⓑ	ⓒ	ⓓ	100	ⓐ	ⓑ	ⓒ	ⓓ

READING COMPREHENSION (PART 5~7)

NO	A	B	C	D	NO	A	B	C	D	NO	A	B	C	D	NO	A	B	C	D	NO	A	B	C	D
101	ⓐ	ⓑ	ⓒ	ⓓ	121	ⓐ	ⓑ	ⓒ	ⓓ	141	ⓐ	ⓑ	ⓒ	ⓓ	161	ⓐ	ⓑ	ⓒ	ⓓ	181	ⓐ	ⓑ	ⓒ	ⓓ
102	ⓐ	ⓑ	ⓒ	ⓓ	122	ⓐ	ⓑ	ⓒ	ⓓ	142	ⓐ	ⓑ	ⓒ	ⓓ	162	ⓐ	ⓑ	ⓒ	ⓓ	182	ⓐ	ⓑ	ⓒ	ⓓ
103	ⓐ	ⓑ	ⓒ	ⓓ	123	ⓐ	ⓑ	ⓒ	ⓓ	143	ⓐ	ⓑ	ⓒ	ⓓ	163	ⓐ	ⓑ	ⓒ	ⓓ	183	ⓐ	ⓑ	ⓒ	ⓓ
104	ⓐ	ⓑ	ⓒ	ⓓ	124	ⓐ	ⓑ	ⓒ	ⓓ	144	ⓐ	ⓑ	ⓒ	ⓓ	164	ⓐ	ⓑ	ⓒ	ⓓ	184	ⓐ	ⓑ	ⓒ	ⓓ
105	ⓐ	ⓑ	ⓒ	ⓓ	125	ⓐ	ⓑ	ⓒ	ⓓ	145	ⓐ	ⓑ	ⓒ	ⓓ	165	ⓐ	ⓑ	ⓒ	ⓓ	185	ⓐ	ⓑ	ⓒ	ⓓ
106	ⓐ	ⓑ	ⓒ	ⓓ	126	ⓐ	ⓑ	ⓒ	ⓓ	146	ⓐ	ⓑ	ⓒ	ⓓ	166	ⓐ	ⓑ	ⓒ	ⓓ	186	ⓐ	ⓑ	ⓒ	ⓓ
107	ⓐ	ⓑ	ⓒ	ⓓ	127	ⓐ	ⓑ	ⓒ	ⓓ	147	ⓐ	ⓑ	ⓒ	ⓓ	167	ⓐ	ⓑ	ⓒ	ⓓ	187	ⓐ	ⓑ	ⓒ	ⓓ
108	ⓐ	ⓑ	ⓒ	ⓓ	128	ⓐ	ⓑ	ⓒ	ⓓ	148	ⓐ	ⓑ	ⓒ	ⓓ	168	ⓐ	ⓑ	ⓒ	ⓓ	188	ⓐ	ⓑ	ⓒ	ⓓ
109	ⓐ	ⓑ	ⓒ	ⓓ	129	ⓐ	ⓑ	ⓒ	ⓓ	149	ⓐ	ⓑ	ⓒ	ⓓ	169	ⓐ	ⓑ	ⓒ	ⓓ	189	ⓐ	ⓑ	ⓒ	ⓓ
110	ⓐ	ⓑ	ⓒ	ⓓ	130	ⓐ	ⓑ	ⓒ	ⓓ	150	ⓐ	ⓑ	ⓒ	ⓓ	170	ⓐ	ⓑ	ⓒ	ⓓ	190	ⓐ	ⓑ	ⓒ	ⓓ
111	ⓐ	ⓑ	ⓒ	ⓓ	131	ⓐ	ⓑ	ⓒ	ⓓ	151	ⓐ	ⓑ	ⓒ	ⓓ	171	ⓐ	ⓑ	ⓒ	ⓓ	191	ⓐ	ⓑ	ⓒ	ⓓ
112	ⓐ	ⓑ	ⓒ	ⓓ	132	ⓐ	ⓑ	ⓒ	ⓓ	152	ⓐ	ⓑ	ⓒ	ⓓ	172	ⓐ	ⓑ	ⓒ	ⓓ	192	ⓐ	ⓑ	ⓒ	ⓓ
113	ⓐ	ⓑ	ⓒ	ⓓ	133	ⓐ	ⓑ	ⓒ	ⓓ	153	ⓐ	ⓑ	ⓒ	ⓓ	173	ⓐ	ⓑ	ⓒ	ⓓ	193	ⓐ	ⓑ	ⓒ	ⓓ
114	ⓐ	ⓑ	ⓒ	ⓓ	134	ⓐ	ⓑ	ⓒ	ⓓ	154	ⓐ	ⓑ	ⓒ	ⓓ	174	ⓐ	ⓑ	ⓒ	ⓓ	194	ⓐ	ⓑ	ⓒ	ⓓ
115	ⓐ	ⓑ	ⓒ	ⓓ	135	ⓐ	ⓑ	ⓒ	ⓓ	155	ⓐ	ⓑ	ⓒ	ⓓ	175	ⓐ	ⓑ	ⓒ	ⓓ	195	ⓐ	ⓑ	ⓒ	ⓓ
116	ⓐ	ⓑ	ⓒ	ⓓ	136	ⓐ	ⓑ	ⓒ	ⓓ	156	ⓐ	ⓑ	ⓒ	ⓓ	176	ⓐ	ⓑ	ⓒ	ⓓ	196	ⓐ	ⓑ	ⓒ	ⓓ
117	ⓐ	ⓑ	ⓒ	ⓓ	137	ⓐ	ⓑ	ⓒ	ⓓ	157	ⓐ	ⓑ	ⓒ	ⓓ	177	ⓐ	ⓑ	ⓒ	ⓓ	197	ⓐ	ⓑ	ⓒ	ⓓ
118	ⓐ	ⓑ	ⓒ	ⓓ	138	ⓐ	ⓑ	ⓒ	ⓓ	158	ⓐ	ⓑ	ⓒ	ⓓ	178	ⓐ	ⓑ	ⓒ	ⓓ	198	ⓐ	ⓑ	ⓒ	ⓓ
119	ⓐ	ⓑ	ⓒ	ⓓ	139	ⓐ	ⓑ	ⓒ	ⓓ	159	ⓐ	ⓑ	ⓒ	ⓓ	179	ⓐ	ⓑ	ⓒ	ⓓ	199	ⓐ	ⓑ	ⓒ	ⓓ
120	ⓐ	ⓑ	ⓒ	ⓓ	140	ⓐ	ⓑ	ⓒ	ⓓ	160	ⓐ	ⓑ	ⓒ	ⓓ	180	ⓐ	ⓑ	ⓒ	ⓓ	200	ⓐ	ⓑ	ⓒ	ⓓ

ANSWER SHEET

시원스쿨 LAB

이름		테스트 회차		날짜	

LISTENING COMPREHENSION (PART 1~4)

NO	ANSWER				NO	ANSWER				NO	ANSWER				NO	ANSWER				NO	ANSWER			
	A	B	C	D		A	B	C	D		A	B	C	D		A	B	C	D		A	B	C	D
1	ⓐ	ⓑ	ⓒ	ⓓ	21	ⓐ	ⓑ	ⓒ		41	ⓐ	ⓑ	ⓒ	ⓓ	61	ⓐ	ⓑ	ⓒ	ⓓ	81	ⓐ	ⓑ	ⓒ	ⓓ
2	ⓐ	ⓑ	ⓒ	ⓓ	22	ⓐ	ⓑ	ⓒ		42	ⓐ	ⓑ	ⓒ	ⓓ	62	ⓐ	ⓑ	ⓒ	ⓓ	82	ⓐ	ⓑ	ⓒ	ⓓ
3	ⓐ	ⓑ	ⓒ	ⓓ	23	ⓐ	ⓑ	ⓒ		43	ⓐ	ⓑ	ⓒ	ⓓ	63	ⓐ	ⓑ	ⓒ	ⓓ	83	ⓐ	ⓑ	ⓒ	ⓓ
4	ⓐ	ⓑ	ⓒ	ⓓ	24	ⓐ	ⓑ	ⓒ		44	ⓐ	ⓑ	ⓒ	ⓓ	64	ⓐ	ⓑ	ⓒ	ⓓ	84	ⓐ	ⓑ	ⓒ	ⓓ
5	ⓐ	ⓑ	ⓒ	ⓓ	25	ⓐ	ⓑ	ⓒ		45	ⓐ	ⓑ	ⓒ	ⓓ	65	ⓐ	ⓑ	ⓒ	ⓓ	85	ⓐ	ⓑ	ⓒ	ⓓ
6	ⓐ	ⓑ	ⓒ	ⓓ	26	ⓐ	ⓑ	ⓒ		46	ⓐ	ⓑ	ⓒ	ⓓ	66	ⓐ	ⓑ	ⓒ	ⓓ	86	ⓐ	ⓑ	ⓒ	ⓓ
7	ⓐ	ⓑ	ⓒ		27	ⓐ	ⓑ	ⓒ		47	ⓐ	ⓑ	ⓒ	ⓓ	67	ⓐ	ⓑ	ⓒ	ⓓ	87	ⓐ	ⓑ	ⓒ	ⓓ
8	ⓐ	ⓑ	ⓒ		28	ⓐ	ⓑ	ⓒ		48	ⓐ	ⓑ	ⓒ	ⓓ	68	ⓐ	ⓑ	ⓒ	ⓓ	88	ⓐ	ⓑ	ⓒ	ⓓ
9	ⓐ	ⓑ	ⓒ		29	ⓐ	ⓑ	ⓒ		49	ⓐ	ⓑ	ⓒ	ⓓ	69	ⓐ	ⓑ	ⓒ	ⓓ	89	ⓐ	ⓑ	ⓒ	ⓓ
10	ⓐ	ⓑ	ⓒ		30	ⓐ	ⓑ	ⓒ		50	ⓐ	ⓑ	ⓒ	ⓓ	70	ⓐ	ⓑ	ⓒ	ⓓ	90	ⓐ	ⓑ	ⓒ	ⓓ
11	ⓐ	ⓑ	ⓒ		31	ⓐ	ⓑ	ⓒ		51	ⓐ	ⓑ	ⓒ	ⓓ	71	ⓐ	ⓑ	ⓒ	ⓓ	91	ⓐ	ⓑ	ⓒ	ⓓ
12	ⓐ	ⓑ	ⓒ		32	ⓐ	ⓑ	ⓒ	ⓓ	52	ⓐ	ⓑ	ⓒ	ⓓ	72	ⓐ	ⓑ	ⓒ	ⓓ	92	ⓐ	ⓑ	ⓒ	ⓓ
13	ⓐ	ⓑ	ⓒ		33	ⓐ	ⓑ	ⓒ	ⓓ	53	ⓐ	ⓑ	ⓒ	ⓓ	73	ⓐ	ⓑ	ⓒ	ⓓ	93	ⓐ	ⓑ	ⓒ	ⓓ
14	ⓐ	ⓑ	ⓒ		34	ⓐ	ⓑ	ⓒ	ⓓ	54	ⓐ	ⓑ	ⓒ	ⓓ	74	ⓐ	ⓑ	ⓒ	ⓓ	94	ⓐ	ⓑ	ⓒ	ⓓ
15	ⓐ	ⓑ	ⓒ		35	ⓐ	ⓑ	ⓒ	ⓓ	55	ⓐ	ⓑ	ⓒ	ⓓ	75	ⓐ	ⓑ	ⓒ	ⓓ	95	ⓐ	ⓑ	ⓒ	ⓓ
16	ⓐ	ⓑ	ⓒ		36	ⓐ	ⓑ	ⓒ	ⓓ	56	ⓐ	ⓑ	ⓒ	ⓓ	76	ⓐ	ⓑ	ⓒ	ⓓ	96	ⓐ	ⓑ	ⓒ	ⓓ
17	ⓐ	ⓑ	ⓒ		37	ⓐ	ⓑ	ⓒ	ⓓ	57	ⓐ	ⓑ	ⓒ	ⓓ	77	ⓐ	ⓑ	ⓒ	ⓓ	97	ⓐ	ⓑ	ⓒ	ⓓ
18	ⓐ	ⓑ	ⓒ		38	ⓐ	ⓑ	ⓒ	ⓓ	58	ⓐ	ⓑ	ⓒ	ⓓ	78	ⓐ	ⓑ	ⓒ	ⓓ	98	ⓐ	ⓑ	ⓒ	ⓓ
19	ⓐ	ⓑ	ⓒ		39	ⓐ	ⓑ	ⓒ	ⓓ	59	ⓐ	ⓑ	ⓒ	ⓓ	79	ⓐ	ⓑ	ⓒ	ⓓ	99	ⓐ	ⓑ	ⓒ	ⓓ
20	ⓐ	ⓑ	ⓒ		40	ⓐ	ⓑ	ⓒ	ⓓ	60	ⓐ	ⓑ	ⓒ	ⓓ	80	ⓐ	ⓑ	ⓒ	ⓓ	100	ⓐ	ⓑ	ⓒ	ⓓ

READING COMPREHENSION (PART 5~7)

NO	ANSWER				NO	ANSWER				NO	ANSWER				NO	ANSWER				NO	ANSWER			
	A	B	C	D		A	B	C	D		A	B	C	D		A	B	C	D		A	B	C	D
101	ⓐ	ⓑ	ⓒ	ⓓ	121	ⓐ	ⓑ	ⓒ	ⓓ	141	ⓐ	ⓑ	ⓒ	ⓓ	161	ⓐ	ⓑ	ⓒ	ⓓ	181	ⓐ	ⓑ	ⓒ	ⓓ
102	ⓐ	ⓑ	ⓒ	ⓓ	122	ⓐ	ⓑ	ⓒ	ⓓ	142	ⓐ	ⓑ	ⓒ	ⓓ	162	ⓐ	ⓑ	ⓒ	ⓓ	182	ⓐ	ⓑ	ⓒ	ⓓ
103	ⓐ	ⓑ	ⓒ	ⓓ	123	ⓐ	ⓑ	ⓒ	ⓓ	143	ⓐ	ⓑ	ⓒ	ⓓ	163	ⓐ	ⓑ	ⓒ	ⓓ	183	ⓐ	ⓑ	ⓒ	ⓓ
104	ⓐ	ⓑ	ⓒ	ⓓ	124	ⓐ	ⓑ	ⓒ	ⓓ	144	ⓐ	ⓑ	ⓒ	ⓓ	164	ⓐ	ⓑ	ⓒ	ⓓ	184	ⓐ	ⓑ	ⓒ	ⓓ
105	ⓐ	ⓑ	ⓒ	ⓓ	125	ⓐ	ⓑ	ⓒ	ⓓ	145	ⓐ	ⓑ	ⓒ	ⓓ	165	ⓐ	ⓑ	ⓒ	ⓓ	185	ⓐ	ⓑ	ⓒ	ⓓ
106	ⓐ	ⓑ	ⓒ	ⓓ	126	ⓐ	ⓑ	ⓒ	ⓓ	146	ⓐ	ⓑ	ⓒ	ⓓ	166	ⓐ	ⓑ	ⓒ	ⓓ	186	ⓐ	ⓑ	ⓒ	ⓓ
107	ⓐ	ⓑ	ⓒ	ⓓ	127	ⓐ	ⓑ	ⓒ	ⓓ	147	ⓐ	ⓑ	ⓒ	ⓓ	167	ⓐ	ⓑ	ⓒ	ⓓ	187	ⓐ	ⓑ	ⓒ	ⓓ
108	ⓐ	ⓑ	ⓒ	ⓓ	128	ⓐ	ⓑ	ⓒ	ⓓ	148	ⓐ	ⓑ	ⓒ	ⓓ	168	ⓐ	ⓑ	ⓒ	ⓓ	188	ⓐ	ⓑ	ⓒ	ⓓ
109	ⓐ	ⓑ	ⓒ	ⓓ	129	ⓐ	ⓑ	ⓒ	ⓓ	149	ⓐ	ⓑ	ⓒ	ⓓ	169	ⓐ	ⓑ	ⓒ	ⓓ	189	ⓐ	ⓑ	ⓒ	ⓓ
110	ⓐ	ⓑ	ⓒ	ⓓ	130	ⓐ	ⓑ	ⓒ	ⓓ	150	ⓐ	ⓑ	ⓒ	ⓓ	170	ⓐ	ⓑ	ⓒ	ⓓ	190	ⓐ	ⓑ	ⓒ	ⓓ
111	ⓐ	ⓑ	ⓒ	ⓓ	131	ⓐ	ⓑ	ⓒ	ⓓ	151	ⓐ	ⓑ	ⓒ	ⓓ	171	ⓐ	ⓑ	ⓒ	ⓓ	191	ⓐ	ⓑ	ⓒ	ⓓ
112	ⓐ	ⓑ	ⓒ	ⓓ	132	ⓐ	ⓑ	ⓒ	ⓓ	152	ⓐ	ⓑ	ⓒ	ⓓ	172	ⓐ	ⓑ	ⓒ	ⓓ	192	ⓐ	ⓑ	ⓒ	ⓓ
113	ⓐ	ⓑ	ⓒ	ⓓ	133	ⓐ	ⓑ	ⓒ	ⓓ	153	ⓐ	ⓑ	ⓒ	ⓓ	173	ⓐ	ⓑ	ⓒ	ⓓ	193	ⓐ	ⓑ	ⓒ	ⓓ
114	ⓐ	ⓑ	ⓒ	ⓓ	134	ⓐ	ⓑ	ⓒ	ⓓ	154	ⓐ	ⓑ	ⓒ	ⓓ	174	ⓐ	ⓑ	ⓒ	ⓓ	194	ⓐ	ⓑ	ⓒ	ⓓ
115	ⓐ	ⓑ	ⓒ	ⓓ	135	ⓐ	ⓑ	ⓒ	ⓓ	155	ⓐ	ⓑ	ⓒ	ⓓ	175	ⓐ	ⓑ	ⓒ	ⓓ	195	ⓐ	ⓑ	ⓒ	ⓓ
116	ⓐ	ⓑ	ⓒ	ⓓ	136	ⓐ	ⓑ	ⓒ	ⓓ	156	ⓐ	ⓑ	ⓒ	ⓓ	176	ⓐ	ⓑ	ⓒ	ⓓ	196	ⓐ	ⓑ	ⓒ	ⓓ
117	ⓐ	ⓑ	ⓒ	ⓓ	137	ⓐ	ⓑ	ⓒ	ⓓ	157	ⓐ	ⓑ	ⓒ	ⓓ	177	ⓐ	ⓑ	ⓒ	ⓓ	197	ⓐ	ⓑ	ⓒ	ⓓ
118	ⓐ	ⓑ	ⓒ	ⓓ	138	ⓐ	ⓑ	ⓒ	ⓓ	158	ⓐ	ⓑ	ⓒ	ⓓ	178	ⓐ	ⓑ	ⓒ	ⓓ	198	ⓐ	ⓑ	ⓒ	ⓓ
119	ⓐ	ⓑ	ⓒ	ⓓ	139	ⓐ	ⓑ	ⓒ	ⓓ	159	ⓐ	ⓑ	ⓒ	ⓓ	179	ⓐ	ⓑ	ⓒ	ⓓ	199	ⓐ	ⓑ	ⓒ	ⓓ
120	ⓐ	ⓑ	ⓒ	ⓓ	140	ⓐ	ⓑ	ⓒ	ⓓ	160	ⓐ	ⓑ	ⓒ	ⓓ	180	ⓐ	ⓑ	ⓒ	ⓓ	200	ⓐ	ⓑ	ⓒ	ⓓ

ANSWER SHEET

시원스쿨 LAB

이름		테스트 회차		날짜	

LISTENING COMPREHENSION (PART 1~4)										READING COMPREHENSION (PART 5~7)									
NO	ANSWER A B C D	NO	ANSWER A B C D	NO	ANSWER A B C D	NO	ANSWER A B C D	NO	ANSWER A B C D	NO	ANSWER A B C D	NO	ANSWER A B C D	NO	ANSWER A B C D	NO	ANSWER A B C D	NO	ANSWER A B C D
1	ⓐ ⓑ ⓒ ⓓ	21	ⓐ ⓑ ⓒ	41	ⓐ ⓑ ⓒ ⓓ	61	ⓐ ⓑ ⓒ ⓓ	81	ⓐ ⓑ ⓒ ⓓ	101	ⓐ ⓑ ⓒ ⓓ	121	ⓐ ⓑ ⓒ ⓓ	141	ⓐ ⓑ ⓒ ⓓ	161	ⓐ ⓑ ⓒ ⓓ	181	ⓐ ⓑ ⓒ ⓓ
2	ⓐ ⓑ ⓒ ⓓ	22	ⓐ ⓑ ⓒ	42	ⓐ ⓑ ⓒ ⓓ	62	ⓐ ⓑ ⓒ ⓓ	82	ⓐ ⓑ ⓒ ⓓ	102	ⓐ ⓑ ⓒ ⓓ	122	ⓐ ⓑ ⓒ ⓓ	142	ⓐ ⓑ ⓒ ⓓ	162	ⓐ ⓑ ⓒ ⓓ	182	ⓐ ⓑ ⓒ ⓓ
3	ⓐ ⓑ ⓒ ⓓ	23	ⓐ ⓑ ⓒ	43	ⓐ ⓑ ⓒ ⓓ	63	ⓐ ⓑ ⓒ ⓓ	83	ⓐ ⓑ ⓒ ⓓ	103	ⓐ ⓑ ⓒ ⓓ	123	ⓐ ⓑ ⓒ ⓓ	143	ⓐ ⓑ ⓒ ⓓ	163	ⓐ ⓑ ⓒ ⓓ	183	ⓐ ⓑ ⓒ ⓓ
4	ⓐ ⓑ ⓒ ⓓ	24	ⓐ ⓑ ⓒ	44	ⓐ ⓑ ⓒ ⓓ	64	ⓐ ⓑ ⓒ ⓓ	84	ⓐ ⓑ ⓒ ⓓ	104	ⓐ ⓑ ⓒ ⓓ	124	ⓐ ⓑ ⓒ ⓓ	144	ⓐ ⓑ ⓒ ⓓ	164	ⓐ ⓑ ⓒ ⓓ	184	ⓐ ⓑ ⓒ ⓓ
5	ⓐ ⓑ ⓒ ⓓ	25	ⓐ ⓑ ⓒ	45	ⓐ ⓑ ⓒ ⓓ	65	ⓐ ⓑ ⓒ ⓓ	85	ⓐ ⓑ ⓒ ⓓ	105	ⓐ ⓑ ⓒ ⓓ	125	ⓐ ⓑ ⓒ ⓓ	145	ⓐ ⓑ ⓒ ⓓ	165	ⓐ ⓑ ⓒ ⓓ	185	ⓐ ⓑ ⓒ ⓓ
6	ⓐ ⓑ ⓒ ⓓ	26	ⓐ ⓑ ⓒ	46	ⓐ ⓑ ⓒ ⓓ	66	ⓐ ⓑ ⓒ ⓓ	86	ⓐ ⓑ ⓒ ⓓ	106	ⓐ ⓑ ⓒ ⓓ	126	ⓐ ⓑ ⓒ ⓓ	146	ⓐ ⓑ ⓒ ⓓ	166	ⓐ ⓑ ⓒ ⓓ	186	ⓐ ⓑ ⓒ ⓓ
7	ⓐ ⓑ ⓒ	27	ⓐ ⓑ ⓒ	47	ⓐ ⓑ ⓒ ⓓ	67	ⓐ ⓑ ⓒ ⓓ	87	ⓐ ⓑ ⓒ ⓓ	107	ⓐ ⓑ ⓒ ⓓ	127	ⓐ ⓑ ⓒ ⓓ	147	ⓐ ⓑ ⓒ ⓓ	167	ⓐ ⓑ ⓒ ⓓ	187	ⓐ ⓑ ⓒ ⓓ
8	ⓐ ⓑ ⓒ	28	ⓐ ⓑ ⓒ	48	ⓐ ⓑ ⓒ ⓓ	68	ⓐ ⓑ ⓒ ⓓ	88	ⓐ ⓑ ⓒ ⓓ	108	ⓐ ⓑ ⓒ ⓓ	128	ⓐ ⓑ ⓒ ⓓ	148	ⓐ ⓑ ⓒ ⓓ	168	ⓐ ⓑ ⓒ ⓓ	188	ⓐ ⓑ ⓒ ⓓ
9	ⓐ ⓑ ⓒ	29	ⓐ ⓑ ⓒ	49	ⓐ ⓑ ⓒ ⓓ	69	ⓐ ⓑ ⓒ ⓓ	89	ⓐ ⓑ ⓒ ⓓ	109	ⓐ ⓑ ⓒ ⓓ	129	ⓐ ⓑ ⓒ ⓓ	149	ⓐ ⓑ ⓒ ⓓ	169	ⓐ ⓑ ⓒ ⓓ	189	ⓐ ⓑ ⓒ ⓓ
10	ⓐ ⓑ ⓒ	30	ⓐ ⓑ ⓒ	50	ⓐ ⓑ ⓒ ⓓ	70	ⓐ ⓑ ⓒ ⓓ	90	ⓐ ⓑ ⓒ ⓓ	110	ⓐ ⓑ ⓒ ⓓ	130	ⓐ ⓑ ⓒ ⓓ	150	ⓐ ⓑ ⓒ ⓓ	170	ⓐ ⓑ ⓒ ⓓ	190	ⓐ ⓑ ⓒ ⓓ
11	ⓐ ⓑ ⓒ	31	ⓐ ⓑ ⓒ	51	ⓐ ⓑ ⓒ ⓓ	71	ⓐ ⓑ ⓒ ⓓ	91	ⓐ ⓑ ⓒ ⓓ	111	ⓐ ⓑ ⓒ ⓓ	131	ⓐ ⓑ ⓒ ⓓ	151	ⓐ ⓑ ⓒ ⓓ	171	ⓐ ⓑ ⓒ ⓓ	191	ⓐ ⓑ ⓒ ⓓ
12	ⓐ ⓑ ⓒ	32	ⓐ ⓑ ⓒ ⓓ	52	ⓐ ⓑ ⓒ ⓓ	72	ⓐ ⓑ ⓒ ⓓ	92	ⓐ ⓑ ⓒ ⓓ	112	ⓐ ⓑ ⓒ ⓓ	132	ⓐ ⓑ ⓒ ⓓ	152	ⓐ ⓑ ⓒ ⓓ	172	ⓐ ⓑ ⓒ ⓓ	192	ⓐ ⓑ ⓒ ⓓ
13	ⓐ ⓑ ⓒ	33	ⓐ ⓑ ⓒ ⓓ	53	ⓐ ⓑ ⓒ ⓓ	73	ⓐ ⓑ ⓒ ⓓ	93	ⓐ ⓑ ⓒ ⓓ	113	ⓐ ⓑ ⓒ ⓓ	133	ⓐ ⓑ ⓒ ⓓ	153	ⓐ ⓑ ⓒ ⓓ	173	ⓐ ⓑ ⓒ ⓓ	193	ⓐ ⓑ ⓒ ⓓ
14	ⓐ ⓑ ⓒ	34	ⓐ ⓑ ⓒ ⓓ	54	ⓐ ⓑ ⓒ ⓓ	74	ⓐ ⓑ ⓒ ⓓ	94	ⓐ ⓑ ⓒ ⓓ	114	ⓐ ⓑ ⓒ ⓓ	134	ⓐ ⓑ ⓒ ⓓ	154	ⓐ ⓑ ⓒ ⓓ	174	ⓐ ⓑ ⓒ ⓓ	194	ⓐ ⓑ ⓒ ⓓ
15	ⓐ ⓑ ⓒ	35	ⓐ ⓑ ⓒ ⓓ	55	ⓐ ⓑ ⓒ ⓓ	75	ⓐ ⓑ ⓒ ⓓ	95	ⓐ ⓑ ⓒ ⓓ	115	ⓐ ⓑ ⓒ ⓓ	135	ⓐ ⓑ ⓒ ⓓ	155	ⓐ ⓑ ⓒ ⓓ	175	ⓐ ⓑ ⓒ ⓓ	195	ⓐ ⓑ ⓒ ⓓ
16	ⓐ ⓑ ⓒ	36	ⓐ ⓑ ⓒ ⓓ	56	ⓐ ⓑ ⓒ ⓓ	76	ⓐ ⓑ ⓒ ⓓ	96	ⓐ ⓑ ⓒ ⓓ	116	ⓐ ⓑ ⓒ ⓓ	136	ⓐ ⓑ ⓒ ⓓ	156	ⓐ ⓑ ⓒ ⓓ	176	ⓐ ⓑ ⓒ ⓓ	196	ⓐ ⓑ ⓒ ⓓ
17	ⓐ ⓑ ⓒ	37	ⓐ ⓑ ⓒ ⓓ	57	ⓐ ⓑ ⓒ ⓓ	77	ⓐ ⓑ ⓒ ⓓ	97	ⓐ ⓑ ⓒ ⓓ	117	ⓐ ⓑ ⓒ ⓓ	137	ⓐ ⓑ ⓒ ⓓ	157	ⓐ ⓑ ⓒ ⓓ	177	ⓐ ⓑ ⓒ ⓓ	197	ⓐ ⓑ ⓒ ⓓ
18	ⓐ ⓑ ⓒ	38	ⓐ ⓑ ⓒ ⓓ	58	ⓐ ⓑ ⓒ ⓓ	78	ⓐ ⓑ ⓒ ⓓ	98	ⓐ ⓑ ⓒ ⓓ	118	ⓐ ⓑ ⓒ ⓓ	138	ⓐ ⓑ ⓒ ⓓ	158	ⓐ ⓑ ⓒ ⓓ	178	ⓐ ⓑ ⓒ ⓓ	198	ⓐ ⓑ ⓒ ⓓ
19	ⓐ ⓑ ⓒ	39	ⓐ ⓑ ⓒ ⓓ	59	ⓐ ⓑ ⓒ ⓓ	79	ⓐ ⓑ ⓒ ⓓ	99	ⓐ ⓑ ⓒ ⓓ	119	ⓐ ⓑ ⓒ ⓓ	139	ⓐ ⓑ ⓒ ⓓ	159	ⓐ ⓑ ⓒ ⓓ	179	ⓐ ⓑ ⓒ ⓓ	199	ⓐ ⓑ ⓒ ⓓ
20	ⓐ ⓑ ⓒ	40	ⓐ ⓑ ⓒ ⓓ	60	ⓐ ⓑ ⓒ ⓓ	80	ⓐ ⓑ ⓒ ⓓ	100	ⓐ ⓑ ⓒ ⓓ	120	ⓐ ⓑ ⓒ ⓓ	140	ⓐ ⓑ ⓒ ⓓ	160	ⓐ ⓑ ⓒ ⓓ	180	ⓐ ⓑ ⓒ ⓓ	200	ⓐ ⓑ ⓒ ⓓ

ANSWER SHEET

시원스쿨 LAB

이름		테스트 회차		날짜	

LISTENING COMPREHENSION (PART 1~4)

NO	ANSWER A B C D	NO	ANSWER A B C D	NO	ANSWER A B C D	NO	ANSWER A B C D	NO	ANSWER A B C D
1	ⓐ ⓑ ⓒ ⓓ	21	ⓐ ⓑ ⓒ	41	ⓐ ⓑ ⓒ ⓓ	61	ⓐ ⓑ ⓒ ⓓ	81	ⓐ ⓑ ⓒ ⓓ
2	ⓐ ⓑ ⓒ ⓓ	22	ⓐ ⓑ ⓒ	42	ⓐ ⓑ ⓒ ⓓ	62	ⓐ ⓑ ⓒ ⓓ	82	ⓐ ⓑ ⓒ ⓓ
3	ⓐ ⓑ ⓒ ⓓ	23	ⓐ ⓑ ⓒ	43	ⓐ ⓑ ⓒ ⓓ	63	ⓐ ⓑ ⓒ ⓓ	83	ⓐ ⓑ ⓒ ⓓ
4	ⓐ ⓑ ⓒ ⓓ	24	ⓐ ⓑ ⓒ	44	ⓐ ⓑ ⓒ ⓓ	64	ⓐ ⓑ ⓒ ⓓ	84	ⓐ ⓑ ⓒ ⓓ
5	ⓐ ⓑ ⓒ ⓓ	25	ⓐ ⓑ ⓒ	45	ⓐ ⓑ ⓒ ⓓ	65	ⓐ ⓑ ⓒ ⓓ	85	ⓐ ⓑ ⓒ ⓓ
6	ⓐ ⓑ ⓒ ⓓ	26	ⓐ ⓑ ⓒ	46	ⓐ ⓑ ⓒ ⓓ	66	ⓐ ⓑ ⓒ ⓓ	86	ⓐ ⓑ ⓒ ⓓ
7	ⓐ ⓑ ⓒ	27	ⓐ ⓑ ⓒ	47	ⓐ ⓑ ⓒ ⓓ	67	ⓐ ⓑ ⓒ ⓓ	87	ⓐ ⓑ ⓒ ⓓ
8	ⓐ ⓑ ⓒ	28	ⓐ ⓑ ⓒ	48	ⓐ ⓑ ⓒ ⓓ	68	ⓐ ⓑ ⓒ ⓓ	88	ⓐ ⓑ ⓒ ⓓ
9	ⓐ ⓑ ⓒ	29	ⓐ ⓑ ⓒ	49	ⓐ ⓑ ⓒ ⓓ	69	ⓐ ⓑ ⓒ ⓓ	89	ⓐ ⓑ ⓒ ⓓ
10	ⓐ ⓑ ⓒ	30	ⓐ ⓑ ⓒ	50	ⓐ ⓑ ⓒ ⓓ	70	ⓐ ⓑ ⓒ ⓓ	90	ⓐ ⓑ ⓒ ⓓ
11	ⓐ ⓑ ⓒ	31	ⓐ ⓑ ⓒ	51	ⓐ ⓑ ⓒ ⓓ	71	ⓐ ⓑ ⓒ ⓓ	91	ⓐ ⓑ ⓒ ⓓ
12	ⓐ ⓑ ⓒ	32	ⓐ ⓑ ⓒ ⓓ	52	ⓐ ⓑ ⓒ ⓓ	72	ⓐ ⓑ ⓒ ⓓ	92	ⓐ ⓑ ⓒ ⓓ
13	ⓐ ⓑ ⓒ	33	ⓐ ⓑ ⓒ ⓓ	53	ⓐ ⓑ ⓒ ⓓ	73	ⓐ ⓑ ⓒ ⓓ	93	ⓐ ⓑ ⓒ ⓓ
14	ⓐ ⓑ ⓒ	34	ⓐ ⓑ ⓒ ⓓ	54	ⓐ ⓑ ⓒ ⓓ	74	ⓐ ⓑ ⓒ ⓓ	94	ⓐ ⓑ ⓒ ⓓ
15	ⓐ ⓑ ⓒ	35	ⓐ ⓑ ⓒ ⓓ	55	ⓐ ⓑ ⓒ ⓓ	75	ⓐ ⓑ ⓒ ⓓ	95	ⓐ ⓑ ⓒ ⓓ
16	ⓐ ⓑ ⓒ	36	ⓐ ⓑ ⓒ ⓓ	56	ⓐ ⓑ ⓒ ⓓ	76	ⓐ ⓑ ⓒ ⓓ	96	ⓐ ⓑ ⓒ ⓓ
17	ⓐ ⓑ ⓒ	37	ⓐ ⓑ ⓒ ⓓ	57	ⓐ ⓑ ⓒ ⓓ	77	ⓐ ⓑ ⓒ ⓓ	97	ⓐ ⓑ ⓒ ⓓ
18	ⓐ ⓑ ⓒ	38	ⓐ ⓑ ⓒ ⓓ	58	ⓐ ⓑ ⓒ ⓓ	78	ⓐ ⓑ ⓒ ⓓ	98	ⓐ ⓑ ⓒ ⓓ
19	ⓐ ⓑ ⓒ	39	ⓐ ⓑ ⓒ ⓓ	59	ⓐ ⓑ ⓒ ⓓ	79	ⓐ ⓑ ⓒ ⓓ	99	ⓐ ⓑ ⓒ ⓓ
20	ⓐ ⓑ ⓒ	40	ⓐ ⓑ ⓒ ⓓ	60	ⓐ ⓑ ⓒ ⓓ	80	ⓐ ⓑ ⓒ ⓓ	100	ⓐ ⓑ ⓒ ⓓ

READING COMPREHENSION (PART 5~7)

NO	ANSWER A B C D	NO	ANSWER A B C D	NO	ANSWER A B C D	NO	ANSWER A B C D	NO	ANSWER A B C D
101	ⓐ ⓑ ⓒ ⓓ	121	ⓐ ⓑ ⓒ ⓓ	141	ⓐ ⓑ ⓒ ⓓ	161	ⓐ ⓑ ⓒ ⓓ	181	ⓐ ⓑ ⓒ ⓓ
102	ⓐ ⓑ ⓒ ⓓ	122	ⓐ ⓑ ⓒ ⓓ	142	ⓐ ⓑ ⓒ ⓓ	162	ⓐ ⓑ ⓒ ⓓ	182	ⓐ ⓑ ⓒ ⓓ
103	ⓐ ⓑ ⓒ ⓓ	123	ⓐ ⓑ ⓒ ⓓ	143	ⓐ ⓑ ⓒ ⓓ	163	ⓐ ⓑ ⓒ ⓓ	183	ⓐ ⓑ ⓒ ⓓ
104	ⓐ ⓑ ⓒ ⓓ	124	ⓐ ⓑ ⓒ ⓓ	144	ⓐ ⓑ ⓒ ⓓ	164	ⓐ ⓑ ⓒ ⓓ	184	ⓐ ⓑ ⓒ ⓓ
105	ⓐ ⓑ ⓒ ⓓ	125	ⓐ ⓑ ⓒ ⓓ	145	ⓐ ⓑ ⓒ ⓓ	165	ⓐ ⓑ ⓒ ⓓ	185	ⓐ ⓑ ⓒ ⓓ
106	ⓐ ⓑ ⓒ ⓓ	126	ⓐ ⓑ ⓒ ⓓ	146	ⓐ ⓑ ⓒ ⓓ	166	ⓐ ⓑ ⓒ ⓓ	186	ⓐ ⓑ ⓒ ⓓ
107	ⓐ ⓑ ⓒ ⓓ	127	ⓐ ⓑ ⓒ ⓓ	147	ⓐ ⓑ ⓒ ⓓ	167	ⓐ ⓑ ⓒ ⓓ	187	ⓐ ⓑ ⓒ ⓓ
108	ⓐ ⓑ ⓒ ⓓ	128	ⓐ ⓑ ⓒ ⓓ	148	ⓐ ⓑ ⓒ ⓓ	168	ⓐ ⓑ ⓒ ⓓ	188	ⓐ ⓑ ⓒ ⓓ
109	ⓐ ⓑ ⓒ ⓓ	129	ⓐ ⓑ ⓒ ⓓ	149	ⓐ ⓑ ⓒ ⓓ	169	ⓐ ⓑ ⓒ ⓓ	189	ⓐ ⓑ ⓒ ⓓ
110	ⓐ ⓑ ⓒ ⓓ	130	ⓐ ⓑ ⓒ ⓓ	150	ⓐ ⓑ ⓒ ⓓ	170	ⓐ ⓑ ⓒ ⓓ	190	ⓐ ⓑ ⓒ ⓓ
111	ⓐ ⓑ ⓒ ⓓ	131	ⓐ ⓑ ⓒ ⓓ	151	ⓐ ⓑ ⓒ ⓓ	171	ⓐ ⓑ ⓒ ⓓ	191	ⓐ ⓑ ⓒ ⓓ
112	ⓐ ⓑ ⓒ ⓓ	132	ⓐ ⓑ ⓒ ⓓ	152	ⓐ ⓑ ⓒ ⓓ	172	ⓐ ⓑ ⓒ ⓓ	192	ⓐ ⓑ ⓒ ⓓ
113	ⓐ ⓑ ⓒ ⓓ	133	ⓐ ⓑ ⓒ ⓓ	153	ⓐ ⓑ ⓒ ⓓ	173	ⓐ ⓑ ⓒ ⓓ	193	ⓐ ⓑ ⓒ ⓓ
114	ⓐ ⓑ ⓒ ⓓ	134	ⓐ ⓑ ⓒ ⓓ	154	ⓐ ⓑ ⓒ ⓓ	174	ⓐ ⓑ ⓒ ⓓ	194	ⓐ ⓑ ⓒ ⓓ
115	ⓐ ⓑ ⓒ ⓓ	135	ⓐ ⓑ ⓒ ⓓ	155	ⓐ ⓑ ⓒ ⓓ	175	ⓐ ⓑ ⓒ ⓓ	195	ⓐ ⓑ ⓒ ⓓ
116	ⓐ ⓑ ⓒ ⓓ	136	ⓐ ⓑ ⓒ ⓓ	156	ⓐ ⓑ ⓒ ⓓ	176	ⓐ ⓑ ⓒ ⓓ	196	ⓐ ⓑ ⓒ ⓓ
117	ⓐ ⓑ ⓒ ⓓ	137	ⓐ ⓑ ⓒ ⓓ	157	ⓐ ⓑ ⓒ ⓓ	177	ⓐ ⓑ ⓒ ⓓ	197	ⓐ ⓑ ⓒ ⓓ
118	ⓐ ⓑ ⓒ ⓓ	138	ⓐ ⓑ ⓒ ⓓ	158	ⓐ ⓑ ⓒ ⓓ	178	ⓐ ⓑ ⓒ ⓓ	198	ⓐ ⓑ ⓒ ⓓ
119	ⓐ ⓑ ⓒ ⓓ	139	ⓐ ⓑ ⓒ ⓓ	159	ⓐ ⓑ ⓒ ⓓ	179	ⓐ ⓑ ⓒ ⓓ	199	ⓐ ⓑ ⓒ ⓓ
120	ⓐ ⓑ ⓒ ⓓ	140	ⓐ ⓑ ⓒ ⓓ	160	ⓐ ⓑ ⓒ ⓓ	180	ⓐ ⓑ ⓒ ⓓ	200	ⓐ ⓑ ⓒ ⓓ

ANSWER SHEET

시원스쿨 LAB

이름		테스트 회차		날짜	

LISTENING COMPREHENSION (PART 1~4)

NO	ANSWER A B C D	NO	ANSWER A B C D	NO	ANSWER A B C D	NO	ANSWER A B C D	NO	ANSWER A B C D
1	ⓐ ⓑ ⓒ ⓓ	21	ⓐ ⓑ ⓒ	41	ⓐ ⓑ ⓒ ⓓ	61	ⓐ ⓑ ⓒ ⓓ	81	ⓐ ⓑ ⓒ ⓓ
2	ⓐ ⓑ ⓒ ⓓ	22	ⓐ ⓑ ⓒ	42	ⓐ ⓑ ⓒ ⓓ	62	ⓐ ⓑ ⓒ ⓓ	82	ⓐ ⓑ ⓒ ⓓ
3	ⓐ ⓑ ⓒ ⓓ	23	ⓐ ⓑ ⓒ	43	ⓐ ⓑ ⓒ ⓓ	63	ⓐ ⓑ ⓒ ⓓ	83	ⓐ ⓑ ⓒ ⓓ
4	ⓐ ⓑ ⓒ ⓓ	24	ⓐ ⓑ ⓒ	44	ⓐ ⓑ ⓒ ⓓ	64	ⓐ ⓑ ⓒ ⓓ	84	ⓐ ⓑ ⓒ ⓓ
5	ⓐ ⓑ ⓒ ⓓ	25	ⓐ ⓑ ⓒ	45	ⓐ ⓑ ⓒ ⓓ	65	ⓐ ⓑ ⓒ ⓓ	85	ⓐ ⓑ ⓒ ⓓ
6	ⓐ ⓑ ⓒ ⓓ	26	ⓐ ⓑ ⓒ	46	ⓐ ⓑ ⓒ ⓓ	66	ⓐ ⓑ ⓒ ⓓ	86	ⓐ ⓑ ⓒ ⓓ
7	ⓐ ⓑ ⓒ	27	ⓐ ⓑ ⓒ	47	ⓐ ⓑ ⓒ ⓓ	67	ⓐ ⓑ ⓒ ⓓ	87	ⓐ ⓑ ⓒ ⓓ
8	ⓐ ⓑ ⓒ	28	ⓐ ⓑ ⓒ	48	ⓐ ⓑ ⓒ ⓓ	68	ⓐ ⓑ ⓒ ⓓ	88	ⓐ ⓑ ⓒ ⓓ
9	ⓐ ⓑ ⓒ	29	ⓐ ⓑ ⓒ	49	ⓐ ⓑ ⓒ ⓓ	69	ⓐ ⓑ ⓒ ⓓ	89	ⓐ ⓑ ⓒ ⓓ
10	ⓐ ⓑ ⓒ	30	ⓐ ⓑ ⓒ	50	ⓐ ⓑ ⓒ ⓓ	70	ⓐ ⓑ ⓒ ⓓ	90	ⓐ ⓑ ⓒ ⓓ
11	ⓐ ⓑ ⓒ	31	ⓐ ⓑ ⓒ	51	ⓐ ⓑ ⓒ ⓓ	71	ⓐ ⓑ ⓒ ⓓ	91	ⓐ ⓑ ⓒ ⓓ
12	ⓐ ⓑ ⓒ	32	ⓐ ⓑ ⓒ ⓓ	52	ⓐ ⓑ ⓒ ⓓ	72	ⓐ ⓑ ⓒ ⓓ	92	ⓐ ⓑ ⓒ ⓓ
13	ⓐ ⓑ ⓒ	33	ⓐ ⓑ ⓒ ⓓ	53	ⓐ ⓑ ⓒ ⓓ	73	ⓐ ⓑ ⓒ ⓓ	93	ⓐ ⓑ ⓒ ⓓ
14	ⓐ ⓑ ⓒ	34	ⓐ ⓑ ⓒ ⓓ	54	ⓐ ⓑ ⓒ ⓓ	74	ⓐ ⓑ ⓒ ⓓ	94	ⓐ ⓑ ⓒ ⓓ
15	ⓐ ⓑ ⓒ	35	ⓐ ⓑ ⓒ ⓓ	55	ⓐ ⓑ ⓒ ⓓ	75	ⓐ ⓑ ⓒ ⓓ	95	ⓐ ⓑ ⓒ ⓓ
16	ⓐ ⓑ ⓒ	36	ⓐ ⓑ ⓒ ⓓ	56	ⓐ ⓑ ⓒ ⓓ	76	ⓐ ⓑ ⓒ ⓓ	96	ⓐ ⓑ ⓒ ⓓ
17	ⓐ ⓑ ⓒ	37	ⓐ ⓑ ⓒ ⓓ	57	ⓐ ⓑ ⓒ ⓓ	77	ⓐ ⓑ ⓒ ⓓ	97	ⓐ ⓑ ⓒ ⓓ
18	ⓐ ⓑ ⓒ	38	ⓐ ⓑ ⓒ ⓓ	58	ⓐ ⓑ ⓒ ⓓ	78	ⓐ ⓑ ⓒ ⓓ	98	ⓐ ⓑ ⓒ ⓓ
19	ⓐ ⓑ ⓒ	39	ⓐ ⓑ ⓒ ⓓ	59	ⓐ ⓑ ⓒ ⓓ	79	ⓐ ⓑ ⓒ ⓓ	99	ⓐ ⓑ ⓒ ⓓ
20	ⓐ ⓑ ⓒ	40	ⓐ ⓑ ⓒ ⓓ	60	ⓐ ⓑ ⓒ ⓓ	80	ⓐ ⓑ ⓒ ⓓ	100	ⓐ ⓑ ⓒ ⓓ

READING COMPREHENSION (PART 5~7)

NO	ANSWER A B C D	NO	ANSWER A B C D	NO	ANSWER A B C D	NO	ANSWER A B C D	NO	ANSWER A B C D
101	ⓐ ⓑ ⓒ ⓓ	121	ⓐ ⓑ ⓒ ⓓ	141	ⓐ ⓑ ⓒ ⓓ	161	ⓐ ⓑ ⓒ ⓓ	181	ⓐ ⓑ ⓒ ⓓ
102	ⓐ ⓑ ⓒ ⓓ	122	ⓐ ⓑ ⓒ ⓓ	142	ⓐ ⓑ ⓒ ⓓ	162	ⓐ ⓑ ⓒ ⓓ	182	ⓐ ⓑ ⓒ ⓓ
103	ⓐ ⓑ ⓒ ⓓ	123	ⓐ ⓑ ⓒ ⓓ	143	ⓐ ⓑ ⓒ ⓓ	163	ⓐ ⓑ ⓒ ⓓ	183	ⓐ ⓑ ⓒ ⓓ
104	ⓐ ⓑ ⓒ ⓓ	124	ⓐ ⓑ ⓒ ⓓ	144	ⓐ ⓑ ⓒ ⓓ	164	ⓐ ⓑ ⓒ ⓓ	184	ⓐ ⓑ ⓒ ⓓ
105	ⓐ ⓑ ⓒ ⓓ	125	ⓐ ⓑ ⓒ ⓓ	145	ⓐ ⓑ ⓒ ⓓ	165	ⓐ ⓑ ⓒ ⓓ	185	ⓐ ⓑ ⓒ ⓓ
106	ⓐ ⓑ ⓒ ⓓ	126	ⓐ ⓑ ⓒ ⓓ	146	ⓐ ⓑ ⓒ ⓓ	166	ⓐ ⓑ ⓒ ⓓ	186	ⓐ ⓑ ⓒ ⓓ
107	ⓐ ⓑ ⓒ ⓓ	127	ⓐ ⓑ ⓒ ⓓ	147	ⓐ ⓑ ⓒ ⓓ	167	ⓐ ⓑ ⓒ ⓓ	187	ⓐ ⓑ ⓒ ⓓ
108	ⓐ ⓑ ⓒ ⓓ	128	ⓐ ⓑ ⓒ ⓓ	148	ⓐ ⓑ ⓒ ⓓ	168	ⓐ ⓑ ⓒ ⓓ	188	ⓐ ⓑ ⓒ ⓓ
109	ⓐ ⓑ ⓒ ⓓ	129	ⓐ ⓑ ⓒ ⓓ	149	ⓐ ⓑ ⓒ ⓓ	169	ⓐ ⓑ ⓒ ⓓ	189	ⓐ ⓑ ⓒ ⓓ
110	ⓐ ⓑ ⓒ ⓓ	130	ⓐ ⓑ ⓒ ⓓ	150	ⓐ ⓑ ⓒ ⓓ	170	ⓐ ⓑ ⓒ ⓓ	190	ⓐ ⓑ ⓒ ⓓ
111	ⓐ ⓑ ⓒ ⓓ	131	ⓐ ⓑ ⓒ ⓓ	151	ⓐ ⓑ ⓒ ⓓ	171	ⓐ ⓑ ⓒ ⓓ	191	ⓐ ⓑ ⓒ ⓓ
112	ⓐ ⓑ ⓒ ⓓ	132	ⓐ ⓑ ⓒ ⓓ	152	ⓐ ⓑ ⓒ ⓓ	172	ⓐ ⓑ ⓒ ⓓ	192	ⓐ ⓑ ⓒ ⓓ
113	ⓐ ⓑ ⓒ ⓓ	133	ⓐ ⓑ ⓒ ⓓ	153	ⓐ ⓑ ⓒ ⓓ	173	ⓐ ⓑ ⓒ ⓓ	193	ⓐ ⓑ ⓒ ⓓ
114	ⓐ ⓑ ⓒ ⓓ	134	ⓐ ⓑ ⓒ ⓓ	154	ⓐ ⓑ ⓒ ⓓ	174	ⓐ ⓑ ⓒ ⓓ	194	ⓐ ⓑ ⓒ ⓓ
115	ⓐ ⓑ ⓒ ⓓ	135	ⓐ ⓑ ⓒ ⓓ	155	ⓐ ⓑ ⓒ ⓓ	175	ⓐ ⓑ ⓒ ⓓ	195	ⓐ ⓑ ⓒ ⓓ
116	ⓐ ⓑ ⓒ ⓓ	136	ⓐ ⓑ ⓒ ⓓ	156	ⓐ ⓑ ⓒ ⓓ	176	ⓐ ⓑ ⓒ ⓓ	196	ⓐ ⓑ ⓒ ⓓ
117	ⓐ ⓑ ⓒ ⓓ	137	ⓐ ⓑ ⓒ ⓓ	157	ⓐ ⓑ ⓒ ⓓ	177	ⓐ ⓑ ⓒ ⓓ	197	ⓐ ⓑ ⓒ ⓓ
118	ⓐ ⓑ ⓒ ⓓ	138	ⓐ ⓑ ⓒ ⓓ	158	ⓐ ⓑ ⓒ ⓓ	178	ⓐ ⓑ ⓒ ⓓ	198	ⓐ ⓑ ⓒ ⓓ
119	ⓐ ⓑ ⓒ ⓓ	139	ⓐ ⓑ ⓒ ⓓ	159	ⓐ ⓑ ⓒ ⓓ	179	ⓐ ⓑ ⓒ ⓓ	199	ⓐ ⓑ ⓒ ⓓ
120	ⓐ ⓑ ⓒ ⓓ	140	ⓐ ⓑ ⓒ ⓓ	160	ⓐ ⓑ ⓒ ⓓ	180	ⓐ ⓑ ⓒ ⓓ	200	ⓐ ⓑ ⓒ ⓓ

ANSWER SHEET

시원스쿨 LAB

이름		테스트 회차		날짜	

LISTENING COMPREHENSION (PART 1~4)

NO	ANSWER A B C D	NO	ANSWER A B C D	NO	ANSWER A B C D	NO	ANSWER A B C D	NO	ANSWER A B C D
1	ⓐ ⓑ ⓒ ⓓ	21	ⓐ ⓑ ⓒ	41	ⓐ ⓑ ⓒ ⓓ	61	ⓐ ⓑ ⓒ ⓓ	81	ⓐ ⓑ ⓒ ⓓ
2	ⓐ ⓑ ⓒ ⓓ	22	ⓐ ⓑ ⓒ	42	ⓐ ⓑ ⓒ ⓓ	62	ⓐ ⓑ ⓒ ⓓ	82	ⓐ ⓑ ⓒ ⓓ
3	ⓐ ⓑ ⓒ ⓓ	23	ⓐ ⓑ ⓒ	43	ⓐ ⓑ ⓒ ⓓ	63	ⓐ ⓑ ⓒ ⓓ	83	ⓐ ⓑ ⓒ ⓓ
4	ⓐ ⓑ ⓒ ⓓ	24	ⓐ ⓑ ⓒ	44	ⓐ ⓑ ⓒ ⓓ	64	ⓐ ⓑ ⓒ ⓓ	84	ⓐ ⓑ ⓒ ⓓ
5	ⓐ ⓑ ⓒ ⓓ	25	ⓐ ⓑ ⓒ	45	ⓐ ⓑ ⓒ ⓓ	65	ⓐ ⓑ ⓒ ⓓ	85	ⓐ ⓑ ⓒ ⓓ
6	ⓐ ⓑ ⓒ ⓓ	26	ⓐ ⓑ ⓒ	46	ⓐ ⓑ ⓒ ⓓ	66	ⓐ ⓑ ⓒ ⓓ	86	ⓐ ⓑ ⓒ ⓓ
7	ⓐ ⓑ ⓒ	27	ⓐ ⓑ ⓒ	47	ⓐ ⓑ ⓒ ⓓ	67	ⓐ ⓑ ⓒ ⓓ	87	ⓐ ⓑ ⓒ ⓓ
8	ⓐ ⓑ ⓒ	28	ⓐ ⓑ ⓒ	48	ⓐ ⓑ ⓒ ⓓ	68	ⓐ ⓑ ⓒ ⓓ	88	ⓐ ⓑ ⓒ ⓓ
9	ⓐ ⓑ ⓒ	29	ⓐ ⓑ ⓒ	49	ⓐ ⓑ ⓒ ⓓ	69	ⓐ ⓑ ⓒ ⓓ	89	ⓐ ⓑ ⓒ ⓓ
10	ⓐ ⓑ ⓒ	30	ⓐ ⓑ ⓒ	50	ⓐ ⓑ ⓒ ⓓ	70	ⓐ ⓑ ⓒ ⓓ	90	ⓐ ⓑ ⓒ ⓓ
11	ⓐ ⓑ ⓒ	31	ⓐ ⓑ ⓒ	51	ⓐ ⓑ ⓒ ⓓ	71	ⓐ ⓑ ⓒ ⓓ	91	ⓐ ⓑ ⓒ ⓓ
12	ⓐ ⓑ ⓒ	32	ⓐ ⓑ ⓒ ⓓ	52	ⓐ ⓑ ⓒ ⓓ	72	ⓐ ⓑ ⓒ ⓓ	92	ⓐ ⓑ ⓒ ⓓ
13	ⓐ ⓑ ⓒ	33	ⓐ ⓑ ⓒ ⓓ	53	ⓐ ⓑ ⓒ ⓓ	73	ⓐ ⓑ ⓒ ⓓ	93	ⓐ ⓑ ⓒ ⓓ
14	ⓐ ⓑ ⓒ	34	ⓐ ⓑ ⓒ ⓓ	54	ⓐ ⓑ ⓒ ⓓ	74	ⓐ ⓑ ⓒ ⓓ	94	ⓐ ⓑ ⓒ ⓓ
15	ⓐ ⓑ ⓒ	35	ⓐ ⓑ ⓒ ⓓ	55	ⓐ ⓑ ⓒ ⓓ	75	ⓐ ⓑ ⓒ ⓓ	95	ⓐ ⓑ ⓒ ⓓ
16	ⓐ ⓑ ⓒ	36	ⓐ ⓑ ⓒ ⓓ	56	ⓐ ⓑ ⓒ ⓓ	76	ⓐ ⓑ ⓒ ⓓ	96	ⓐ ⓑ ⓒ ⓓ
17	ⓐ ⓑ ⓒ	37	ⓐ ⓑ ⓒ ⓓ	57	ⓐ ⓑ ⓒ ⓓ	77	ⓐ ⓑ ⓒ ⓓ	97	ⓐ ⓑ ⓒ ⓓ
18	ⓐ ⓑ ⓒ	38	ⓐ ⓑ ⓒ ⓓ	58	ⓐ ⓑ ⓒ ⓓ	78	ⓐ ⓑ ⓒ ⓓ	98	ⓐ ⓑ ⓒ ⓓ
19	ⓐ ⓑ ⓒ	39	ⓐ ⓑ ⓒ ⓓ	59	ⓐ ⓑ ⓒ ⓓ	79	ⓐ ⓑ ⓒ ⓓ	99	ⓐ ⓑ ⓒ ⓓ
20	ⓐ ⓑ ⓒ	40	ⓐ ⓑ ⓒ ⓓ	60	ⓐ ⓑ ⓒ ⓓ	80	ⓐ ⓑ ⓒ ⓓ	100	ⓐ ⓑ ⓒ ⓓ

READING COMPREHENSION (PART 5~7)

NO	ANSWER A B C D	NO	ANSWER A B C D	NO	ANSWER A B C D	NO	ANSWER A B C D	NO	ANSWER A B C D
101	ⓐ ⓑ ⓒ ⓓ	121	ⓐ ⓑ ⓒ ⓓ	141	ⓐ ⓑ ⓒ ⓓ	161	ⓐ ⓑ ⓒ ⓓ	181	ⓐ ⓑ ⓒ ⓓ
102	ⓐ ⓑ ⓒ ⓓ	122	ⓐ ⓑ ⓒ ⓓ	142	ⓐ ⓑ ⓒ ⓓ	162	ⓐ ⓑ ⓒ ⓓ	182	ⓐ ⓑ ⓒ ⓓ
103	ⓐ ⓑ ⓒ ⓓ	123	ⓐ ⓑ ⓒ ⓓ	143	ⓐ ⓑ ⓒ ⓓ	163	ⓐ ⓑ ⓒ ⓓ	183	ⓐ ⓑ ⓒ ⓓ
104	ⓐ ⓑ ⓒ ⓓ	124	ⓐ ⓑ ⓒ ⓓ	144	ⓐ ⓑ ⓒ ⓓ	164	ⓐ ⓑ ⓒ ⓓ	184	ⓐ ⓑ ⓒ ⓓ
105	ⓐ ⓑ ⓒ ⓓ	125	ⓐ ⓑ ⓒ ⓓ	145	ⓐ ⓑ ⓒ ⓓ	165	ⓐ ⓑ ⓒ ⓓ	185	ⓐ ⓑ ⓒ ⓓ
106	ⓐ ⓑ ⓒ ⓓ	126	ⓐ ⓑ ⓒ ⓓ	146	ⓐ ⓑ ⓒ ⓓ	166	ⓐ ⓑ ⓒ ⓓ	186	ⓐ ⓑ ⓒ ⓓ
107	ⓐ ⓑ ⓒ ⓓ	127	ⓐ ⓑ ⓒ ⓓ	147	ⓐ ⓑ ⓒ ⓓ	167	ⓐ ⓑ ⓒ ⓓ	187	ⓐ ⓑ ⓒ ⓓ
108	ⓐ ⓑ ⓒ ⓓ	128	ⓐ ⓑ ⓒ ⓓ	148	ⓐ ⓑ ⓒ ⓓ	168	ⓐ ⓑ ⓒ ⓓ	188	ⓐ ⓑ ⓒ ⓓ
109	ⓐ ⓑ ⓒ ⓓ	129	ⓐ ⓑ ⓒ ⓓ	149	ⓐ ⓑ ⓒ ⓓ	169	ⓐ ⓑ ⓒ ⓓ	189	ⓐ ⓑ ⓒ ⓓ
110	ⓐ ⓑ ⓒ ⓓ	130	ⓐ ⓑ ⓒ ⓓ	150	ⓐ ⓑ ⓒ ⓓ	170	ⓐ ⓑ ⓒ ⓓ	190	ⓐ ⓑ ⓒ ⓓ
111	ⓐ ⓑ ⓒ ⓓ	131	ⓐ ⓑ ⓒ ⓓ	151	ⓐ ⓑ ⓒ ⓓ	171	ⓐ ⓑ ⓒ ⓓ	191	ⓐ ⓑ ⓒ ⓓ
112	ⓐ ⓑ ⓒ ⓓ	132	ⓐ ⓑ ⓒ ⓓ	152	ⓐ ⓑ ⓒ ⓓ	172	ⓐ ⓑ ⓒ ⓓ	192	ⓐ ⓑ ⓒ ⓓ
113	ⓐ ⓑ ⓒ ⓓ	133	ⓐ ⓑ ⓒ ⓓ	153	ⓐ ⓑ ⓒ ⓓ	173	ⓐ ⓑ ⓒ ⓓ	193	ⓐ ⓑ ⓒ ⓓ
114	ⓐ ⓑ ⓒ ⓓ	134	ⓐ ⓑ ⓒ ⓓ	154	ⓐ ⓑ ⓒ ⓓ	174	ⓐ ⓑ ⓒ ⓓ	194	ⓐ ⓑ ⓒ ⓓ
115	ⓐ ⓑ ⓒ ⓓ	135	ⓐ ⓑ ⓒ ⓓ	155	ⓐ ⓑ ⓒ ⓓ	175	ⓐ ⓑ ⓒ ⓓ	195	ⓐ ⓑ ⓒ ⓓ
116	ⓐ ⓑ ⓒ ⓓ	136	ⓐ ⓑ ⓒ ⓓ	156	ⓐ ⓑ ⓒ ⓓ	176	ⓐ ⓑ ⓒ ⓓ	196	ⓐ ⓑ ⓒ ⓓ
117	ⓐ ⓑ ⓒ ⓓ	137	ⓐ ⓑ ⓒ ⓓ	157	ⓐ ⓑ ⓒ ⓓ	177	ⓐ ⓑ ⓒ ⓓ	197	ⓐ ⓑ ⓒ ⓓ
118	ⓐ ⓑ ⓒ ⓓ	138	ⓐ ⓑ ⓒ ⓓ	158	ⓐ ⓑ ⓒ ⓓ	178	ⓐ ⓑ ⓒ ⓓ	198	ⓐ ⓑ ⓒ ⓓ
119	ⓐ ⓑ ⓒ ⓓ	139	ⓐ ⓑ ⓒ ⓓ	159	ⓐ ⓑ ⓒ ⓓ	179	ⓐ ⓑ ⓒ ⓓ	199	ⓐ ⓑ ⓒ ⓓ
120	ⓐ ⓑ ⓒ ⓓ	140	ⓐ ⓑ ⓒ ⓓ	160	ⓐ ⓑ ⓒ ⓓ	180	ⓐ ⓑ ⓒ ⓓ	200	ⓐ ⓑ ⓒ ⓓ

ANSWER SHEET

시원스쿨 LAB

이름		테스트 회차		날짜	

LISTENING COMPREHENSION (PART 1~4)

NO	ANSWER A B C D	NO	ANSWER A B C D	NO	ANSWER A B C D	NO	ANSWER A B C D	NO	ANSWER A B C D
1	ⓐ ⓑ ⓒ ⓓ	21	ⓐ ⓑ ⓒ	41	ⓐ ⓑ ⓒ ⓓ	61	ⓐ ⓑ ⓒ ⓓ	81	ⓐ ⓑ ⓒ ⓓ
2	ⓐ ⓑ ⓒ ⓓ	22	ⓐ ⓑ ⓒ	42	ⓐ ⓑ ⓒ ⓓ	62	ⓐ ⓑ ⓒ ⓓ	82	ⓐ ⓑ ⓒ ⓓ
3	ⓐ ⓑ ⓒ ⓓ	23	ⓐ ⓑ ⓒ	43	ⓐ ⓑ ⓒ ⓓ	63	ⓐ ⓑ ⓒ ⓓ	83	ⓐ ⓑ ⓒ ⓓ
4	ⓐ ⓑ ⓒ ⓓ	24	ⓐ ⓑ ⓒ	44	ⓐ ⓑ ⓒ ⓓ	64	ⓐ ⓑ ⓒ ⓓ	84	ⓐ ⓑ ⓒ ⓓ
5	ⓐ ⓑ ⓒ ⓓ	25	ⓐ ⓑ ⓒ	45	ⓐ ⓑ ⓒ ⓓ	65	ⓐ ⓑ ⓒ ⓓ	85	ⓐ ⓑ ⓒ ⓓ
6	ⓐ ⓑ ⓒ ⓓ	26	ⓐ ⓑ ⓒ	46	ⓐ ⓑ ⓒ ⓓ	66	ⓐ ⓑ ⓒ ⓓ	86	ⓐ ⓑ ⓒ ⓓ
7	ⓐ ⓑ ⓒ	27	ⓐ ⓑ ⓒ	47	ⓐ ⓑ ⓒ ⓓ	67	ⓐ ⓑ ⓒ ⓓ	87	ⓐ ⓑ ⓒ ⓓ
8	ⓐ ⓑ ⓒ	28	ⓐ ⓑ ⓒ	48	ⓐ ⓑ ⓒ ⓓ	68	ⓐ ⓑ ⓒ ⓓ	88	ⓐ ⓑ ⓒ ⓓ
9	ⓐ ⓑ ⓒ	29	ⓐ ⓑ ⓒ	49	ⓐ ⓑ ⓒ ⓓ	69	ⓐ ⓑ ⓒ ⓓ	89	ⓐ ⓑ ⓒ ⓓ
10	ⓐ ⓑ ⓒ	30	ⓐ ⓑ ⓒ	50	ⓐ ⓑ ⓒ ⓓ	70	ⓐ ⓑ ⓒ ⓓ	90	ⓐ ⓑ ⓒ ⓓ
11	ⓐ ⓑ ⓒ	31	ⓐ ⓑ ⓒ	51	ⓐ ⓑ ⓒ ⓓ	71	ⓐ ⓑ ⓒ ⓓ	91	ⓐ ⓑ ⓒ ⓓ
12	ⓐ ⓑ ⓒ	32	ⓐ ⓑ ⓒ ⓓ	52	ⓐ ⓑ ⓒ ⓓ	72	ⓐ ⓑ ⓒ ⓓ	92	ⓐ ⓑ ⓒ ⓓ
13	ⓐ ⓑ ⓒ	33	ⓐ ⓑ ⓒ ⓓ	53	ⓐ ⓑ ⓒ ⓓ	73	ⓐ ⓑ ⓒ ⓓ	93	ⓐ ⓑ ⓒ ⓓ
14	ⓐ ⓑ ⓒ	34	ⓐ ⓑ ⓒ ⓓ	54	ⓐ ⓑ ⓒ ⓓ	74	ⓐ ⓑ ⓒ ⓓ	94	ⓐ ⓑ ⓒ ⓓ
15	ⓐ ⓑ ⓒ	35	ⓐ ⓑ ⓒ ⓓ	55	ⓐ ⓑ ⓒ ⓓ	75	ⓐ ⓑ ⓒ ⓓ	95	ⓐ ⓑ ⓒ ⓓ
16	ⓐ ⓑ ⓒ	36	ⓐ ⓑ ⓒ ⓓ	56	ⓐ ⓑ ⓒ ⓓ	76	ⓐ ⓑ ⓒ ⓓ	96	ⓐ ⓑ ⓒ ⓓ
17	ⓐ ⓑ ⓒ	37	ⓐ ⓑ ⓒ ⓓ	57	ⓐ ⓑ ⓒ ⓓ	77	ⓐ ⓑ ⓒ ⓓ	97	ⓐ ⓑ ⓒ ⓓ
18	ⓐ ⓑ ⓒ	38	ⓐ ⓑ ⓒ ⓓ	58	ⓐ ⓑ ⓒ ⓓ	78	ⓐ ⓑ ⓒ ⓓ	98	ⓐ ⓑ ⓒ ⓓ
19	ⓐ ⓑ ⓒ	39	ⓐ ⓑ ⓒ ⓓ	59	ⓐ ⓑ ⓒ ⓓ	79	ⓐ ⓑ ⓒ ⓓ	99	ⓐ ⓑ ⓒ ⓓ
20	ⓐ ⓑ ⓒ	40	ⓐ ⓑ ⓒ ⓓ	60	ⓐ ⓑ ⓒ ⓓ	80	ⓐ ⓑ ⓒ ⓓ	100	ⓐ ⓑ ⓒ ⓓ

READING COMPREHENSION (PART 5~7)

NO	ANSWER A B C D	NO	ANSWER A B C D	NO	ANSWER A B C D	NO	ANSWER A B C D	NO	ANSWER A B C D
101	ⓐ ⓑ ⓒ ⓓ	121	ⓐ ⓑ ⓒ ⓓ	141	ⓐ ⓑ ⓒ ⓓ	161	ⓐ ⓑ ⓒ ⓓ	181	ⓐ ⓑ ⓒ ⓓ
102	ⓐ ⓑ ⓒ ⓓ	122	ⓐ ⓑ ⓒ ⓓ	142	ⓐ ⓑ ⓒ ⓓ	162	ⓐ ⓑ ⓒ ⓓ	182	ⓐ ⓑ ⓒ ⓓ
103	ⓐ ⓑ ⓒ ⓓ	123	ⓐ ⓑ ⓒ ⓓ	143	ⓐ ⓑ ⓒ ⓓ	163	ⓐ ⓑ ⓒ ⓓ	183	ⓐ ⓑ ⓒ ⓓ
104	ⓐ ⓑ ⓒ ⓓ	124	ⓐ ⓑ ⓒ ⓓ	144	ⓐ ⓑ ⓒ ⓓ	164	ⓐ ⓑ ⓒ ⓓ	184	ⓐ ⓑ ⓒ ⓓ
105	ⓐ ⓑ ⓒ ⓓ	125	ⓐ ⓑ ⓒ ⓓ	145	ⓐ ⓑ ⓒ ⓓ	165	ⓐ ⓑ ⓒ ⓓ	185	ⓐ ⓑ ⓒ ⓓ
106	ⓐ ⓑ ⓒ ⓓ	126	ⓐ ⓑ ⓒ ⓓ	146	ⓐ ⓑ ⓒ ⓓ	166	ⓐ ⓑ ⓒ ⓓ	186	ⓐ ⓑ ⓒ ⓓ
107	ⓐ ⓑ ⓒ ⓓ	127	ⓐ ⓑ ⓒ ⓓ	147	ⓐ ⓑ ⓒ ⓓ	167	ⓐ ⓑ ⓒ ⓓ	187	ⓐ ⓑ ⓒ ⓓ
108	ⓐ ⓑ ⓒ ⓓ	128	ⓐ ⓑ ⓒ ⓓ	148	ⓐ ⓑ ⓒ ⓓ	168	ⓐ ⓑ ⓒ ⓓ	188	ⓐ ⓑ ⓒ ⓓ
109	ⓐ ⓑ ⓒ ⓓ	129	ⓐ ⓑ ⓒ ⓓ	149	ⓐ ⓑ ⓒ ⓓ	169	ⓐ ⓑ ⓒ ⓓ	189	ⓐ ⓑ ⓒ ⓓ
110	ⓐ ⓑ ⓒ ⓓ	130	ⓐ ⓑ ⓒ ⓓ	150	ⓐ ⓑ ⓒ ⓓ	170	ⓐ ⓑ ⓒ ⓓ	190	ⓐ ⓑ ⓒ ⓓ
111	ⓐ ⓑ ⓒ ⓓ	131	ⓐ ⓑ ⓒ ⓓ	151	ⓐ ⓑ ⓒ ⓓ	171	ⓐ ⓑ ⓒ ⓓ	191	ⓐ ⓑ ⓒ ⓓ
112	ⓐ ⓑ ⓒ ⓓ	132	ⓐ ⓑ ⓒ ⓓ	152	ⓐ ⓑ ⓒ ⓓ	172	ⓐ ⓑ ⓒ ⓓ	192	ⓐ ⓑ ⓒ ⓓ
113	ⓐ ⓑ ⓒ ⓓ	133	ⓐ ⓑ ⓒ ⓓ	153	ⓐ ⓑ ⓒ ⓓ	173	ⓐ ⓑ ⓒ ⓓ	193	ⓐ ⓑ ⓒ ⓓ
114	ⓐ ⓑ ⓒ ⓓ	134	ⓐ ⓑ ⓒ ⓓ	154	ⓐ ⓑ ⓒ ⓓ	174	ⓐ ⓑ ⓒ ⓓ	194	ⓐ ⓑ ⓒ ⓓ
115	ⓐ ⓑ ⓒ ⓓ	135	ⓐ ⓑ ⓒ ⓓ	155	ⓐ ⓑ ⓒ ⓓ	175	ⓐ ⓑ ⓒ ⓓ	195	ⓐ ⓑ ⓒ ⓓ
116	ⓐ ⓑ ⓒ ⓓ	136	ⓐ ⓑ ⓒ ⓓ	156	ⓐ ⓑ ⓒ ⓓ	176	ⓐ ⓑ ⓒ ⓓ	196	ⓐ ⓑ ⓒ ⓓ
117	ⓐ ⓑ ⓒ ⓓ	137	ⓐ ⓑ ⓒ ⓓ	157	ⓐ ⓑ ⓒ ⓓ	177	ⓐ ⓑ ⓒ ⓓ	197	ⓐ ⓑ ⓒ ⓓ
118	ⓐ ⓑ ⓒ ⓓ	138	ⓐ ⓑ ⓒ ⓓ	158	ⓐ ⓑ ⓒ ⓓ	178	ⓐ ⓑ ⓒ ⓓ	198	ⓐ ⓑ ⓒ ⓓ
119	ⓐ ⓑ ⓒ ⓓ	139	ⓐ ⓑ ⓒ ⓓ	159	ⓐ ⓑ ⓒ ⓓ	179	ⓐ ⓑ ⓒ ⓓ	199	ⓐ ⓑ ⓒ ⓓ
120	ⓐ ⓑ ⓒ ⓓ	140	ⓐ ⓑ ⓒ ⓓ	160	ⓐ ⓑ ⓒ ⓓ	180	ⓐ ⓑ ⓒ ⓓ	200	ⓐ ⓑ ⓒ ⓓ

시원스쿨 토익 실전 1500제, 이런 분들께 추천!

해야 할 공부가 너무 많아!

토익에 많은 시간을
쓸 수 없는 분

학원에 교재에 응시료에…

토익 목표를 경제적으로
달성하고 싶으신 분

토익은 트렌드가 중요해!

토익 기출 트렌드가 반영된
문제로 공부하고 싶으신 분

가장 합리적인 비용으로
빠른 토익 목표 달성! 시원스쿨 토익 실전 1500제

시원스쿨 토익 실전 1500제, 선택의 이유!

1 최다 실전 문제
- 토익 실전 모의고사 15회분 (LC, RC 각 1500제)
- 국내 토익 실전서 중 단권으로 최다 문제 수록

2 기출 트렌드 반영
- 토익 기출 빅데이터 정밀 분석에 따른 문항 구성
- 실제 토익 시험 완벽 구현
(문제 유형/구성/토픽/길이와 난이도 등 시험 요소 반영)

3 놀라운 가성비
- 무료 해설 제공(별도 구매 필요 없음)
- 무료 MP3/오답노트 제공
- 무료 학습 서비스(토익 데일리 퀴즈/적중 특강/해설 특강)

4 편리한 온라인 학습
- 실전 전략과 중요 포인트를 정확하게 짚어내는 온라인 강의(유료)
- QR코드를 통해 해설 바로 확인
- 온라인 공부질문 게시판 운영

세상 어디에도 없다!

토익을 시작하는 분들을 위한 맞춤형 환급반

첫 토익에
목표 달성하세요!

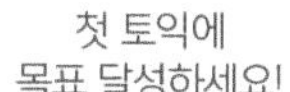

토익 응시료까지 아낌없이 지원합니다.

하루라도 빠지면
환급 NO?

출석 미션이 없으니 원할 때 공부하세요.

토익은 처음인데
성적이 있어야만 환급?

점수 제한 없이 환급! 부담 없이 도전하세요.

토익 점수가
내 맘같지 않을 때

365일 수강기간 연장 여유있게 공부하세요.

혼자 공부하기
막막하면

선생님과의 1:1 카톡스터디로 물어보세요!

목표 달성 후기가 증명합니다.

고민하지 말고 지금 시작이반 하세요!

3주 만에 855점 달성 송*형 | 토익 855점 달성

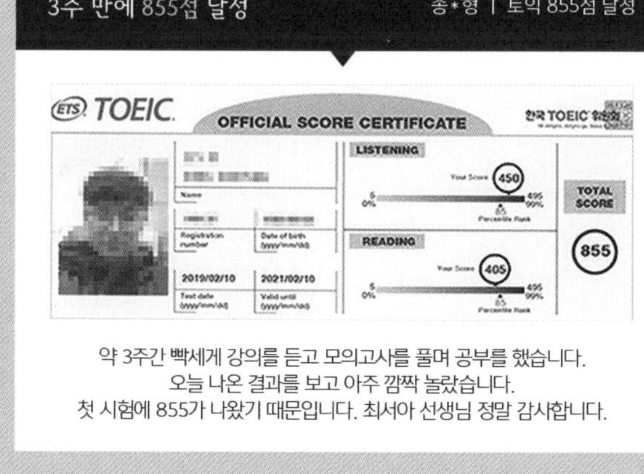

약 3주간 빡세게 강의를 듣고 모의고사를 풀며 공부를 했습니다.
오늘 나온 결과를 보고 아주 깜짝 놀랐습니다.
첫 시험에 855가 나왔기 때문입니다. 최서아 선생님 정말 감사합니다.

첫 토익 한 달만에 880점 후기 오*경 | 토익 880점 달성

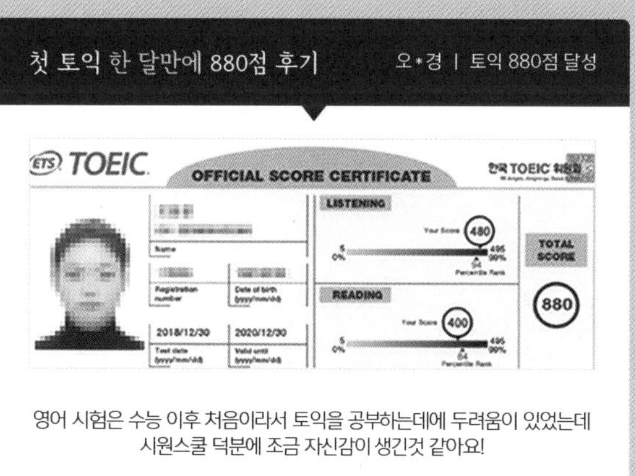

영어 시험은 수능 이후 처음이라서 토익을 공부하는데에 두려움이 있었는데
시원스쿨 덕분에 조금 자신감이 생긴것 같아요!

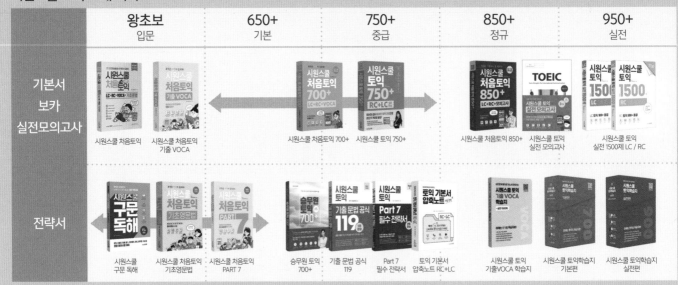